INTRODUCTION TO
ECONOMIC GEOGRAPHY

Bulk transport by rail. A freight train, nearly one and a quarter miles in length, heads towards St John, New Brunswick, with 8,000 tons of prairie grain. (*Canadian Pacific.*)

INTRODUCTION TO

ECONOMIC GEOGRAPHY

BY

E. H. COOPER, M.A.

HEAD OF GEOGRAPHY DEPARTMENT, MARPLE HALL BOYS' GRAMMAR SCHOOL

UNIVERSITY TUTORIAL PRESS LTD

9-10 GREAT SUTTON STREET, LONDON, E.C.1

Published 1968

SBN: 7231 0144 2

PRINTED IN GREAT BRITAIN BY UNIVERSITY TUTORIAL PRESS LTD, FOXTON NEAR CAMBRIDGE

PREFACE

This book is written primarily to meet the needs of students pursuing advanced courses in Geography in the Sixth Forms of schools, and in Technical Colleges and Colleges of Education. Its aim, briefly, is to lead these students, whom it is assumed have acquired at least an elementary knowledge of World Geography, towards an understanding of the factors which interact to produce the patterns of production found in the modern world. The treatment is systematic. Each of the major types of economic activity is described in turn, and while lengthy accounts of certain areas are included by way of example or illustration, no attempt has been made to write a Regional Economic Geography.

The manner in which man earns a living has always been influenced by the physical environment in which he finds himself. He can, for instance, only engage in coal mining where known deposits of coal are found, or grow peaches in the open air where the climate is appropriate to the cultivation of the peach tree. On a world scale, the type of agriculture found in the tropics is very different from that of the temperate lands, and so on. But the works of man are conditioned by more than factors of physical geography. History, social and cultural practices, religious beliefs, political philosophies, and the general level of economic development all have a bearing on the location of productive activities. Furthermore, in these days of advanced technologies man is able to a degree unknown in the past to modify natural environments, and to create artificial environments to suit his own purposes. The factors underlying the choice of site for a particular factory, or the combination of crops to be grown on a particular farm, are therefore apt to be complex, and can rarely be explained in simple terms of "raw materials", "transport", "climate", etc.

There are no laws of Economic Geography as there are laws of Physics and Chemistry. One cannot, for example, draw up a list of requirements for the successful production of a commodity, and then assert that they will be valid in all circumstances. It may be the case that the cultivation of rice in the Ganges Delta requires so much rain per year, or a growing season of so many days. But the same conditions would not apply to rice production in California, northern Italy, or the south of France where the plant is grown by very different methods. One can only be dogmatic to the point of stating that a certain combination of factors will give rise to a situation in which rice will (to use the jargon of the economist) *tend* to be an important crop. But one must not be surprised to find rice being produced very successfully in areas where these conditions do not obtain.

It must be remembered that a community will try and utilise its resources (natural resources such as climate, soils, mineral, and fuel deposits, etc., and its acquired resources such as labour skills and capital) in the manner which best suits its current needs. It must also be borne in mind that no commodity can be produced without a cost. If conditions change, if costs of production rise or fall (and they are rarely static for very long) then the pattern of production is likely to alter. In the matter of production costs the activities of the central government must be considered. Government encouragement to industry and agriculture is very common now-a-days, and the hand of the state is often to be found behind some of the apparently anomolous distribution patterns one finds at the present time.

A note about the statistics used in this book. Most of the Tables have been taken from officially published lists, and are as up to date as they can be at the time of writing. In each case where published sources have been used the source has been quoted and hence students wishing to undertake further work on their own will find the task of research simplified. Many publications, particularly the *Yearbooks* of the United Nations and the *Statistical Abstract of the United States*, will be found to be mines of information.

I wish to express my thanks to many colleagues at Marple Hall Boys' Grammar School for the help they have given in the preparation of this book. In particular I would record my indebtedness to Mr R. W. Knight, Assistant Geography Master; Mr G. C. Walters, Head of the Science Department; and Mr D. M. Hannah, former Head of the Economics Department, and now of International Computors and Tabulators. I would also thank the many commercial firms who have provided statistical material, photographs, maps, and diagrams. Acknowledgement has been made where appropriate in every case.

E. H. C.

CONTENTS

ILLUSTRATIONS

TABLES

CHAPTER I

POPULATION

THE WORLD DISTRIBUTION OF POPULATION

There are approximately ten acres of land, excluding the ice cap regions of Greenland and Antarctica, to each of the world's 3,300 million inhabitants. In the year 1700 there were some sixty acres, in 1900 there were twenty, and if the present upward trend in population continues until the end of the present century, there will then be five.

A cursory glance at the population map (Fig. 1) is sufficient to show that the world's peoples are distributed very unevenly. In fact, fully one quarter of the earth's land area contains less than one person per square mile, and a further quarter less than five. At the other extreme, densities exceeding 10,000 per square mile are found in every large city and town in the world, and even some predominantly agricultural regions support upwards of 3,000 per square mile. Furthermore the closely settled areas are tending to become more congested as the world population grows, while most of the empty lands are attracting settlement but slowly, and some hardly at all. Why is it that human beings have spread themselves so unevenly across the surface of the globe? The first part of this chapter is an attempt to explain.

REGIONS OF HIGH POPULATION DENSITY

More than three quarters of the world's inhabitants are concentrated into three major continental groupings. The first, and largest, embraces the lands of Monsoon Asia; the second Britain, and the countries of continental Europe; and the third—much smaller than the other two—the states of north-eastern U.S.A., and the southern fringes of eastern Canada. The Asian peoples live primarily by agriculture. In Europe and North America agriculture is also an important industry, but only very locally is it of over-riding significance. The people of these two regions depend rather for their livelihood on mining, manufacture, and commerce (see Table 15, p. 91).

High rural population densities in Monsoon Asia

The problems of over-population, land hunger, and poverty are associated in the minds of men everywhere with the countries of the

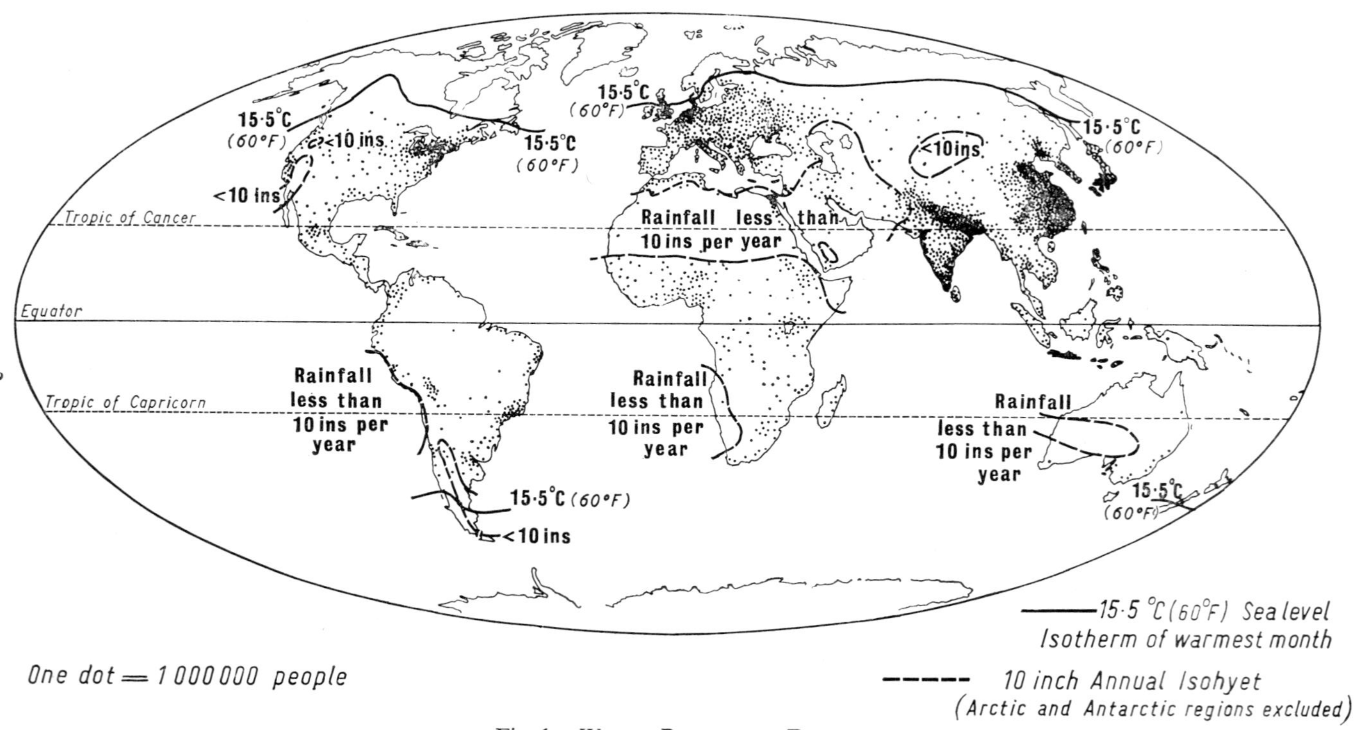

Fig. 1.—World Population Distribution.

Far East, where one half of the world's people live. The population of China alone is estimated to be approaching 800 million, whilst a further 490 million dwell in India. These totals are enormous by comparison with any of the countries of the Western World. However, the fact should not be overlooked that the area of China is double that of all the European states (excluding the Soviet Union) combined, and India is equivalent in size to that part of Europe lying west of the Iron Curtain. Average population densities are in fact lower in China and most Asian countries than in Britain, Holland, Belgium, Germany, and Italy (Table 1).

TABLE 1

COMPARISON BETWEEN (*a*) TOTAL POPULATIONS, (*b*) POPULATION DENSITIES IN SELECTED ASIAN AND EUROPEAN COUNTRIES

ASIA			EUROPE		
	Total population (in thousands)	Density per sq. mile		Total population (in thousands)	Density per sq. mile
Formosa	12,400	892	Holland	12,300	880
Japan	97,900	686	Belgium	9,400	800
Ceylon	11,600	458	West Germany*	58,800	613
India	492,000	390	United Kingdom	54,000	574
Pakistan	100,700	276	Italy	52,500	451
China			East Germany	17,000	408
(mainland)	755,000	204	Switzerland	6,000	378
Thailand	30,600	154	Luxembourg	329	330
Burma	24,700	94			

* including West Berlin.

Superficial densities taken without reference to resources and techniques of production are, however, quite meaningless. The intense and mounting population pressures in India and China stem not directly from the enormous numbers inhabiting these lands, but from the fact that people are compelled by the difficult conditions of their environment, and the poor agricultural techniques which are at their disposal, to congregate in the valleys and deltas where fertile soils and water are found. One usually finds a rapid falling off in population density along the margins of the uplands, and a more gradual thinning out in the direction of lower rainfall. The reason is that the hills and drier regions are of limited value to a peasantry ill-equipped with devices that make extensive agriculture possible. The characteristic Asian type farming, based essentially on "spade" cultivation, is inappropriate if more than a few acres need to be worked in order to support a family. In Europe, North America, and Australia, farmers have profitably occupied marginal land by bringing a large acreage into use, and cultivating it with labour-saving machinery. The poverty of the majority of Asian farmers makes this type of adaptation very difficult, if not impossible.

The importance of relating population densities to the productive, rather than the superficial area will be evident from Table 2.

TABLE 2

POPULATION DENSITIES IN CHINA IN RELATION TO SUPERFICIAL AND PRODUCTIVE LAND AREAS

Total land area (thousand acres)	2,333,000
Total productive area* (thousand acres)	904,600
Total arable area (thousand acres)	222,800
Overall density per thousand acres	300
Density per thousand acres of productive land	775
Density per thousand acres of arable land	3,150

* productive area includes arable, permanent pasture, forest, and woodland.

Densities which exceed 3,000 per thousand acres (nearly 2,000 per square mile) are very high indeed for a nation in which some 80 per cent. of the people live on farms, and obtain the greater part of their food supply from the soil they cultivate. Less than half an acre of crop land per head, which is all that is available in many parts of China and other Asian countries, can sustain human life only if the land is fertile, well watered (either by rainfall or irrigation), and is capable of being intensively, and more or less continuously, cultivated throughout the year.

Intensive cultivation is not of course practised only in Asia, but is commonplace on fertile soils in closely settled areas throughout the world. Multiple cropping, too, is carried on in all market gardening regions wherever winters do not impose too severe a check on the growth of plants. But 2,000 or more people do not inhabit each square mile of farm land in the Imperial Valley, California; or south Cornwall. Important as intensive multiple cropping might be in helping to sustain high population densities, it could not support the numbers present in Monsoon Asia at the level of nutrition enjoyed by the average Englishman or North American. Neither could it support them on a diet having a high content of meat, milk, and eggs, which are wastefully and expensively produced by domestic animals from cereals and other cultivated plants. Maize, for instance, feeds three times as many people if consumed *as* maize, as it feeds after conversion into animal products. It is the willingness of the Asian peasant to eat little, and to subsist mainly on vegetables, that permits such large numbers to live directly from the land they cultivate (Fig. 2).

Other continents

In marked contrast to Monsoon Asia, the tropical and subtropical sections of Africa, Latin America, and Oceania are thinly populated. The territory in these three continents lying between latitudes 30° north and south represents more than one third of the world's land area, but contains only 7 per cent. of its human population. Furthermore, such dense population clusters as do exist are predominantly urban. The great exception is the valley and delta

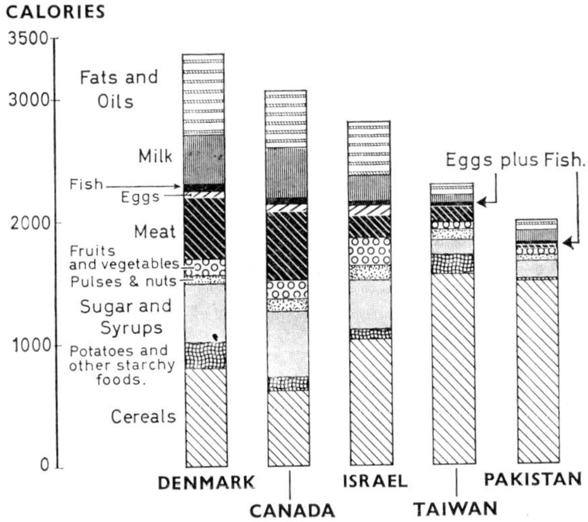

Fig. 2.—Daily per capita Intake of Food in Selected Countries.
Source: *F.A.O. Production Year Book*, 1965.

region of the Nile in Egypt where 27 million people, 70 per cent. of whom depend primarily on agriculture for a livelihood, occupy 13,600 square miles of irrigable crop land hemmed in between the desert and the sea. Meticulous attention to every detail of cultivation, the existence of a valuable export crop, cotton, which can be exchanged on favourable terms for food, and, as in Asia, a stoical acceptance of a miserable standard of material well-being, make life possible for such numbers.

Population densities exceed 500 per square mile on rural land on some of the Antilles Islands, notably Barbados and Puerto Rico; in the forest belt of southern Ghana and Nigeria; and locally on the Lake Victorian Plateau. As in Egypt, the production of commercial crops is important in all these regions—sugar-cane in Barbados and

Puerto Rico, cocoa and the oil palm in Ghana and Nigeria, and cotton on the Lake Victoria Plateau—crops which are sold to obtain some of the food requirements. In Europe, the Plain of Flanders, the *huerta* lands of southern and eastern Spain, and the Plain of Naples also support comparatively high population densities on agricultural land. Market gardening and commercial fruit production are important enterprises here.

Regions of high population density based primarily on mining, manufacturing, and commerce

Settlements which are supported wholly by an extractive industry are seldom permanent. They must inevitably be dispersed once the mineral deposit is exhausted, or when it is no longer profitable to work. This is likely to happen sooner rather than later if the ore body is small, and mining operations speculative. The existence of innumerable ghost towns in Australia and the American West, where gold and silver were once produced, is testimony to this fact.

On the other hand, some mining regions have attracted and held large populations. The coalfields particularly have become areas of permanent settlement. The coal-producing industry is itself a large employer of labour, but of even greater importance is the fact that, after the invention of the steam engine, coal became the only fuel capable of supplying the energy requirements of most types of manufacturing industry. Factories tended, therefore, to be drawn towards locations where coal could be obtained cheaply. The importance of coal as a fuel is now declining, and new industrial centres are appearing at points remote from the mines. However, the great coal-based conurbations—the Ruhr, South East Lancashire, Tyneside, Pittsburgh-Youngstown, to name but a few—not only persist, but in some cases continue to expand. The reasons why they do so are numerous, but not the least among them is the enduring attraction for almost every kind of enterprise of a large and diversified labour force, and the market for goods and services that the population of a major conurbation provides.

The livelihood of town and city dwellers depends ultimately on the existence of a well developed network of communications and on ample opportunities for trade. If the supply lines are cut, an urban centre perishes. An industrial town functions as a great workshop, drawing in raw materials, sometimes from the four corners of the earth, processing them, and then re-exporting them in a changed form, and with their value increased many times. In return it receives (among other things) its food supply. A city the size of Manchester or Pittsburgh is fed from perhaps a million acres of crop land scattered across the globe, and not, as is the village in Bengal or on the Yangtze plains, from land within its own boundaries. A situation of this sort permits of population densities far in excess of those possible in predominantly agricultural areas, no matter how frugally the farmers may live or how intensive their cultivation may be.

The employment structure of towns

The diversity of employment in any town, even in the so-called "one industry" town, is surprisingly great. It is most unusual to find one half of the working population engaged in the basic industry—primary metal smelting, engineering, textiles, or whatever it may be. Perhaps the most noteworthy feature is the importance of the "non-productive" or tertiary industries. The larger and more prosperous a centre becomes, the more rapidly the number of workers in occupations such as banking and insurance, transport, the distributive trades, and entertainment, proliferate. If a town also serves as a social and economic centre for the surrounding region, the tertiary industries may well—in terms of the volume of employment they create—overshadow the manufacturing industries. More than two-thirds of all males employed in Manchester, for instance, are in occupations other than manufacturing industry, and in Norwich some 14 per cent. of the total labour force find work in the distributive trades alone. The employment structure for a "railway" town—Crewe—is illustrated in Fig. 3.

THE NEGATIVE REGIONS

Lands which are virtually devoid of human habitation at the present time correspond broadly to certain major natural regions, viz. the polar ice caps (where permanent settlement is impossible outside the highly artificial environment of, for example, a research station), the tundra and northern forest lands, the hot and temperate deserts, and the tropical rain forests. The high mountains and plateaus are also scantily peopled, although there are important exceptions, especially within the low latitudes.

The tundra and northern forests

Circling the globe, for the most part within the Arctic latitudes, is a vast expanse of treeless waste, where in the absence of developed mineral resources, or military bases and weather stations established during the last quarter century, man is compelled to depend for his livelihood upon the animal population that subsists on the poor seasonal pastures or which lives in the sea. The capacity of the tundra to support grazing animals is very low, and human populations are consequently small. Life is essentially nomadic, whether based on hunting, fishing, or the herding of domesticated reindeer. The shortness of the growing season, and the low temperatures that prevail during the summer months preclude cultivation of any sort.

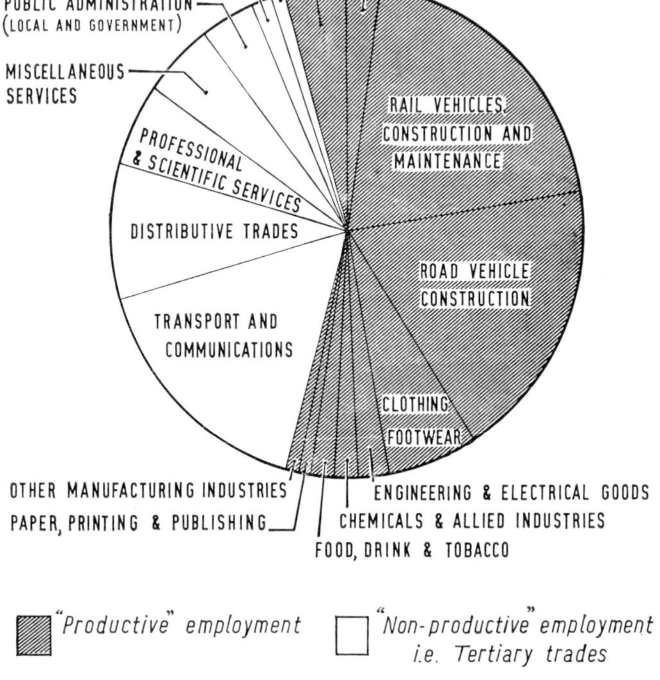

Fig. 3.—EMPLOYMENT STRUCTURE OF CREWE.

Marginal to the tundra lies a great zone of coniferous forest. Isolated and remote, and handicapped by a climate only slightly less harsh than the tundra itself, the northern forest region is also hostile to human settlement, except again where there are minerals to be worked. Southwards across the forest lands the population density increases, although in North America country supporting less than one person per square mile reaches to within fifty miles of Lake Superior.

The arid regions

Aridity imposes limitations on human settlement over far greater areas than does cold. Regions receiving an annual rainfall of under ten inches are to be found in every continent, and in every latitude, from the inter-tropical zone to the Arctic Circle, and beyond. In the hot deserts the scanty precipitation and exceptionally high rates of evaporation combine to produce some of the worst possible conditions for the growth of economically useful plants. Here life centres upon the oases, where a water supply is assured from springs or from rivers fed by head streams rising in moister uplands beyond the desert. In more humid parts of the world there is a gradual transition in the type and intensity of land use from one locality to another. This is not so in the arid lands. The line separating the desert from the sown is sharp, and cultivation begins and ends abruptly against an irrigation ditch (Fig. 4). Away from the oases, only the extensive herding of a restricted range of animals—sheep, goats, and camels—is possible, except where the chance occurrence of minerals creates the opportunity for alternative employment.

The tropical rain forests

Whilst cold deters human settlement in the tundra and high mountain regions, and a scanty precipitation makes life precarious in the deserts, the combination of heat and moisture creates immense difficulties for man in some of the hot wet lands. The rain forest is most extensively developed in the Amazon Basin, a region of broad, flat plains subject to periodic flooding and covered with dense stands of broad-leaved, evergreen trees. Away from the rivers the forest has remained largely undisturbed since Tertiary times. The population clings to the rivers, which are the only highways, and apart from Belem (300,000), Manaus (165,000), and Iquitos (54,000), settlements are small and primitive. The region is poor in known natural resources, apart from timber, for which there is little demand at present. The thin, heavily leached soils do not support the continuous cropping of shallow rooted plants. Few fish are of economic importance, and as most of the animal life is tree-dwelling, even hunting is difficult. Human energy is sapped by an enervating climate and by disease. In spite of development schemes put in hand by Brazil, Peru, and Bolivia, the population of Amazonia, inclusive of the large towns, is less than 3 million.

The rain forests of Africa and southern Asia.—Large population vacuums occur in the remoter parts of the Congo, and on the forested mountainous islands of the East Indies. In general, however, equatorial Africa and Asia have proved to be more attractive regions for human habitation than Amazonia, and in certain countries, notably Java and Nigeria, population densities are high. Indeed

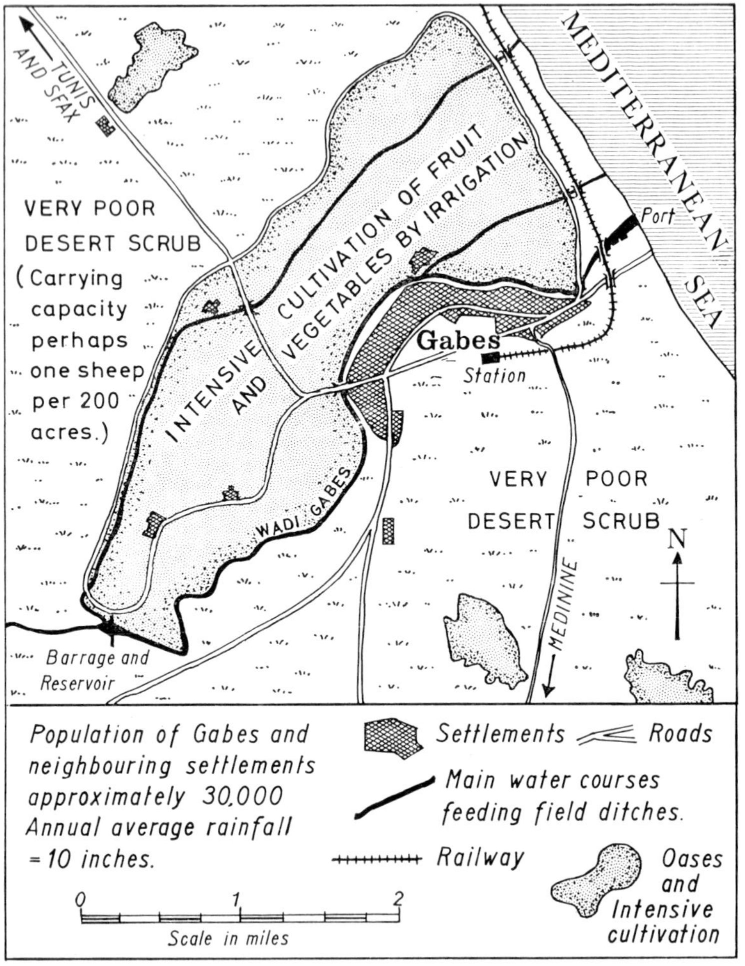

Fig. 4.—The Oasis of Gabes.

Java is the most densely populated island in the world. The reasons would appear to be:

1. The generally lighter forest cover in Africa and Asia that presented, and still presents, fewer problems of land clearance.

2. The higher level of native culture and social organisation in the Old World, particularly in Asia, which have enabled the inhabitants to overcome the natural environmental handicaps.

3. The stimulus given to commercial agriculture and mining by the trading connections established between West Africa and the East Indies on the one hand, and Europe and the countries of continental Asia on the other.

The higher mountain and plateau lands.—Regions of high relief, more especially in the colder parts of the world, are thinly populated. Within the tropics, however, mountains often provide a more favourable human habitat than the plains. The Peruvian and Bolivian Andes, and the Plateau of East Africa are more closely settled than the lowlands that lie on their flanks. Nevertheless, over most of the world mountains tend to repel human settlement because:

1. Climatically they are unsuitable for agriculture. Above a certain height which varies with latitude, and locally with aspect and exposure, temperatures become too low and the growing season too short for tillage. Above the cultivable zone settlement thins out, and eventually ceases at the snow line. Mountains which rise above the level of permanent snow are as devoid of habitation as the ice caps, which in a small way they resemble.

2. A large proportion of their surface area is in steep slopes which would be difficult and expensive to bring under cultivation, even if the climate permitted it.

3. Communications are difficult. Mountain villages are often isolated from each other, and from the lowlands beyond. The opportunities for engaging in industry and commercial agriculture are restricted by the restraints imposed on trade by the relief. Poor communications are, of course, more often than not the consequence rather than the cause of sparse settlement. Where roads and railways can be justified economically they are built, in spite of the difficulties of the terrain.

4. At heights above 12,000 to 15,000 ft, physical and mental exertion is possible only with extreme difficulty because of the reduced atmospheric pressure. The highest human dwellings are probably in Tibet at about 16,000 ft. Over the greater part of the world, however, climatic factors inhibit settlement at much lower altitudes than these.

The future of the empty lands

The tundra and northern forests hold deposits of useful minerals. Some of these deposits are already being exploited; others are known to exist, and their utilisation awaits only the development of an economic method of extraction or the provision of adequate transport; still others will undoubtedly be discovered as the regions are more thoroughly explored. The deserts of the Middle East contain nearly two-thirds of the world's proven oil reserves, although by no means all are in areas devoid of population at the present time. Rich strikes of oil have also been made in the Sahara during the last decade. Nitrates and copper have been mined for more than a century in the Atacama. Gold, silver, copper, many of the base metals such as tin, zinc, and lead, as well as iron ore are found in many localities in the desert interior of Australia and are present in many of the high mountain regions. The Amazon Basin is imperfectly known geologically, but as it occupies one of the great sedimentary depressions of the world, the possibilities of eventually finding oil there must be considered good.

The empty lands, then, contain a great store of mineral wealth that is likely to be drawn upon increasingly as the more readily accessible reserves become depleted. An extension of mining will inevitably lead to a growth in the population of these regions, but any really significant increase in numbers can be anticipated only if manufacturing industry can be attracted. Manufacturing industry, however, is expanding most rapidly in areas that are already developed, industrially, and which are relatively densely settled. New industrial plants are springing up almost daily in California and on the Gulf Coast of the U.S.A., but very few have been urged into Labrador or to the shores of the Hudson Bay. It seems most probable, therefore, that unless the state itself directs industry into these isolated territories (perhaps for strategic or military reasons as in the Soviet Union) they will continue, as far as one can foretell, to play the role of primary producers to the established manufacturing regions.

What of the possibilities of settling farmers in some of the regions now unoccupied by man? It is unlikely that agricultural science will progress to the point where the cultivation of the tundra becomes feasible, at least in the foreseeable future. On the other hand a further small reduction in the length of the growing season of certain hardy plants (probably by the technique of vernalisation, whereby the life cycle of the plant is quickened by subjecting the seed to temperatures a few degrees above freezing point for several weeks before sowing) would open up the possibility of utilising the milder fringes. Cultivation is now technically possible within the Mackenzie Basin of Canada, and Soviet farmers have grown barley successfully within the Arctic Circle. In the deserts, there is scope for extending the area of canal and well irrigation; and the desalination of sea water, at present too costly a process to provide water in the quantities needed by the farmer, may become an economic proposition in the future. Experiments now being undertaken in soil-less plant culture will, if successful, be of particular value to desert agriculture. The problems of the rain forests are of course wholly different, but basically less difficult to solve. The reclamation of the Amazon region calls for the application of no technique not proven in broadly similar forested areas of South East Asia and West Africa. The cost of development, however, would be enormous.

That man now has, or very soon will have, the means to push forward the frontiers of settlement into the empty lands there can be little doubt. Finance will be the main stumbling block, particularly as the nations who would have to find the money for development are not those most in need of the food these regions could be made to supply. It is important to note that there are few similarities between the pioneer lands of the last century—the Pampas, the Prairies, and the Murray Basin—and the territories under consideration. The nineteenth-century settlers moved into virgin areas of great agricultural potential, and developed them with comparative ease. There is no cheap way of opening up the Arctic fringes, the deserts, and the equatorial rain forests. The position at present, although it will not always necessarily be so, is that extra food or agricultural raw materials, if needed, can be obtained at less cost by intensifying production in areas already in cultivation than by breaking new land in these difficult regions. This fact alone will put a brake on their development for some considerable time.

Population densities—a summary

The number of people, then, that a region is able to support ultimately depends on:

1. The wealth of the natural resources that can be exploited by existing techniques of production.

2. The extent to which the population is able to draw upon the resources of other regions for its food and other means of subsistence.

3. The living standards of the population. The lower these are (provided they do not fall below subsistence level) the greater the number of inhabitants that can be supported.

THE GROWTH OF POPULATION

Past and present trends

Our knowledge of population numbers and trends prior to the eighteenth century is scanty, but such information as exists points to a world total of about 550 million in 1700, and a rate of increase that

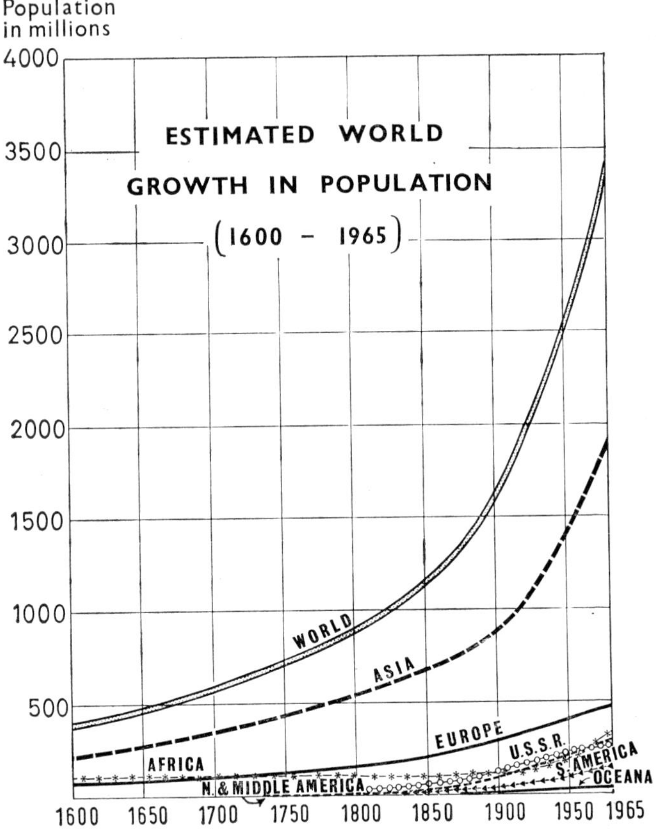

Fig. 5.

was both slow and spasmodic. In Britain numbers probably increased from 1·5 million to 6 million during the six hundred years that followed the Domesday Survey of 1086. Early in the eighteenth century in Britain, and a little later on the continent of Europe, there began a period of expansion that continued at an accelerating pace until after 1900, when the rate of growth slackened. It is estimated that the population of Europe (excluding European Russia) increased from about 100 million in 1700 to more than 300 million in 1900. In most West European countries the growth virtually ceased during the 1930s, although the upward trend has been resumed since the Second World War. In Eastern Europe the increase also continues, but at a slower rate than formerly.

In the under-developed continents—Asia, Africa, and Latin America—the expansion in population occurred much later than in Europe, and in Africa it did not begin until well into the present century. Census taking in backward countries with poorly developed communications and illiterate inhabitants is an exceedingly difficult exercise, however, and it is not a simple matter to determine the extent to which the very rapid growth in numbers which has apparently occurred recently is to be ascribed to a real increase, or is simply due to better methods of enumeration. China is an exceptional case, but for years official agencies—apparently oblivious to changes that were known to be taking place in other countries of the Far East—continued to regard 400 million as a reasonable estimate of the population of China. The world was not taken entirely by surprise, therefore, when the 1954 census—the first complete census ever to be taken in the country—revealed no fewer than 580 million Chinamen. The most recent United Nations estimate puts the number at 755 million. Probably these figures are still subject to an error in the order of 20 per cent. Almost certainly the population could not have nearly doubled in twenty years.

The situation is again different in North America and Australasia. In North America the rate of growth was phenomenal during the nineteenth century, and showed a five-fold increase between 1800 and 1850, and a three-fold increase between 1851 and 1900. Since then the population has more than doubled, and at the present time the United States records a rate of increase which is among the highest in the world. The nineteenth and early twentieth centuries were periods of massive immigration into the U.S.A. and Canada. Nearly 30 million settlers arrived from Europe alone. A high proportion of these were young adults who married and had children—children who, had there been no migration, would have been born in Europe.

Future growth of population

It is notoriously difficult, and probably quite pointless, to issue population forecasts for more than a few decades hence. Predictions can go badly awry. In 1950, for example, calculations based on all available evidence pointed to a world total of between 3,000 million and 4,000 million people by the end of the present century. In the event, the figure had already exceeded 3,300 million by 1965, and revised estimates indicate a population of 6,000 million likely by the year A.D. 2000. No doubt further substantial adjustments will be made during the next thirty-five years.

Forecasting can only be based on the assumption that birth and death rates and the age and sex structure of populations will remain unchanged, or will follow patterns that are predictable. It is by no means certain, of course, that past and present trends will continue into the future. A substantial increase in the supply of food to countries where birth and death rates are still high, particularly if accompanied by improved medical services and better sanitation and water supplies, would make nonsense of any forecasts being made to-day. So would the widespread acceptance of birth control practices.

Birth and death rates are expressed as the number of live births, and the number of deaths, occurring each year per thousand of the population (Table 3). Birth rates are high among non-industrial, peasant communities. In many parts of Asia, Africa, and Latin America, and to a less extent in the more retarded areas of southern Europe, children are still looked upon as an economic asset. They can be put to work at an early age on the land or in domestic workshops, and thus contribute to the family income. This indeed happened in Britain before and during the early phases of the Industrial Revolution. The high mortality rate in backward countries is, paradoxically, also a factor which encourages large families, as the only way of being reasonably sure that three of one's children will survive into adulthood is to produce six.

Rising living standards are normally accompanied by a falling birth rate. Economic development is often associated with a shift of the working population into factories where children would be less able to play a useful role, even if the law allowed them to make the attempt. At the same time there is usually a lengthening of the period of full-time education during which young people must be maintained by their parents. Instead of being an asset, economically, children thus become a liability. A family's standard of living declines as its size increases, and the attitude of parents towards having children is thereby radically affected. The significant rise in the birth rate that has occurred in Britain, and other advanced countries since the Second World War can be attributed, at least in part, to the policy of spreading some of the cost of bringing up a family over the community in general. The granting of income tax rebates and child allowances and the provision of subsidised school meals are three of the ways by which it is done.

Death rates also fall as material prosperity increases, and they invariably fall more rapidly than birth rates. This is the reason why the populations of so many Asian and Latin American countries are growing so alarmingly at the present time. Death rates respond quickly to changes in the quality of nutrition and medical care. Improved food and water supplies, better housing conditions, more doctors, nurses, and hospitals can be relied upon absolutely to increase a person's chances of survival at any age, but especially in the early years of life when he is more likely to succumb to the effects of malnutrition and disease. It should be noted that the increase in the length of life expectancy that has occurred in Britain since 1850 (from about forty-five to seventy years) has come about as a result of a dramatic decline in the mortality rates among children, not among the old. The chances of surviving to the age of 100 are only marginally higher now than they were a century ago.

TABLE 3

BIRTH RATES, DEATH RATES, AND EXPECTANCY OF LIFE AT BIRTH IN SELECTED COUNTRIES

	BIRTH RATE (per thousand of population)	DEATH RATE (per thousand of population)	LIFE EXPECTANCY (in years)
Ivory Coast	56·1	33·3	35·0
Morocco	46·1	18·7	49·6
Haiti	43·6	21·6	32·6
India	40·9	22·0	45·9
Canada	24·8	7·8	70·2
England and Wales	18·3	11·9	72·0
France	18·2	11·7	70·7
Sweden	14·8	10·1	73·4

Source: *U.N. Demographic Yearbook.*

Net reproduction ratios

The capacity of a community to reproduce itself is determined primarily by the number of women in the population who are of child-bearing age. The *net reproduction ratio* is a measure of the rate at which women of the present generation are being replaced by daughters who themselves are likely to have children. The following examples are given as illustrations.

	Number of children born per 1,000 women in the present generation	Number of Boys*	Number of Girls*	Gross Reproduction Ratio	Number of daughters expected to survive to age of forty-five	Net Reproduction Ratio	Future Population Trends
A	2,050	1,050	1,000	1·0	800	0·8	Population will decline†
B	2,460	1,260	1,200	1·2	1,000	1·0	Population will remain unchanged†
C	5,330	2,730	2,600	2·6	2,000	2·0	Population will double during the next generation†

* Approximately 1,050 boys are born for every 1,000 girls.
† Provided birth and death rates remain unchanged and there is no net gain or loss through migration.

TABLE 4

GROSS AND NET REPRODUCTION RATIOS, AND PRESENT AND FUTURE POPULATIONS IN SELECTED COUNTRIES

	Reproduction Ratio* (Gross)	(Net)	Present Population	Population one generation hence† (*c.* 1990-2000)
Japan	0·95	0·90	97,960,000	88,160,000
Sweden	1·07	1·05	7,730,000	8,120,000
England and Wales	1·35	1·30	46,100,000	59,900,000
Cyprus	1·69	1·52	590,000	887,000
U.S.A.	1·77	1·70	194,200,000	330,100,000
Panama	2·80	2·39	1,240,000	2,964,000
Costa Rica	3·58	2·84	1,420,000	4,033,000

* In 1961, except Cyprus (1962) and Costa Rica (1960).
† Provided birth and death rates remain unchanged, and there is no net gain or loss through migration.

Source: U.N. Statistical Office.

Age structure of populations

The age compositions of the population of (i) the African continent, (ii) Europe, excluding the U.S.S.R., and (iii) Oceania, are illustrated graphically in Fig. 6. The age pyramid for Africa is seen to be broadly based, with the proportion of the total population in any given age group substantially larger than in the group immediately above it. This pattern is due, first, to the high mortality rates in

Africa which significantly reduce the size of each generation as it passes through life, and secondly to the fact that the younger age groups were numerically larger at birth than the groups that preceded them. The pyramid is characteristic of a population which is grow-

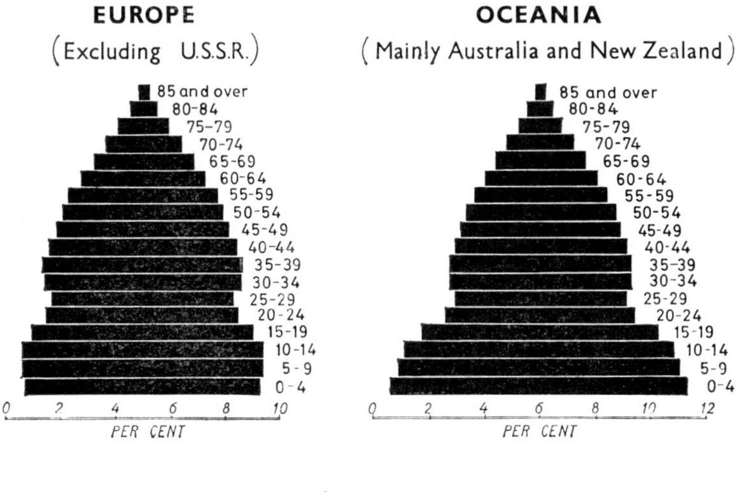

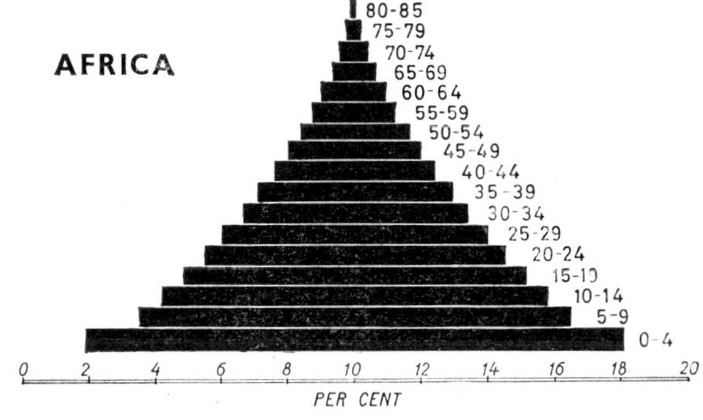

Fig. 6.—POPULATION PYRAMIDS FOR AFRICA, EUROPE, AND OCEANIA. (The length of each bar is proportional to the percentage of the total population in the given age group.)

ing rapidly by natural increase, but which still experiences a high death rate.

The age structure of the European countries resembled that of Africa during the eighteenth and early nineteenth centuries but to-day it is strikingly different. Persons under the age of fifteen comprise

25 per cent. of the total in Europe, as against 41 per cent. in Africa, but the proportion of elderly people (over sixty-five) in Europe is four times as great as in Africa. The proportion within the economically unproductive age groups that have to be supported wholly or in part by the rest of the community is roughly the same in each continent, however. A feature of the European pyramid is the deficiency within the 20-24, and 25-29 age groups. These generations were born during the Second World War and the depression years of the late 1930s, when the birth rate in Europe was lower than at any time in its history.

The age structure of Oceania (mainly Australia and New Zealand) broadly resembles that of Europe, the main difference being the higher percentage of young people in Oceania. Here we have an example of a population which is being increased by immigration. As already noted, immigrants are on the whole drawn from the young adult groups, among whom the birth rate is high.

The growth of population, and the Malthusian theory

Now and again during the past 200 years, a prophet has arisen to warn mankind of the dangers of uncontrolled human reproduction. One such man, who sensed keenly the approach of disaster, was Thomas Robert Malthus, clergyman, and Fellow of Jesus College, Cambridge. In 1798 he published his *Essay on the Principle of Population* in which he sought to show that whilst a nation's means of subsistence (its food, and raw materials) tends to increase in arithmetic progression—1.2.3.4.5.6, etc., its population grows in geometric progression—1.2.4.8.16.32, etc. From this he drew the conclusion that a community *living within a defined area, and drawing the whole of its sustenance therefrom*, must sooner or later increase in numbers up to the limit of its means of subsistence, and that any further increase would be prevented by what he called the positive checks of famine, disease, misery, and war.

Malthus based his theory on a study of conditions in England at the end of the eighteenth century. The population of the country at that time was still small (about 10 million) but was increasing rapidly. Living standards were low, and even a small curtailment in the supply of food brought considerable suffering, if not actual starvation, in its train. The threat of famine was real, as it had been throughout history. There is much evidence to suggest that the Black Death of 1348 and the Great Plague of 1665—which were but two of a host of pestilences that ravaged Britain and the continent during the Middle Ages—followed in the wake of bad harvests when people's resistance to disease was seriously impaired. Malthus's opinions were thus well grounded in historical fact. Events, however, were to prove him utterly wrong as far as Britain and the countries of continental Europe were concerned. The nineteenth and twentieth centuries were to see developments of a scope and nature beyond the wildest dreams of Malthus or any one else living at the time—developments which were to allow a population several times the size of 1790 to live in a state of unimagined prosperity. They were:

1. Enormous improvements in the techniques of production which eventually resulted in a spectacular increase in crop yields, and which also allowed previously uncultivable land to be brought into use.

2. The opening up of virgin territories in the Americas and Australia, made possible by a revolution in transport. The people of Europe thus came to draw a substantial proportion of the food and raw materials they consumed from land they did not inhabit or cultivate.

3. The decline in the rate of population growth, brought about, not by a rise in the death rate as Malthus had predicted, but by a fall in the birth rate.

If Malthus has been proved wrong in Europe, and other economically advanced regions, one cannot be too confident that he will not even yet be vindicated by happenings in many Asian countries. In those lands, the checks of which he wrote—famine, disease, misery, if not war—are operating to prevent a population explosion that would really stagger the world. India's birth rate, for example, coupled with the survival rate now prevailing in Britain would serve to treble her numbers by the end of the present century. In the absence of an increase in her food supply little short of miraculous this cannot happen. Starvation is already widespread in the country. The Bengal famine of 1944 and the recent famine of 1965-6 have been blamed on drought, a breakdown in communications and distribution, and on that handy scapegoat—the administration, but basically they were a consequence of a population outstripping the capacity of the land to support it. Furthermore, unless there is a fall in the country's birth rate comparable to that which occurred in Europe half a century or more ago, they will not be the last of the Indian famines of which we shall hear.

"Optimum" populations

Any discussion on the size, density, or rate of growth of populations is of little value without reference to the resources and techniques of production in the country under consideration. A region peopled by backward tribesmen may be over-populated with a density of ten persons per square mile, whilst another country, no better endowed by nature but inhabited by an enterprising community may comfortably support many times that number.

The population of a country may be said to have reached its optimum when it has grown to, but has not gone beyond, the point at which the law of diminishing returns begins to operate so strongly that per capita production, and consequently standards of living, begin to fall. The discovery of additional resources or improvements in the techniques of production may allow extra people to subsist without a decline in material living standards, but the tendency to diminishing returns is always present. If this were not so, it would be possible for a country to produce the whole of its food supply from one small farm, or the whole of its coal from a single face simply by increasing the number of workers and other factors employed upon it (Table 5).

TABLE 5

OUTPUT OF LABOUR (IN UNITS OF COAL FROM FACE OF GIVEN SIZE) PER WORKING DAY

NUMBER OF WORKERS	TOTAL PRODUCT (per day)	MARGINAL PRODUCT (*i.e.* the product of each additional worker)	DAILY WAGE PER WORKER (at £1 per 10 units of coal produced)
1	10	10	£1
2	22	12	£1·1
3	40	18	£1·33
4	60	20	£1·5
5	85	25	£1·7
6	109	24	£1·82
7	129	20	£1·84
8	144	15	£1·8
9	154	10	£1·71
10	158	4	£1·58
11	154	– 4	£1·4
12	144	– 10	£1·2
13	120	– 24	£0·92
14	90	– 30	£0·64

It is easy to recognise cases of extreme over-population. Many of the rice-growing areas of Asia have far surpassed their optimum levels as defined above. They could make substantial reductions in the number of agricultural workers without appreciably affecting the total output of food. They are in the position of the coalface manager who has taken on the tenth and eleventh man. Land hunger and poverty lie behind the call for industrialisation in these lands.

Manufactured products could be exported, always assuming that markets could be found, in exchange for foreign food.

At the other end of the spectrum stand Australia and Canada as examples of countries whose populations are below the level required for the most effective development of their resources. In each case the application of additional labour would produce more than a proportional increase in the value of output, and a rise in the standards of living would follow. Hence Australia and Canada are doing what they can to encourage immigration.

The migration of populations

Migration has been a feature of human life from the earliest times. Many of the great population movements of history have been, and still are, prompted by economic motives. Men have travelled from place to place in search of new land for their crops and animals, driven perhaps by adverse climatic conditions or increasing pressure on the soil. The Old Testament wanderings and the Mongol incursions into China, Russia, and Eastern Europe were of this type. Between 1820 and 1950 the desire for economic betterment induced some 40 million Europeans to cross the Atlantic to the United States: nearly 9 million made the journey during the first decade of the present century. The same motives have lain behind the migration of the southern Italians and French to North Africa; of Englishmen to the Commonwealth; and of West Indians to Britain.

Some migrations have been a direct consequence of war. One might note the movement of more than 15 million Muslims and Hindus who in 1948 found themselves on the wrong side of the frontier in a partitioned and strife-torn India, or the 25 million Europeans who were uprooted from their homes during and after the Second World War. Migrations of this type are often hurried and unplanned. The people involved are frequently unwelcome in the country where they seek refuge, and become a political and economic embarrassment to its government.

Slave raiding, and the forced transfer of labour have been responsible for mass migrations. Slavery was commonplace in parts of Africa as recently as the beginning of the present century, and there was a strong element of compulsion about the exodus of Russians and others to Siberia during the Tzarist and subsequent periods. One of the most important and spectacular of all forced transfers, however, was the movement of African negroes to the New World. This migration, which spanned nearly three centuries, and involved some 10 million people, has left an indelible imprint on the ethnic, social, and economic structure of the Southern states of the U.S.A., and large areas of Latin America.

Migration as a solution to the problem of over-population

Population pressures have seldom been relieved more than temporarily by migration. Ireland in fact is the only example of a country which has suffered a permanent decline in numbers as a result of emigration. Elsewhere, as far as can be ascertained, losses have been more than off-set by natural increase. As a means of reducing the burden on the over-taxed resources of some of the more hard-pressed Asian countries, emigration lies outside the sphere of practical policies, if only because of the vast numbers that would have to be transferred to give any significant relief. The population of India, for example, is increasing at the rate of about 8 million a year, or some 23,000 a day. The *Queen Elizabeth* has a peace-time capacity of 2,500 passengers, and could be adapted to carry four or five times this number if the need arose. Two vessels then, each the size of the *Queen Elizabeth*, would have to sail from an Indian port, outward bound with emigrants every twenty-four hours, merely to hold the Indian population at its present level. Even if a country willing to accept, house, and feed such multitudes could be found, the sheer impossibility of providing transport on such a scale would prevent it making more than a well-intentioned gesture.

British migrations since 1800

Between 1800 and 1930, approximately 20 million people left Britain for the U.S.A. and the Commonwealth. To some extent this loss was balanced by immigration from Ireland and the Continent, but over the period as a whole 10 million more people left than arrived. Since 1930 the flow has been reversed, and the net movement has been inwards. Returning British nationals, refugees from Europe, Irishmen, and coloured Commonwealth citizens, have made up most of the arrivals. At the 1961 census, 2·1 million residents in the United Kingdom were found to have been born abroad.

Internal migrations

The movement of people *within* national territories is usually free from the kind of restraints (customs and language barriers, restrictive immigration laws, etc.) that inhibit migration to foreign countries. In Britain, a sizeable proportion of the population changes its place of residence every year, particularly in prosperous times. In 1961 one person in every ten persons moved home, although the majority moved only to other houses in the same district. In the short term the number of people who leave a particular area is more or less balanced by the numbers that arrive. Certain long-term trends, however, are plainly discernible in practically every country in the world, viz.

1. The movement from the countryside into the cities.

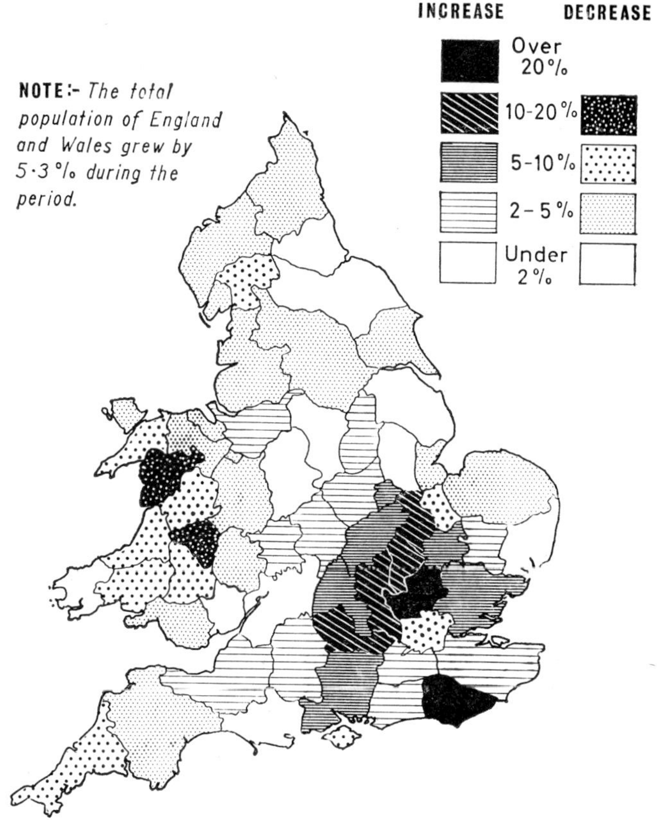

Fig. 7.—Percentage Changes in Population of England and Wales, 1951-61.

2. The movement from the centres and inner suburbs of large cities to the outer suburbs, or to towns beyond the city boundaries.

3. The movement from regions of declining economic importance to regions of economic growth (Fig. 7).

Population and economic demand

In an economic sense a community can only demand what it can afford. The demands of people living at subsistence level are small, and tend to concentrate on the bare essentials of life—food, clothing, shelter, and fuel. As the purchasing power of such people is low, goods must be cheap. This is one of the reasons for the shoddiness of some of the products made in the poorer lands of the Far East. An increase in wealth alters the pattern of demand. It results first of all in a growing desire to possess commodities that could not be afforded initially—footwear, bicycles, and perhaps radio sets—and later in a demand for more expensive substitutes. Thus in a prosperous society, motor vehicles come to replace bicycles; television sets are bought rather than radio sets; meat, butter, eggs, milk, and fresh fruit are preferred to the "filler" foods such as potatoes and cereals; holidays are taken abroad rather than at home.

The modern state is able, by means of its own direct spending of money obtained from its citizens by taxation and through the medium of subsidies, to determine the pattern of supply and demand to a degree unknown in the past. Whether this is desirable or not is outside the primary concern of the economic geographer, but as it influences the manner in which a country's productive resources are employed it is something of which he must take account. One might consider, for instance, whether the demand for armaments, space vehicles, the dispensations of the National Health Service, education, and so on would be as great as it is, or even whether it would exist at all in some cases, if the community were not persuaded or compelled by the State to "consume" the goods or services it provides.

Population and the supply of labour

The production of goods and services is impossible without labour, and an intelligent and adaptable labour force is the most valuable economic asset that a country can possess. The size of a nation's labour force will be determined, obviously, by the total size of the population, but also by such factors as age and sex structure, the extent to which society permits or encourages women to engage in work outside the home, and the age at which employment normally begins and ends. Its efficiency will depend on labour attitudes to work (which in turn are conditioned by religious beliefs, tradition, the influence of trade unions, etc.), health, standards of education, the competence of the management, the amount of machine-power behind each worker, and the quality of the machines at his disposal. Generally speaking, productivity (*i.e.* the value of output per worker per day) will be high in the technically advanced countries where a high ratio of capital to labour is employed, and low in the under-developed lands, where labour is cheap in relation to other factors of production, and where, because of its cheapness, it is often employed wastefully.

Wage rates and the cost of labour

It is essential to appreciate that there is no direct relationship between wage rates on one hand, and the cost of labour on the other. Low wages do not necessarily mean that labour is cheap, neither do high wages imply that it is expensive. An industry can be said to enjoy the advantages of cheap labour (or suffer from the handicaps of expensive labour) only when the labour cost component in that industry is lower (or higher) than in other similar industries. For example, the total production costs of two factories turning out equal quantities of identical products may be compounded as follows:

Factory A.	Wages of 200 men at £10 each per week = £2,000	All other processing costs (power, depreciation on plant, etc.) = £2,000	Labour cost component as percentage of total value added by manufacture $= \frac{2,000}{4,000} = 50\%$
Factory B.	Wages of 50 men at £20 each per week = £1,000	All other processing costs = £2,000	Labour cost component as percentage of total value added by manufacture $= \frac{1,000}{3,000} = 33\frac{1}{3}\%$

It is clear in this particular instance, that B's smaller wage bill results not from the greater input of mechanical energy, or the use of labour saving machinery (fuel costs and plant depreciation, etc., are the same in each case) but that it is due solely to the fact that the labour employed at Factory B is either working harder, working for longer hours, or simply working more effectively. Whatever the reason, labour at Factory B, in spite of the higher wages it receives, is cheaper in the real sense of the word than at Factory A.

Labour costs expressed as a proportion of the total value added by manufacture vary greatly from one type of industry to another, as well as from factory to factory within a given industry. Industries in which the labour cost component is high, and which at the same time (*a*) are not attracted strongly to the source of their raw materials (as is cement making), (*b*) are not tied closely to the markets for their products (as is bespoke tailoring, bread, and soft drink manufacture), (*c*) possess no specialised site requirements (as does shipbuilding) tend to be pulled towards centres where labour costs are genuinely low. Such industries include textiles and the ready-made clothing trades. The last hundred years has witnessed a major shift in the areas of cotton manufacturing from New England to the low wage regions of the South, and from Britain to the countries of eastern Asia. Towns in which there is a limited opportunity for unskilled female work are often attractive to firms seeking low-cost labour. The rise of the silk industries of Scranton and Wilkes Barre (Pennsylvania), and the clothing trades of Crewe (Fig. 3) is due at least in part to the presence of surplus female labour in centres of predominantly male employment.

Labour skills

In a number of industries, a considerable proportion of the total labour force is made up of skilled craftsmen. The production of machine tools, fine metal goods, certain types of pottery, furniture, watches, and made-to-measure clothing, is not possible without the application of manual skills learned during a long period of apprenticeship. The constructional and maintenance trades also depend on skilled bricklayers, electricians, plumbers, and joiners. Increasingly in modern industry, however, as machines take over work formerly done by craftsmen, and as industrial processes become more and more a matter of applying flow-line techniques to the production and assembly of standardised components, the need for the old, traditional skills declines. In many factories to-day the great majority of the workers are unskilled or semi-skilled men and women who have received only a few weeks' or even days' training for the work in which they are currently engaged, and perform tedious, repetitive tasks which call for little practical ability.

The replacement of skilled men by machines which are simple to operate is making both labour and industry increasingly mobile. Transfer from one job to another is not particularly difficult if a long period of re-training is unnecessary. The ease with which women took to unfamiliar work in munition factories during the Second World War is an indication of how adaptable modern labour has become. The migration of industry to new areas is not inhibited in the way it once was by the absence in those areas of skilled craftsmen. The majority of industries (the craft industries noted above are obvious exceptions) are now relatively "footloose" as far as their labour requirements are concerned. A firm seeking a location for a new factory looks not so much for a pool of skilled labour (as the skills it possesses will probably be inapplicable in any case) but for a pool of surplus labour or even a pool of relatively poorly paid labour that can be weaned from other industries by the offer of higher wages. Key personnel—managers, scientists, design experts, etc., are, of course, a different matter. Most firms employ a nucleus of highly trained men. Their numbers, however, are usually small, and they can be attracted to the point where they are needed by the payment of high salaries, the provision of houses, travel allowances, and other inducements.

CHAPTER II

TRANSPORT

Transport is essential to all types of economic activity. Even the most primitive and self-sufficient individual must "consume" transport in one form or another, for otherwise he would have to provide with his own hands all the necessities and luxuries of life, and what is more, would have to provide them from resources in his own back yard.

When advanced, industrial nations are considered, it becomes apparent that their needs are so great and varied that they can only be satisfied when goods and services are drawn from a very wide area indeed. No country, however large and well endowed by nature, can produce all that it requires. Trade is essential, and trade cannot take place without means of transport. Modern industry, too, has become so complex, and labour specialisation so fine, that even the simplest article is likely to be manufactured in stages, each stage more or less dispersed geographically, and each utilising the various factors of production (labour, capital, and natural resources) in varying ratios and in different ways. The essential function of transport in industry is to link together each stage of production from the winning of the raw material to the emergence of the finished article, and then to distribute the finished article to as wide a market as possible.

Some consequences of transport inventions

The growth of every nation's economy has been closely bound up with improvements in its transport system. The steam ship and the railway in the nineteenth century, for example, made the Industrial Revolution possible in Britain, and later in Europe and North America. Together these new inventions provided for the first time in history the means whereby bulk cargoes could be carried safely, cheaply, and quickly over long distances. They opened up new lands to mining and agriculture, and helped to spread perhaps 50 million Europeans over all the temperate, and many of the tropical, regions of the world, and with them Western methods of farming, industry, and commerce. The railways in particular performed a service of incalculable value in the development of the great continental interiors of North America and Siberia. It is scarcely an exaggeration to say that they built the United States.

In the twentieth century the motor vehicle and the aircraft—both novelties before the First World War—are having an effect no less revolutionary than did their predecessors a hundred years ago. To-day many countries, especially the smaller ones, rely more on the roads than the railways for inland freight movements. Through the medium of the privately owned truck and car, firms and individuals have been provided with a means of transport which frees them from the routes and schedules of the public carriers. Goods and people can move where and when they please. Deliveries can be arranged to suit the convenience of customers. The need for firms and wholesalers to carry large stocks has been reduced, thus releasing capital for productive use. The retailing of goods has also been greatly simplified.

The impact of air transport during the last twenty years, particularly of long-distance passenger transport, on the world's economic and political life has, of course, been spectacular. New York can now be reached from London in five hours, and the cities of Australia in two days. Within a decade these times will probably have been reduced by half. The aircraft is also changing the lives of thousands living in isolated farming and mining communities in Australia and Northern Canada; and in the backward and thinly populated parts of Africa, Asia, and Latin America, where distances are great and surface communications poorly developed, the light aeroplane is proving a boon to government officials, scientists, and engineers (to whom time is precious), if not as yet to the common people.

The present century has also seen the development of pipeline transport on a massive scale. Each day it carries untold quantities of water, oil, natural gas, slurried coal, chalk, limestone, and shale without the majority of the population beneath whose feet these commodities pass being aware of its existence. The economies of many countries would collapse if the pipelines ceased to operate.

Finally, one should not overlook the simpler transport inventions of the last 150 years. Few vehicles can have had such an impact on the lives of ordinary people as the bicycle. Before, and during the Second World War a sizeable proportion of Britain's labour force rode to its daily work on bikes, not in cars; and in parts of the world to-day—in rough jungle country within the tropics, for instance, and even in some congested European towns these cheap, uncomplicated, and yet wonderfully flexible machines give men a degree of mobility that no other vehicle could possibly give.

An efficient transport system should be able to meet all the demands that are made upon it. It should contain elements able to move bulk materials cheaply; others capable of high speeds over both long and short journeys; and yet others adaptable enough to carry large and small consignments anywhere, and at any time. Water, rail, road, and air transport, as well as the specialised carriers all have a part to play in a modern economy. They must be regarded as complementary as well as competing transport media, and an abundance of any one type does not adequately compensate for the insufficiency of another.

Transport costs

The cost *to a carrier, i.e.* to a transport company, of moving a consignment of goods from A to B comprises the following elements:

(1) The cost of loading into the transport vehicle. This cost, which is largely determined by the ease with which the goods can be handled, bears no relationship to the distance travelled, and does not vary with it.

(2) Movement costs. These vary to some extent with the type of route being traversed, otherwise they increase directly with the distance travelled.

(3) Trans-shipment costs, as occur when freight is transferred from one vehicle to another.

(4) The cost of unloading at the destination.

(5) Insurance charges.

The rates charged by hauliers do not necessarily reflect the true cost of providing a particular service. It does not follow, for example, that because factory X is situated at twice the distance from a pit-head as factory Y it will pay twice as much for the carriage of its coal. The reason why rates cannot be calculated on a simple ton-mileage (or for that matter passenger-mileage) basis is because an element of cross-subsidisation enters into the price structure of the public transport undertakings, and occasionally into those of the private hauliers. There are numerous every-day examples of the consequences of the cross-subsidisation of services. It costs a person no more, for instance, to send a parcel by post from London to Aberdeen, than from one part of London to another, or even to the house next door. Children under the age of fourteen travel at half-fare by bus or train, although they occupy a seat, and are as expensive to carry as an adult. The standard first- or second-class rail fare takes no account of the cost of providing the particular service for which the charge is made, and the users of the main line expresses in effect provide a handsome subsidy to those who travel by branch line, and to many who use the commuter trains. The railways which operate a nation-wide network of routes are in the strongest position to implement a policy of discriminatory pricing, and until recently in Britain they were under a statutory obligation to do so on their freight as well as on their passenger services. The Railway Act of 1921 divided the several categories of merchandise into twenty-one classes, and commodities in Class I, which included ashes for road repair, and waste tips, bulk chalk, and iron ore, were carried at a much lower rate than gold and silver which were placed in Class 21. The aim was to encourage the maximum use of the rail system, and at the same time to raise as much revenue as possible by charging the various types of traffic as much as, but no more, than they could bear.

Transport companies sometimes offer preferential rates in order to attract and retain business. A well-known case is the rail rate on Californian oranges. The Californian grower pays considerably less per ton mile to have his fruit carried to the eastern markets than his rival grower in Florida pays. If it were otherwise many of the Californian fruit farmers would go out of business, and the railways would lose the revenue that now accrues from the orange traffic. The existence of competing transport services can also affect freight rates. Goods passing by rail along the Hudson Valley thus move more cheaply than they undoubtedly would if the New York State Barge Canal did not run parallel to the tracks. Very low rates can also be secured at times on commodities carried as a "return cargo" on a vehicle that would otherwise run empty, and on goods carried in bulk, regularly in full vehicle loads, or during periods when the transport system is under utilised.

The cost of haulage is the largest, but not the only factor in transport costs. The cost of documentation and packaging, insurance rates, the cost of providing warehouse space, and holding stocks are also charges against transport in the fuller meaning of the term. If a particular type of transport can produce a saving on any one of these items, by, for example, offering a safer, more regular, and reliable service it may well be preferred, even though its rates are not the lowest. It is considerations of this sort that have convinced many firms of the advantages of operating their own fleets of road vehicles instead of relying on the public carriers, in spite of the fact that the price of maintaining the fleets may be a very high one.

TYPES OF TRANSPORT

1. OCEAN TRANSPORT

While road, rail, canal, and to a less extent air, transport companies have for many years competed for internal traffic, the shipping services have held until very recently a complete monopoly of all freight and passenger movements that have had to cross water. Air transport is to-day making inroads into the overseas passenger business, both

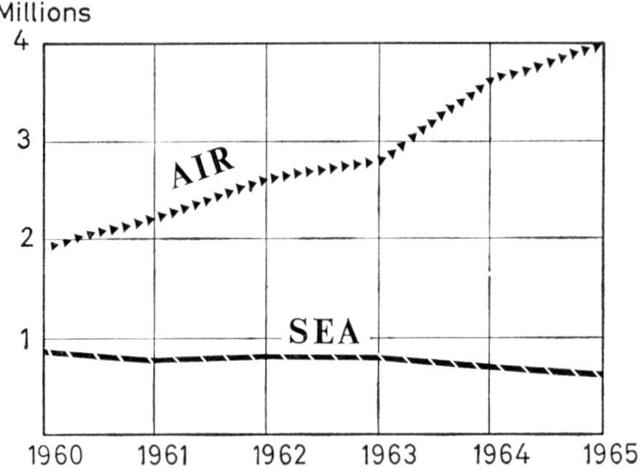

Fig. 8.—Transatlantic Passenger Traffic (1960-65).

on long and short journeys. Its share of the transport of valuable articles of freight is also increasing. Seven per cent. of British exports (by value) were carried by air in 1965, compared with under 3 per cent. ten years ago. But the ship remains the only transport vehicle able to carry the vast majority of cargoes that pass over the oceans. 99·98 per cent. by weight of Britain's exports, for example, are still sent by sea.

Types of ocean transport

Liner and tramp services.—A liner is a vessel that works to a regular and advertised schedule. It may be a passenger or a freight vessel, or it may carry both passengers and freight. A tramp on the other hand, plies for hire, sailing where it can pick up a cargo. Its voyage is likely to be triangular in character. It might sail to Denmark carrying Welsh coal, and return to a South Wales port with a shipment of Finnish timber. Liner charges are made from published tariffs. Tramp rates are a matter for negotiation between the owners of the vessel and those chartering it. Liners are of value principally to passengers and to traders who ship goods in small consignments to regular destinations, whereas tramps are best suited to homogeneous cargoes moving in bulk. Because of the different nature of the cargoes carried in each class of vessel, the tramp features most prominently in Britain's import trade, and the liner in her export trade.

SPECIALISED CARRIERS.—Certain commodities are carried satisfactorily only in specially equipped vessels. Meat and bananas have to be transported in holds where temperatures can be carefully controlled. Oil is conveyed in compartment vessels in which stringent precautions are taken to guard against the risk of fire. Liquefied natural gas cannot possibly be shipped except in specially designed tankers. Some commodities which were formerly carried in general cargo ships are now moved in such bulk that it has become economically worthwhile to build carriers specifically to handle them, and to equip the terminals with specialised loading and discharging gear. Iron ore, coal, grain, and sugar are now coming increasingly into this category.

Costs of ocean transport

Movement costs by water are extremely low—a consequence of the small amount of energy required to move a vehicle through water compared with movement on land. On a capacity-cost basis, large vessels are cheaper to build and maintain, consume less fuel, and can be handled by fewer men than small ones. The advantage of the large vessel is evident from the fact that the cost of carrying each ton of oil in a 160,000 ton tanker is only one-third the cost incurred by a 20,000 ton tanker. The size of ships, especially the bulk carriers, has increased rapidly in recent years owing to the economies of scale that result from the use of bigger transport units. The upward limit on their size, however, is set by two factors:

(i) the berthing facilities available in ports, and the depth of water in their approaches. Where ship canals have to be navigated, *e.g.* on the Great Lakes, the size of the locks also effectively restricts the tonnage of vessels that can use the route.

(ii) the size of the payload. Economies of scale are realised only when a ship can be loaded to, or nearly to, its full capacity. A large vessel operating with its holds only one-quarter full is not a paying proposition.

Terminal charges at ports are high, and for short voyages may exceed movement costs. This makes sea transport expensive, and generally uncompetitive with road or rail on coastwise services over distances of less than a few hundred miles.

Ocean ports.—The function of a port is to provide facilities for the discharge, storage, re-sorting, and trans-shipment of cargoes, and the transfer of passengers from water to land transport, and vice versa.

Ideally, a port should be situated in a harbour spacious and deep enough to accommodate simultaneously, and without congestion, several of the largest and hundreds of the smaller vessels at any state of the tide. In addition, the harbour should afford protection from the weather, be free from ice and fog, have a low tidal range, and enjoy easy communications with a rich hinterland which creates and receives the traffic passing through the port. A situation on or near a busy shipping lane so that vessels do not have to make a wide detour to reach port is a further asset. Because of the relative cheapness of ocean transport for most kinds of cargo, commercial ports tend to be established as near the head of navigation on a river or estuary as possible in order to reduce the distance that goods must travel over-land to their ultimate destination. In some cases outports have grown up to serve vessels that cannot reach the main port. Tilbury (London), Cuxhaven (Hamburg), Bremerhaven (Bremen), Ijmuiden (Amsterdam), and Avonmouth (Bristol), are examples.

The harbour.—Natural harbours exist as nature created them, and are usable without need for any, or only minor, improvements. Of the world's natural harbours able to accommodate large ocean-going vessels, those of Southampton, Milford Haven, Rio de Janeiro, Sydney, and Hong Kong are among the finest. Most of the world's harbours are artificial to a greater or lesser degree. Improvement has been carried out by deepening or increasing the area of the harbour, as at Los Angeles, dredging the approaches as at Liverpool and New York (and in a special way at Rotterdam and Amsterdam, where the old channels became totally inadequate to cope with the increasing size of ships wishing to use the ports, and new artificial approaches had to be constructed), or by building break-waters to give additional protection from rough seas. The harbours of Tema and Takoradi on the exposed coast of Ghana, and the harbour at Dover are entirely artificial, and are protected in this way.

The hinterland.—The region tributary to the port constitutes its hinterland. This may be essentially local and specialised (Blyth and Fowey), regional (Newcastle), national (New York and London), or international (Rotterdam, Singapore, and Hong Kong). The influence of a port declines with increasing distance from it. Two points, however, should be noted, viz.:

1. There is always a considerable over-lapping of the hinterlands of adjacent ports.

2. For certain commodities the hinterland may extend over the greater part of the country in which the port is situated. The hinterland is more extensive in the case of high value products which are not deterred by heavy overland charges, and those for which highly specialised handling and storage facilities are needed, than it is for low grade commodities which tend to be shipped from or to the port nearest their place of origin or destination. Cross haulage is uncommon for tramp cargoes which can be handled at almost any port, but not unusual for cargoes that are shipped by a particular liner service that may operate from one port only. Thus Liverpool, with well-established liner connections with the Far East, handles most of the east-bound liner traffic originating in the United Kingdom.

The nature of internal communications is important in determining the extent of a port's hinterland. Ports well situated in relation to road, rail, or inland water routes are likely to outstrip their rivals. New York, on a site at the seaward end of the easiest crossing point of the Appalachians, with access by all forms of surface transport to the Mid-West, has grown at the expense of Boston and Baltimore. The alignment of the British railway network, which radiates spoke-like from London, has favoured London and Liverpool rather than Bristol and Hull; while on the Continent the Rhine and its tributaries have bestowed enormous advantages upon the ports on the main river, and particularly those situated near its mouth.

Specialised ports

A PACKET STATION—DOVER.—Dover has functioned as a port since the Romans established an anchorage in a tiny harbour carved in the chalk cliffs by the River Dour. The natural harbour has for long been useless because of silting, but a man-made harbour has been constructed over the centuries to give one of the largest areas of artificially protected water in the world. Dover has become the largest passenger port in the British Isles because of its position on the narrow seas, commanding the shortest route to the Continent (Fig. 9). For passenger traffic, the short crossing has the double advantage of saving time (as sea travel is slower than road or rail) and sparing travellers the discomfort of several hours at sea in a small ship. A train ferry links London with Paris via Dover and Dunkirk, and a number of car ferries are in operation. Cargoes handled at the port are generally of a high value in relation to bulk, and those for which rapid transit is essential. Of the bulky commodities, oil and pit props are the most important. When eventually a Channel tunnel is built,

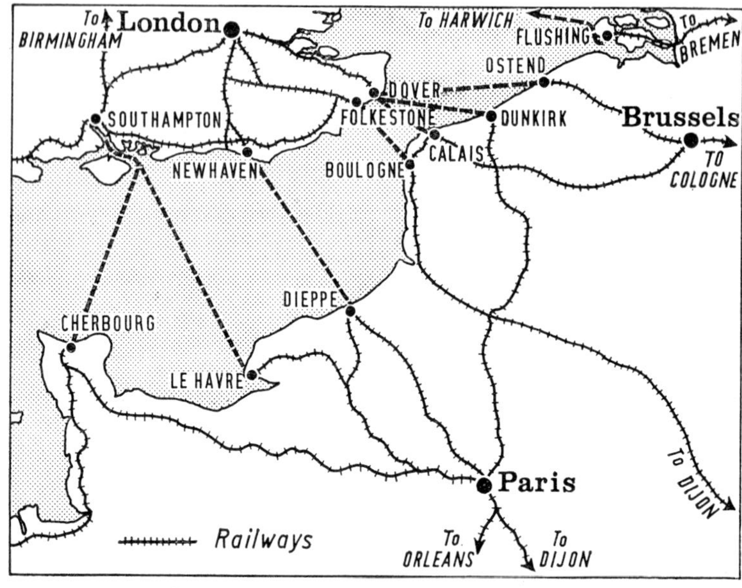

Fig. 9.—Ferry Ports on the Narrow Seas.

Dover will become a rail head, passing cargoes from many parts of Great Britain to the Continent much more quickly, and probably at lower cost, than they move at present by sea.

Blyth—a specialised port with a restricted hinterland.—Blyth is situated towards the northern apex of the Northumberland and Durham coalfield at a point where the Blyth River reaches the sea. The trade of Blyth is highly specialised: shipments of coal comprise more than 97 per cent. of the cargoes passing through the port (Table 6). The coal originates at some twenty collieries lying within a few miles of the town, and is transported to the harbour by rail. Bulk handling equipment allows coal to be emptied directly from rail trucks into waiting colliers. The important coal export trade of the pre-war years has now been reduced to small proportions, but coastwise shipments to the Thames, and the East Anglian, Channel, and Scottish ports have been well maintained. The great excess of out-going over incoming cargoes is a noteworthy feature of the trade of Blyth, and involves the return of most vessels in ballast.

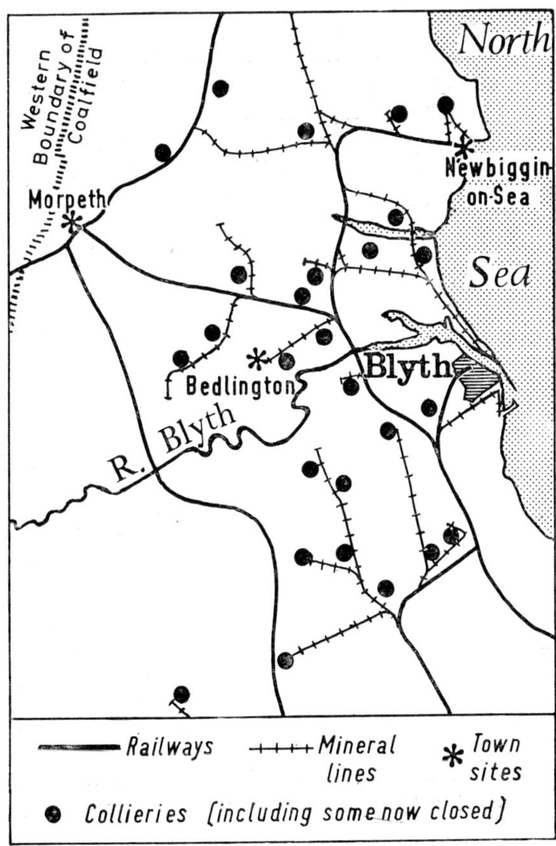

Fig. 10.—Colliery Sites near Blyth, Northumberland.

TABLE 6

THE TRADE OF BLYTH, 1965
(in tons)

INWARD		OUTWARD	
Cement	35,909	Coal	4,584,797
Pit props	14,868	Barley	3,573
Deals, battens, and boards	7,524	Firebricks and fireclay	699
Machinery and other iron goods	2,026	Scrap iron	2,170
Tiles	1,199	Fuel oil	5,563
Oil fuel	3,561	Iron and steel	219
Fertilisers	820	Marine Seismex	509
Miscellaneous	394	Provisions	1,062
		Miscellaneous	85
Total	66,301	Total	4,598,677

Source: Blyth Harbour Commission.

SINGAPORE—A GREAT ENTREPÔT.—Singapore first became important early in the nineteenth century as a base of the East India Company. The subsequent development of the port was due to its large, deep water harbour, and its position at the very tip of the Malay Peninsula, where shipping routes from Europe and India to South East Asia, the Far East, and Australia diverge after passing along the narrow corridor of the Malacca Straits (Fig. 11).

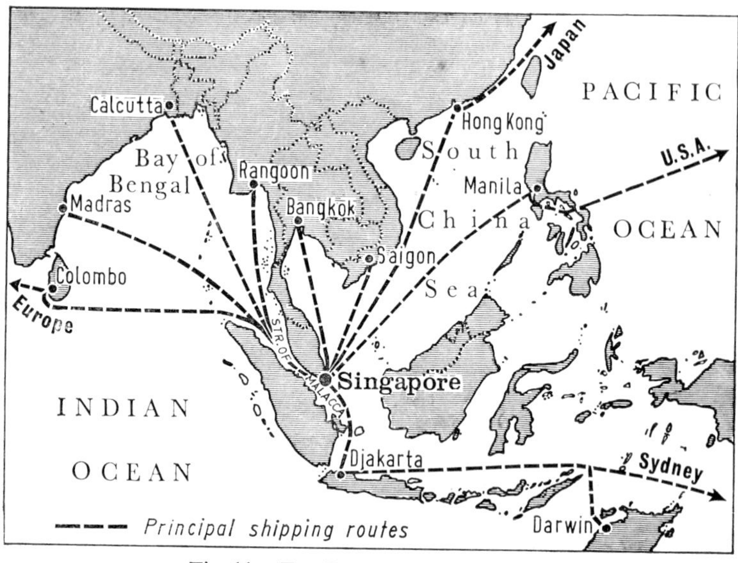

Fig. 11.—THE POSITION OF SINGAPORE.

The trade of Singapore is essentially of an entrepôt character. The port acts as a great depot for the region, collecting rubber, tin, copra, timber, rice, pepper, palm oil, and other primary commodities from continental and insular South East Asia, and then sorting and re-exporting them to Europe and North America. Bulk shipments of machinery, textiles, and Western foodstuff are also broken down at Singapore and distributed. A feature of this type of trade is the similarity between the import and export lists of the port (Table 7). Singapore is a city of merchants and middlemen, of offices, banks, and finance houses. Manufacturing industry is of small but growing importance. The insular character of much of South East Asia, and the difficulties of land communications across predominantly forested and mountainous terrain have directed trade to the sea, so that the bulk of traffic passing through Singapore is waterborne, the collecting and distributing part of the business being done by thousands of small craft. Until 1959, when some protective tariffs were imposed by the new government, the city was a free port, and commodities were landed without payment of duties. Freedom from artificial restraints on trade was a significant factor in the rise of the city.

TABLE 7

SELECTED LIST OF COMMODITIES PASSING THROUGH SINGAPORE IN 1964
(in tons except where otherwise stated)

	IMPORTS	EXPORTS
Tin blocks, ingots, bars, and slabs (unwrought)	442	605
Coconut oil, crude and refined	7,900	14,800
Copra cakes	6,900	3,770
Pepper, unground, black and white	10,900	14,800
Palm oil	35,500	36,900
Pineapples, canned	40,750	50,300
Rice (thousands of tons)	260	107
Wheat flour	51,200	56,300
Biscuits (thousands of hundredweights)	68	70
Condensed milk (thousands of pounds)	59,000	23,000
Fish, dried or salted	8,700	5,580
Beer and ale (thousands of gallons)	980	2,490
Cigarettes (thousands of pounds)	3,400	2,370
Flashlight batteries (thousands)	26,100	51,600
Sewing machines, industrial and household (thousands)	38	21
Cotton piece goods (millions of square yards)	164	118

Source: *Monthly Digest of Statistics, Singapore.*

General cargo ports

MERSEYSIDE.—Merseyside, rather than Liverpool, is the more appropriate term for the port which extends along both banks of the Mersey estuary, and which lies within the county boroughs of Liverpool, Bootle, Birkenhead, and Wallasey.

Liverpool, where most of the port installations are situated, first became important in the thirteenth century as a military base against the Irish. For more than 400 years its growth was retarded by the presence of Chester, twenty miles to the south, which syphoned off most of the region's trade. Liverpool's rather isolated position on the seaward side of a belt of enveloping marshland was also an impediment to its development in the early years.

A number of factors contributed to the growth of Liverpool after 1700. Chester was finally abandoned as a port during the eighteenth century after attempts to improve navigation on the Dee had failed. The eighteenth and nineteenth centuries brought forth a great upsurge of mining and manufacturing activity in Lancashire and Cheshire, and with it the development of an important export trade in salt, coal, and factory products. The canal, and later the railway, extended Liverpool's influence eastward to the Pennines, and beyond, and southwards into the Midlands. Abroad, commercial connections were established with the temperate and tropical food and raw material producing countries of both hemispheres. Liverpool's trade, which during the early period had been conducted with Ireland, France, and Spain, became world-wide in character.

Birkenhead began to share in the activities of Liverpool during the nineteenth century when the port extended across the river. The harbour facilities on both banks are now owned and managed by the

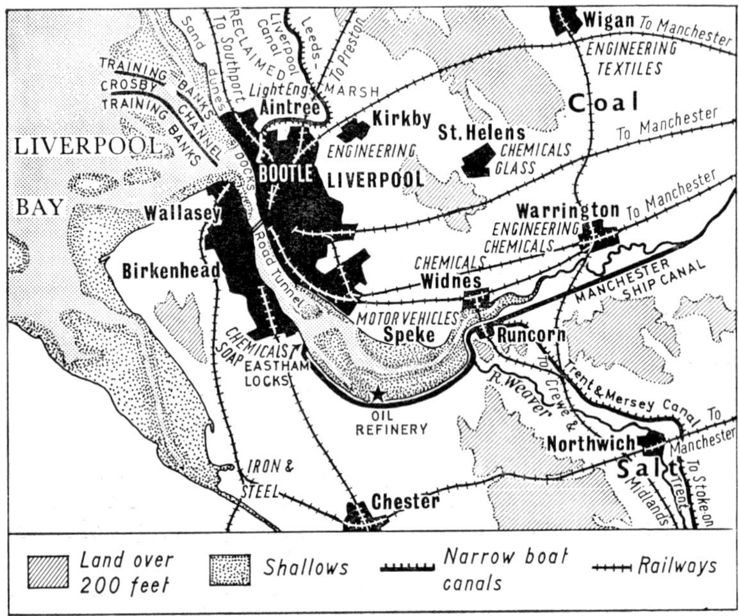

Fig. 12.—Part of the Hinterland of Liverpool.

Mersey Docks and Harbour Board, with the exception of the railway docks at Garston. These passed to the control of the Transport Commission in 1948.

Merseyside's main physical asset is the great depth of water in the "Narrows"—the 1,000-yard-wide stretch of river between Liverpool and Birkenhead. The constriction of the estuary at this point increases the speed of both the flood and ebb tides, and removes any tendency towards silting. The approaches to the harbour, on the other hand, are obstructed by shallows, and before dredging began in 1890 there was a depth of only ten feet over the bar at low water. Constant dredging, and the construction of training walls along the

Crosby and Queen's Channels, now help to maintain a minimum depth of twenty-five feet, and a navigable passage over a mile wide at any state of the tide.

The great tidal range, which has been known to exceed thirty feet, and the speed at which the flow enters and leaves the estuary constitute a problem and a hazard with which vessels and harbour authorities have had to contend since earliest times. Instead of quays, tidal basins, and riverside wharves which are the normal structures at ports where the range of the tide is low, an elaborate system of docks has had to be built (Fig. 13). Within the docks ships can load and

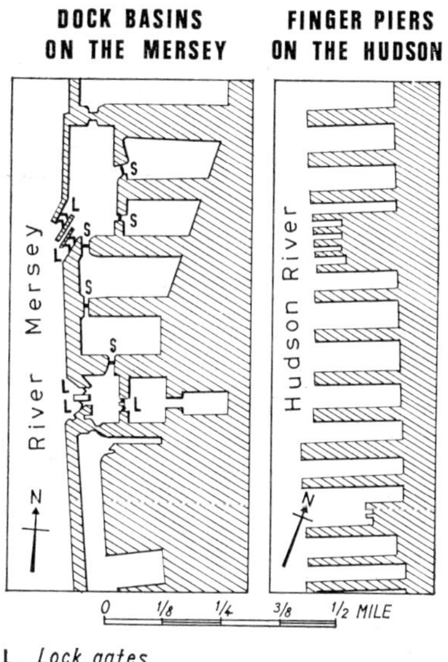

Fig. 13.—PORT STRUCTURES AT LIVERPOOL AND NEW YORK.

discharge without interference from the fluctuating level of the river, but the larger vessels are able to enter and leave dock only during a short period on each side of high water.

As a manufacturing centre Merseyside has attracted the normal assemblage of "port" industries, based to a large extent on the working up of imported raw materials. Grain milling, sugar refining, cattle and poultry food processing, oil seed crushing, margarine manufacture, and the production of newsprint are among the industries in this group. Shipbuilding and repairing are the main industrial activities of Birkenhead. At a few points on the Cheshire bank only, can vessels discharge directly on to factory premises. On the Liverpool side docks line the entire waterfront. Factories occupy a zone to the rear of the docks, and off-loading from ship to lorry is necessary. In this respect Liverpool is at a disadvantage compared with the port of Manchester, which has access to almost unlimited space for industrial development along the thirty-seven miles of Ship Canal between the terminal docks and Eastham.

TABLE 8

THE TRADE OF LIVERPOOL

IMPORTS (in £ millions)

	1963	1964
Food, drink, and tobacco	*292·0*	*301·0*
Meat and meat preparations	25·4	29·9
Cereals and cereal preparations	32·6	32·2
Fruit and vegetables	53·3	54·1
Sugar and sugar preparations	57·5	48·5
Animal feedstuffs	10·4	10·6
Coffee, tea, cocoa, spices	24·0	20·9
Tobacco and tobacco manufactures	23·9	20·9
Wine, beer, and spirits	7·3	7·7
Crude materials (inedible) except fuel	*214·0*	*226·0*
Oil seeds, oil nuts, and oil kernels	17·9	16·0
Crude rubber	22·7	21·6
Wood, lumber, and cork	20·0	26·4
Textile fibres and their wastes	107·5	104·0
Metalliferous ores and scrap	4·9	6·1
Hides, skins, and furs	6·2	7·0
Mineral fuels, lubricants, and related materials	*54·0*	*57·0*
Petroleum and petroleum products	53·5	56·8
Animal and vegetable oils and fats	*24·0*	*29·0*
Animal oils and fats	7·6	11·8
Fixed vegetable oils and fats	15·1	16·3

EXPORTS (in £ millions)

	1963	1964
Food, drink, and tobacco	*40·0*	*41·0*
Dairy produce and eggs	3·9	3·4
Cereals and cereal preparations	3·4	3·6
Sugar and sugar preparations	7·4	6·3
Wine, beer, and spirits	11·2	13·4
Tobacco and tobacco manufactures	4·5	4·5
Crude materials (inedible) except fuel	*48·0*	*43·0*
Textile fibres and their wastes	39·2	34·8
Mineral fuels, lubricants, and related materials	*11·0*	*10·0*
Petroleum and petroleum products	9·2	8·4
Coal, coke, and briquettes	1·5	1·6
Animal and vegetable oils and fats	*3·8*	*2·8*

TABLE 8 (*continued*)

Imports (in £ millions)	1963	1964
Chemicals	*28·0*	*35·0*
Chemical elements and compounds	10·7	12·6
Plastics, etc.	7·9	11·6
Machinery and transport equipment	*41·0*	*57·3*
Machinery, non-electric	32·7	45·8
Electrical machinery	5·6	6·9
Transport equipment	2·9	4·6
Manufactured goods	*147·0*	*187·0*
Textile yarn, fabrics, and articles	44·4	58·3
Non-ferrous metals	77·8	88·3
Miscellaneous manufactured articles and unclassified commodities	*26·0*	*39·2*
TOTAL IMPORTS	*826·0*	*932·0*

Exports (in £ millions)	1963	1964
Chemicals	*111·0*	*123·0*
Chemical elements and compounds	36·2	38·9
Dyeing and tanning materials	15·7	17·3
Medicinal and pharmaceutical products	9·8	9·8
Plastics, etc.	17·4	20·6
Machinery and transport equipment	*394·0*	*404·0*
Machinery, non-electric	216·9	225·2
Electrical machinery	74·1	69·2
Transport equipment	103·2	109·8
Manufactured goods	*264·0*	*287·0*
Rubber manufactures	15·2	13·2
Paper and paper-board	8·3	8·2
Textile yarn, fabrics, and articles	82·5	92·3
Non-metallic mineral manufactures	27·7	30·6
Iron and steel	47·8	54·0
Non-ferrous metals	34·3	39·9
Manufacture of metals	42·8	43·9
Miscellaneous manufactured articles and unclassified commodities	*54·0*	*58·0*
TOTAL EXPORTS	*926·0*	*969·0*

N.B. The slight inaccuracies in the totals are due to "rounding" of the values in the principal groups.

Source: *Port Statistics of the Foreign Trade of the United Kingdom*, Part III 1964.

2. INLAND WATERWAYS

Rivers and canals

Rivers are where nature placed them, and this is not always where they are of greatest value to man. Besides navigability—which is influenced by such factors as depth and width of the channel, seasonal fluctuations in flow, and climatic hazards—the economic significance of a river depends upon its alignment in relation to population centres, natural resources, and established trade routes. However easily navigated a river might be, it will have little commercial value unless it traverses a region where there are commodities to be carried. The Amazon with its tributaries constitutes the finest system of natural highways in the world, but because it drains an area of jungle and swamp it is commercially of little worth (Fig. 14). Even the Mississippi, the greatest river of the North American continent, and once its main commercial artery, lost much of its importance when the railway channelled trade away from its productive basin eastwards to the Atlantic ports. On the other hand a river that links densely settled areas, or taps rich agricultural, mining, or industrial hinterlands, and which discharges into a sea that is not a commercial backwater, provides a means of communication whose significance can scarcely be over-estimated. Such rivers include the Rhine,

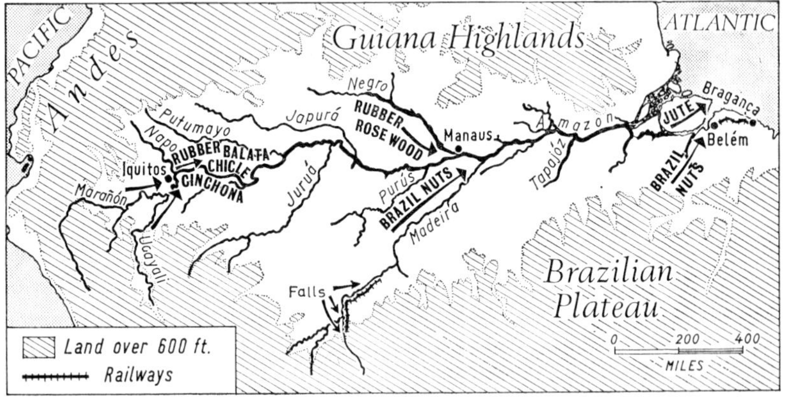

Fig. 14.—THE NAVIGABLE REACHES OF THE AMAZON AND ITS TRIBUTARIES.

which penetrates the heart of industrial Europe, and the St Lawrence-Great Lakes, which bears ocean-going vessels 2,000 miles into Canada and the United States.

Few important rivers exist entirely in their natural state. Most have been dredged, locked, deepened, straightened, or by-passed by canals along difficult stretches. Many of the major river dams—those on the Tennessee and St Lawrence, for example, were constructed with the improvement of navigation as one of the main objectives. Canals have been built to act as feeders to rivers, and to join river basins together. The North Sea, Baltic, Mediterranean, and Black Seas are inter-connected by navigable water, much of it capable of passing barges of several hundred tons capacity.

In few regions of the world is such intensive use made of an inland water system as on the North European Plain. Here, across an area of featureless lowland, well supplied with water from a number of large rivers, canal construction was easy. Unfortunately the North

European canals, like others in the cooler parts of the world, suffer badly from ice in severe winters. During freezes it becomes necessary to fall back on the roads and railways for the movement of essential commodities (Fig. 15).

The inland waterways of Britain

The rivers of Britain, unlike many on the continent of Europe and North America, are of very restricted value for navigation in their

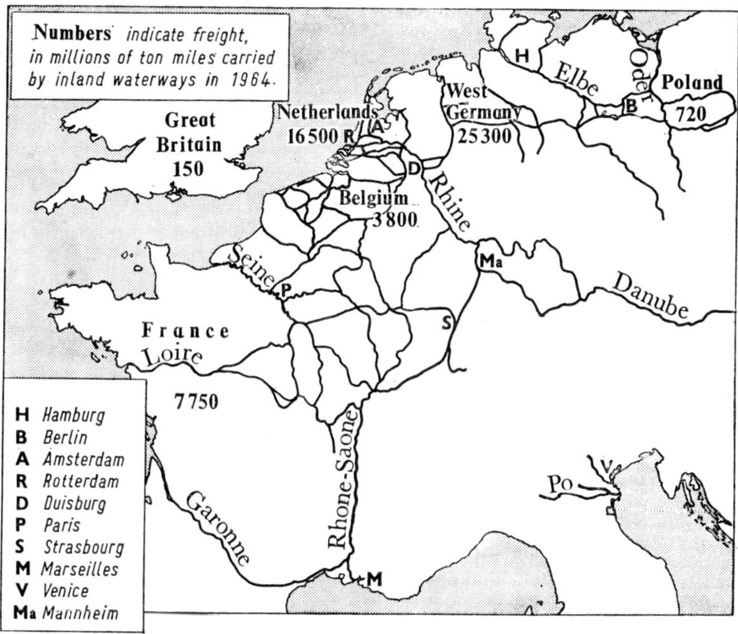

Fig. 15.—THE PRINCIPAL INLAND WATERWAYS OF WESTERN AND CENTRAL EUROPE.

natural state. Estuaries are broad and deep, and Britain's coastline affords many excellent sites for deep-water ports. But above their tidal limits rivers are small and shallow, and especially on the western side of the country are obstructed by sharp changes of gradient. These conditions are a consequence of the hilly topography of these islands, and the small size of their drainage basins.

Work to improve navigation on rivers, by digging cuts across meander loops, removing obstructions such as fords and low bridges, and constructing weirs to raise water levels, became important after the middle of the seventeenth century, and by 1850 most of the major waterways could be negotiated by barge or small boat for several miles inland. But the interior of the country derived few benefits from these improvements. Trade continued to be directed outwards to the coast, and the sea became more important than ever as the main artery of English commerce.

The coming of the Industrial Revolution, and the demand for coal that was created by the upsurge of manufacturing, made apparent the need for a system of communications that could give rather better access to the coalfields than was provided by the roads of the day—roads that had seen little improvement since the Roman period, and which were apt to become impassable every time it rained. The first true canal was dug in 1761 to carry coal from the collieries of Worsley to Manchester. Its success marked the beginning of an era of feverish building. The Mersey and the Humber were linked by the Grand Trunk Canal (the Trent and Mersey), and the Leeds-Liverpool, and Aire-Calder Canals. The Kennet and Avon joined Bristol with the navigable reaches of the Thames. The coalfield regions of Lancashire, the West Riding, and the West Midlands soon became threaded with waterways (Fig. 16). Construction went ahead, often without the backing of adequate financial resources, and in rural areas where the prospects of attracting sufficient traffic to make canals viable propositions were slender indeed, until further expansion was checked abruptly in the second quarter of the nineteenth century by the advent of the railway.

British inland waterways in the twentieth century

The reasons for the decline of the canal in face of competition from the railways was not due wholly to the superiority of the newer form of transport. The exorbitant rates charged by some carriers, and the railway companies' practice of eliminating competition by buying up sections of canal and closing them to traffic, played a part. No less than one third of the canal system passed into the ownership of the railways in this way. Equally damaging was the attitude of Parliament. Until 1845 the canal companies were forbidden by law to act as carriers. Haulage was in the hands of a host of independent men, operating mainly on local routes. The organisation of through traffic was therefore very difficult, and the quotation of through rates almost impossible.

As industrialisation increased and as traffic grew both in volume and diversity, the inadequacy of the English canal system became more and more apparent. To-day it is little used, and such traffic that it has managed to retain is local, limited to a few commodities, and confined almost entirely to the broad waterways. Revenue from commercial traffic on the narrow boat canals amounted to only £64,000 in 1964.

Most British canals are generally unsuited to modern needs for the following reasons:

1. Approximately 1,000 miles (two thirds of the system) are suitable only for the narrow boat—a vessel with a beam of seven feet, and a payload capacity of twenty-five to thirty tons. The gauge is determined by constrictions at bridges and locks rather than on the "levels" which are usually wide enough to accommodate larger craft. Increasing the gauge would be costly, especially on canals running through congested industrial areas. Facilities for handling freight are also often antiquated. The narrow boat does not lend itself to mechanised loading and discharging, and more often than not cargoes have to be dealt with by hand.

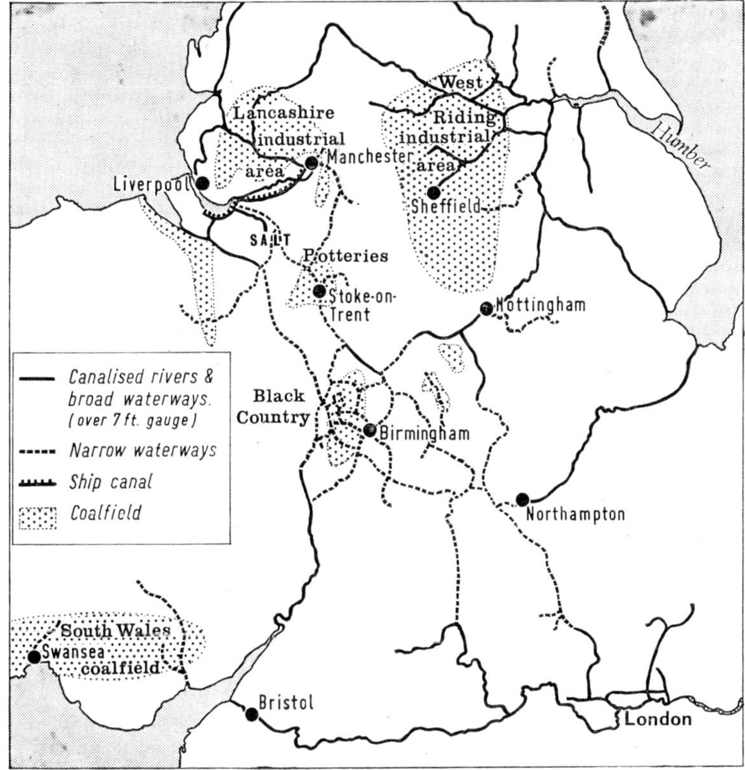

Fig. 16.—Inland Waterways of the North of England and the Midlands.

2. Canal transport is slow, but not necessarily slower than some types of rail traffic which are delayed for long periods at marshalling yards. The slowness arises from restrictions on the speed of boats passing along a narrow channel, from the time-consuming business of negotiating locks, and from the circuitous routes taken by canals in order to follow the contour. It should be noted that time does not cease to be a commercial factor simply because most canal cargoes are non-perishable and can be stored; for example:

Return journey from pit head to factory = 120 miles.

1 30-ton barge moving at 3 m.p.h. (ignoring turn-about times) will deliver 30 tons of coal every 40 hours.

1 10-ton lorry travelling at 20 m.p.h. (again ignoring turn-about times) will deliver 30 tons of coal every 18 hours.

20 barges, therefore, will be required to perform the same work as 9 lorries.

Which of the two vehicles—the barge or the lorry—will provide the cheaper form of transport now turns on the relative costs of purchasing, maintaining, and operating twenty of the one against nine of the other; on handling costs, and the costs of maintaining the "track". In most circumstances to-day these factors will be in favour of the lorry.

3. Canal navigation is impeded by frost and drought. The effect of severe winter weather is well known, but the problem of supplying water during a prolonged drought can raise difficulties equally acute, especially on watersheds where there are no large rivers to act as feeders to the canal. Some 25,000 gallons of water pass down a canal each time a narrow lock is used, and a broad lock consumes twice this amount. The quantity of water available determines the number of craft that can use the canal in a given time. It was the water supply factor that helped to convince the early canal engineers of the advantages of building on the narrower gauge.

4. Canal transport is inflexible. It is self-evident that barges can only move where there is water, and most waterways are poorly aligned to serve industry as it is located to-day. The cost of building a branch canal would be much higher than the cost of constructing a road or branch railway.

Canals and industrial location

Eighteenth- and early nineteenth-century industry was attracted to the canal bank where commodities could be loaded directly on and off boats, and so avoid trans-shipment charges. Many factories of the early industrial period still line the narrow waterways of the

Midlands and North, but have long forsaken the canal as a mode of transportation, and have turned instead to the roads and railways. Others erected more recently on canal bank sites have never had any organic connection with the waterway on which they are situated,

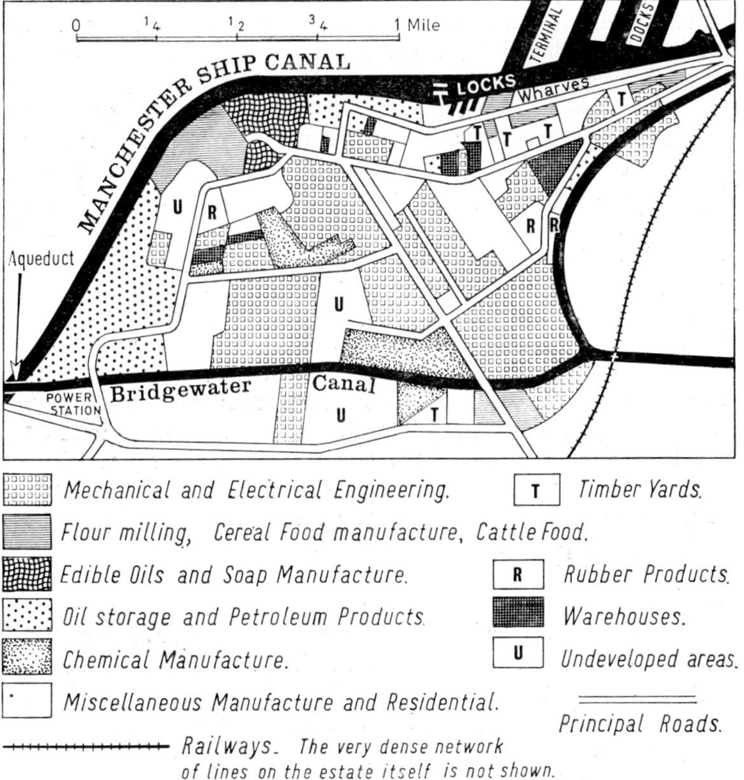

Fig. 17.—Industrial Location on the Trafford Park Estate, Manchester.

but owe their waterside location to the chance occurrence of vacant plots of land. The factories along the Bridgewater Canal are of this type (Fig. 17).

3. RAILWAYS

Choice of route and gauge

The cost of railway construction—which is likely to be considerable whatever the circumstances—will be lowest when the track can be laid in a more or less straight line across firm, level land without large rivers. Conditions approaching this ideal were found on the Pampas, on parts of the North American Prairies, and along the route of the trans-continental railway of Australia. In broken country the track will tend to conform to the relief, making use of valley routeways through hills, avoiding lakes, and crossing rivers where the underlying rock can support the weight of heavy bridges. In areas of all but the most subdued relief, it will be necessary to grade the track by means of cuttings, embankments, and tunnels.

About 60 per cent. of the world's railways, including those of Britain, North America, and most of the European countries are constructed on the standard gauge of four feet eight and a half inches. The remainder employ gauges of between two feet and five feet six inches. The narrow gauge railway is of value in thinly populated and mountainous country, as it can be of lighter construction, and can negotiate steeper gradients, and sharper curves than broader gauge railways. It does, however, impose a limit on the speed and capacity of the trains that pass over it. In some countries a number of gauges are in use. Unco-ordinated development among the states of Australia resulted in the construction of lines on three different gauges, with the result that the role the railway was able to play in the opening up of the country was seriously restricted. To-day the Australian state governments are expensively converting the main routes to the standard gauge to avoid trans-shipment at break-of-gauge points.

Traction

Most of the advanced nations of the world are abandoning steam in favour of diesel or electric traction. The last of the steam trains disappeared from the U.S.A. railways in 1960, and conversion should be complete in Britain by late 1967. Diesels are three or four times as expensive to buy as steam locomotives, but they are much more economical in the use of fuel, simpler to operate, spend less time out of service for maintenance, and do not require the provision of stocks of fuel and water at depots along the route. In short they are much cheaper to run. The running costs of electric trains are very low, but the high capital charges, which must cover the cost of new track, and signalling equipment, as well as overhead wiring if maximum benefits from main line electrification are to be obtained, make this form of traction economically justifiable only on routes carrying heavy traffic.

Railways and human settlement

The British railway companies of the last century built their lines where they believed they could pick up traffic. They were constructed to serve existing centres of mining and industry. Few railways penetrated the Highlands of Scotland, mid-Wales, and the south-west because there was little freight and few passengers to be carried in those regions, and not because engineering problems were particularly difficult. These were no more difficult than in the southern Pennines, which have a close network of routes. In some parts of the world railways preceded settlement and were the cause of it. Such was the case in Canada and the United States. Here, tracks were driven westwards with the aid of government grants, usually land grants, which the railway companies used to attract farmers, in the knowledge that grain and other agricultural products would soon flow back along the lines to the eastern cities and ports.

The burden of maintaining routes that must cross large expanses of thinly populated territory has to be borne by the settled areas at each end. The two trans-continental railways of Canada traverse nearly 1,000 miles of negative "shield" country of forest and lakes before breaking out on to the Prairies, and further 500 miles of uninhabited mountain land before reaching the Pacific coast. The people of south-east and south-west Australia are joined by a track laid across 1,000 miles of arid waste. In these, and other similar cases, the state normally assumes some responsibility for the route, usually by the payment of a subsidy.

The economics of railway operation

Technically, the railway is a highly efficient form of transport. It is capable of moving both passengers and freight in larger numbers and volume, at higher speeds, and with greater safety than any other form of land transport that man has yet devised. Its technical superiority derives from the self-guiding nature of rail vehicles, the low rolling friction of a steel wheel running on a steel track, and the high loading capacity of a train, which is limited only by the power of the locomotive to haul the coaches or trucks without mishap. The actual work of haulage can also be performed by a very small labour force—a matter of growing consequence in times of rising labour costs—and it is the only form of transport suited to a high degree of automation.

In spite of these very considerable advantages, many railways (not only those of Britain) continue to lose business to the roads and airlines (Fig. 18). Some of the reasons are:

1. Overhead or fixed costs of railway operation are very high. Fixed costs are costs that have to be met whether the system is used much or little. They do not vary, or vary only slightly with the volume of traffic passing over the lines. Track, bridges and tunnels,

signalling installations, stations, and terminal facilities have to be maintained even though a route may be used by only a few trains a day. Where fixed costs can be spread over a large volume of traffic, operating costs are very low indeed (they were estimated to be only one third of a penny per passenger-mile on busy main line routes in Britain in 1950), but if they have to be borne by one or two trains loaded to only a fraction of their capacity, as they must on many branch lines, operating costs are then very high.

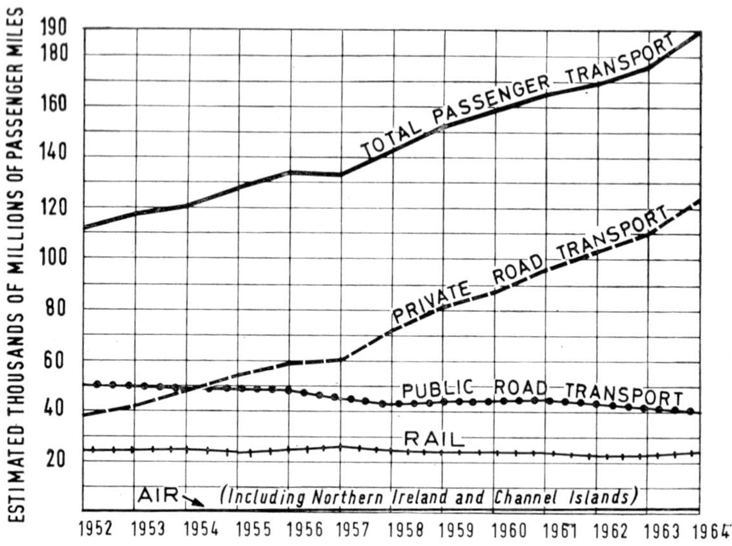

Fig. 18.—Passenger Transport—Great Britain, 1952-64.

2. Traffic, particularly passenger traffic, rarely moves in even flows. It makes a great deal of difference to a railway company's finances whether a route is called upon to handle, say, 20,000 passengers spread over sixteen hours a day, or 20,000 passengers all bent on travelling at more or less the same time. The latter situation is characteristic of the commuter routes, and lies at the heart of their problems. One electrified line out of Manchester has to contend with 85 per cent. of its passenger movements between 7.30 a.m. and 9 a.m., and between 4 p.m. and 6 p.m. The provision of a service of this type is extremely costly, as train capacity and crews have to be found to meet conditions of peak demand, but have little opportunity for productive employment for the rest of the day. Main line services are beset with the same problem, if to a lesser degree.

Until a year or two ago nearly one-third of British Railways' fleet of main line corridor coaches were held in reserve solely for use at the height of the holiday season, and were brought out on fewer than eighteen occasions during the course of the year.

3. British Railways, and also the railways of some other countries, are saddled with services for which they took responsibility during the very different transport conditions of the last century. Rivalry among competing companies led to a proliferation of routes, some of which were a financial embarrassment from the beginning. Many of these routes are still open to traffic, but are hopelessly under-utilised. The Beeching Report showed that half the route mileage carried only 5 per cent. of the freight and 4 per cent. of the passengers of the entire system, and was losing money on a scale that no commercial undertaking could possibly withstand. The future of many of these uneconomic lines is still undecided. British Rail would like to close them, but are not permitted to do so because it is held that they are essential to the welfare of communities living in isolated places. Many rural areas would indeed suffer if the trains ceased to run, but it is nevertheless impossible to escape the illogicality of a situation in which the railways are on the one hand required by statute to pay their way, and on the other to go on providing a social service which involves running half their system at a crippling loss. Almost half of British Rail's deficit in 1965 was incurred on services which B.R. had tried to eliminate, but which the State insisted it must maintain.

4. Rail transport is comparatively inflexible, and for some purposes unsuited to modern needs. The railway is not, and never has been, of any value for local collection and delivery work. Unless firms originating traffic possess their own sidings, which increasing numbers do not as industry tends to become road- rather than rail-based, rail transport involves a road haul and trans-shipment, thus adding to total movement costs. The greatest economies on rail are obtained when freight moves long distances in full train loads, and when loading and discharging can be mechanised. British Rail is trying to develop this type of traffic by means of the block train and liner train. Many consignments, however, still move in small lots requiring individual handling, and in these conditions it becomes necessary to dispatch mixed cargoes for different destinations behind the same locomotive, and then to re-sort them *en route*, a procedure which is both time-consuming and expensive.

4. ROADS

The car and the lorry are the most flexible of all transport vehicles. The road network is invariably denser than the network of railways, canals, and air routes, and vehicles of all sizes from light vans to the heaviest lorries permitted on the highway can be used, as appropriate, to accommodate cargoes of all types, and almost every size.

The economics of road transport

Road vehicles run on a public track, provided and maintained by the community in general, which is open on equal terms to all comers provided they pay a tax for its use, and abide by the traffic regulations of the land. Herein lies a fundamental difference between roads and railways. Railway companies are responsible for the upkeep of their entire system: road hauliers only for the operation of their own vehicles. The cost of running the first train is enormous, but the cost thereafter decreases with each additional train, until it becomes very low indeed on a heavily used route. The overheads of the road haulier are low by comparison with those of a railway company, but his operating costs vary in almost direct proportion to the number of vehicles he has in use.

The public sector of the road haulage business in Britain is in the hands of some 5,000 individual and usually very small firms who together control about 250,000 (fifteen per cent.) of the goods vehicles on the roads. This sector, however, accounts for nearly half the freight ton-mileage, mainly because the vehicles are fairly large and are engaged on the longer hauls. Eighty-five per cent. of the commercial vehicles in Britain carry "C" licence plates, and are run by firms solely for the carriage of their own merchandise. For the most part they are concerned with local collection and delivery work.

Because most haulage firms are so small, and individually handle only a tiny fraction of the nation's freight, they are in no position to cross-subsidise services. Road rates are based on the cost of making each particular journey after all factors have been taken into account—distance, nature of the route, the cost of over-night accommodation for the driver, the possibility of picking up a return cargo, etc., and not on what the traffic can bear.[1] If a commodity cannot stand the cost of road transport it will not be carried by road. It was the road hauliers' understandable reluctance to accept traffic that was not profitable to them that was the undoing of many of the railways'

[1] Road transport costs, as borne by the haulier (or private motorist), do not of course take into account what has been termed "social cost". This is not easy to calculate, but in 1966 the cost to the community of road accidents was estimated to be £267,000,000, and road congestion as much as three shillings per vehicle mile in cities and towns during peak travel hours.

freight-carrying services. Until 1953 British Railways (and their predecessors, the private companies) were legally bound to accept any traffic offered, and to carry it at a rate not in excess of the scheduled rate for the particular class into which it was placed. The result was that the lucrative traffics which were surcharged by rail passed to the roads, while the low grade commodities which were of value to no-one were retained by the railways.

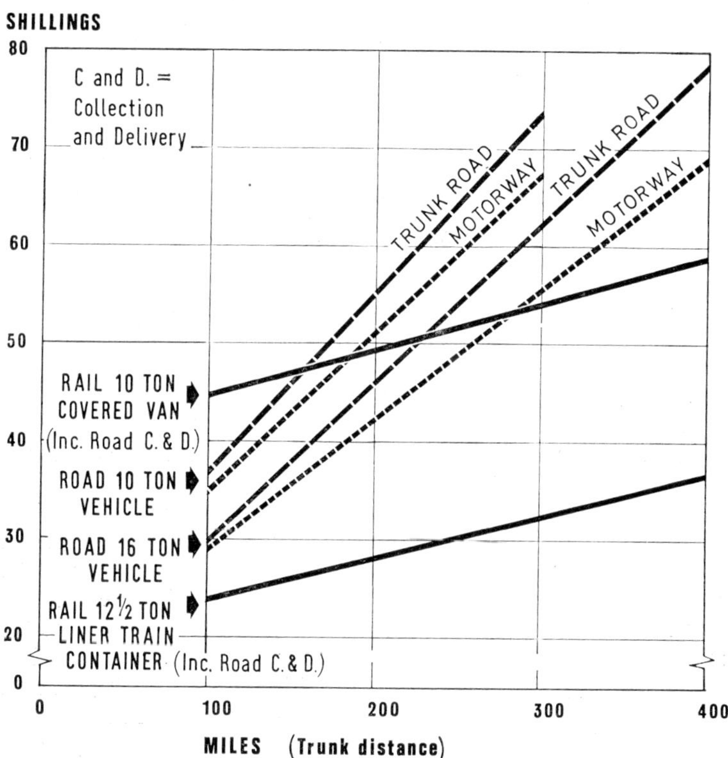

Fig. 19.—(Reproduced by permission of British Railways Board)

About 80 per cent. of the freight-tonnage in Britain is currently handled by the roads. On a ton-mileage basis, however, their share is somewhat less (Table 9). In larger countries roads play a rather smaller part in inter-city freight movements than they do in Britain. The break-even point, *i.e.* the distance at which road and rail costs are equal, varies with the type of route and the nature of the cargo, but at distances over 200-250 miles costs are generally in favour of rail (Fig. 19).

TABLE 9

GOODS TRANSPORT IN GREAT BRITAIN
(in millions of ton-miles)
1952-65

	1952	1957	1965
Road	18,800	22,900	41,000
Rail (excluding freight by passenger train)	22,400	20,900	15,400
Coastal shipping	9,000	9,800	11,300
Inland waterways	200	200	100
Pipelines (excluding lines less than ten miles in length and movements of gas by pipeline)	100	100	800
Total	50,500	53,900	68,600

Source: *Annual Abstract of Statistics.*

TABLE 10

VOLUME OF INTER-CITY FREIGHT TRAFFIC IN THE U.S.A., 1965
(in millions of ton-miles)

Rail	720,800	(43%)
Road	370,800	(22%)
Inland water	256,000	(15%)
Pipelines	310,100	(19%)
Air	1,900	(0·1%)

Source: *Statistical Abstract of the U.S.A.*, 1967.

5. AIR TRANSPORT

The aircraft is the only vehicle that can operate over both land and water. Indeed, within the limits of its range it is able, as far as technical factors apply, to move anywhere.

In practice, its movement is rather closely circumscribed. The air is free only over the oceans, and the right to operate over foreign territories is a matter for negotiation between the interested parties. All but the lightest aircraft require large and well maintained airfields on which to land, and the larger and faster machines become, so the number of airports able to accommodate them declines. The location of airports, as well as the position of ground navigational aids, in fact hold commercial aircraft to well defined tracks.

The economics of air transport

Aircraft are expensive vehicles to build and maintain. The initial cost of research may run into hundreds of millions of pounds if the machine is of revolutionary design, even before the prototype is flown. It is expected that the development costs of the controversial "Concord" will exceed £700 million before it makes its maiden flight—enough to build 1,000 miles of motorway or to electrify one-third of Britain's rail network. The construction costs even of large conventional aircraft are upwards of £1 million.

When in flight, fuel consumption is high, and much energy is expended merely to keep the machine airborne. The payload capacity is also small, and as operating costs increase in almost direct proportion to size, there are fewer economies of scale to be realised than with surface vehicles. On the other hand the high speeds attained by modern aircraft compensate to a considerable degree for their low payload capacity, by enabling the actual work of haulage to be performed by a small number of operating units. Three or four airliners can carry as many passengers in a given time as a large Cunarder.

The location of airports

Commercial airports are normally owned and maintained by state or municipal authorities, and not by the airway companies that make use of them. The latter are therefore spared the enormous capital outlay that their construction and operation involves. Ideally, an airport should be built on level ground, with ample room for expansion, in an area free from obstructing buildings and hills, and near to a large centre of population. It is rare to find a site that meets all these requirements, or meets them for very long. As machines become larger and faster they demand longer runways and more elaborate terminal facilities, and when an existing airport is no longer able to provide them it is abandoned, or relegated to a secondary role, and a new one is built in open country. Airports therefore tend to move farther and farther from the cities they are meant to serve, so that for short journeys the time taken travelling to and from the airport often exceeds the duration of the flight. On short hauls, the low loading factor and high terminal charges also make the aircraft uncompetitive with surface vehicles in terms of fare charges (Table 11).

TABLE 11

COMPARISON BETWEEN AIR AND RAIL PASSENGER FARES IN THE UNITED KINGDOM

July 1966

		AIR (tourist class single, including coach to and from airport)	RAIL (second class single)
		£ s. d.	£ s. d.
LONDON TO	Manchester	6 13 0	2 10 0
	Edinburgh	9 1 6	4 15 0
	Aberdeen	11 16 0	6 0 0

Some airports have developed as refuelling centres at strategic points on important air routes. Anchorage (Alaska) is thus conveniently placed on a route between Europe and the Far East that avoids the Soviet Union and China. Such bases lose their importance as the range of aircraft increases. Gander and Shannon, for example, were established as jumping-off points for the early trans-Atlantic flights, but are now over-flown by most machines operating between Europe and centres in North America.

The principal air routes radiating from Western Europe are shown in Fig. 20. On this map great circles appear as straight lines.

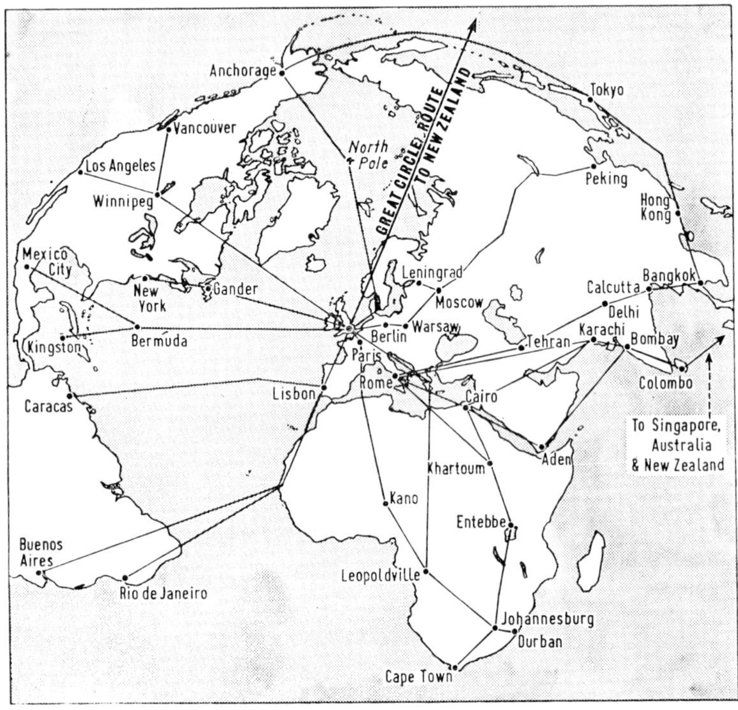

Fig. 20.—Principal Transcontinental Air Routes Radiating from London.

It should be noted that the air routes between Europe and the west coast of North America approximate to a great circle, using Winnipeg as a convenient refuelling station. On the other hand the air route to Australia lies almost parallel to the traditional shipping lanes. Airline companies do not always find the shortest route the most profitable. Like other transport undertakings they must operate where they can pick up the maximum traffic.

6. PIPELINES

Pipelines have been accepted for decades as the only satisfactory means of conveying domestic and industrial water supplies from reservoirs to consuming areas. For a commodity such as water, which is of low value and consumed in enormous quantities, this method of transport is unchallenged. For the carriage of most other materials, however, the pipeline must compete with water, rail, and road transport.

The first oil pipeline was laid in Pennsylvania in 1861 to avoid high rail rates on petroleum. This line, and others that were constructed in the early years of the oil industry, served local purposes only, such as the collection from wells for delivery to a central refinery, or to a rail head for forwarding. As the economy of the U.S.A. developed the value of the pipeline for the transport of crude oil in bulk, and later for refined products, became realised. In the deserts of the Middle East and North Africa and also in other oil-producing regions where conventional transport was inadequate, the pipeline became indispensable to the movement of petroleum from inland fields to refineries and ocean terminals.

The economics of pipeline operation

These are dominated by the extreme inflexibility of the system and the high installation charges. A natural gas pipeline was estimated to cost 150,000 dollars per mile in the U.S.A. in the 1950s, and the 30-inch, 1,000-mile oil pipeline which links the Saudi Arabian fields with Sidon on the Mediterranean was laid at a cost of £80 million (see Fig. 73). Once in position a pipeline cannot be transferred to another route should there be a shift in the geographical location of either the producing region or the market. The range of products it can carry is also limited, and there is no possibility of its being used to carry, say, wool or butter. Finally, extra capacity can only be provided by laying a larger, or additional, line in its entirety. Road, rail, and tanker companies can add extra vehicles to their fleets as the need arises, and at a cost which, by comparison, is low.

A pipeline becomes a sound economic investment once the market it serves has expanded sufficiently to make capacity working possible, but even at this stage transport by large tanker is still cheaper for journeys of comparable length. The great advantage of the pipeline is that it can be used to shorten what would otherwise be a circuitous voyage by sea, as for example, from the Gulf fields to Chicago, or from the Middle East fields to the Levant coast.

The market for crude oil is always larger than the market for individual refined products. To ship crude oil to market, oil companies have merely to provide for the transport of a bulk commodity from the wells to the refinery. The marketing of refined products, on the other hand, involves their separate distribution to several consuming points which are likely to be geographically separated. For this reason most of the world's oil pipelines are designed to carry crude oil, and companies rely on road and rail for distribution from the refineries.

Exceptions, however, are found in the "island" markets of Britain and Japan which are well served by ocean transport, and which have located their refineries on the coast. In these cases product, rather than crude pipelines are the rule. Product lines link the Thames and Fawley refineries with London and the Midlands, and the Stanlow refinery with the Midlands and south Lancashire.

Pipelines are now used extensively for the long-distance transport of natural gas. They have also proved their value for the carriage of solid materials in certain circumstances. Slurried coal, for example, is pumped for more than 100 miles from Cadiz (Ohio) to Cleveland at the rate of 1 million tons per year. Crushed shale and limestone often arrive at a cement works by pipeline.

Human and animal transport

Man and his domestic animals are still important transport media over wide areas of the earth's surface. Often their use is complementary to mechanical forms of transport. Goods are carried, for instance, on the backs of human beings or pack animals to the nearest road or rail head, or to navigable water. Ghanaian cocoa, Colombian coffee, and Saharan dates often begin their journey to the outside world in this way. Animals can pull or drag more than they can carry, and hence the efficiency of animal haulage is considerably increased if roads capable of taking wheeled vehicles exist, or if the ground is snow-covered for much of the year. It should be noted that animals are excluded from large areas of Africa by the tsetse fly, and that in such areas human porterage is the only form of non-mechanical transport available away from water.

Transport as a factor in the location of industry

Transport costs tend to comprise a high proportion of the total costs of manufacture in industries where a large quantity of bulky raw material has to be assembled, or heavy, unwieldy finished products distributed, and a low proportion in the case of industries where both raw materials and finished products have a high value in relation to bulk and weight. It is obviously in the interests of manufacturers to keep transport costs as low as possible, and it is particularly important that they do so in industries of the first type. It can be done in the following ways:

1. *By reducing the volume of freight to be moved.*—Many raw materials suffer a considerable loss of weight during processing. For example, some minerals and metals comprise only a tiny proportion of the ore in which they are held. The gold content of some of the Rand ores is less than 0·001 per cent. The average metal content of the Zambian copper ore deposits is only 5 per cent., and of Bolivian tin 3 per cent. Transport of the ore as mined would in these cases involve the movement of millions of tons of useless rock, and in order to save on freight costs, the first stage of manufacture, *i.e.* the separation of the metal from its ore, is undertaken at the site of the mine.

Certain agricultural and forest products are also concentrated prior to transport. The extraction of juice from sugar cane and beet, fruit drying and canning, cotton ginning, and the coagulation of latex are all processes which bring about a reduction in the weight or bulk of the product, and are characteristic activities of the producing areas.

Some goods, on the other hand, gain in weight and bulk during manufacture, and there is a saving in overall transport costs if such goods are produced near the point of consumption. The manufacture of lemonade and sulphuric acid require the addition of a nearly ubiquitous commodity, water, on which it is pointless to pay transport costs, and are thus industries of the market areas. Bread and confectionery are not only bulkier than the flour and sugar from which they are made, but are also less durable, and again are produced near to centres of population. The production of tin boxes is related to the food packing industries, rather than to the centres of tin-plate manufacture. Motor vehicle and agricultural machinery assembly plants are also frequently located in regions of consumer demand, rather than in the areas of primary engineering. Many types of farm machinery are particularly awkward to handle, and take up much space in the transport vehicle. Freight charges can invariably be reduced if such machinery is carried in a "knocked down" or unassembled state.

2. *By reducing the length of the haul.*—The total distance that a product needs to be transported between the point where its initial stages of manufacture are undertaken and its ultimate destination, must be kept to a minimum. The haulage distance can be reduced

by locating the plant engaged in the final processing or assembly operations within, or sometimes on the edge of, the market area. If most of the raw materials arrive at the plant along roughly the same route, a location on the edge of the market area may produce a substantial saving in overall transport costs (Fig. 21). The experience of an American firm seeking a location for a new cotton picking machinery assembly plant illustrates the point. The firm chose Memphis as the most suitable site for the plant. Memphis lies on the northern margin of the Cotton Belt in the direction of Chicago where most of the components originated. The firm found that a more southerly location in the heart of the Cotton Belt would have resulted in higher overall transport costs, as such a location would have meant hauling the assembled machines back over the route already covered by the component parts.[1]

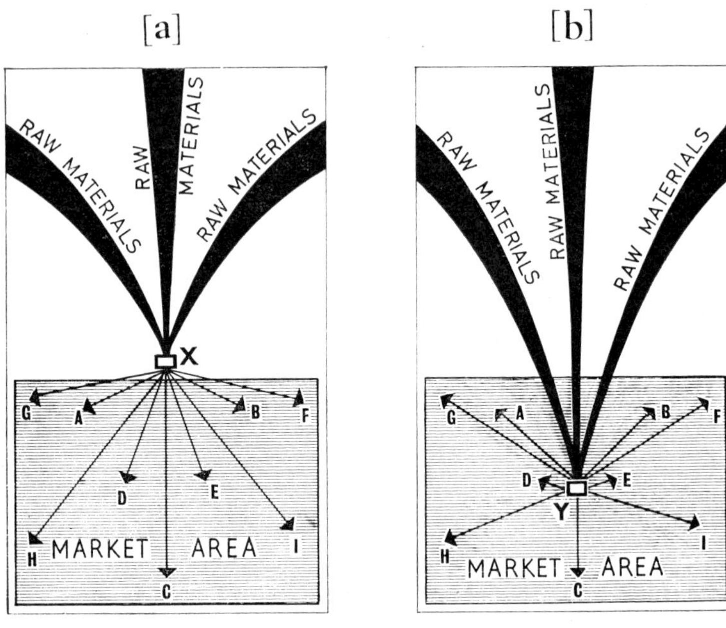

Fig. 21.—Two Industrial Locations. (*a*) On the edge of the market area, (*b*) in the middle of the market area. The total haulage distance from raw material sources to markets (as indicated by the points of the arrows) is less in the case of the industry situated at X than in that of the industry situated at Y.

[1] Mclaughlin and Robock—*Why Industry moves South*, Washington, D.C., 1949.

Above: Industrial development on the banks of the Manchester Ship Canal. The large plant in the middle distance is the Lancashire Steel Corporation's integrated iron and steel works at Irlam, Lancashire. (*Aerofilms and Aero Pictorial Ltd.*)

Below: Modern, road-based industry at Kirkby, Lancashire. (*Aerofilms and Aero Pictorial Ltd.*)

Above: The Plessey Company's Allen Clark Research Centre at Caswell, Northants, which is concerned with research on materials for electronics and mechanical devices. (*Aerofilms and Aero Pictorial Ltd.*)

Below: Aerial view of a sugar mill at Cinclaire, Louisiana. Note the factory surrounded by cane fields, the workers' homes, and the large area of unreclaimed woodland. (*USIS.*)

This desire to eliminate as far as possible what the Americans call "backhaul" is one of the reasons why many developing British firms are reluctant to move into certain of the older manufacturing regions of this country. These regions neither supply in sufficient quantity the kind of raw materials such firms require, nor provide a large enough market for the type of goods such firms produce. A location, for example, in Newcastle, Aberdeen, or Belfast of a car assembly plant would involve the transport northwards of components produced in the Midlands, and the return of most of the vehicles to the southern half of England, where the principal market for cars is found.

3. *By locating an industry where an appropriate form of transport is available.*—Industries handling bulky materials find that procurement and distribution costs are generally lowest when a site on navigable water is chosen. Thus blast furnaces consuming imported ore are drawn to the coast. The same factor determines the location of flour mills, sugar refineries, and pulping plants at ports, and the siting of oil refineries and electricity generating stations on tide water, in instances where they depend on sea-borne materials.

By contrast, industries engaged in the manufacture of goods of high value-bulk ratio, especially if the goods are dispatched to customers in small batches at irregular but frequent intervals, tend towards a road-side location. Such industries, which include all types of patent foods, pharmaceutical products, plastic goods, electrical equipment, and scientific instruments, are to be found in the suburbs of all large and most medium sized towns, usually on a trunk highway. For them, the flexibility of road transport is very attractive.

Break of bulk locations

Industries situated at a point where materials are transferred from one transport vehicle to another are in a favourable position to intercept the flow of goods, and to save the cost incurred in their trans-shipment. Any port is a trans-shipment point, and port industries are at break of bulk locations. Sometimes a situation occurs where a port is passing materials for a particular industry in each direction, both to and from the hinterland. In this case, plants utilising these materials are likely to develop at the trans-shipment point. Examples are the iron-smelting centres of the Lower Lake shores, where Superior ore and Appalachian coal are transferred from freighter to rail car, and vice versa.

CHAPTER III

WATER SUPPLY

Introduction

Civilised man uses a lot of water. Each person in Britain consumes on average some sixty gallons of pure water each day, exclusive of the amount required to grow his food. In the United States daily *per capita* consumption is now no less than 150 gallons. However, only a tiny fraction—about four pints per head per day—of the total water usage is actually drunk. The rest is used in and about the household, and on the individual's behalf by the local authorities (for sewage disposal, putting out fires, irrigating grass and flower beds in public parks, etc.), and by the industries that provide him with manufactured goods, and power supplies.

Nevertheless, consumption is trifling when measured against the earth's reserves of water—estimated at more than 300 million cubic miles, or some 22,000 million gallons for each of its human inhabitants. Furthermore, water resources are not wasting assets like coal, oil, or iron ore, and are not destined to inevitable exhaustion by continued use. Every drop consumed by man, animals, crops, factories, and power stations is sooner or later evaporated into the atmosphere and returned to earth as rain.

In view of this, it is something of a paradox that every continent should be experiencing a water shortage which, in some cases, is proving serious enough to galvanise international organisations into action. The problem of dwindling supplies is not confined to the semi-arid lands, where periodic drought has been accepted as one of the facts of life since the beginning of time. It is afflicting the humid regions as well. We in Britain, in spite of the 30 billion gallons of water that fall annually on our islands, grow apprehensive at what a few weeks of rainless summer weather might bring. The difficulty of meeting demands for water—a difficulty that becomes more acute every year as the population grows and as standards of living rise—stems basically from the following causes:

1. Existing techniques of recovery allow only a tiny fraction of the earth's total resources to be harnessed for direct use by man. Over 99·5 per cent. of the reserves are held in the oceans, or locked away in the ice caps, or underground (Fig. 22).

2. The increasing degree of urbanisation of human society, which is producing a situation in which local resources are daily becoming

more and more incapable of meeting the demands made upon them. Cities and towns are being forced to depend increasingly upon distant supplies which are expensive to harness and transport. The general unwillingness of people to pay more than a nominal price for what they consider to be a free gift of nature also militates against a more substantial investment in water undertakings. The capital expenditure on water supply in the United States is only 1 per cent. of the expenditure on coal and natural gas.

3. The pollution of many rivers and streams by industrial effluent.

4. The spread of irrigation farming which is a prodigious user of water.

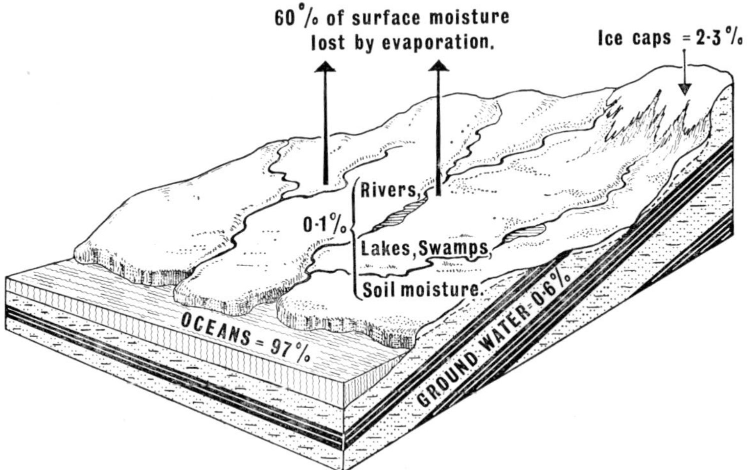

Fig. 22.—Water Resources of the Earth.

Sources of supply

Ground water.—Water held in the pore spaces and fissures of rock is termed ground water. Much of the enormous store of ground water has accumulated during the geological past, but is being currently added to by rainfall, and by seepage from rivers and swamps. Most of the rain water that is not lost by evaporation percolates underground, and only a small fraction enters the streams and rivers direct. The ratio of percolation to run-off varies according to the local geology and topography. Rain falling on dry soil is immediately absorbed by the upper few inches where it remains until released by evaporation. Once the surface layers have become saturated run-off begins, and when the soil is saturated throughout, the recharge of the underground reservoir or *aquifer* commences. Percolation rates are comparatively high on level or nearly level tracts of permeable sedimentary strata, and low in mountainous regions where impermeable bed-rock predominates. Well-bedded and jointed sandstones and limestones favour the accumulation of large reserves of subterranean water, and at the same time facilitate their movement from the catchments to regions remote from them. Thus water is transferred from beneath the Chilterns and North Downs to the centre of the London Basin, and from the Eastern Highlands of Australia to the arid interior of the continent. Thick deposits of coarse sands and gravels, which are characteristic of many alluvial fans at the base of the Alps, Himalayas, Andes, and other high

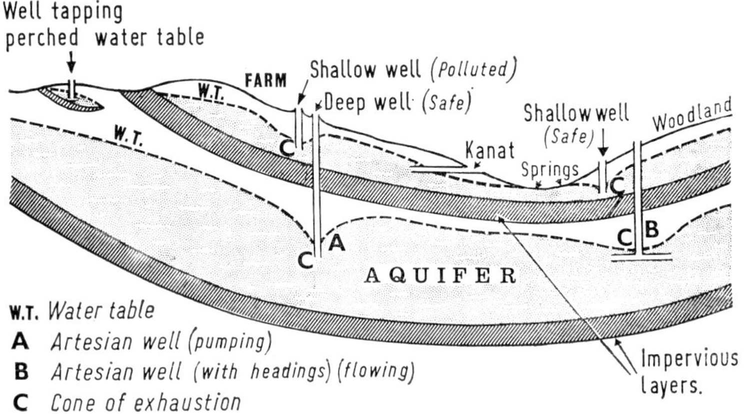

Fig. 23.—The Recovery of Ground Water.

mountain ranges, also make excellent aquifers as they are charged by local rainfall and by seepage water from streams flowing across them.

Cool season rainfall is more effective than summer rain in replenishing underground supplies. A dry winter creates more difficulties for people depending on springs and shallow wells than does a dry summer because the greater part of the summer precipitation, be it heavy or light, is lost by evaporation.

Wells.—Since time immemorial, man has tapped the earth's reserves of ground water by means of wells. Millions of them, mostly shallow, and dug by hand, are in daily use in many parts of the world, and countless numbers of people depend upon them absolutely for their drinking water. It is estimated by the World

Health Organisation that upwards of 90 per cent. of the rural population in seventy-five of the under-developed countries is without access to a tap, and must rely primarily on shallow wells. In Britain, the almost ubiquitous public supply has released us from dependence on the backyard or village pump, except perhaps in a few outlying districts, but it was otherwise in many a rural area as recently as the 1930s. In the U.S.A. wells still supply the greater part of the farmer's domestic and stock requirements, and in regions where the cost of bringing in surface water is high, they are the main, and sometimes the only, source of irrigation water.

The main advantage of the shallow well is that it is cheaply and easily constructed. On the other hand it is liable to fail during periods of prolonged drought, and unless care is taken the supply may become polluted. The supply from wells which penetrate an aquifer sealed from above by an impervious stratum is less affected by the vagaries of the rainfall, and safer from surface contamination (Fig. 23). Some 45,000 million gallons, or one fifth of the nation's supply is pumped daily from such wells in the U.S.A. Most small towns and some cities, *e.g.* Houston and Memphis, are supplied entirely from wells. New York and Chicago obtain large quantities of drinking water from wells, as do London, Berlin, and other European capitals. Most of the Dutch supplies are drawn from underground. Wells also furnish much of the water consumed in south-east England and the Midlands (Fig. 24).

In rocks such as chalk and limestone, where the flow of water is commonly channelled along open joints and fissures, the yield of a well may be increased by driving horizontal adits or "headings" from its base. Wells supplying Brighton and Eastbourne have such headings driven into the chalk. Their construction is not without its hazards, and it is not unknown for workmen to have to abandon their equipment in a hurry and run for safety when a large fissure is struck.

More than half a million square miles of territory in central Australia is underlain by water held under pressure beneath impervious layers of shale. Bores sunk into the aquifer bring water to the surface without need for pumping. These are true artesian wells. Parts of the London and Paris basins are able to obtain water in a similar manner.

A serious problem has developed in many areas as a result of over-pumping. A local lowering of the water table, or a *cone of exhaustion*, develops at the base of each well as water is withdrawn. Deepening the well broadens the cone. Withdrawal from a number of wells at a rate in excess of the rate of replenishment lowers the water table overall. This has happened in the London area where certain wells on the outskirts of the city have ceased to yield, whilst others near the centre that were formerly artesian now have to be pumped. In some coastal districts of California, the water table has fallen below sea level, resulting in an intrusion of sea water

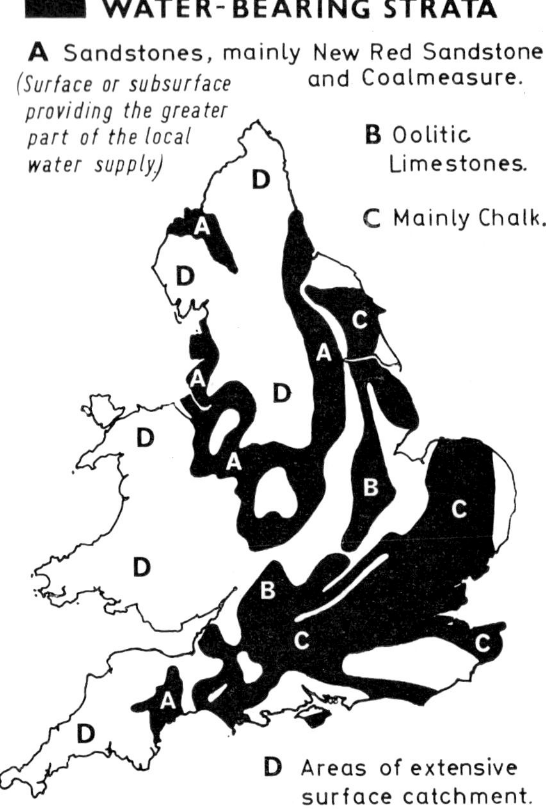

Fig. 24.—The Main Water Bearing Strata of England and Wales (generalised).

into the aquifer. It has proved feasible in certain cases to counter this by constructing a line of injection wells between the pumping wells and the coast into which fresh water is deliberately charged. In this manner a ridge of fresh water has been built up behind which pumping can continue safely. The artificial recharge of an aquifer is also possible, given suitable geological conditions, by spreading surplus run-off over the surface during periods of low irrigation demand.

SPRINGS.—Springs are still important to many communities. It is common, however, for "spring line" settlements—if they are not now served by a public supply—to draw water from shallow wells rather than from springs as such unless the springs happen to be strongly flowing. As often as not spring lines are little more than seepage zones. Springs are most productive when located on open-jointed or cavernous rock in country enjoying a heavy rainfall. In limestone areas they often yield prolifically. The Fontaine de Vaucluse (France) and Silver Springs (Florida) each produce some 500 million gallons daily. Such springs are, in fact, the resurgences of limestone rivers.

FOGGARAS AND KANATS are tunnels driven into an alluvial fan or hillside to intersect with the water table. Water flows along the tunnels by gravity to the point where it is needed. Foggaras are traditional Persian devices for obtaining drinking and irrigation supplies. They are also very common in the arid lands of North Africa and India.

Characteristics of ground water

The properties of ground water vary according to the depth to which the water has penetrated, the time spent underground, and the nature of the geological formations comprising the aquifer. Water drawn from very shallow wells or springs may be very similar, chemically, to the surface water of the area, while conversely a stream or reservoir maintained largely by the flow of springs will possess most of the characteristics of the ground supply. The following generalisations regarding ground water, however, may be noted:

1. Water drawn from deep wells will have been filtered during its passage through the rocks, and is less likely to be contaminated by objectionable surface materials than are surface supplies. It will also be of a more uniform temperature which will be an advantage if the water is to be used for refrigeration purposes. On the other hand it may be mineralised to an extent that adversely affects its usefulness for certain industrial purposes and for irrigation, and occasionally it may be dangerous to drink. Water containing dissolved calcium or magnesium salts is unsuitable (unless treated, which adds to operating expenses) for use in boilers, laundries, tanneries, or in the manufacture of dyes, viscose rayon, high quality paper, and textiles. Concentrations of sodium or boron in irrigation

water are harmful to the well-being of crops: one of the factors retarding the extension of irrigation farming in the arid lands is the saline nature of many desert aquifers. Highly mineralised waters are sometimes an economic asset, however. Supplies containing dissolved calcium sulphate have positive advantages in the brewing industry. There is, for example, a nice correlation between the distribution of the gypsum-bearing Keuper Marl in the English Midlands, and the location of important beer making centres. The brewing industries of Dublin, Dortmund, Pilsen, and Munich also owe much to the quality of the local water. In a different field, spa towns such as Lourdes, Bath, and Buxton have become famous because of the therapeutic qualities of their mineral springs.

2. Several weeks, months, or even years may elapse before surface water percolates to the site of a deep well. It probably takes as long as three years for water to flow from beneath the Chilterns to the centre of the London Basin. Reserves held in large aquifers, therefore, do not reflect short-term fluctuations in rainfall to anything like the same degree as reserves impounded behind a dam. During the exceptional year of 1959, when cities and towns supplied by upland reservoirs were experiencing acute water shortages, authorities drawing on subterranean supplies had little difficulty in meeting normal demand.

Surface water

The greater part of the world's fresh-water requirements are met by diverting surface streams and rivers. To insure against periods of drought, and to meet conditions of heavy demand, storage reservoirs are constructed, commonly by building a dam across a river, or by raising the natural barrier at the outlet of a lake.

Dam sites

Large storage reservoirs are generally located in mountain, plateau, or foothill country, where valleys are deep and sharply incised, and where outcrops of resistant, impermeable rock afford a sound foundation for the dam. A reservoir in such country exposes only a small surface area to the atmosphere in relation to its volume, and water losses through evaporation are consequently relatively small—a matter of some importance in the hot regions of the world. The loss of farm land is likely to be less serious than would be the case if the reservoir were constructed on the plains, and the flooding of an isolated valley creates comparatively few re-settlement problems. Upland water supplies are also reasonably free from pollution. Against these advantages must be set the high construction costs in remote areas (where labour, food, and most of the materials needed for the project may have to be imported from a distance) and the expense of laying pipelines, or building canals, to carry water to the point where it is needed.

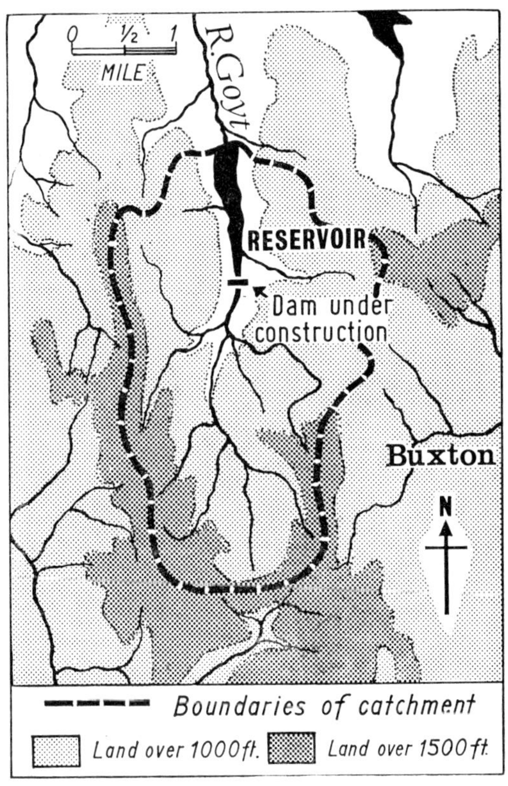

Fig. 25.—Sketch Map of the Goyt Reservoir near Buxton, Derbyshire.

Total area of catchment	5,234 acres
Average annual rainfall over catchment	49·48 inches
Average annual loss by evaporation and percolation	15·60 inches
Average annual run-off 33·88 inches: 14,760 acre-feet:	4,809 million galls.
Compensation water at 2·51 million gallons per day	916 million galls.
Water available for passing into supply during average year	3,893 million galls.
Capacity of present reservoir	1,095 million galls.
Number of days' capacity	186
Quantity passed into supply in 1964	2,139 million galls.
Capacity of reservoir under construction	935 million galls.

Data supplied by the Stockport and District Water Board.

Factors influencing the size of reservoirs.—Engineers will have the following considerations in mind when drawing up plans for any reservoir:

1. The discharge of the river at the site of the dam. Upon this will depend the volume of water available for storage, and for passing into supply. The discharge from a small catchment area can be calculated simply by multiplying the area of the catchment by the average depth of water available for run-off (rainfall minus evaporation and percolation). (See Fig. 25.)

2. The proportion of the natural flow of the river that must be allowed to pass the dam for the benefit of users downstream. This is known as "compensation water", and in Britain amounts to about one third of the average annual discharge.

3. The present and likely future demand for water in the consuming centres.

4. The extent to which it is necessary to provide storage. In regions where run-off is regular and dependable, and demand steady, a few weeks' storage capacity will normally suffice. On the other hand it may be provident to construct a reservoir capable of holding several years' supply in a region afflicted by recurring droughts.

IRRIGATION

Irrigation is the artificial and controlled application of water to the land, the object being to replace moisture lost from the soil by the combined processes of evaporation and transpiration (*evapo-transpiration*), and thus to provide as far as possible optimum conditions for plant growth.

Edaphic and climatic factors

The amount of water that a soil can hold against gravity, *i.e.* its *field capacity*, varies with the soil's depth and texture. A coarse, sandy soil stores between 0·75 and 0·90 inches of water per foot depth, whereas a finely textured clay-loam can retain more than twice this amount before its field capacity is reached.

Research into the behaviour of plants indicates that as far as their moisture requirements are concerned, optimum conditions for growth occur when they are losing moisture at their maximum or *potential* rate. Potential evapo-transpiration rates vary principally with temperature, relative humidity, wind conditions, and length of daylight, and to a less extent with the nature of the soil and the type of plant under cultivation. They are higher for alfalfa than they are for barley, and also higher when barley is growing rapidly than when it is ripening. An estimate of the actual water loss from tobacco plants in the southern states of U.S.A. gives 0·1 inch per day as the average in April, rising to 0·17 inches per day in July. These values may of course be doubled during a heat wave.

A cultivator intending to employ irrigation must, unless his efforts are to be less than wholly successful, have some means of ascertaining the moisture requirements of his crops. Given the potential evapo-transpiration rates for the district in which the farm is situated (which are published by the Ministry of Agriculture in the case of Britain) and the rainfall (which the farmer can measure for himself), then:

Potential evapo-transpiration rates—rainfall = water deficit in soil, or the balance to be made good by irrigation. The yield of many crops, however, is not materially affected until the water deficit exceeds half an inch, and from an economic standpoint little is gained from irrigation until this level has been reached.

TABLE 12

POTENTIAL EVAPO-TRANSPIRATION RATES (*A*), AVERAGE MONTHLY RAINFALL (*B*), AND SOIL-WATER DEFICIT (*C*) FOR THREE STATIONS IN BRITAIN DURING THE SUMMER

		April	May	June	July	August	Sept.	Total
Sittingbourne	(*A*)	1·95	3·10	3·85	3·90	3·30	1·80	17·90
(North East	(*B*)	1·70	1·80	2·25	2·30	2·35	2·10	12·50
Kent)	(*C*)	0·25	1·30	1·60	1·60	0·95	– 0·30	5·40
Falmouth	(*A*)	2·10	3·10	3·50	3·35	3·15	1·80	17·00
(South	(*B*)	2·60	2·60	1·95	2·80	3·05	3·05	16·05
Cornwall)	(*C*)	– 0·50	0·50	1·55	0·55	0·10	– 1·25	0·95
Aberdeen	(*A*)	1·70	2·60	3·05	2·85	2·35	1·35	13·90
(North East	(*B*)	2·25	2·60	2·05	3·35	2·85	2·95	16·05
Scotland)	(*C*)	– 0·55	0·00	1·00	– 0·50	– 0·50	– 1·60	– 2·15

Source: Ministry of Agriculture and *Monthly Weather Report*.

Regions deriving benefit from irrigation

Some 350 million acres of crop and pasture land are to-day under some form of irrigation throughout the world (Fig. 26). Environments in which it is practised are:

1. The deserts, where rainfall is so slight that without irrigation cultivation is impossible.

2. The Great Plains of North America, the Murray Basin of Australia, and other similar regions, where rainfall is adequate for some form of cultivation, but where irrigation offers an insurance against drought, and also makes possible the production of crops with high water requirements (Table 13).

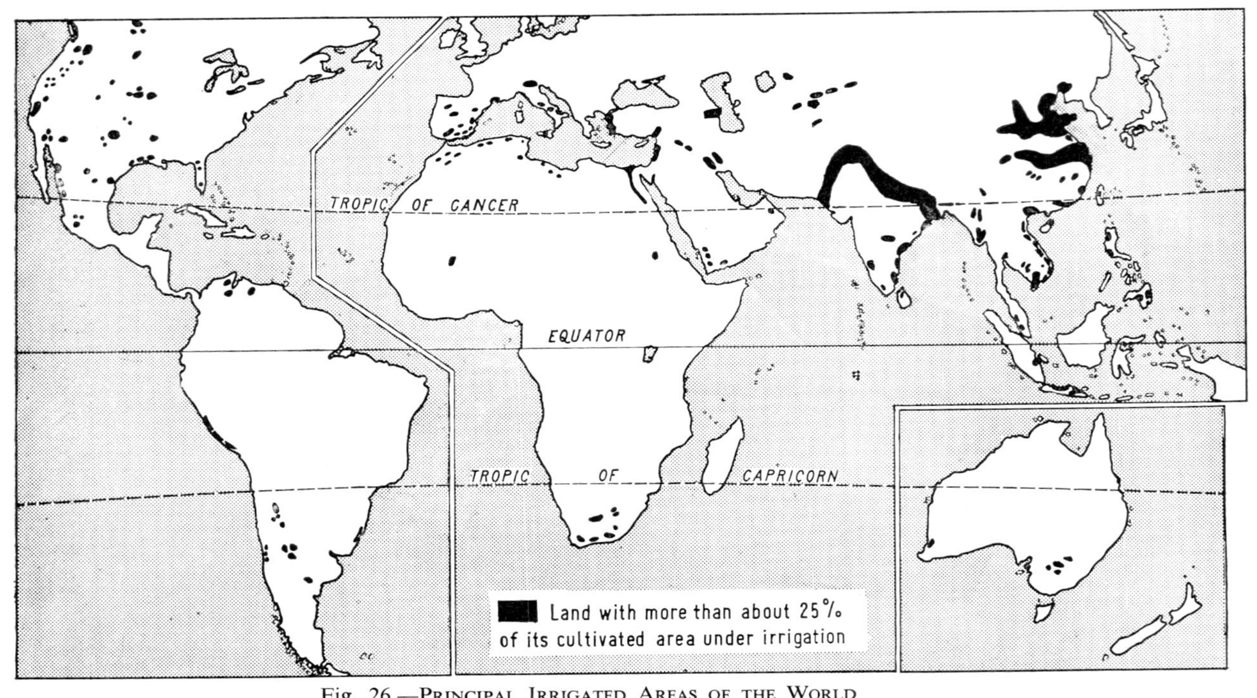

Fig. 26.—Principal Irrigated Areas of the World

3. The Mediterranean and Monsoon lands which suffer from prolonged seasonal drought, but which enjoy a moderate and sometimes a copious rainfall for a few months each year. Irrigation during the dry season makes round-the-year cropping possible.

4. The humid lands which experience a well distributed and seemingly abundant rainfall. Irrigation is practised here in order to improve the type of cultivation already in existence, rather than to introduce a wholly different form of land use, which is the aim in the arid regions. In Florida, for example, where few areas receive less than fifty inches of rain annually, upwards of 1,000 million gallons of water are being applied daily during the summer months to high value crops such as citrus, tobacco, and vegetables. Yields on some farms have been doubled as a result. Experiments have also shown that irrigation is needed in nine years out of ten in south-east England if maximum yields are to be obtained from grass, and in seven years out of ten (during May and June) to provide optimum conditions for the Cornish early potato crop (Table 12). In all, about 150,000 acres are under irrigation at present in Britain, and as these represent only about one tenth of the area from which an economic return from investment in irrigation plant can be expected, a further considerable expansion is likely in future.

TABLE 13

NORMAL SEASONAL REQUIREMENTS FOR (*a*) ALFALFA, (*b*) CORN (MAIZE) (*c*) ORCHARDS, ON A TYPICAL FARM NEAR MONTROSE, COLORADO

	ALFALFA	MAIZE	ORCHARDS
Total water consumed by plant during growing season (in inches)	26·45	19·66*	20·23
Water available during growing season from rainfall (in inches)	4·72	3·64	4·72
Irrigation water consumed (in inches) ..	21·73	16·02	15·51
Irrigation efficiency†	60%	55%	60%
Irrigation water required on a 10-acre plot (in millions of gallons)	8·2	6·6	5·8

* The comparatively low consumption is a consequence of the shorter growing season for maize.

† Irrigation efficiency $= \frac{\text{vol. of water reaching roots of plants}}{\text{vol. delivered at the farm}} \times 100.$

Water is lost by evaporation and seepage from ditches, and by percolation caused by over-watering. For furrow irrigation, an efficiency of 60% is good.

Source: *U.S. Yearbook of Agriculture 1955: Water.*

Methods of irrigation

1. PRIMITIVE LIFTING DEVICES.—The shaduf, sakia (Persian wheel), and the Archimedean Screw have been used in eastern countries for thousands of years. They employ animal or human energy to lift water from a well, canal, or river, and to empty it into a field ditch

for distribution. The area that can be irrigated by these appliances is small. A sakia, for example, can command between half an acre and two acres per day, depending on the height of the lift.

2. Pumps.—Steam, diesel, and electrically driven pumps are used on a number of large, public irrigation schemes in Egypt, Sudan, and many other countries. They have also proved to be of immeasurable

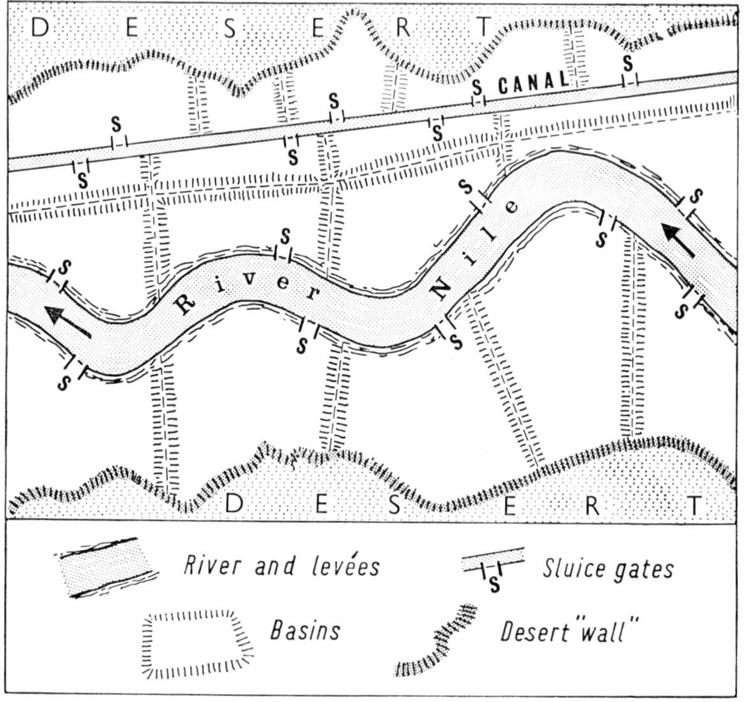

Fig. 27.—Diagram to Illustrate the Basin System of Irrigation on the Nile. The canal taking off from the river well upstream is able to deliver water to basins near the margins of the flood plain which might not otherwise be reached by the flood.

value on tens of thousands of farms throughout the world which have no access to public supplies, but whose sole source of irrigation water is the privately owned well.

3. Basin irrigation has been practised in Egypt since the time of the Pharoes, and although its importance has now been declining for a hundred years, it is still essential to the cultivation of more than a million acres of farmland above the Isna Barrage. Simply,

but effectively, the system achieves a limited degree of control over the Nile flood. As the river rises in late summer, its waters are impounded within shallow compartments or *basins* enclosed by earthen walls. The movement of water from one basin to another can be regulated by opening and plugging gaps in the walls. The higher basins on the outer margins of the plain which lie above the reach of the average flood, are supplied by canals taking off from the river upstream (Fig. 27).

For about six weeks each year the Nile valley is submerged to a depth varying from a few inches to several feet, and the soil is soaked to capacity. In early November surplus water is allowed to drain back into the river, which by this time is subsiding, and crops are sown broadcast in the mud. An autumn sowing only can be made, as summer water is not available except near the river or in localities where wells have been sunk.

In the U.S.A. the term basin irrigation is applied to the controlled flooding of dyked fields from canals, and is associated mainly with rice cultivation, although other crops, notably alfalfa and orchard fruit, are often irrigated in this way.

4. TANKS are small reservoirs held behind stone or earth dams, and are common in Ceylon and the southern portion of the Indian peninsula. They are rarely large enough to provide year-round storage, but are of value in so far as they supplement the water supply during the rains, and permit an extension of the cropping period into the first few weeks of the subsequent dry season.

5. FLOOD WATER CONSERVATION IN DESERTS.—A feature of desert rainfall is its concentration into heavy downpours of short duration, with the result that run-off, especially on bare, rocky slopes, is high and exceptionally rapid. It is a truism, of course, that desert rainfall is low. However, an annual fall of five inches over a catchment of one square mile represents no fewer than 70 million gallons of water, and if only one tenth of this volume could be conserved, and directed to, say, ten acres of potentially fertile land on the valley floor, then those ten acres would receive the equivalent of thirty inches of rain—sufficient to sustain at least drought-resistant crops even when allowance has been made for the very high evaporation rates that prevail in the hot deserts. The technique of collecting and storing water from flash floods, and then using it to raise crops of grain, fruit, and vegetables before it had chance to escape to the sea or become swallowed up in the sand was known to, and practised by, the Roman colonists in North Africa, and the Nabattean farmers in the Negev, more than 2,000 years ago (Fig. 28). It is currently being revived

by the Israelis. A modern refinement of the method involves the use of chemicals to render the soil impervious, and thereby increase the volume of run-off.

6. CANAL IRRIGATION.—All the major irrigation schemes in the world are based on canals. The simplest, but generally the least satisfactory system makes use of the *inundation canal* which intercepts the flood waters only of a river, and hence is effective but for a limited period each year. Inundation canals are still common in northern

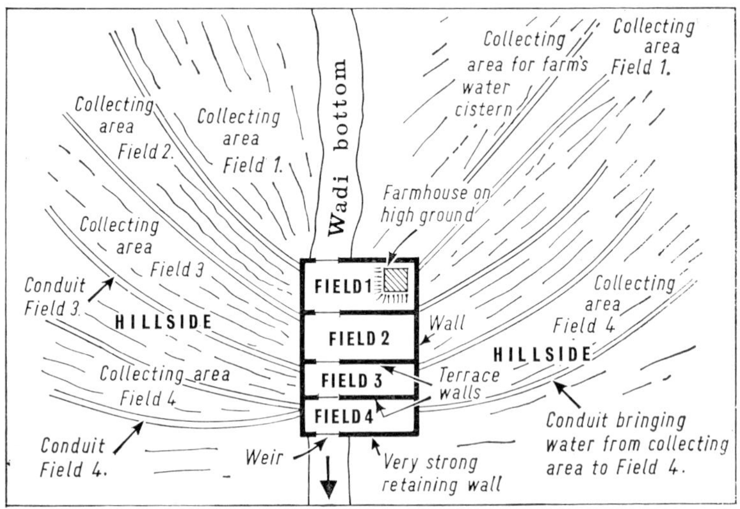

Fig. 28.—IRRIGATION ON A NABATEAN FARM ABOUT A.D. 100. The farm is built in a wadi valley bottom. Water from the valley sides is led down from different areas to the fields. One section collects water for the farm house cistern. The wadi, too, provides water in the wet season. The water overflows, if there is excess, through the weirs from field to field. In this way the soil is retained in the field. (Reproduced by permission of the *New Scientist*.)

India and Pakistan. The earliest *perennial canals* were dug deep enough at their heads to divert part of the dry season flow of a river. They thus made round-the-year cultivation possible, but their depth below ground level at the take-off point necessitated laborious lifting of water on to the fields, and the channels also became rapidly choked with silt. Modern perennial canals take water from behind a barrage (Fig. 29). The function of a barrage is not primarily to store water, although many have a considerable storage capacity, but to raise the level of a river to the point at which it can be diverted into a high level canal. Regulators control the flow past the barrage, and into the

Above: The Archimedean Screw. An age-old method of lifting water from ditches on to fields—the Nile Valley, Egypt. (*Paul Popper.*)

Below: An irrigation canal in the Salt River Valley, Arizona. Cotton, citrus fruit, alfalfa, and kitchen vegetables are under cultivation. Note the areas of unreclaimed desert on the left of the picture. (*USIS.*)

Above: An overhead sprinkler system irrigating potatoes, Oregon, U.S.A. (*Paul Popper.*)
Below: Tea gardens occupying steep slopes above the flooded rice paddies in the valley. Note the terraced hill sides. Japan. (*Paul Popper.*)

canals. From the main canals water is fed into branch canals, and from branch canals into distributaries, and from distributaries into field ditches from which the farmer obtains his supply. Both the capital and working costs of such a system are high, because in addition to the heavy construction charges, an army of engineers,

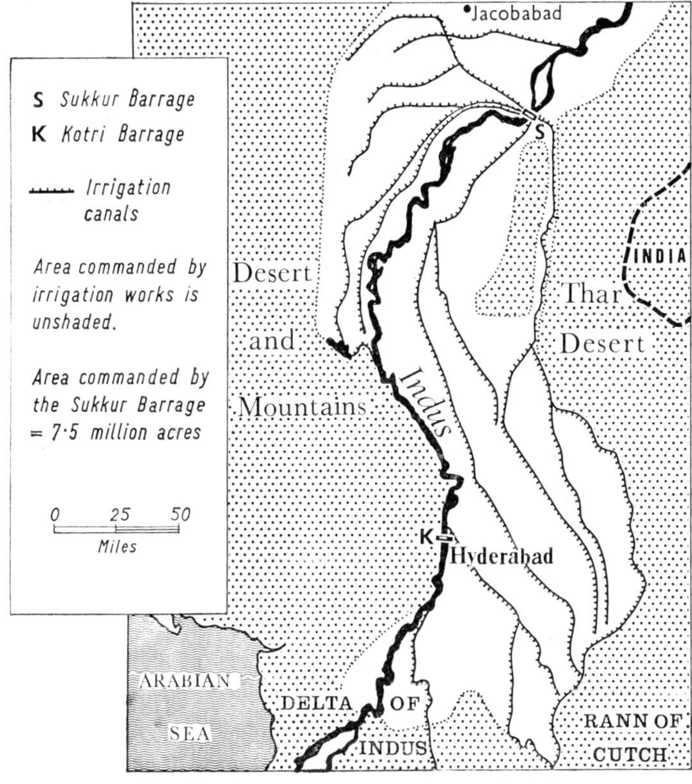

Fig. 29.—Irrigation on the Lower Indus.

hydrologists, and administrators is needed to maintain the works, and to ensure a fair distribution of available water.

Perennial irrigation on the Nile.—The aim of a perennial system of irrigation must be to deliver water to the fields at the time when it can be of greatest benefit to the farmer. This objective is unlikely to be achieved, except in the unlikely event of the peak of the flood coinciding with the period of maximum irrigation demand, unless substantial storage reservoirs are constructed to even out the flow of the river.

On the Nile such reservoirs are impounded behind the dams at Aswan, Jebel Aulia, and Sennar, from which water is released during the season of low natural discharge to the barrages in Egypt and (in the case of Sennar) to the Gezira irrigation area in the Sudan. The Roseires dam, now under construction, will eventually irrigate 4 million acres near Manaqil and Kenana. These dams, however, are large enough to hold back only a fraction of the Nile flood in a normal year, and only by imposing strict limitations on the use of water from February to May, the critical spring sowing period, can reserves be eked out. The situation becomes even more serious if the flood is very weak. In really poor years the total discharge of the Nile falls below the combined water requirements of Egypt and Sudan: hence the interest in what has come to be called "over-year" storage, *i.e.* the storage of one year's surplus for use in the next. The key installations in Egypt's over-year storage plans are the Owen Falls and the Aswan High Dams. The latter, begun in 1960, will ultimately impound twenty-five times the volume of water held behind the existing Aswan Dam. Other proposals include the erection of dams at the outlets of Lakes Albert, Kioga, and Tana, and a canal to hasten the passage of the Nile waters through the swamps of the Sudd (Fig. 30).

The Nile is an international river whose drainage basin embraces parts of seven countries. Uganda's concern is primarily with the development of the power potential of the Victoria Nile—a concern which does not conflict with the interests of Egypt and the Sudan to whom irrigation is of first importance. The river system is of little economic value to the remaining countries at present, although the power resources of the Blue Nile in Ethiopia may be harnessed in the future. The division of water between Egypt and Sudan is now governed by the 1959 Nile Water Agreement which replaced the earlier 1929 Agreement. The revised 1959 Agreement apportioned a greater share of the water to Sudan than she previously enjoyed, thereby recognising the growing importance in that country of irrigated agriculture,

e.g. *by the 1929 Agreement*

Egypt 48,000 million cubic metres.
Sudan 4,000 million cubic metres.

by the 1959 Agreement

Egypt 55,500 million cubic metres.
Sudan 18,500 million cubic metres.

7. Sprinkler or spray irrigation was first employed in the United States about the turn of the present century. It has proved

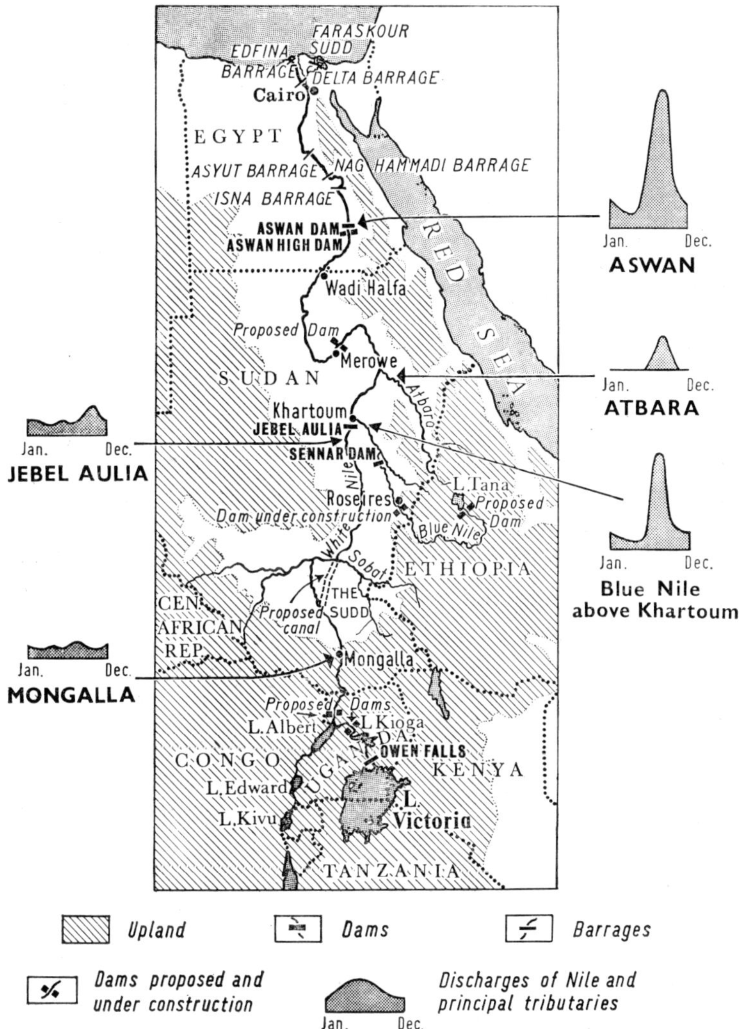

Fig. 30.—The Control of the Nile.

to be a highly efficient method of irrigating crops in widely differing conditions. It can be used on all types of land without preliminary levelling or the construction of ditches. The quantity of water used, and the rate of application, can be finely controlled, thereby reducing wastage, and minimising the risk of erosion on slopes. If mains water is available, the system is independent of streams or irrigation channels. The initial cost of the equipment is, however, rather high, and as most sprinklers are designed only to work at high pressure a considerable amount of power is required to operate the pump when working from a pond or stream. The sprinkler system is the only type in extensive use in Britain.

The problem of water loss

In irrigated areas generally, only one gallon of water out of every three that leave the reservoir reaches the roots of plants. The other two are lost by evaporation or by seepage from unlined channels. Annual evaporation rates within the tropics approach and in places exceed 100 inches. In practical terms these values represent a considerable volume of water. Of the rain that falls on Lake Victoria, for instance, only one quarter eventually flows over the Owen Falls Dam; and as the Nile picks its way through the Sudd marshes its volume shrinks by a half. In each case the villain is evaporation. A deep reservoir loses a smaller proportion of its water than a shallow one, but a deep reservoir is more costly to construct. A less expensive method of reducing wastage in certain conditions is to spray an insoluble chemical on to the water. Appreciable savings have followed the adoption of this practice in Australia. Stock losses have been reduced, and the cost of additional pumping from rivers and streams into city reservoirs in drought seasons curtailed.

Methods of countering water loss by seepage are also costly. Puddled clay, concrete, plastics, bitumen, and chemicals are employed to seal the floors of some reservoirs and canals. The use of concrete practically eliminates seepage loss from irrigation canals, which in some cases amounts to 40 per cent. of the total water transported.

The problem of saline soils

The use for irrigation purposes of water containing only a normal concentration of soluble minerals (sodium chloride, calcium, magnesium, boron, etc.) is likely to lead eventually to the accumulation of a noxious saline deposit on the surface, and in the upper few inches of the soil. This condition, to which soils in arid regions are particularly prone, arises because the natural drainage in dry regions is ill adjusted to deal with the copious waterings that irrigated areas receive. Instead of percolating freely into stream channels, which in dry lands are rather widely spaced, surplus moisture accumulates underground, and causes a rise in the water table. From the high water table strong salt solutions are drawn upwards by evaporation, and the salts precipitated within the root zone of plants. Hundreds of thousands of acres of good farm land in the Punjab, the Gezira, the American West—indeed in most regions under perennial canal irrigation, are menaced by this particular type of soil poisoning, and in several instances land has been forced out of cultivation.

The answer to the problem lies in the construction of a network of drainage ditches or pipe drains, parallel to, but at a lower level than, the irrigation channels. Spent irrigation water can then seep into these drains, and be led back into the river or main canal. The water table is lowered, and the concentration of salts in the ground water reduced. In the better farmed districts of the Nile Valley, drainage ditches are now set at fifty-yard intervals, and may occupy as much as 10 per cent. of the cultivated area.

Multi-purpose schemes

Supplying water to the arid lands is an extremely expensive undertaking. The cost of the Columbia River Basin project directly attributable to irrigation was estimated at $280 million, and the cost of irrigation works associated with the new Aswan High Dam project will approach $600 million. It is unlikely these and other schemes of a similar magnitude could ever have been contemplated if the burden of repayment had had to fall entirely on the shoulders of the farmers. However, by combining irrigation with other river-based projects—power development, flood control, and navigation improvement—the cost can be spread over a much wider field, and furthermore spread in such a way that the consumers of the various services that such a project provides pay according to their means. Thus it is not uncommon to find the prices of electricity and irrigation water so manipulated that the users of electricity pay more than, and the users of irrigation water less than the true cost of providing each commodity. In other words a part of the charge attributable to agriculture is defrayed by manufacturing industry and by the consumers of domestic power.

Other major multi-purpose schemes include projects on the Colorado (Fig. 31), Tennessee, and St Lawrence Rivers in North America; the Rhone in Europe; the Dnieper and Volga in the Soviet Union; the Snowy in Australia; the Zambesi (Kariba) in Africa, and the Bhadra in India.

Domestic water supplies.—Dissolved mineral salts which are so often injurious to plants are seldom detrimental to the health of man. The essential requirement of water intended for human consumption is that it be free from disease-producing bacteria. Enteric diseases such as typhoid, cholera, and dysentery are endemic in countries where drinking water is polluted, and are among the main causes of death, as they once were in Europe. The World Health Organisation estimates that 500 million people suffer each year from fatal or disabling illnesses contracted through drinking contaminated water.

A safe supply could be made available to the populations of the backward countries only at a cost that would place an enormous burden on resources that are already over-taxed. The task is not

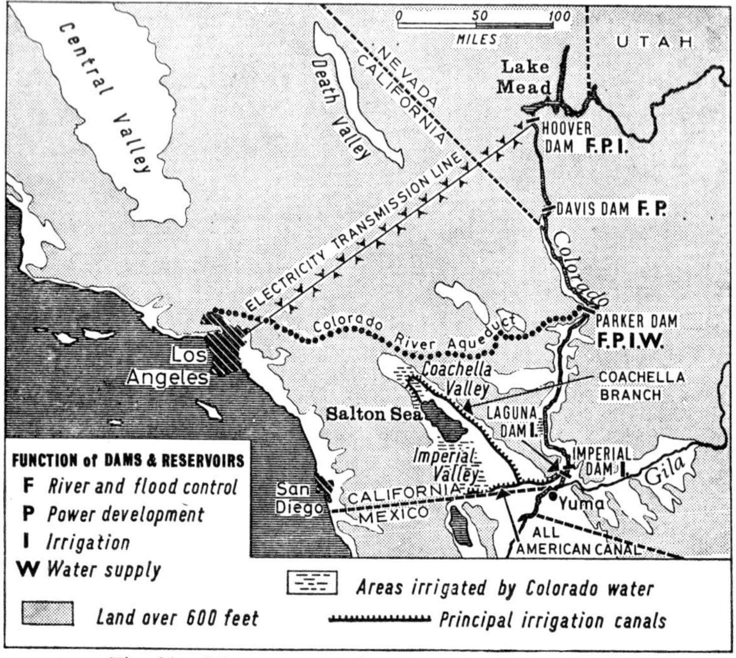

Fig. 31.—Multi-purpose Schemes on the Colorado.

impossible, however, and the return on investment in the form of better health (and poor health, it should be remembered, is one of the contributing factors to the low productivity of labour in the under-developed countries) would make any such project well worth while.

The desalination of sea water.—97 per cent. of the earth's water is held in the oceans. It is not surprising therefore, in view of the increasing difficulties of harnessing fresh supplies, that scientists should be actively searching for methods of removing salt from sea water at a cost that is commercially attractive. So far, desalination plants have proved economically feasible only in areas where fresh water supplies are absent or very scarce. They have been installed in Kuwait, on the island of Guernsey, and at the U.S.A. naval base at Guantanamo, Cuba. Others are under construction at Gibraltar and in Israel. In 1964 it was estimated that plant was in use throughout the world capable of desalting some 62 million gallons of water per day.

At the present rate of technological change it is impossible to forecast what the position will be in, say, twenty years' time. It is likely that distilled sea water will be used increasingly by mining communities, and by the producers of high-valued industrial products in regions where water is not at present available. In countries such as Britain, barrages across bays and estuaries rather than desalination plants are more likely to provide the long term solution to our water problems. Projects such as the Morecambe Bay Barrage would at present yield water at less than half the cost incurred by the most up-to-date desalination plant, although the margin is narrowing. Desert agriculture would benefit enormously if irrigation projects could be extended, but unfortunately agriculture is less able than industry to absorb the costs that the use of distilled sea water would involve. Only a drastic reduction in the price of water would benefit the peasant farmer.

Water in industry

Manufacturing industry consumes water on an enormous scale. The chemical industries of Britain alone use some 800 million gallons per day. Blast furnaces, steel mills, oil refineries, aluminium reduction mills, and nuclear and thermal electricity generating stations also consume copious amounts. Access to an abundant and cheap source of water is one of the most important localising factors in these and many other industries.

Some of the main industrial uses of water are:

1. For cooling purposes. Cooling water need not be of high quality, and can generally be abstracted directly from a river, lake, or in some cases from the sea, and used without any prior treatment.

2. For steam raising.

3. As an ingredient in the product, *e.g.* in many chemicals, processed foods, and drinks.

4. As process water in textile, pulp and paper, leather, and synthetic fibre production.

5. For the transportation in suspension of certain minerals, *e.g.* limestone, coal, shale, and kaolin.

6. For cleaning and washing out utensils.

CHAPTER IV

AGRICULTURE

Agriculture is the largest and most important of man's economic activities, and directly supports 60 per cent. of the world's population, or some 1,800 million people. The great majority of these people are sedentary cultivators or stock rearers and their dependants who in different ways, and with varying degrees of success, have set out to modify their natural environment with the object of providing for crops and animals the best conditions that their techniques allow. A further small and declining number depend upon the land for their livelihood but have not formed any close attachment to it, and have not made any conscious effort to improve it, in spite of centuries of occupation. Such are the nomads and shifting cultivators. The pure hunters and the gatherers of wild fruit and vegetables, although numbered among the world's producers of food, are in no sense of the word agriculturalists, and we shall not be concerned with them in this chapter.

Classification of the world's land resources

Table 14 indicates the percentage of agricultural land in the world as a whole, and in each of its major regions. A word of caution is necessary, however, before one begins to interpret statistics, especially any as generalised as these. Statistics of any kind can be misleading, and this is truer of those relating to agriculture than to most other industries. Compilation errors arise, for instance, from the incompleteness of the data upon which records are based and from differences in accounting methods employed from one country to another. Figures relating to the under-developed parts of the world are highly suspect. Much of the production from peasant farms often goes unrecorded (it is worth observing here that our own Ministry of Agriculture excludes from its returns data for holdings of less than one acre), and the recorded production that finds its way into official publications is often based on estimates or random sampling. There is then the very considerable difficulty of interpreting such material as may be available. Table 14 illustrates some of the problems very well. The Food and Agricultural Organisation puts the percentage of "arable land including fallow and orchards" at 10 per cent., and "permanent meadows and pastures" at 19 per cent. of the total land area of the world. But what is one to understand by these terms? The cultivated but eroded hill slopes of southern Italy and the rich fenlands of Cambridgeshire are both classified as arable, but they are in no way comparable as far as their cropping potential is concerned. The classification "permanent meadow and grassland" also embraces such diverse regions as the Cheshire Plain and the unimproved ranges of western Texas—the former including some of the best pasture land in the world, and the latter some of the poorest. The dangers of too literal an interpretation of the data given in Table 14, however, is best illustrated by reference to the entries against the Near East. With no less than 50 per cent. of its land area classified as "grassland", the region appears to be among the best endowed in the world, when in fact it is among the worst, as much of the grazing is little better than desert scrub, fit only for the nomadic herdsman for a few weeks each year.

TABLE 14

CLASSIFICATION OF THE WORLD'S LAND RESOURCES
(percentages)

	Agricultural Land		Non-Agricultural Land	
	Arable (including fallow) and orchards	Permanent meadow and grassland	Forest and woodland	Built-on, water, unused waste, and other
WORLD	10	19	31	40
Africa	9	23	26	42
U.S.S.R.	11	16	39	34
North America ..	10	12	34	44
Far East	18	13	24	45
Latin America ..	5	18	47	30
Oceania	8	17	12	63
Near East	4	50	6	40
Europe	32	16	30	22

Source: *F.A.O. Agriculture in the World Economy.*

After all allowances have been made for the over-generalised nature of Table 14, the very striking fact emerges, particularly in view of the prevailing world shortage of food, that more than 70 per cent. of the earth's land area is used for purposes other than agriculture, or is not used at all.

Forest and woodland comprise upwards of one quarter of the area in each region, with the exception of the Near East and Oceania, where the climate is not generally conducive to tree growth. Forests are a valuable economic resource. They also render a service to the farmer by protecting slopes from erosion and bottom lands from excessive flooding and silting. In the interests of agriculture, as well as the wood-using industries, forest conservation is being given a high priority in many parts of the world.

The second category of non-agricultural land includes the deserts, ice caps, much of the tundra, and many of the high mountain regions, as well as land that has been transferred from agriculture to other uses—urban development, road and railway construction, mines, quarries, waste-tips, etc. In Britain alone some 2 million acres of farm land have been lost since 1900, and during the building boom of the 1930s the countryside was being devoured at the rate of 60,000 acres per year. Estimates indicate that between 5 and 6·5 million acres of British farmland, representing between 12 and 20 per cent. of the total area of the country, will pass from agricultural to urban use during the present century.

Grasslands include both the natural grasslands of the tropics and temperate belts, and the sown pastures of formerly forested and wooded regions. With very few exceptions the areas under grass in Britain have been seeded. Many are in fact occupied by temporary leys in an arable rotation.

There remains the 10 per cent. of the world's land area classified as arable. Arable land produces (i) crops for direct human consumption, (ii) grains, roots, and rotation grasses for livestock feed, (iii) industrial crops such as cotton, flax, and jute. Europe has a larger proportion of crop land than any other continent. Moreover, because of Europe's temperate, humid climate, and the care that for centuries has been devoted to conserving and improving its soils, much of this land is of high quality. Over the world as a whole, however, the percentage of arable is very low, a fact that can be attributed to the scarcity of land in nearly every region that with present techniques repays the cost of cultivation.

Agriculture as an employer of labour

More people find employment in agriculture than in all other industries combined. The proportion of agricultural workers to the total employed population varies considerably from country to country, but tends to be high in the undeveloped and low in the advanced industrial lands (Table 15). Industrialisation is generally accompanied by a decline in the numbers who earn a living on farms, although not by a fall in agricultural production. The growth of manufacturing industry in fact benefits agriculture by making available equipment that performs farm operations more quickly, more efficiently, and often at lower cost than is possible by manual labour. Manufacturing industry also provides an outlet for labour displaced from the countryside (Fig. 32).

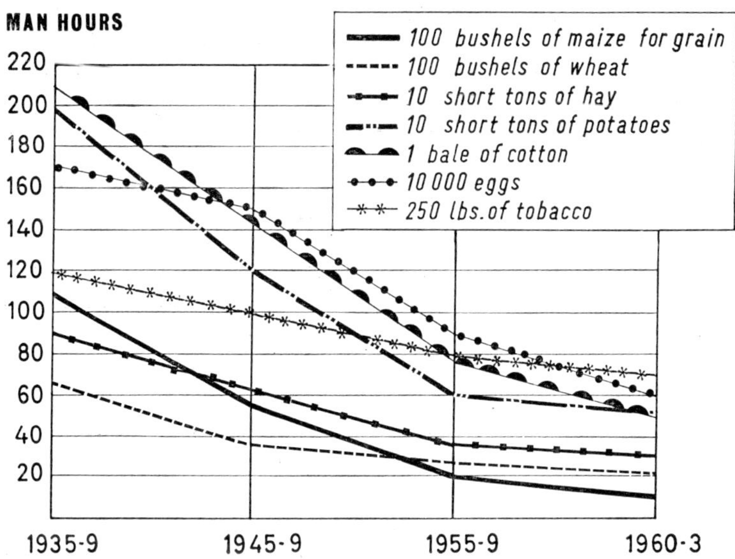

Fig. 32.—NUMBER OF MAN-HOURS REQUIRED TO PRODUCE GIVEN VOLUMES OF AGRICULTURAL PRODUCE IN THE UNITED STATES.

TABLE 15
POPULATION ENGAGED IN AGRICULTURAL OCCUPATIONS
(in thousands)

	Year	Number in Agriculture	Percentage of Total Active Population	Year	Number in Agriculture	Percentage of Total Active Population
Turkey	1935	6,460	82	1965	10,700	72
Philippines.. ..	1939	4,450	73	1965	6,105	59
Brazil	1940	9,453	67	1965	12,565	48
U.S.S.R.	1939	39,470	50	1965	38,910	33
Japan	1930	14,130	48	1965	12,955	27
France	1936	7,200	36	1965	3,600	18
Canada	1941	1,080	26	1965	635	9
Australia	1933	548	19	1965	455	10
U.S.A.	1940	8,370	19	1965	4,555	6
England and Wales	1931	1,260	6	1965	940	4

Source: *F.A.O. Production Yearbook.*

TYPES OF AGRICULTURE

INTENSIVE AND EXTENSIVE AGRICULTURE.—Land which is farmed *intensively* normally gives a high product yield per unit area. Such land accounts for only a small proportion of the total area in cultivation or grazed by animals; its distribution is patchy, but it can be found in every continent and in varied physical environments. It is associated with the richest as well as with the poorest of the world's farming communities, and supports most of the crops known to man and many of his domestic animals. In sharp contrast, large areas of the world are characterised by an *extensive* form of agriculture, in which the output per unit area is low, sometimes very low, while the output per man or machine is often, but not necessarily, high. Extensive farming is typical of regions having indifferent climates for crops, poor soils, difficult lines of communication with the outside world, and comparatively few inhabitants.

Characteristics of intensive farming

1. There is a heavy investment in the land, which is scarce relative to the other factors of production.

2. Farming may be labour-intensive as in Japan, southern China, and Egypt, or machine intensive as in Britain where it competes severely with manufacturing industry for labour. In both cases, the input of energy per unit area of land is high.

3. Intensive *subsistence* farming generally corresponds with regions of high population pressure. In these regions stark hunger is often the incentive to a maximum use of the land at no matter what cost in terms of time and labour. Intensive *commercial* agriculture, on the other hand, is normally associated with high living standards, and often with dense urban populations. It is frequently practised close to large cities, which provide a profitable outlet for farm products. In the case of certain speciality crops with exacting climatic requirements, however, farm and market may be widely separated.

4. Farms are commonly small. The average holding in Japan is less than three acres. More than three quarters of the farms in Britain are under 100 acres (Fig. 33), and the standard unit in the Corn Belt of the United States is the "quarter" (160 acres). Small farms are the result of vigorous competition for land, which forces up its price. On productive soils the area needed to support a family is also small.

Characteristics of extensive farming

1. Land is plentiful and cheap, the scarce factor of production in this case being labour. Hence there is a tendency to mechanise

farm processes, or to engage in activities which make little demand upon labour resources, *e.g.* livestock ranching.

2. There is little investment in the land, and its capacity to support crops or animals is low. An average annual yield of five to ten bushels of hardy cereals per acre, or one livestock unit[1] per fifty acres is not untypical. An increase in farm output is achieved by bringing a larger area into production, rather than by intensifying the system.

3. Where land yields so poorly, the economic unit must be very large. In the arid south-western states of the U.S.A., ranches average more than 10,000 acres, and some of the cattle stations of Northern Australia exceed 5,000 square miles.

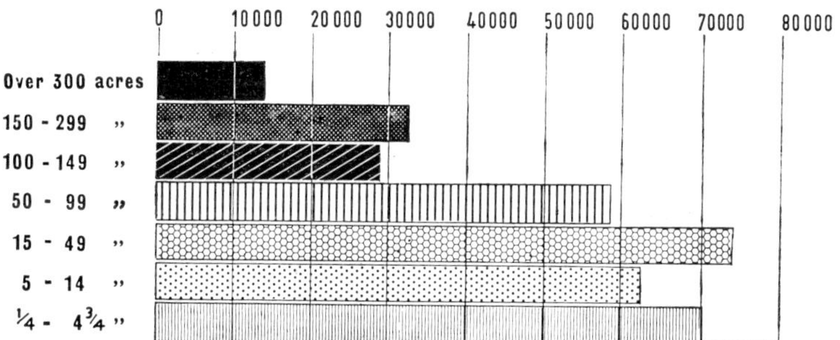

Fig. 33.—Number and Size of Agricultural Holdings in England and Wales (1961).

4. The type of crop that can be raised successfully by extensive farming methods is limited. Wheat, for instance, suffers only loss of yield when grown by this system: the quality of the flour milled from the grain is unimpaired. On the other hand, kitchen vegetables, tobacco, and most kinds of fruit not only crop badly if starved of water, or if cultivated on poor soils, but the quality of the produce itself is inferior and cannot readily command a market.

Subsistence and commercial agriculture.—Subsistence agriculture is concerned primarily with the production of food for consumption on the farm. By contrast, commercial agriculture entails the production of farm commodities for sale on commercial markets. The former is characteristic of the peasant economies of the Far East, Africa, and Latin America, and the latter of the agricultural enterprises of Europe, North America, the Soviet Union,

[1] A "livestock unit" may be taken as the equivalent of one horse, one cow, seven sheep, seven goats, or five pigs.

and the plantation areas of the tropics. On many farms, certain crops are grown mainly for subsistence, and others as cash crops for sale. The encouragement of cash cropping on native farms in colonial and former colonial territories is now accepted policy. Peasants are gradually being persuaded of the advantages of planting coffee, rubber, sugar-cane, etc., and tending them alongside their maize, rice, and cassava. In Europe and North America farmers engage in subsistence agriculture to the extent to which they raise crops of fruit and vegetables for use in their own households.

Examples of subsistence agriculture

(A) SHIFTING CULTIVATION

Shifting cultivation is a system of agriculture in which forest or bush land is cleared and cropped intermittently. It is practised widely by primitive people in the equatorial forests and the wet savanas, and is an appropriate system of tillage in conditions of poor soils, backward techniques, and low population densities (Fig. 34).

The method.—A patch of land which is to bear crops is chosen as close to the cultivator's village as possible. If suitable land cannot be found in the neighbourhood, the village itself may have to be moved. Trees are felled and brushwood cleared with whatever tools happen to be available. Trees too large to tackle are left standing. Cut material is gathered into the centre of the cleared area, and burnt when dry. Crops are sown without any preparatory cultivation, simply by making holes with a digging stick and dropping in a few seeds, or alternatively by scattering seeds on small mounds made by drawing up the soil with a hoe. A variety of crops is often sown together, so that once begun, harvesting is more or less continuous. A harvest spread over the year helps to solve the difficult problem of storage in a hot, humid climate. After a few years it becomes necessary to abandon the plot, either because the effort of keeping it clear of weeds and the encroaching jungle outweighs the return from further cultivation, or more likely because of a declining soil fertility which manifests itself in lower yields. Once the land has been abandoned, it is quickly covered with a canopy of creepers, bushes, and trees; and over the years the cycle of growth, leaf-fall, and decay restores to it a measure of fertility. The time taken for complete restoration varies with local conditions, but it is unlikely to be less than twenty or thirty years. At the end of this period, the plot may be re-cleared and re-cultivated.

Shifting cultivation is capable of supporting only a low population density. Land that is cropped for only three years out of thirty cannot, on the assumption that one acre is needed to feed a man for a

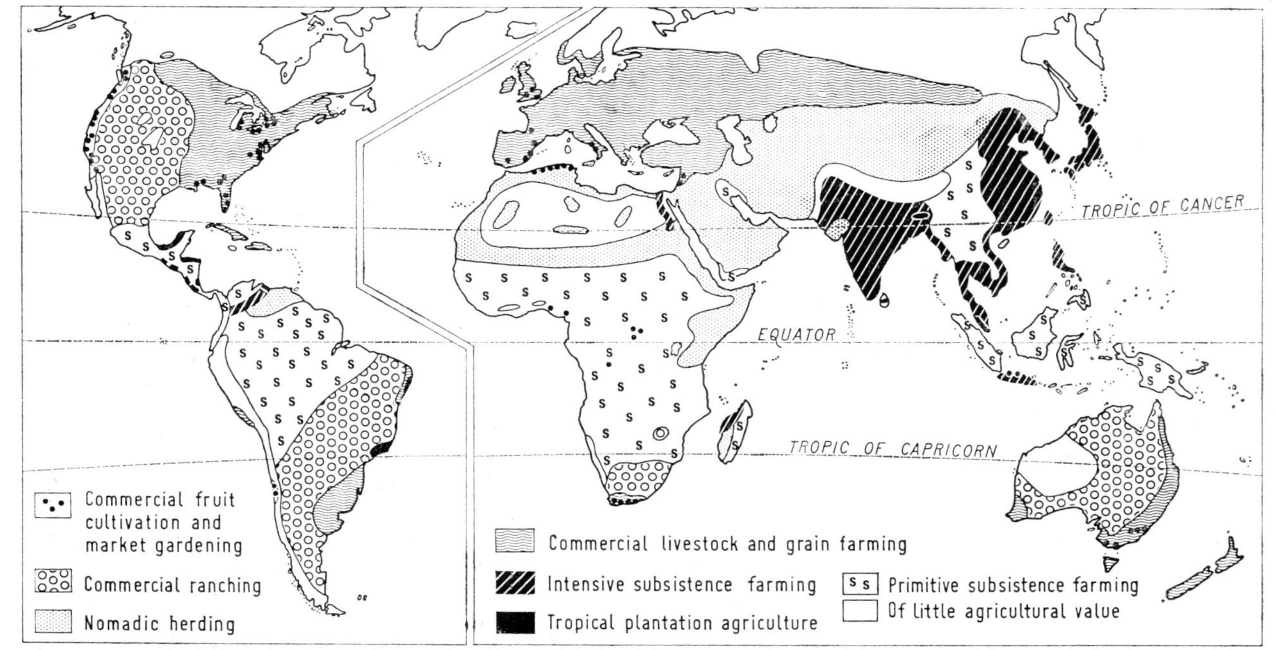

Fig. 34.—World Agricultural Regions.

year, sustain more than sixty-four persons per square mile. However, it matters little whether one or only half an acre suffices. The fact remains that a farming system which by its nature is incapable of being intensified, will set a fairly rigid upward limit to the numbers it can support on a given area if an adequate resting period for recuperation is to be allowed. A reduction in the length of the fallow consequent upon increasing pressure on the land is likely to lead to soil impoverishment, and ultimately to erosion, thereby undermining the very basis of the community's existence. This is the weakness of shifting agriculture during a time of rising populations.

Once regarded as a system whereby agricultural production could be maintained indefinitely in the tropics without danger to the soil, shifting cultivation is now considered by experts to be wasteful of natural resources, and even a menace to society as a whole. Soil conservationists and forest land administrators are becoming increasingly alarmed at the activities of the shifting cultivators, particularly when they are operating on steep slopes adjacent to densely settled plains, as is frequently the case in southern and South East Asia. The worst effects of their "slash and burn" techniques can be mitigated if burning is controlled, and if seedlings of useful trees are planted and tended as part of the cropping system. Not all efforts to convince the shifting cultivator of the value of forest conservation have failed. In India considerable areas of woodland have been restored by planting sal, a useful timber tree resembling teak. In the Philippines, tung trees (the source of a vegetable oil used in the manufacture of paints and varnishes) have been used to replace economically valueless forest; and in Malaya *Hevea* seedlings have been established. The introduction of conservation methods obviously involves fundamental changes in the farming system, and change is apt to be a slow process among peoples living on the margins of civilisation. If only for this reason, shifting cultivation is likely to persist in its traditional form for many years, especially in the more remote parts of the world.

(B) Intensive subsistence agriculture—the example of Oriental agriculture

The intensive production of subsistence food crops has reached its highest level of development on the plains and deltas, and in some instances also on the uplands of Monsoon Asia. This great farming region extends, albeit with several interruptions, from West Pakistan to Japan, and southwards to the islands of Indonesia. In a few areas commercial farming has taken root—sometimes on native farms, sometimes on foreign-owned and managed plantations, but over the greater part of the Far East, agriculture is geared to supplying local needs, and few products find their way into commercial markets.

Unless the growing season is short, as in northern China, or rainfall is deficient, as in parts of western India and Pakistan, rice is the almost universal summer crop. In the hotter and better watered parts, one, or even two crops of summer rice may be followed by a cool or dry season sowing of wheat, barley, pulses, rape, or vegetables. Population pressure is such that every square foot of land that can possibly be brought into cultivation is put under crops. Tiny, irregular-shaped fields, often too small for efficient working, are cultivated right up to the boundary fence or irrigation ditch. Villages are sited on levées, infertile patches, coastal spits, or on uncultivable hill sides above the fertile valley alluvium, and beyond the reach of irrigation water. In the better farmed lowlands of China and Japan, every ounce of manure that can be scraped together is used to fertilise the fields. Slopes in hilly districts are laboriously terraced. Little machinery is used, and implements are simple. Hence the amount of human energy expended on these and other operations—lifting water, preparing the land, planting, weeding, harvesting, and threshing is prodigious. A very high crop yield indeed would be expected in these circumstances, and in some favoured areas it is achieved. But high yields are not universal in the Orient, in spite of the intensity of the farming. In India, for example, where farmers are handicapped by poor water supplies and impoverished soils, rice yields, on average, at only one quarter the level attained in Japan, and bad harvests in parts of the country are the rule rather than the exception (Table 26, p. 141). The problem facing subsistence cultivators here, and in many areas of the Far East, is that the limits of intensification have been reached with existing agricultural techniques. An improved water supply, better seed, more fertilisers, larger units of production, and in some instances fewer farm workers, would result in an increase in output, bringing with it a rising living standard for the rural population. Indeed, the problem of food supply in the Orient would be largely solved if the rice fields of India, Pakistan, Ceylon, Indonesia, and many other monsoon countries could be made to yield as prolifically as those of Japan, or only one third as bountifully as some experimental plots in the United States where the latest strains of rice have produced up to six tons per acre.

(c) Pastoral nomadism

Nomadism has survived from pre-historic times in regions where cultivation is precarious, and where the commercial stock rearer has not penetrated (Fig. 34). Over a wide range of natural environments, from the Arctic to the equatorial regions, men, usually grouped into tribal units, are constantly on the move in search of pastures for their animals. The principle on which their economy is based is simple. Owing to aridity or cold, human beings are unable to live directly from the land, but grazing animals can: hence, according to region, reindeer, yaks, horses, camels, sheep, goats, donkeys, and cattle are herded in order to furnish their keepers with food, clothing, shelter, and transport.

The nomad does not wander aimlessly, but his migrations follow regular tracks. In arid country in summer they lead towards a river or oasis, or upwards to the higher valleys where rain and the accumulation of moisture from winter snows help to support better grazing. Along the southern margins of the Sahara, cattle herders move southwards on to the savana during the period of summer rains, and northwards to the desert margins in the cooler season. In the Arctic, migration is southward to the shelter of the taiga in winter, and back on to the tundra in summer.

The art of cultivation is known to and practised by some nomadic peoples. The Kirghiz and Kazak of central Asia tend patches of cultivated, and sometimes irrigated, land which produce cereals in the early summer. Nomadic tribes of south-western Asia plant crops, and harvest them between seasonal migrations. By contrast, the Bedouin engage in little or no cultivation, but obtain grain and fruit from the oasis dwellers, either in exchange for animals and animal products, or, in difficult times, by raiding. The Masai of East Africa despise tillage absolutely. Tending crops is considered unmanly, degrading work—an activity best left to the women-folk, whilst the men get on with the serious business of fighting and stealing each others' cattle.

To-day, pastoral nomadism is on the wane. In all but the harshest environments sedentary farmers are encroaching upon the nomad's traditional grazing grounds. Mobile, resourceful, and often aggressive, the nomad has always held a tactical advantage over his settled neighbour. The latter, however, mainly owing to the support given him by national governments who are anxious to foster an ordered way of life, has triumphed in the end. In the Soviet Union nomadism is now virtually extinct. During the last half-century most of the tribesmen of central Asia have been converted to law-abiding stockmen or cultivators.

(D) Commercial agriculture

Unlike the subsistence farmer, whose chief concern is to feed his family from his own land, the commercial farmer (except in certain countries where the economy is tightly controlled by the state) must sell his products on an open market where he competes with other producers of like and substitute products. His prosperity depends not only on the capacity of his land to support crops or animals, and on his skill as a cultivator or stockman, but also on his ability to respond to market conditions which are constantly changing. A domestic market may be protected. A farmer may be cushioned by subsidies against unexpected or rapid falls in prices at home. But if he depends heavily on overseas outlets for the sale of the bulk of his crop his fortunes will rise and fall with the level of foreign demand, the prosperity of the population in the importing countries, and the trading policies of their governments. Fortunately for the farmer only a small proportion of the output of most agricultural commodities enters international trade, but the producers of those commodities which are traded in substantial quantities are particularly vulnerable to the consequences of booms and slumps (Tables 16 and 17).

Physical and economic limits of cultivation

The limits within which a crop can be produced commercially are set by two factors. The first is physical, and of the physical

TABLE 16

WORLD EXPORTS OF CERTAIN AGRICULTURAL PRODUCTS

(*a*) in thousands of metric tons

(*b*) as a percentage of total recorded production

(1965)

	EXPORTS (Thousands of metric tons)	PERCENTAGE OF TOTAL RECORDED PRODUCTION
Wheat	49,900	19
Maize	25,100	11
Rice	7,800	3
Barley	8,080	8
Cotton	3,690	31
Bananas	4,730	20
Potatoes (for consumption only)	2,810	1
Coffee	2,750	60
Oranges	3,600	17
Copra	1,400	43
Apples	1,990	10
Oats	1,730	3
Cocoa beans	1,315	105
Jute	860	26
Sisal	619	76
Tea	632	55

Source: *F.A.O. Trade Yearbook.*

TABLE 17

EXPORTS OF CERTAIN AGRICULTURAL COMMODITIES FROM SPECIFIC COUNTRIES

(*a*) in thousands of metric tons
(*b*) as a percentage of total recorded production
(1965)

	COUNTRY	EXPORTS (Thousands of metric tons)	PERCENTAGE OF TOTAL RECORDED PRODUCTION
Wheat	Canada	11,882	63
Maize	U.S.A.	15,160	15
	Argentina	2,804	55
Rice	Burma	1,347	17
Barley	France	1,743	24
Cotton	Sudan	106	71
Bananas	Ecuador	1,200	37
Potatoes	Netherlands	463	14
Coffee	Colombia	338	71
Oranges	Spain	1,155	61
Copra	Philippines	1,849	85
Tea	Ceylon	224	98
Apples	Italy	486	22
Oats	West Germany	562	27
Cocoa beans	Ghana	501	119
Jute	Pakistan	758	65
Sisal	Tanzania	213	97

Source: *F.A.O. Trade Yearbook.*

controls, climate is by far the most important. Whilst most plants are tolerant of a wider range of climatic conditions than is commonly realised, a point is reached beyond which they will not grow. The lemon, for instance, does not succeed in regions of winter frost; the olive fails outside the areas of Mediterranean climate; and the oil palm has never been acclimatised to conditions of dry heat or cold. Within the boundaries described by physical geography are the more restricted limits set by economic factors beyond which it does not *pay* to produce a crop. These limits are subject to constant, and often considerable, modification. A change in the techniques of production, a change in space relationships resulting from a relative improvement or worsening of communications, switches in the agricultural policies of a government, and fluctuations in demand brought about, perhaps, by the use of a substitute product will sooner or later be reflected in an increase or decrease in the area devoted to the production of a particular commodity, or group of commodities. For instance, the invention of the cotton gin ultimately brought about the decline of flax as a major European crop; New York State ceased to be an important producer of wheat once the Erie Canal and the railway opened up the Middle West; the "Grow More Food" campaign in war-time Britain increased the arable acreage by 50 per cent. within a few years, with a corresponding decline in the area under grass; and the advent of synthetic rubber, if it has not yet resulted in a reduction in the output of natural rubber has at least prevented the expansion that otherwise would have taken place. Even the controls of climate are relaxed when a new variety of plant better able to withstand drought, frost, or climate-induced disease is introduced, or when the land is irrigated or even drained. Agriculture is dynamic. Patterns of cultivation change, both in the long and short term. Land utilisation maps therefore, and maps depicting "crop belts", become outdated unless constantly revised.

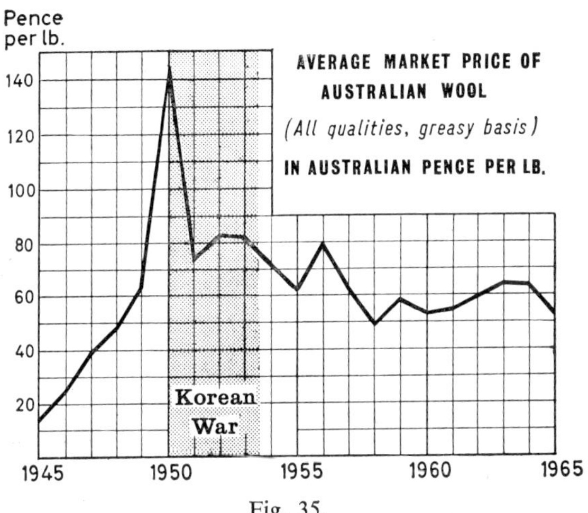

Fig. 35.

The instability of agriculture

Commercial agriculture has been bedevilled for years by short-term, and often violent, fluctuations in the market prices of commodities (Fig. 35). Several factors account for this:

1. The volume of production coming on to the market is determined to a considerable extent by forces which the farmer cannot control—frost, drought, insect damage, etc. (Fig. 36).

2. Many agricultural products are the raw materials of manufactured articles which are themselves subject to fluctuating prices.

3. The demand for many farm products, especially those for which there is no close substitute, *e.g.* sugar, wheat, tobacco, and in some markets, coffee, is *inelastic*, *i.e.* the quantity demanded is unaffected (or only slightly affected) by a small change in price.

A substantial price reduction would be necessary to dispose of large surpluses, with serious consequences for the producers (Fig. 37).

4. The cycle of production in agriculture is long. This is particularly so in the case of animal products, and crops borne on

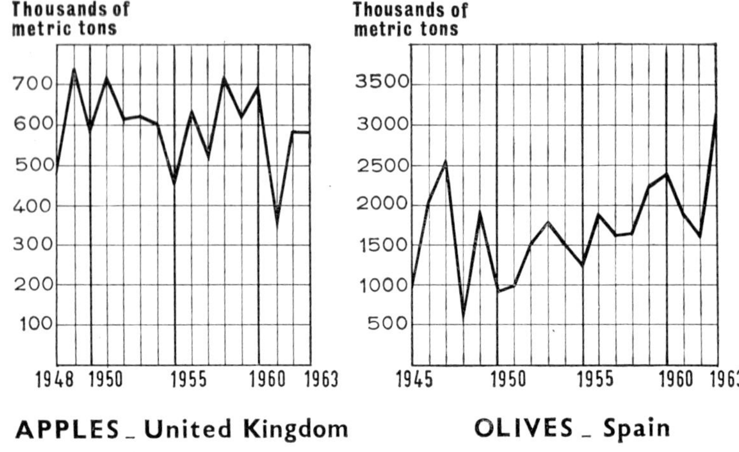

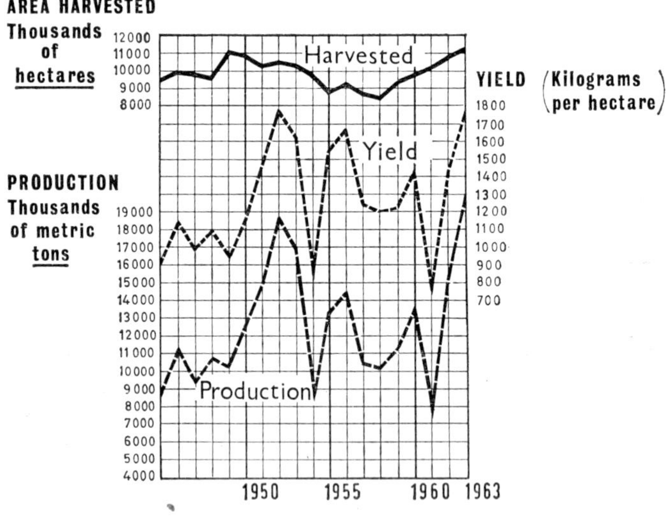

Fig. 36.—FLUCTUATIONS IN THE OUTPUT OF CERTAIN AGRICULTURAL COMMODITIES SINCE THE SECOND WORLD WAR.

perennial plants, where current yields represent the return on investments made several years earlier. It is not as easy to stop, or curtail, production on a farm as it is in a factory. Tea bushes and coffee shrubs do not stop bearing because the market for tea and coffee is glutted, and sheep still have to be sheared even if there is no demand for wool. Supply, then, as well as demand, is inelastic. Adjustments in agricultural production to changing conditions are therefore inevitably slow.

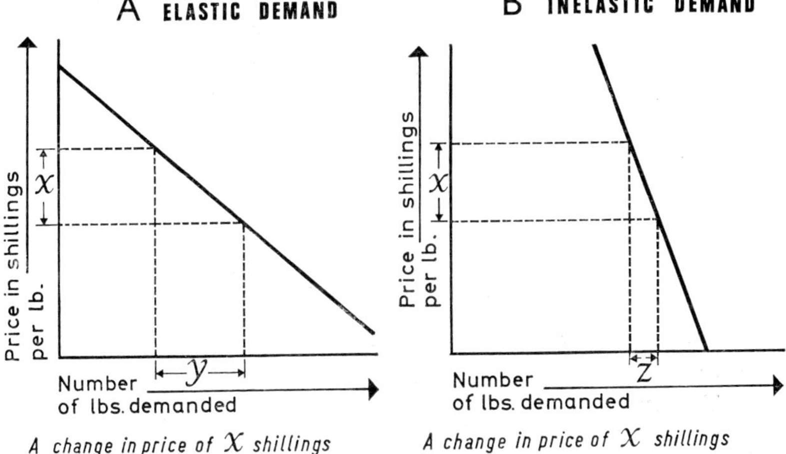

Fig. 37.—ELASTICITY OF DEMAND.

5. Certain products do not store well, and have to be sold almost as soon as they are harvested whether the market is favourable to the producer or not.

6. Agriculture (state farms and plantations are exceptions) is still largely the preserve of the independent farmer, and is organised in small, often very small, units of production. In bad times, labour cannot be readily discharged, as management and labour are often invested in the same person. Co-operation for mutual advantage among an infinite number of small, competing producers, scattered over the five continents, is also far more difficult to organise than it is in manufacturing industry, where production units are normally much larger and geographically more concentrated.

Government intervention in agriculture

International commodity agreements.—It is one of the paradoxes of our time, that in a world where nearly half the population is under-fed, the recurring problem in commercial agriculture should be over-production. For various reasons market prices tend to fall periodically below the level at which it pays the farmer to produce. Before the First World War, some of the exporting countries (which were often the least developed countries) sought to arrest this tendency by limiting the volume of goods coming on to the market. During the depression years of the 1930s, national governments became directly involved. In some cases they paid farmers not to bring in the harvest. In others they bought up crops, and stored them in anticipation of more favourable trading conditions later. Frequently such measures served only to aggravate the situation. Many farmers, aware that the state would purchase unsaleable surpluses at guaranteed prices, actually increased their production, while the state itself became encumbered with stocks it could not release except at the risk of depressing prices further. A position was sometimes reached when stocks had become so large, and the prospects of disposing of them so remote, that there appeared no other solution but to destroy them. This is what Brazil in fact did. In that country some 70 million bags of coffee were burnt during the late 1930s and the early years of the Second World War.

The need for commodity agreements negotiated internationally, and embracing all the major producing and consuming countries, became evident if any real degree of stability were to be achieved. There was little point in a group of countries curtailing production and exports if an outsider were going to take advantage of the improved marketing conditions to dispose of her entire crop. Some pre-war agreements were, in fact, undermined by actions of this sort.

Before 1939, international agreements involving some or most of the major producers and importers of wheat, sugar, tea, coffee, and rubber were concluded. They were allowed to lapse during the war, and since 1945 only four new agreements that are truly international in character have been re-negotiated. They concern wheat, sugar, coffee, and olive oil. Other agreements, *e.g.* the Commonwealth Sugar Agreement, regulate production and trade among certain *groups* of producers and importers. The main objective of all agreements is to equate supply with demand by means of export quotas and fixed prices.

Agriculture in Britain—a policy of protection.—British agriculture began to feel the full force of world competition towards the end of the last century when technical developments in transport opened the markets of this country to low-cost producers in the New World and Australasia. One solution to the problem created for the British farmer by the new situation would have been to erect high tariff barriers against the type of foreign-grown food that could be produced at home. Such a solution was not practical, however, as reducing imports would inevitably have meant an increase in the price of food to the expanding urban population, and, more seriously, would have resulted in a decline in the export trade which had become vital to the well-being of the British people as a whole. By the late 1920s, however, the situation had become critical enough for the government to intervene on behalf of the farmers, and various forms of protection and aid were given. These continued until the outbreak of war.

The position of agriculture in the national economy changed radically after 1940. During the war itself, food imports were cut to a minimum. The period of scarcity continued into the post-war years when Britain found herself competing for inadequate world food resources with the devastated countries of Europe and the Far East whose own agriculture had been disrupted by the conflict. The situation both during and after the war required that output from British farms be increased at almost any cost. Heavy subsidies were paid to farmers to intensify production and to bring marginal land into cultivation. In order to provide a fair standard of living for farmers and agricultural workers, and at the same time to keep food prices steady, the government purchased all foodstuffs, and released them on ration at low, controlled prices. The difference between the artificially low market price and the price paid to farmers was met out of taxation. This practice continued until the end of food rationing, when government control over production and marketing was relaxed.

Since the end of rationing, emphasis has been placed on the production of commodities demanded by the consumer, rather than on products that best met the needs of a people living in a state of semi-siege. Output has continued to rise, and the proportion of food purchased overseas has declined. Britain now produces about 50 per cent. of its food at home, whereas in 1939 it produced about 30 per cent. (Fig. 38). The farm support policy has also continued, although in recent years it has been severely criticised on the grounds that £300 million per year (its present cost) is too high a price to pay in order to keep the farmers happy. The arguments in favour of continuing the present policy are, however, quite formidable, and may be summarised as follows:

1. That it is in the national interest to preserve a healthy and vigorous rural way of life, and to be as self-supporting in food as possible in case of war or other emergency. To allow the industry to run down at this stage would gravely impair its future potential.

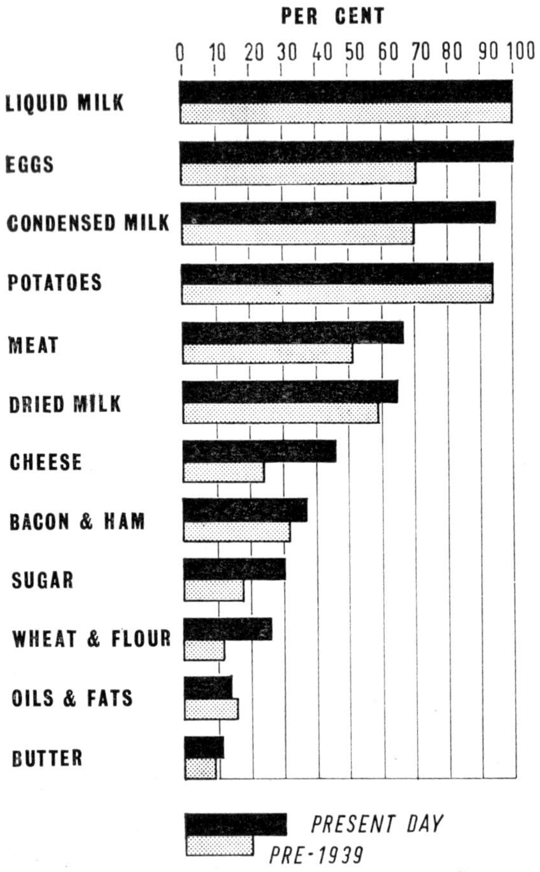

Fig. 38.—PERCENTAGE OF TOTAL UNITED KINGDOM FOOD SUPPLIES PROVIDED BY HOME AGRICULTURE.

2. That the government, having directed and controlled agriculture during the war and post-war years, and having imposed a certain pattern of production upon it, has a moral obligation to continue its support.

3. That the production of food at home assists the balance of payments problem by reducing the amount of foreign currency

needed to finance imports. This argument, of course, ignores the possibility that the balance of payments problem might be more readily solved if scarce national resources were employed to raise the efficiency of the exporting industries, rather than to subsidise the production of high-cost food.

4. That agriculture operates with certain inherent disadvantages compared with manufacturing industry. The farmer is to a large extent at the mercy of the weather and other forces he cannot control. The small size of the farm unit also reduces the opportunities for labour specialisation, and large economies of scale cannot be realised as easily as they can in manufacturing industry. Because work is seasonal, certain machines must stand idle for much of the year, and for some operations mechanisation is inappropriate. For these reasons, productivity in agriculture tends to lag behind productivity in other industries, and farmers tend to receive a decreasing share of the nation's wealth unless some form of support is given.

The nature of the agricultural support policy.—Tariff protection for agriculture has found little favour in Britain. It is felt that such a policy would offend Commonwealth producers who rely heavily on the United Kingdom market. Tariffs on principal foodstuffs are low or absent, and where they exist they are designed to discriminate in favour of one group of exporters (mainly the Commonwealth and Colonial territories), and against another. Government support is therefore by subsidy (whose effect on the exporting countries, it should be noted, is substantially the same as a tariff), and takes the following forms:

(i) *Price guarantees or deficiency payments.*—The farmer receives a guaranteed price in respect of each major product, and the difference between the guaranteed price and the world market price (*i.e.* the price Britain would pay for the imported product) is met by the exchequer. The effect is to keep the cost of food to the consumer lower than it would be if home production were protected by a tariff (as it tends to be on the continent of Europe), and as the subsidy is financed out of taxation the burden of payment is shifted on to the shoulders of the wealthier sections of the community. The main economic objection to the price support policy is that efficient and inefficient producers are equally rewarded, with the consequence that farming remains a profitable venture for many who without a subsidy would be forced to leave the industry.

(ii) *Production and improvement grants.*—Production grants, *e.g.* the fertiliser grant and the lime subsidy, are paid to assist current production. Improvement grants are intended to aid long-term capital improvements. Improvement grants are made only for specific purposes, and then only after the improvements have been carried out. In so far as they help to raise farm efficiency they reduce costs, and can be justified on economic grounds.

(iii) *Research grants.*—These too have the ultimate effect of increasing efficiency. However, they amount to only a very small fraction of the total support costs.

Agricultural policies in the Dependent Territories, and the under-developed Commonwealth.—Most of the territories for which Britain assumes, or until recently assumed, political and economic responsibility are situated within the tropics. Some of these territories, through the fortunate accident of geology or location, have developed important mining or commercial enterprises, but the great majority continue to be producers of food and agricultural raw materials, both for subsistence purposes and for exchange.

In some of these lands, foreign-owned plantations or estates worked by independent white farmers are well established, and make a contribution to the economic well-being of the territory in which they are located out of all proportion to their size or number. However, agriculture is primarily in the hands of native peasant farmers, and in too many cases it is retarded by archaic methods of cultivation, by systems of land tenure inimical to progress, by lack of capital for improvement, and by distance from, or poor communications with, potential markets. The difficulties of organised marketing and the price fluctuations in primary commodities have also made commercial farming appear a less attractive and less secure proposition to the peasant than subsistence farming.

In 1940, the first of a series of Colonial Development and Welfare Acts was passed, and in 1948 the Colonial Development Corporation was established. This later became the Commonwealth Development Corporation in order to bring the newly independent territories within the scope of its activities. Through these agencies considerable capital sums have been made available to the colonies and under-developed Commonwealth members with the object of increasing their general productivity and trade. Grants have also been made by the British government to colonies at the time of their independence. In addition, the World Bank, the United Nations, and other international bodies have contributed considerable sums.

Plans for agricultural development have laid stress on giving the native farmer practical self-help and advice. New land has been brought into cultivation, model farms and co-operatives established, new strains of economic crops developed, research undertaken into animal and plant diseases, the problem of soil erosion tackled, water supplies improved, holdings re-organised, and facilities for the efficient collection, grading, and marketing of commodities provided. Care has been taken to prevent an imbalance developing in the agricultural economy. Over-dependence on cash cropping can be dangerous, and the importance of the staples is not overlooked. Thus in Kenya, native plantings of coffee are restricted initially to 100 trees per family, and only when peasant farmers have proved themselves capable of managing these without detriment to food production, and without inflicting damage on the soil, is permission for further plantings granted.

There has been little emphasis placed on farm mechanisation. A distinguishing feature of native tropical agriculture is its dependence on non-mechanical energy. Power is provided by draught animals and by the farmer and his family. Farm implements consist of a hoe and simple plough. The number of tractors in the whole of Africa probably does not exceed a quarter of a million, and the majority of these are on European farms in the Republic of South Africa. Britain, by comparison, has nearly 500,000 tractors exceeding 10 h.p. In the conditions that exist at present in most underdeveloped tropical countries, it is questionable whether any significant increase in the use of mechanical energy would be justified on economic grounds. Farm mechanisation would consume capital resources that could be put to better use in improving water supplies and providing fertilisers. To replace men by machines would be to replace a plentiful factor of production (labour) with a scarce factor (capital), and to substitute an expensive form of energy (mechanical power) for a cheap form (man-power). These acts would be unlikely to lead to the increase in production which alone would warrant their consideration. They would, however, be likely to increase the problem of rural unemployment unless alternative work could be provided in manufacturing industry. But, again, manufacturing industry cannot be developed without substantial capital investment.

Farm mechanisation in regions of plentiful labour is likely to bring economic benefits to the community as a whole if and when:

(i) Machines can be used to clear land that cannot be cleared by human labour.

(ii) It speeds up certain operations at a critical time of the year. If the growing season is short the use of a machine may reduce the time taken to plant, and thus allow a crop to be cultivated that could not be cultivated if the planting season were prolonged by the employment of slower hand labour.

(iii) It helps to clear labour bottlenecks during periods of intense activity. The busiest time of the year in the tropics usually coincides with the season of rapid plant growth, when constant weeding is necessary. The mechanical weeding of standing crops, however, is virtually impossible.

If it is established with reasonable certainty that benefits will accrue from the mechanisation of farm operations, it is then important to take measures which will ensure that labour is properly trained and equipped to handle and care for the machines. One does not turn an illiterate Kikuyu tribesman into a competent mechanic simply by seating him astride a tractor. Even elementary skills are not easily acquired by people living in a hoe and digging-stick civilisation. One recalls the case of an African labourer who was found to be using lubricating oil on a mowing machine to a value in excess of what he was earning in wages. Technical education must always precede the introduction of mechanical equipment, otherwise machines, no matter how simple (and many exported from Europe to the tropics are needlessly complicated), will be luxuries.

The United States—A policy of protection and conservation.—The problems which to-day face United States' agriculture stem basically from its efficiency. In recent decades technological developments have resulted in production outstripping demand, in spite of a growing population. An attempt was made to curtail farm output in President Roosevelt's New Deal programme of 1933, by setting an acreage quota on all basic commodities (maize, cotton, peanuts, rice, and tobacco), and by paying a guaranteed minimum price for crops harvested, provided the acreage was not exceeded. The policy was taken a stage further in 1955 with the setting up of the "Soil Bank" into which a farmer could retire a proportion of his allotted acreage, and receive an annual payment so long as it remained there. By 1960, some 28 million acres had been withdrawn from cultivation, and had been grassed or planted with trees.

As a conservation measure, the concept of a "soil bank" is unquestionably sound. But it has failed to solve the problem of over-production for the simple reason that farmers have intensified their production methods, and now produce substantially the same volume as before, but from a smaller area. The Federal Government now holds surplus stocks worth several billion dollars, which, in the absence of normal commercial outlets, it seeks to dispose of by barter agreements and by making gifts to famine relief organisations. An unfortunate consequence of giving away food, or selling it cheaply, is that the economies of established commercial producers can sometimes be undermined. In 1956, for instance, and again in the early 1960s, the United States sold millions of tons of grain to India and Pakistan at about half the cost of production. Australia, a part of whose "natural market" is the Far East, found it extremely difficult to sell some of her wheat crop in face of competition of this kind.

Types of farm organisation

OWNER OCCUPATION AND TENANCY.—Approximately 40 per cent. of the world's farmers are tenants, working land they do not own. Census returns show that 65 per cent. of the farmers in England and Wales are tenants, 77 per cent. in Scotland, 53 per cent. in India, and 5 per cent. in West Germany and Denmark.

Tenancy is not necessarily a symbol of agricultural poverty. In fact the correlation between status (owner-occupier or tenant), on the one hand, and living standards on the other is slight. The percentage of tenant farmers in the United Kingdom and the Mid-West states of the U.S.A. is high, and so are the standards of living. They are manifestly higher than they are in Thailand, where in some areas more than 95 per cent. of the farmers own their own land. It is the nature rather than the fact of tenancy that is important. Prosperity depends on security. Short leases, or worse, leases that can be terminated abruptly, do not encourage long-term planning, farm improvement schemes, and the careful husbanding of soil resources that are essential to the proper use of the land. Few tenants are anxious to invest on behalf of successors who are not to be members of their own family. The extent to which short-lease tenants have contributed to the problem of soil erosion in the world cannot be measured, but it must be very considerable.

Recognition of the problem has led governments to pass legislation giving greater security of tenure to farmers. The payment of compensation for capital improvements undertaken by the tenant should he no longer wish to occupy the farm is now obligatory in many countries. The United Nations, through the Food and Agricultural Organisation, assists under-developed lands in financing their tenancy improvement schemes.

Most tenants in Britain are cash tenants. A rent paid to the landlord gives them exclusive right to work the land, and to the produce therefrom. Tenure is for life, or for as long as they continue to practise what the law calls "good husbandry". The legal relationship between landlord and tenant differs from country to country. In the United States the following types of lease are common:

(i) *Cash tenancy.*

(ii) *Crop-share tenancy.*—This differs from cash tenancy in that rent is paid by surrendering a proportion of the crop.

(iii) *Share-cropping.*—Share-cropping is commonest in the South, where it evolved in conditions of economic bankruptcy that followed the Civil War (1861-5). In a situation where plantation owners were without resources to pay wages to the freed slaves, and the former slaves without capital to purchase land, the only solution that appeared feasible was to break up the plantations into lots of twenty to fifty acres for cultivation by negro and white tenant farmers. The owner furnished machinery, fertilisers and seed, and the tenant his labour. Owner and tenant each took a share of the crop. This form of tenure has persisted down to the present, and lies at the root of many of the agrarian problems of the South. In all, some 250,000 United States farmers, representing 25 per cent. of the tenant farmers of the country, are to-day share-croppers.

Co-operative farming.—The agricultural co-operative system was pioneered in Denmark during the middle decades of the last century. In various forms it has spread to most countries of the world, although the economic incentive for farmers to combine co-operatively has tended to be greater in the exporting countries than in countries like Britain where most of the farm production is consumed internally.

Through co-operatives, some of the advantages of large-scale organisation can be achieved without individuals surrendering their independence. The bargaining power of the small-holder is immeasurably increased if he combines with others. Cheaper seed, fertilisers, implements, etc., and better prices for products can be obtained as a result of collective buying and selling. The co-operative can also fulfil necessary functions which are beyond the scope of the individual farmer acting alone, and which in its absence would come under the control of independent operators. Dairies, slaughter houses, bacon factories, egg and fruit grading and packing stations are in many cases owned co-operatively, and profits accruing from their activities used to provide improved services to members. Co-operatives are also a valuable source of farm credit. Well-run co-operatives also afford one of the best means of raising the standards of rural life in the economically backward regions of the world.

Collective and state farms: the Soviet Union.—The collectivisation of land in the Soviet Union began in 1928 with the introduction of the First Five Year Plan. Two forms of property were created: immense state farms (*sovkhozy*) and collective farms (*kolkhozy*).

The *sovkhozy* are controlled by a state-appointed management, and worked by hired labour. They tend to specialise in a particular branch of agriculture, *e.g.* wheat cultivation and livestock breeding, and are the means whereby virgin land has been broken in. The *kolkhozy* are worked by peasants who as a condition of joining are required to pool their land, livestock, implements, and other factors of production, including their labour, for which they are paid. The initial rules concerning the possession of private property have been relaxed and the farmer is now allowed to own a small plot of land close to his house, and to dispose of its produce as he wishes. The production from the *kolkhozy* is purchased by the state.

In 1917, Russian agriculture was in a poor way. Its low productivity was partly a consequence of war and revolution, but it stemmed also from the fact that most of the land was farmed by an illiterate and ill-equipped army of 20 million peasants who battled against a capricious climate and indifferent soils in much the same manner as their forebears had done in the Middle Ages. On the larger estates of the Ukraine, which were owned by a number of prosperous landowners, farming was more advanced, and prior to 1914 large quantities of cereals were exported annually from the Black Sea ports. The aim of the First Five Year Plan (and subsequent Five Year Plans) was to revolutionise agricultural techniques, and to increase production through collectivisation and by the mechanisation of farm operations. In setting its production targets, however, the Soviet government reckoned without the peasants, particularly the class of rich peasants or *kulaks*. Outraged by being compelled to surrender their property to a government they hated, many resorted to acts of sabotage, and then proceeded to work with as little effort and enthusiasm as they dared. The First Five Year Plan ended (at the end of four and a half years as it turned out), not only with its targets unrealised, but with production considerably below the level of 1928. The animal population fell by a half during this period. Another decade was to pass before the advantages of the collective farm were manifest to the Russian peasant, and before farm production regained its pre-Revolution levels.

ISRAEL.—Most of the agricultural land of Israel is organised into communal and co-operative settlements, of which the *kibbutz* is the most common. A *kibbutz* has between a few dozen and several hundred members who work without formal payment in return for spending money, housing, clothing, medical attention, and education for the young. Many are pioneer settlements created to absorb Jewish immigrants from Europe before and after the partition of

Palestine in 1949. The *kibbutz* and other communal-type settlements to-day supply 80 per cent. of Israel's food.

THE TROPICAL PLANTATION.—Within the tropics and sub-tropics, a type of farm organisation known as the plantation has developed, primarily in response to a demand in the cooler regions of the world for tropical crops that could not be produced in sufficient volume by existing native methods of cultivation.

Plantations occupy only a tiny fraction of the cultivated area within the hot lands, but account for the greater proportion of tropical agricultural products that enter international trade. Plantations are particularly well suited to crops whose cultivation demands a fair degree of skill and which require processing prior to export. Rubber, palm oil, sisal, coffee, tea, cane sugar, pineapples, and bananas are characteristic plantation commodities, although in many areas their production has now passed into the hands of independent farmers. Rubber, for example, is being grown by an increasing number of Malaysian peasants who sell to the plantation factory. Much of Brazil's coffee is now produced by small farmers. In the West Indies there has been an increase in the number of cane growers who farm land held on lease from the sugar company, and sell to the company's crushing mill. The United States Cotton Belt is the outstanding example of a region which during the span of a few decades abandoned the plantation economy in favour of the commercial production of cotton by the small farmer.

Plantations have been established in areas where natural lines of communications exist with the markets of Europe and North America. The insular and peninsular regions of the Caribbean and South East Asia are favoured in this respect as few parts lie at any great distance from ocean transport.

The cost of developing a plantation is high. Ten years ago the United Fruit Company estimated that 1,000 to 1,250 dollars per acre were required to bring virgin land in Latin America into banana production. Land clearance and frequently drainage and irrigation schemes have to be undertaken, and in pioneer territory services such as roads, water, and power supplies, houses, schools, and hospitals provided before planting can begin. After planting there may be a wait of several years before the first crop is harvested, and in the meantime wages and salaries have to be paid. Labour costs are always high, and can amount to as much as 50 per cent. of the total costs on some plantations. Only companies backed by extensive capital resources, and with considerable managerial skills at their disposal, are likely to succeed in this sort of venture.

CHAPTER V

AGRICULTURAL PRODUCTS, I—THE INDUSTRIAL CROPS

(*a*) VEGETABLE FIBRES

Despite the spectacular rise in the output of man-made fibres during the present century, and the still considerable production of wool and hair from animals, the vegetable kingdom continues to provide some three-quarters of the world supply of fibres coming on to commercial markets (Fig. 98, p. 364).

Vegetable fibres are obtained from the hair surrounding the seeds of fruit (cotton, coir, kapok); from stems (flax, jute, hemp, and ramie); leaves (sisal, abaca); and occasionally from roots. Seed, fruit, and stem fibres are generally soft, and used in fabric manufacture. Leaf fibres are normally hard and tough, and find their way into the making of such products as twine, rope, and nets.

Cotton

Cultivated varieties of cotton have been developed from wild strains native to the Americas and the Old World. Annual production of ginned cotton from all sources now exceeds 24,000 million pounds (11 million metric tons). Of this, more than 40 per cent. is from the fields of the United States and the Soviet Union.

Most types of cotton now in cultivation are annuals. Perennial varieties, however, are found in some tropical countries. The cotton plant does best when the growing season is long. Cultivation on the cooler side of the 200-day frost-free line is risky, as in more years than not spring or autumn frosts cause considerable damage. The mean temperature of the hottest month should exceed 25° C. (77° F.), but somewhat cooler conditions are beneficial during the harvesting months. Water requirements are not high, and a total of fifteen inches distributed over the season of active growth is normally sufficient, unless the evaporation rate is excessive. Heavy late summer and autumn rains splash and stain the lower bolls, and encourage the growth of leaves and shoots at the expense of fibre. Ill-drained areas are also unsuitable. The cotton plant is a heavy feeder, and soil exhaustion quickly follows upon cultivation unless the land is naturally very fertile, or large applications of manure are given.

Until twenty-five years ago, all but a tiny proportion of the world's cotton crop was grown by methods involving hand labour,

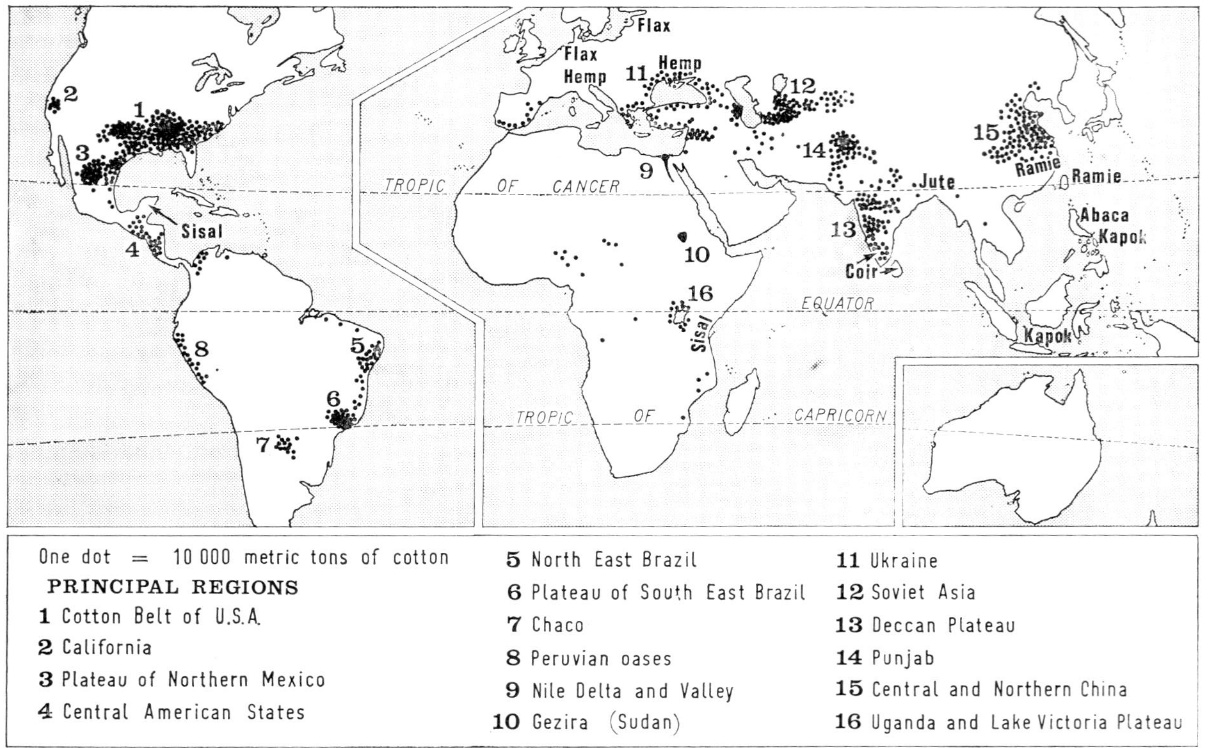

Fig. 39.—Distribution of Cotton and other Textile Fibres

and even to-day in the U.S.A. where mechanisation has proceeded farthest, two-thirds of the crop is still picked by hand. The late arrival upon the scene of planting and harvesting machinery can be attributed to the location of the main areas of cultivation in economically retarded regions where peasant farmers have few capital resources. In the U.S.A. cotton is the traditional crop of the South, an area of comparative poverty and backwardness. The introduction of mechanical pickers and strippers has also had to await the development of strains of cotton that ripened their bolls simultaneously, rather than over an extended period. Now that such equipment is available it can be employed profitably only on large farms in areas of open country: the twenty-acre peasant holding in the Gezira (Sudan) and the "one mule farm" of the Southern States are not suited to the operation of large machines. The greatest advances in mechanised cotton farming have been, not surprisingly, in the new cotton lands of Texas, Arizona, New Mexico, and California, and in the Soviet Union.

Cotton is sown in drills twelve to twenty-four inches apart. On irrigated sections sowing is done on low ridges, the intervening furrows being used to distribute water over the field. After sowing, work involves thinning out seedlings, hoeing between drills, keeping down weeds, destroying pests, and where necessary irrigating the crop. Irrigation is undertaken every ten to fourteen days in arid areas. The harvest period extends from August to October in the northern hemisphere, or until the first autumn frost kills the plant. Several pickings may be taken from each field during the season.

Cotton is prey to a host of insect pests. No region is free from them. The pink boll-worm has caused more damage to some Asian crops than all other insect pests combined. The most destructive in North America is the boll weevil, which entered the United States from Mexico in 1892, and within a few years had infested practically the whole of the South. The small Sea Island cotton-growing industry of the islands lying off the coast of Georgia was wiped out by the insect. Chemical sprays are employed to control infestations if circumstances warrant their use. The magnitude of the problem, however, becomes apparent when it is realised that one pair of boll weevils can produce some 13 million off-spring during the course of a single season. Insect damage to the United States' cotton crop alone, plus the cost of control measures, has amounted in exceptional years to nearly 1,000 million dollars. The boll weevil's greatest enemies are frost and drought, and the development of strains of cotton tolerant of the drier climates and shorter growing seasons of north-west Texas and Oklahoma have permitted the extension of cultivation into areas comparatively free from the pest. The western Prairies are also virtually treeless, and the insect is thus deprived of its hibernating quarters in forests and woodlots.

The quality of cotton depends upon the length of the fibre. The longer the fibres, the finer they are, and the higher the grade of fabric that can be made from them. Short staple cotton has a fibre length of less than seven-eighths of an inch; medium staple seven-eighths to one and a quarter inches; and long staple from one and a quarter to two and a half inches. Many producers of the coarser, shorter staples are endeavouring to introduce long staple varieties. One problem is to prevent cross-pollination from inferior strains growing in an adjacent field. The highest quality, long staple cottons are to-day produced in Egypt, Sudan, Peru, and the West Indies.

TABLE 18

PRODUCTION OF RAW (GINNED) COTTON

(in thousands of metric tons)

	1948-52 (average)	1963	1964	1965
U.S.A.	3,100	3,340	3,305	3,256
U.S.S.R.	970	1,750	1,800	1,908
China	868	n/a	n/a	n/a
Brazil	395	650	590	662
India	485	980	1019	847
Mexico	220	460	550	577
Egypt	390	440	504	520
Pakistan	245	420	380	417
Turkey	120	250	326	325
Peru	76	n/a	139	140
Syria	30	155	176	178
Iran	26	115	121	140
Sudan	75	100	102	150
Argentina	120	100	99	138
WORLD TOTAL	7,600	11,400	11,428	11,769

n/a—not available

Source: *F.A.O. Production Yearbook.*

Jute

India and Pakistan supply the greater part of the world's raw jute. Until recently the state of East Bengal, which was absorbed by Pakistan following the partition of the sub-continent in 1947, was the main region of production. Since independence, however, encouragement has been given to jute cultivation in India, particularly in West Bengal and in the neighbouring states of Bihar, Orissa, and Assam, and also in Uttah Pradesh, with the result that output from Indian sources now equals and will very soon exceed that from Pakistan.

Jute is a tall-growing, tropical plant, demanding humid heat and heavy rainfall during its growing season of four or five months. It does well on land suited to rice cultivation, and is frequently grown as a cash crop by rice farmers. In Bengal it occupies about one quarter of the rice acreage. Broadcast sowing is carried out in spring, early enough to allow the crop to ripen before the fields become too deeply submerged beneath the delta floods. Thinning and weeding are done several times during the season. When mature, the plant is cut, taken to retting pools, and allowed to soak until the bark can be removed from the woody centre of the stalk. The fibres, which lie beneath the bark, are then stripped, washed, dried, and baled. About 1,000-1,500 pounds of fibre are obtained per acre.

Most of the fibre passes into commercial markets. Calcutta and Chittagong are the main exporting ports. Calcutta is also the largest jute manufacturing centre in the world. Important jute manufacturing and jute-using industries are also located at Dundee and in many textile centres on the continent of Europe and in the United States.

Jute is a coarse textile, unsuited to the manufacture of garments, but because of its cheapness finds acceptance as a packing and wrapping fabric. It is used as a backing material for carpets and linoleum. In small quantities it is employed also in twine and rope making, paper manufacture, and as an insulating medium in the electricity industry.

Jute is produced in a few countries besides India and Pakistan, notably in China, Thailand, and Brazil. Physical conditions are suitable for its cultivation over wide areas of the wet tropics, but new producers must face the problem of competition from established areas of production which enjoy the advantages of abundant, low-cost labour.

TABLE 19

WORLD PRODUCTION OF JUTE
(in thousands of metric tons)

	1948-52 (average)	1963	1964	1965
Pakistan	1,015	1,085	967	1,154
India	640	1,070	1,084	805
Brazil	15	44	51	62
Burma	—	13	10	15
China (Taiwan) ..	12	10	13	13
Thailand	2	12	7	7
WORLD	2,260	3,100	3,272	3,274

Source: *F.A.O. Production Yearbook.*

Flax

As a fibre plant, flax attains its greatest importance in the temperate regions, although it is cultivated on a small scale as a winter crop within a few tropical countries. A growing season of eighty to a hundred days, a mean summer temperature of 15° C. (59° F.), and a moderate rainfall, provide adequate conditions for growth.

Although the leading fibre plant of the cool temperate zone, flax has now declined to the status of a minor crop, and has disappeared from many areas where it was once important. Flax fibre is superior to cotton in smoothness, strength, and durability, but in normal times is unable to compete in terms of price. The small flax-growing industry that was revived in England for strategic reasons during the Second World War is now virtually extinct. Flax is no longer grown in Northern Ireland, and the Belfast linen industry relies on fibre imported from the Continent (Table 101, p. 375). Three-quarters of the world production at the present time comes from the Soviet Union (Table 20).

TABLE 20

PRODUCTION OF FLAX FIBRE
(in thousands of metric tons)

	1948-53 (average)	1963	1964	1965
U.S.S.R.	255	380	346	443
France	30	72	86	59
Poland	40	52	46	57
Belgium	31	40	46	31
Netherlands	30	34	40	27
United Kingdom	10	nil	nil	nil
East Germany	n/a	6	4	6
WORLD	480	650	646	691

n/a—not available

Source: *F.A.O. Production Yearbook.*

Other fibres

Hemp.—Hemp is a soft fibre, obtained from the bark of a tall growing annual of the warmer sections of the temperate zone. The U.S.S.R. and China are the leading producers. Hemp is employed for similar purposes to flax. The plant is also the source of a vegetable oil, and of the drug marijuana.

Abaca.—Abaca, or manila hemp, is in no way related to the true hemp, but is a plant of the banana family. Land cleared of tropical rain forest or abandoned banana country is suitable for its cultivation. The fibre, which is obtained from the leaves, is exceptionally strong, hard, and resistant to salt water. It is used in the making of cords, cables, ropes, fishing nets, and binder twine. Approximately 85 per cent. of the world production of abaca comes from the Philippine Islands (Table 21).

Sisal.—The sisal plant is a large perennial, rosette-shaped bush that produces several dozen spiky, fibrous leaves of up to five or six feet in length. Commercially, the fibre is similar to abaca. Sisal is a tropical plant, and is well suited to cultivation on plantations. The East African countries, Yucatan, Java, and other islands in the East Indies, account for most of the world production. In favourable conditions the plant continues to yield marketable fibre for as long as twenty years.

Coir.—Coir is obtained from the shell of the coconut. The western coastal areas of India and Ceylon, and some of the Pacific Islands are important producers and exporters.

Ramie.—Ramie, or "China grass", is cultivated principally in the Far East, but small quantities originate in North America. Its fibres are strong and durable, but can only be separated with extreme difficulty from the gummy material which binds them together. World production is small.

Kapok.—Resilient, moisture-proof fibres from the seeds of the kapok tree are used in the manufacture of life jackets and insulating material. Most of the commercial production comes from countries of the Far East.

TABLE 21
PRODUCTION OF HEMP, ABACA, AND SISAL
1965
(in thousands of metric tons)

HEMP		ABACA		SISAL	
India	56	Philippines	108	Brazil	242
Yugoslavia	49	Malaysia	3	Tanzania	218
Hungary	22	Indonesia	0·3	Mexico	175
Italy	10			Kenya	60
Rumania	13			Angola	50
				Mozambique	31
				Madagascar	28
				Haiti	17
WORLD	330	WORLD	111	WORLD	687

Source: *F.A.O. Production Yearbook.*

(*b*) VEGETABLE OILS

Oil-bearing plants can be grouped, from an economic standpoint, into two categories:

(i) those from which oil is obtained as the major product, *e.g.* the olive.

(ii) those that do not repay the cost of cultivation for oil alone but which yield oil as an important by-product, *e.g.* the cotton plant.

In certain regions of primarily subsistence agriculture, oil-producing plants have been important for centuries. The oil palm and groundnut of West Africa, the soyabean of northern China, and the olive of southern Europe, have been to the people of those lands what the pig and cow have been to the people of northern Europe—providers of edible fats. The large scale commercial production of vegetable oil, however, is a comparatively new development; as recently as the end of the last century the volume of oil entering international trade was very small. Oils were generally of poor quality, and their uses in manufacturing industry limited. They were also generally unacceptable outside the areas of production as substitutes for animal fats in food preparation.

The situation has changed fundamentally during the last 100 years. Technical advances have resulted in vastly greater quantities of higher grade oil coming on to the market. Demand for it in the manufacturing and food processing industries has increased, so much so that wild sources of supply are now totally inadequate, and dependence upon cultivated plants is virtually complete. The present century has also witnessed a shift in the major areas of commercial production from the tropics to the temperate regions: it is significant that the most important oil plant is no longer the oil palm or the coconut, but the soyabean (Table 22). As far as one can foretell, however, the tropics will always remain important to the economies of industrial countries like Britain, whose climates are unsuited to the cultivation of oil plants but who nevertheless are relying upon them increasingly as a source of essential raw materials.

SOURCES OF VEGETABLE OIL

Of the many and varied oil plants of commercial significance, the following are of prime importance:

The oil palm

Palm oil and palm kernel oil are two distinct products obtained respectively from the pericarp and kernel of the fruit of this plant.

The oil palm flourishes in a tropical climate enjoying a heavy and well distributed rainfall and abundant sunshine. Soil factors are not critical provided drainage is good. The wild tree sometimes grows to fifty feet or more, but cultivated varieties, bred with an eye to making harvesting as simple an operation as possible, attain only half this height. Fruit is borne in large golden-red clusters at the base of the frond. Good trees on well-managed estates each produce 200 pounds of fruit, representing a yield of some twenty-five cwt of oil annually per acre.

As early as the eighteenth century, palm oil was being exported from West Africa for use in the manufacture of low grade soap, candles, and as an anti-corrosive agent in the production of tin-plate.

However, the long period that elapsed between gathering and processing the fruit, and the failure to prevent impurities entering the oil during extraction, resulted in a product that, as time went on, was unable to meet the more exacting requirements of manufacturers in the importing countries. It soon became apparent that a much greater control over all stages of production and transport would be necessary if quality were to be improved. Ultimately this led to two developments:

(i) The establishment in the Congo (in 1911) and later in South East Asia and West Africa, of plantations concerned solely with the production of high-grade oil.

(ii) The setting up outside the plantation areas of research stations, the introduction of government controlled systems of grading and inspection, and the building of extraction plants to replace inefficient native presses. Nigeria, whose production comes mainly from native-owned trees, has benefited enormously from these developments. Low-grade oil which was becoming increasingly difficult to sell in the years prior to the Second World War has now been virtually excluded from the market.

The main producers of palm oil and palm kernel oil are Nigeria, Congo, and Indonesia (Table 22). In these and other countries in the rain-forest zone, reserves of suitable land for oil palm cultivation are almost limitless, and could be developed, if needed, to satisfy the growing demand for vegetable oil in the industrial nations.

The coconut palm

The coconut is important commercially for its copra, the dried kernel from which oil is obtained, and coir, a hard fibre produced from the husk. Groves of both wild and cultivated palms thrive on the beaches and low-lying island coasts in the Pacific and Indian Oceans. The palm has been acclimatised to certain inland areas, but yields in these localities are generally poor. A hot, tropical climate with abundant rain and sunshine, and a situation near the sea are essential for its proper development.

Once the coconut comes into bearing (at about five or six years), fruiting is continuous. Fifty nuts, yielding twenty-five pounds of copra and one gallon of oil, can be expected annually from a mature palm. Copra is prepared by drying the kernel in the sun, or by a hot air process in plantation factories. The extraction of the oil is undertaken in the large market centres of the producing countries, *e.g.* Singapore and Manila, or at the ports of the importing countries, *e.g.* at Marseilles. The main producers are the Philippines, Ceylon, Malaya, and the British Dependencies in the South Seas (Table 22).

The olive

The olive tree is one of the most characteristic of all Mediterranean plants, and has been cultivated in southern Europe, South West Asia, and North Africa since antiquity (Fig. 40). Its introduction to other regions of Mediterranean climate, however, has been recent, and in South Africa its acclimatisation has been only partially successful.

Hot, arid summers, winters without severe frost, and rain only in the cooler months are essential conditions for growth. The tree is highly drought-resistant, although the heaviest yields come from regions of moderate rather than scanty rainfall and from irrigated groves. Irrigation is a feature of the small olive-growing industry

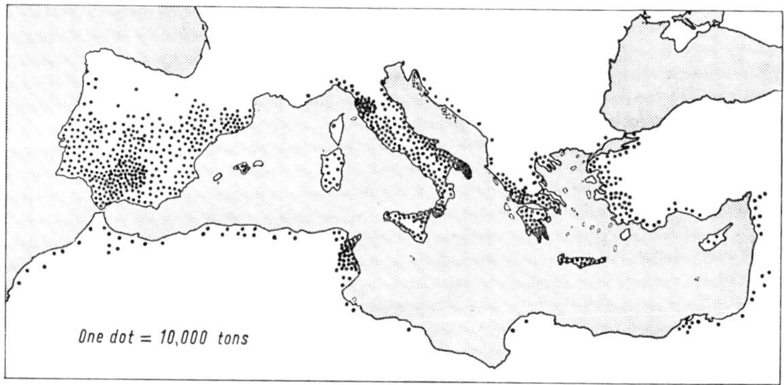

Fig. 40.—Production of Olives in the Mediterranean Basin, 1963-4.

of California, but is exceptional elsewhere. Useful crops can be obtained with as little as eight inches of rain per year, provided measures are taken to conserve winter run off, by, for example, throwing up low earthen embankments round the trees. The olive is tolerant of most types of soil as long as drainage is not impeded, and it succeeds on dry, stony hill slopes where most other crops would fail. These characteristics make it a plant of particular importance in southern Europe, where by accident of geology, fertile soils and extensive lowland plains are rare. The light foliage of the olive tree and open formation of most of the groves permit intercropping with winter cereals on the better land.

The olive develops slowly, and comes into production only after ten to fifteen years, but once established requires little attention,

The harvest season is late summer, when the ripe fruit (which resembles a small greenish-black plum) is stripped from the branches or shaken into sheets placed on the ground. The oil must be expressed within a few hours of harvesting if the highest grade is to be obtained.

In the lands of southern Europe and North Africa, where natural pastures are unsuited to stock rearing and animal products are scarce, olive oil has assumed great significance. Apart from its many uses in industry, it is employed in the areas of production for cooking, frying, and as a dressing on green vegetables. The comparative ease with which butter and lard can now be imported from the north has not reduced its importance in food preparation to any great extent, as any visitor from Britain with a delicate digestion will be quick to discover. Even boiled food in some areas is invalid diet, given only to the sick and convalescing.

More than 95 per cent. of the world's olive crop comes from the countries surrounding the Mediterranean Sea. One of the most concentrated areas of production is the Sahel of Tunisia—the semi-arid plains lying between Sfax and Susa, where during the present century the French have planted millions of trees on the former grazing grounds of nomadic herdsmen.

The groundnut

The groundnut, or peanut, is an easily cultivated, high-yielding annual of the pea and bean family, that grows best on light, sandy soils within the tropics and warm temperate belt. It is a native plant of Brazil, but the main areas of cultivation are now northern China, the Deccan region of India, and the savana lands of West Africa. In these areas it is a peasant crop. Substantial acreages are also cultivated by mechanical farming methods in the Cotton Belt of the United States.

Outside the actual areas of production, the main consuming countries are in Europe, where most of the oil extraction plants are located. Since the Second World War, crushing mills have been erected in India and Nigeria to process the local crop. In the United States, cotton-seed oil extraction mills are used to crush groundnuts.

The groundnut is associated in the minds of many with the East African Groundnut Scheme of the immediate post-war years. In an attempt to relieve a world shortage of edible oils, the British government embarked on an ambitious plan to grow the plant on some 3 million acres of bushland in Tanganyika. In the event, the scheme achieved little. The remoteness of the area, the poor supply lines, lack of technical skill on the part of the African tractor drivers and mechanics, and much administrative bungling contributed to the

TABLE 22

PRINCIPAL SOURCES OF VEGETABLE OILS, PRODUCTION, AND USES

	Production (in thousands of metric tons) 1948-9 to 1952-3 (average)	1963	1964	1965	Oil Content	Main Uses of Oil	By-products
Palm Oil							
Nigeria	345	415	510	515	(of pericarp) 65-70%	Soap, margarine, cooking fat, candles, tin plate industry.	Fertilisers.
Congo (Leopoldville)	172	224	223	209			
Indonesia (estates only)	114	148	161	163			
Malaysia (estates only)	49	125	126	122			
World	970	1,200	1,337	1,318			
Palm Kernels							
Nigeria	372	420	420	407	35-50%	Margarine, cooking oil, soap.	Fertilisers, fuel in plantation mills.
Congo (Leopoldville)	117	102	122	96			
Sierra Leone	75	54	53	50			
Dahomey	43	50	56	54			
Cameroon	28	35	22	21			
Indonesia	29	33	35	36			
Malaysia	10	31	31	35			
World	890	1,040	1,062	1,046			
Copra							
Philippines	875	1,510	1,428	1,446	35-50%	Margarine, soap, cooking oil, candles.	Livestock feed.
Indonesia	714	403	450	450			
India	202	254	264	270			
Ceylon	230	250	320	266			
World	2,600	3,300	3,325	3,269			
Olive Oil							
Spain	360	638	116	323	(of Olive) 15-40%	Cooking oil, soap, pharmaceuticals.	Livestock feed.
Italy	253	594	334	455			
Greece	120	230	141	191			
Turkey	48	102	122	60			
Tunisia	53	89	108	60			
World	1,000	1,900	987	1,287			

GROUNDNUTS							
India	3,200	5,290	5,889	4,022	35-40%	Margarine, cooking oil, soap, peanut butter.	Livestock feed.
China (mainland)	2,060	1,900	n/a	n/a			
Nigeria	690	1,390	1,252	1,542			
Senegal	560	950	1,019	1,122			
U.S.A.	840	920	952	1,081			
Brazil	140	410	470	743			
Indonesia	280	400	435	465			
WORLD	9,600	15,000	16,123	15,315			
SOYABEANS							
U.S.A.	7,310	19,000	19,076	23,014	15-20%	Margarine, cooking oil, soap, paints, lubricants.	Livestock feed, fertilisers.
China (mainland)	7,280	10,400	n/a	n/a			
Indonesia	270	375	390	355			
Japan	375	320	240	230			
U.S.S.R.	165	300	285	410			
WORLD	16,000	31,400	32,300	36,600			
LINSEED							
U.S.A.	1,030	790	620	900	30-40%	Paints, varnishes, linoleum, oil-cloth, soap.	Livestock feed.
Argentina	515	770	815	570			
India	385	385	380	500			
Canada	240	540	515	740			
WORLD	3,100	3,400	3,550	3,645			
COTTONSEED							
U.S.A.	5,300	5,600	5,660	5,550	30-35%	Cooking and salad oil, margarine, soap.	Livestock feed, paper (from hulls), cellulose (from linters), explosives, fertilisers.
U.S.S.R.	1,900	3,450	3,485	3,720			
India	970	1,900	2,050	1,705			
Brazil	750	1,250	1,120	1,160			
WORLD	13,900	21,200	21,100	21,850			

n/a — not available.

Source: *F.A.O. Production Yearbook*.

failure. Much blame also attaches to the fact that, in their haste to show results, the authorities paid insufficient heed to the importance of preparatory soil and climatic surveys. The scheme at least demonstrated the risks involved in attempting to introduce cultivation techniques proven in Europe into the very different conditions of the tropics, and the need for scientifically managed pilot schemes before contemplating an enterprise of this scope and nature.

The soyabean

Soyabean production to-day is concentrated in three areas of the world; in China and Manchuria, where it is of ancient culture, and the U.S.A., where it is of recent introduction. As late as the 1920s, the soyabean was unimportant commercially in North America, but by the middle of the century it had become the leading oil-bearing plant of the continent. It is primarily a crop of the Maize Belt. It has substantially the same requirements for growth as maize, with which it is rotated. It is exceptionally rich in protein, and after the oil has been extracted the cake residue makes excellent livestock feed. The plant haulm can also be harvested as "hay". The bean yields oil at the rate of about two hundredweight per acre.

Linseed

Linseed oil is obtained from the seed of the flax plant. Varieties grown for their oil are shorter in the stem, produce more seeds, and flourish in warmer and drier climates than those cultivated for fibre. The principal producers are the U.S.A., the U.S.S.R., and the Argentine.

Cottonseed

Cottonseed oil is a by-product of cotton ginning, and the quantity coming on to the market is dependent on the production of cotton fibre. The by-products of the cotton plant are almost as valuable as the fibre for which the plant is principally grown. In addition to oil, the seed is an important source of cattle food (from the hulls and meal); and the small, hairy fibres or *linters* that adhere to the seed after ginning, become raw materials of the paper, rayon, synthetic rubber, explosives, and other industries.

Other plants that yield oil in significant quantities include the castor oil plant, sesame, the sunflower, rape, maize, the Brazil nut tree, and the tung tree. *Essential oils* are also expressed from the flowers, fruit, and foliage of many plants, *e.g.* from the rose, lavender, clove, nutmeg, sandlewood, and camphor tree, and from the rind of the orange and lemon. Essential oils are used in perfumery, flavouring, and medicine.

Above: An olive grove in the wide flat plains of the Sahel in Tunisia. (*Tunisian Embassy.*)
Below: Typical narrow-bench terraces on steep Apennine slopes overlooking the Mediterranean. Vines and vegetables are under cultivation. Liguria, Italy. (*Paul Popper.*)

Above: Intensive arable farming on English Fenlands—Downham Market, Norfolk (*Aerofilms and Aero Pictorial Ltd.*)

Below: Rice being harvested by combine, Stuttgart, Arkansas. (*USIS.*)

CHAPTER VI

AGRICULTURAL PRODUCTS, II—CEREALS

Cereals are the most important of man's food crops. They occupy about half the world's arable acreage, and are grown in practically every country outside the tundra lands (Fig. 41). There are a number of reasons for their wide distribution, and for their predominance in most agricultural economies:

1. Being nutritious, heavy yielding, and generally easy to cultivate and store, one or other of them has become the staple food of all but a tiny proportion of the world's peoples. Cereals or cereal products comprise one half of the calorific value of all food consumed, although there are significant variations from country to country according to economic and social conditions. As a general rule, the importance of cereals in man's diet declines relative to other foods as his standard of living rises (see Fig. 2). Cereals are also a major source of livestock feed, and vast and increasing acreages of the feed grains (maize, barley, oats, and sorghums) are in cultivation in many countries. In North America they occupy roughly twice the combined area of wheat, maize, and rice grown for direct human consumption.

2. Cereals are annual plants which complete their life cycle in a single season, and often in only a few weeks. There are thus comparatively few regions where the growing period is not long enough for at least one of the species to thrive.

3. Not only is each of the main species naturally adapted to specific climatic belts—rice to the tropics, maize to the warm temperate, and wheat to the cool temperate lands, but innumerable varieties of each species have been successfully developed by plant scientists with the object of extending their range into environments which originally were unsuitable. Some strains of rice, for example, can now be cultivated as far north as latitude 50° in the Ukraine.

WHEAT

Wheat probably originated in South West Asia, whence it spread northwards and westwards into Europe and eastwards into India and the Far East. It was introduced to the Americas and Australasia by European colonists. To-day it is the leading cereal in terms of acreage and production, although it is eaten by fewer people than rice.

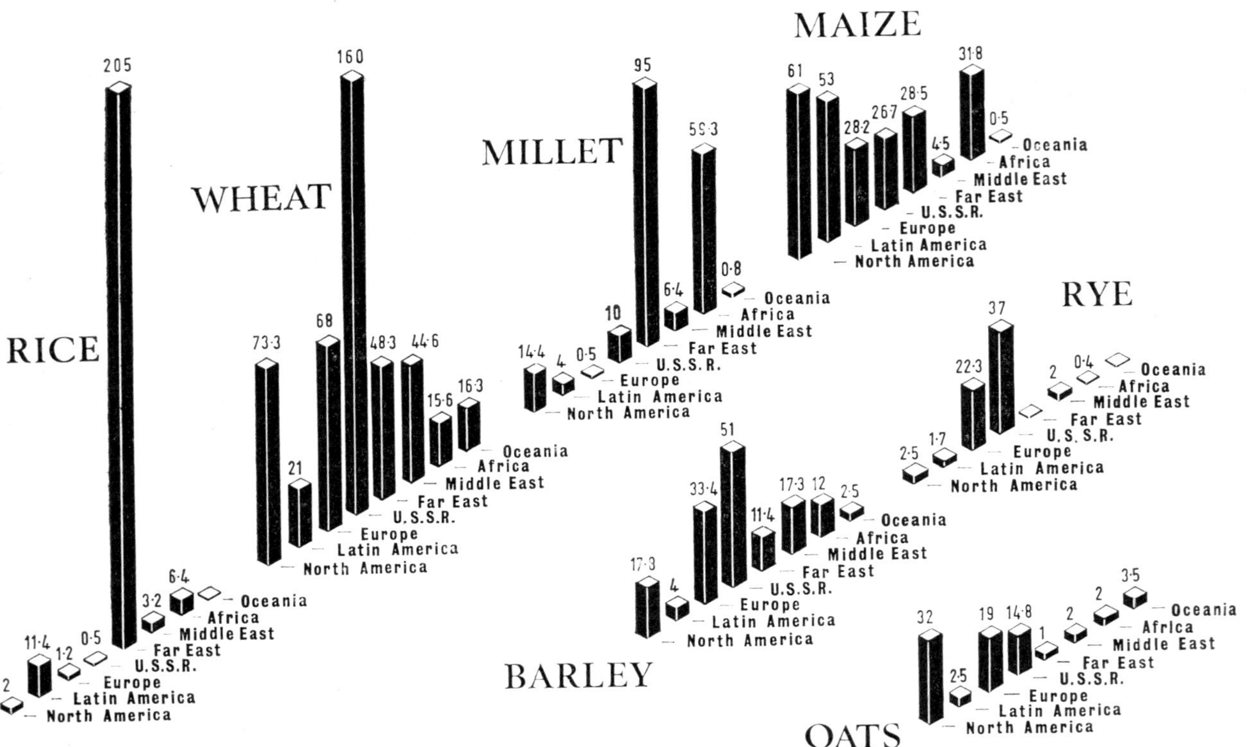

Fig. 41.—Area Occupied by the Principal Cereal Crops in each of the World's Major Regions. In thousands of hectares, 1963-4.

Wheat is essentially a human food, valued for the fine, light-textured bread that can be made from its flour. It has a restricted use in industry, although small quantities are used in the manufacture of starch, malt, dextrose, and alcohol. Surplus or damaged wheat is frequently fed to animals.

The cultivation of wheat

Wheat production has become firmly established in the temperate grassland and deciduous forest regions of the world, where rainfall is moderate or low and where summers are warm but not hot (Fig. 42). High temperatures, especially when associated with high humidities, are damaging and hence the plant has a restricted distribution within the tropics. If grown at all in this zone, it is invariably as a cool-season crop. A well-drained, heavy to medium loamy soil containing lime is also beneficial.

Two main classes of wheat can be recognised. First there are the *winter wheats* which are always sown at the onset of the cooler season, but early enough to allow the plant to develop a strong root system and to make substantial top growth before the winter cold temporarily checks development. Growth is resumed with the return of warmer weather in the spring. The harvest season is from late spring to late summer depending on the region. Winter wheats are unsuited to very mild climates, as a degree of winter chilling is essential if the plant is to flower. For this reason spring varieties are cultivated in the tropics. Winter wheat is hardy, but can rarely tolerate the severe frosts of the continental interiors unless protected by a thick blanket of snow.

In Canada, the North Central states of the U.S.A., most parts of the Soviet Union, and northern China *spring wheats* are cultivated. These are sown as soon as possible after the thaw. Some strains mature in as little as ninety days. Spring wheats rarely yield as heavily, however, as the slower-maturing autumn-sown varieties, and the latter are nearly always grown in preference if the winter cold is not too intense.

Wheat is produced in the moister parts of the temperate belt where it competes with other crops for land, and takes a place in a system of intensive rotational farming. In these conditions yields are high, 35 cwt to the acre not being unusual in Britain and the countries of Western Europe. On the other hand it is grown on an extensive basis in many sub-humid regions where the rainfall is too low and precarious for intensive cropping. In these circumstances yields are commonly low. In Australia they averaged 6·9 cwt per acre in the decade 1940-50, and 9·0 cwt between 1950 and 1960.

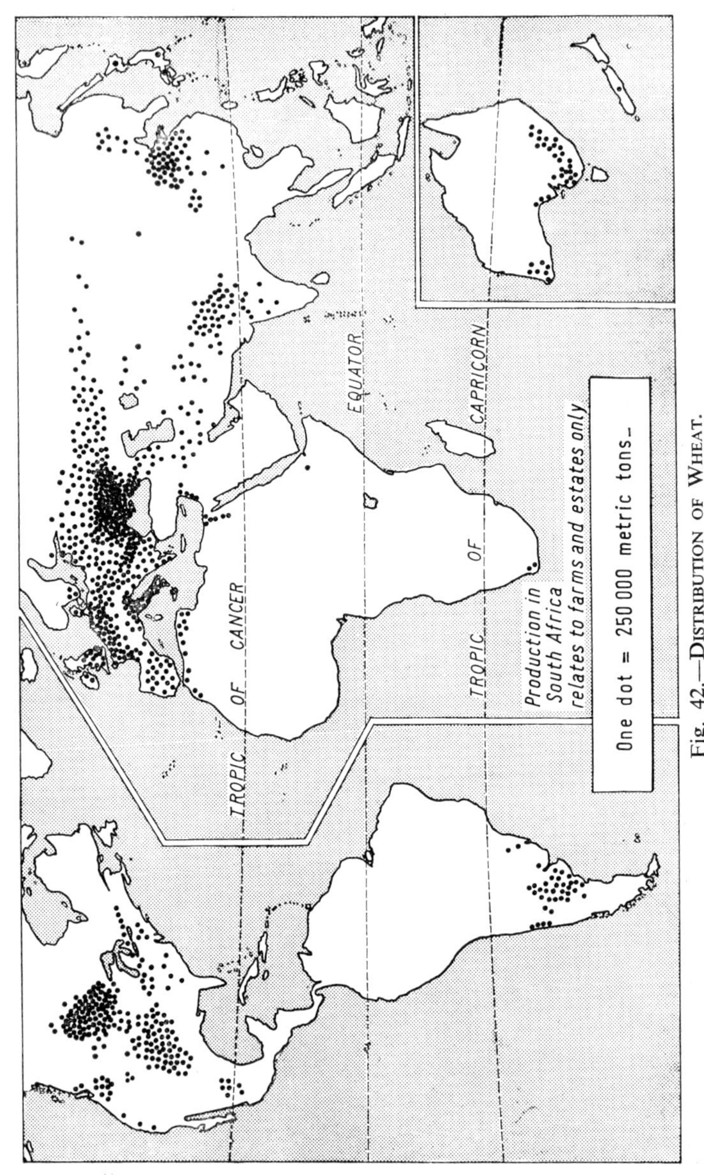

Fig. 42.—Distribution of Wheat.

Most types of wheat resist drought well, and can be grown without recourse to dry farming techniques provided upwards of eight inches of rain fall during the growing season. Even lower totals may suffice if a winter snowfall can be held on the ground until the spring thaw without being removed by the wind. Much wheat, however, is produced near to or beyond the safe limits of cultivation, and in such regions farmers stand to lose disastrously in years of low precipitation. The experience of thousands of Americans who had to abandon their homesteads on the High Plains during the 1930s, and of the many Soviet wheat growers who are now threatened with drought in the "virgin lands" of Kazakhstan illustrates the dangers of pushing cultivation too far into the semi-arid zones.

The cost of wheat production is lowest when the processes of cultivation are mechanised. The use of large-scale labour-saving machinery is essential in regions of low population, especially as sowing and reaping are concentrated into a few weeks of the year. Large machines require open, level country in which to work, and land firm enough to support them. Heavy rain in late summer may necessitate postponing the harvest until the ground has frozen hard enough to allow heavy equipment to be taken into the fields. By this time the crop will have been frosted, and its value reduced. A combine harvester cuts, threshes, and then pours the grain into a waiting truck in a single operation. The crop, however, must be fully ripe before a combine can be used, and consequently the machine is best suited to regions where a dry summer season is reasonably assured. It is not without significance that the combine is an Australian invention. If there is risk of damage by wind and rain, the crop is often cut ten to fourteen days before maturing, and left to ripen on the ground, or "in the swab" as the Canadian farmers say. A "pick-up" combine then completes the work of harvesting.

World trade in wheat

The great volume of wheat entering international trade arises because of the heavy demand for the product as the only satisfactory bread cereal, because some countries are naturally surplus-producing, whilst others cannot meet their needs, and because the grain can be transported easily, and stored almost indefinitely (Table 25). Bulk transport by rail and water is cheap as grain can be handled as a liquid cargo. Wheat too is a heterogeneous commodity. The hard wheats of high protein content from the drier lands make an excellent bread flour, whilst the softer wheats of the moister countries are better suited to the manufacture of biscuits, pastries, and cakes. Thus the United Kingdom and other producers of soft wheats could not entirely rid themselves of the dependence on imports, even if output from their own farms were substantially increased.

TABLE 23

WORLD PRODUCTION OF WHEAT
(in thousands of metric tons)

	1948-52 (average)	1958	1963	1965
U.S.S.R.	32,700	76,500	49,700	59,600
U.S.A.	31,000	39,500	31,000	35,805
China (mainland)	15,900	28,900	n/a	n/a
Canada	13,400	10,800	19,700	17,661
France	7,800	9,600	10,250	14,760
Australia	5,100	5,800	9,000	7,067
Argentina	5,100	6,700	8,950	5,400
India	6,200	8,000	10,800	12,290
Italy	7,200	9,800	8,100	9,776
Turkey	4,700	8,600	10,100	8,630
Pakistan	3,600	3,600	4,200	4,625
Spain	3,600	4,500	4,850	4,718
WORLD	171,000	257,000	245,000	265,808

n/a—not available

Source: *F.A.O. Production Yearbook.*

MAIZE

Maize is one of the greatest gifts of the New World to the Old. It was introduced to Europe and Africa in the years following the discovery of the Americas, and within half a century it had spread across Asia to China to become the staple food of millions of people. Because maize has been successfully adapted to a wide range of climatic environments; because of its heavy-yielding characteristics and its low unit costs of production; and because of its usefulness as a human food and a fattening grain for animals, it has come to occupy an acreage almost as extensive as wheat, and has attained a wider geographical distribution than any other cultivated crop, with the exception of the sown grasses (Fig. 43). Nearly one half of the world's commercial maize, however, is grown in the United States.

The Corn Belt

In no other extensive region in the world are conditions so favourable for the cultivation of maize as in the belt of country 900 miles long and 300 miles wide that extends from the Ohio River to the borders of Nebraska. Here, on the flat or gently rolling tall grass Prairie, with its deep, fertile, lacustrine and till soils, maize takes first place on nearly every farm. The Corn Belt farmer, however, markets little of the crop as grain. The bulk is used to feed and fatten livestock, particularly cattle and pigs, and to a less extent poultry, and it

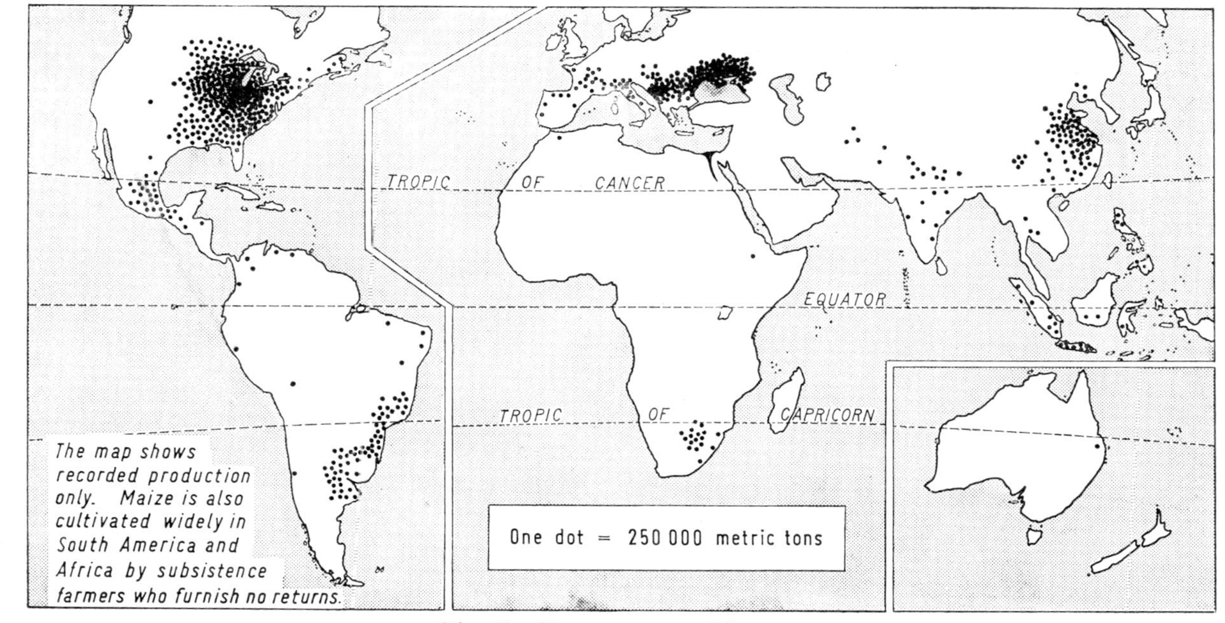

Fig. 43.—Distribution of Maize.

TABLE 24
WORLD PRODUCTION OF MAIZE
(in thousands of metric tons)

	1948-52 (average)	1958	1963	1965
U.S.A.	74,300	85,200	103,900	103,746
U.S.S.R.	5,700	16,700	23,500	7,800
Brazil	5,900	7,800	9,400	12,112
Mexico	3,000	5,200	6,400	8,865
Rumania	2,300	3,600	6,000	5,877
Yugoslavia	3,100	3,950	5,400	5,920
Argentina	2,500	4,900	5,300	5,140
India	2,300	3,450	4,500	4,632
South Africa	2,400	3,650	4,200	4,490
Italy	2,300	3,600	3,700	3,317
Hungary	2,050	2,800	3,550	3,564
France	452	1,700	3,800	3,468
WORLD	138,000	192,000	227,000	226,153

Source: *U.N. Statistical Yearbook.*

is from the sale of animals and animal products that most of his income derives.

Corn Belt agriculture is intensive and mixed, maize being rotated with oats, hay, clover, winter wheat, and soyabeans (Fig. 44). On a typical farm, maize will occupy between one third and one quarter of the land in any given year. The alternate crops help to maintain soil fertility, and are an insurance against a failure of maize through frost or drought. The limits of the commercial Corn Belt are reached when any one of these alternative crops replaces maize as the leading crop. In present economic conditions, maize predominates where rainfall exceeds about eight inches during June, July, and August, where the mean July temperature is above 22° C (72° F.), and where the growing season (*i.e.* the period free from a frost severe enough to injure growing plants) is longer than 140 days. Warm, humid nights are also favourable. Drought is a limiting factor in the west and south-west where wheat becomes dominant, and oats and hay are more profitable in the cooler and moister north: here the emphasis shifts from a stock fattening to a dairying economy. Maize also declines in importance in the hilly Appalachian country; on the Ozarks; and on the driftless region of Kentucky to the south.

Maize is cultivated throughout the South as a human food, although its importance as a bread grain is declining. Maize flour makes an inferior, crumbly loaf. The grain is also deficient in vitamin B, so that populations over-dependent on it are subject to pellagra, a disease which can be fatal, and which was once one of the curses of the South. Throughout the United States, and in many parts of the world, small quantities of maize are eaten as a green vegetable and as pop corn, sweet corn, and a breakfast cereal. In the northern regions of the U.S.A. and in Canada, where summers are too cool to allow the plant to ripen satisfactorily, it is cut green, and used as silage. About 10 per cent. of the U.S.A. crop is consumed annually by the manufacturing industries. Starch, adhesives, oil, and alcohol are some of the products made from the grain. Hard-

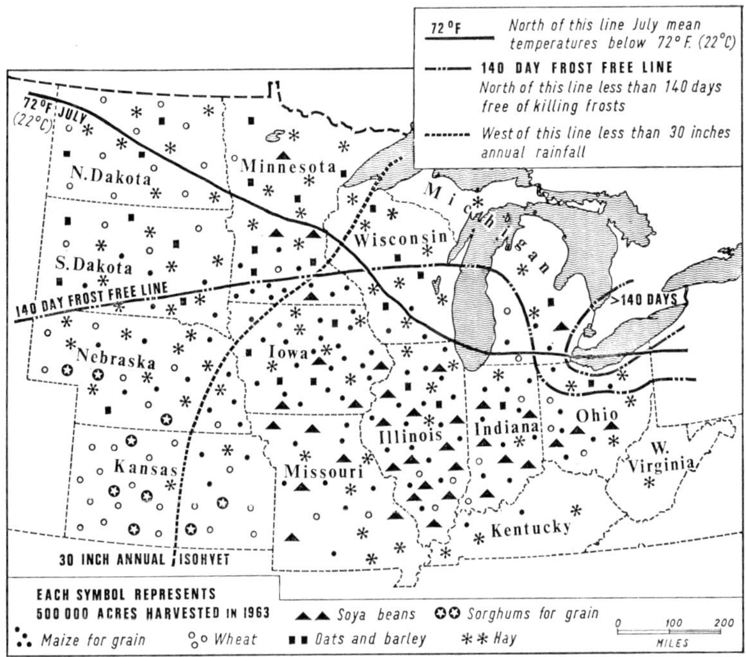

Fig. 44. Distribution of the Principal Crops in the American Corn Belt and Adjacent States.

board and paper are produced from the stems. The cobs can be utilised in the preparation of industrial solvents, and for making charcoal.

Outside North America, areas of concentrated maize production are found in the moister parts of the warm temperate belts between latitudes 40-45° N. and 30-35° S. These regions are climatically similar in the warm season to the Corn Belt. The most important are the Lombardy Plain of Italy (where the crop is grown intensively by irrigation in spite of a substantial summer rainfall); the plains of

Hungary, Rumania, and Yugoslavia; the "Maize Triangle" of South Africa; south-eastern Brazil; and the Pampas region of the Argentine. Between the two world wars the Pampas produced some 75 per cent. of all maize that was traded internationally. Flint varieties, which have a low moisture content, and which can be transported easily, were grown. In more recent years the Argentine has fallen far behind the U.S.A. as an exporter of maize (Table 25).

TABLE 25

FOREIGN TRADE IN WHEAT, WHEAT FLOUR, MAIZE, AND RICE
(in thousands of metric tons)

Chief Exporting Countries	1934/5 to 1938/9 (av'ge)	1959	1965	Chief Importing Countries	1934-5 to 1938/9 (av'ge)	1959	1965
			Wheat				
U.S.A.	963	9,725	17,700	U.K.	5,232	4,340	4,409
Canada	4,214	7,175	11,881	India	56·2	3,550	6,533
Australia	2,045	1,480	5,714	Japan	251	2,400	3,645
U.S.S.R.	563	6,050	1,662	U.S.S.R.	61·4	430	6,375
Argentina	3,176	2,400	6,660	Brazil	959	1,820	1,876
			Wheat flour				
U.S.A.	363	1,250	1,397	Egypt	—	425	610
Canada	400	750	615	U.K.	415	380	238
Western Germany				U.S.S.R.	—	31	289
	16·4*	520	456	Cuba	90	85	361
Australia	592	425	544	Ceylon	16·2	260	215
			Maize				
U.S.A.	797	5,560	15,158	Italy	153	1,075	5,152
Argentina	6,526	2,680	2,803	U.K.	3,285	2,975	3,259
S. Africa	333	410	326	Japan	196	900	3,434
U.S.S.R.	34·8	150	551	Netherlands	934	1,100	1,789
			Rice				
Burma	n/a	1,700	1,348	Indonesia	n/a	600	190
Thailand	n/a	1,100	1,947	India	n/a	300	783
U.S.A.	n/a	680	1,549	Ceylon	n/a	580	530
Cambodia	n/a	200	473	Japan	n/a	280	967

* Includes East Germany

n/a—not available

Source: *F.A.O Trade Yearbook.*

RICE

Throughout East and South East Asia, wherever well watered and more or less level land is found, rice has established itself as the outstanding crop. Several hundred million people have come to depend upon it for their daily food, and to an extent that is not always appreciated in the Western World. Among rural communities in parts of Bengal and southern China, breakfast, dinner, and tea mean rice, and very little else. Lightly milled rice is very nutritious. In the Orient it is generally boiled and eaten with sauces. Polished rice, the product so familiar to the people of Britain, is rarely seen in the East.

Rice cultivation in Monsoon Asia

Rice is invariably grown as a hot-season crop. A temperature of 21° C. (70° F.) in the warmest month, however, is sufficient—a value which is exceeded over most of lowland Asia south of latitude 45° N. The growing season need not be longer than 100 days for certain varieties of rice. The critical factor is water, as some thirty to fifty inches are required during the growing period. Water supply is not a function of rainfall alone. Evaporation, soil porosity, the height of the water table, the seasonal flooding of rivers, and the availability of irrigation have to be taken into account, and in areas of marginal rainfall they will determine whether rice can be grown or not, and whether a second crop is possible. The date of sowing depends on the time the rains can be expected, or on the flooding of a river: the two do not necessarily coincide. When a second crop is to follow the first, the length of the growing season also becomes important, as the hardiest type of rice requires a temperature of at least 10° C. (50° F.) during the coldest month in which it is in the ground.

Rice is normally sown in nursery plots, rather than directly on to the paddy field where it is to mature. The use of a nursery plot has certain advantages:

1. Land is released for another crop until the seedlings are large enough to need transplanting.

2. Once the rice crop has been sown, the ground must be flooded. It is clearly a simpler matter to provide water for a few square yards of land than for a whole field. If the rains upon which flooding depends are late, transplanting can be deferred without damage to the young plants until they arrive.

3. It permits a more efficient use of manures and fertilisers. If these are scarce, it is better to apply them intensively to a small

seedling patch rather than thinly over a larger area. Furthermore, a maturing crop can succeed on poor soils, but a young plant rarely recovers from a bad start.

Before the seedlings are transferred to the paddy field, the land is flooded, and the soil well stirred. Transplanting takes place when the young plants are from three to six weeks old in a back-breaking

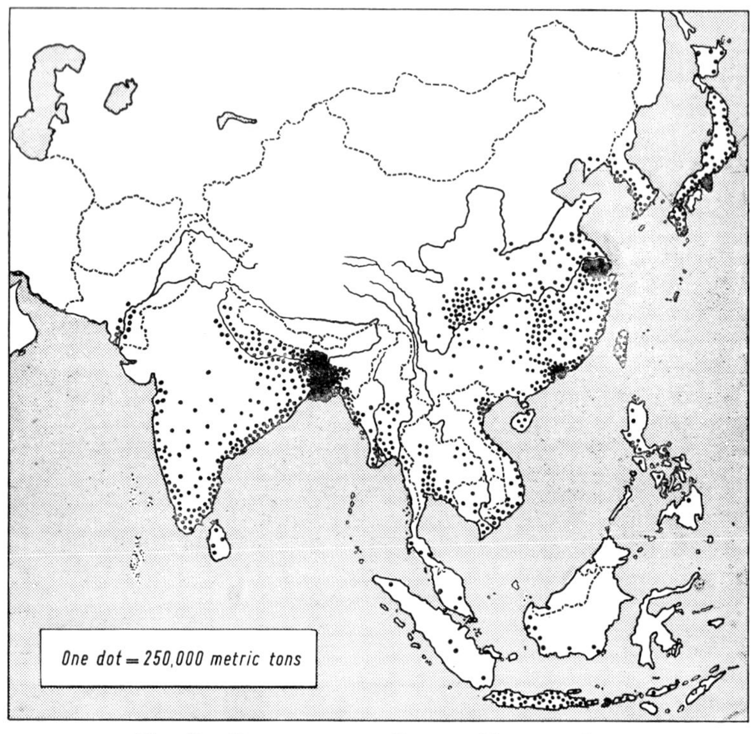

Fig. 45.—DISTRIBUTION OF RICE IN MONSOON ASIA.

manual operation. However, simple planting machines are being developed, and nearly 2·5 million were reported to be in use in China in 1960. Their value lies in the fact that they speed up the work, which may be a matter of some importance if a second crop is to have time to mature before the end of the summer. At harvest time the paddy field is drained, and the grain is cut with a knife or sickle, often in two operations; the ears first, and then the straw.

Upland rice—The cultivation of lowland or swamp rice requires the even flooding of the field to a depth of a few inches, for which naturally flat or terraced land is essential. In hilly country, types of rice which succeed without the need for levelling, or the construction of dykes and bunds, can be grown provided the rainfall is heavy. Upland varieties yield lightly, and are apt to fail in dry years, or if the rains arrive late. They account for only a tiny proportion of the world's rice crop.

Commercial rice production—On the deltaic flats of the Irrawaddi, Menam, and Mekong, production exceeds local demand, and there is an export to the rice-deficient regions of India, China, Japan, Indonesia, and Malaya. Most of the trade passes through the ports of Rangoon, Bangkok, and Saigon. The delta regions have been reclaimed from swamp and jungle during the last 100 years, and are still thinly populated by Asian standards. The same hand-methods of cultivation are employed as in the subsistence rice areas.

Mechanised rice farming—Although characteristically associated with the monsoon lands, rice cultivation is by no means confined to those regions, and Asian methods of cultivation are not necessarily applied in every part of the world where the plant is grown. In California, Arkansas, and along the Gulf Coast lowlands of the U.S.A.; in the Murrumbidgee irrigation areas of New South Wales; in parts of the Ukraine and south-western Siberia; and between the Ticino and Po rivers of northern Italy, rice is being successfully grown by mechanised grain-farming techniques. Some of the Russian and Californian crop is even sown from the air. By these means labour demands are kept to a minimum. Eighty man-days per acre are lavished upon the rice fields of North Vietnam, while two man-days per acre suffice in California. However, the rice yield in California is twice that of North Vietnam, and more than three times the average for India—a striking illustration of the economic inefficiency of much of Oriental intensive subsistence agriculture (Table 26).

TABLE 26

YIELD OF RICE

(in hundreds of kilograms per hectare)

(1965)

Spain	59·3	U.S.A.	47·7	Ceylon	17·7
Italy	40·2	Yugoslavia	42·0	Pakistan	16·8
Japan	49·5	Taiwan	37·8	India	13·1
Egypt	41·8	Indonesia	18·0		

One hectare equals approximately two and a half acres.

Source: *F.A.O. Production Yearbook.*

Total production however, is small in the Western World. The people of Europe and North America prefer wheat to rice, and the area suitable for rice cultivation is restricted. The leading world producers are almost without exception the countries of Asia (Table 27). There is a small, but growing, export from the United States to the Far East, and from Australia to the Far East and the United Kingdom.

TABLE 27

WORLD PRODUCTION OF RICE (in thousands of metric tons)

	1948-52 (average)	1958	1963	1965
China (mainland) ..	58,100	88,000	n/a	n/a
India	34,000	46,200	54,700	45,900
Pakistan	12,400	12,000	17,700	17,800
Japan	12,700	16,000	17,100	16,100
Indonesia	9,500	12,000	12,500	13,200
Thailand	6,800	7,000	10,100	9,600
Vietnam	n/a	9,000	9,600	9,400
Burma	5,400	6,600	7,500	8,050
Brazil	3,000	4,100	5,400	7,580
Philippines	2,700	3,750	3,800	4,070
South Korea ..	2,550	3,250	3,750	4,730
Cambodia	1,250	1,150	2,750	2,500
U.S.A.	1,925	2,000	3,150	3,460
Egypt	950	1,000	2,000	1,860
WORLD	165,600	227,900	260,000	254,200

n/a—not available

Source: *F.A.O. Production Yearbook.*

OATS

Oats have never ranked with wheat, rice, or maize as a human food. Apart from small quantities which are used to produce oatmeal and breakfast cereals, they are consumed almost entirely as animal feed. Oats are cultivated as a valuable rotation crop in most temperate mixed farming regions, but only become dominant on the cooler and moister margins of the wheat belts, especially on tracts of poorer soil. North-western Britain, the North European Plain, the Baltic lands, and the northern Prairies of Canada are leading producing regions (Table 28). The replacement of the farm horse by the tractor (oats were primarily a feed for horses) has been in part responsible for the decline in oat production during recent years. New strains of barley also yield more heavily than oats, and are tending to displace them on land which can equally well support either.

TABLE 28

PRODUCTION OF OATS, BARLEY, RYE, AND MILLETS
(in thousands of metric tons)

OATS	1948-52 (average)	1965	BARLEY	1948-52 (average)	1965
U.S.A.	18,950	13,450	U.S.S.R. ..	6,350	20,200
Canada	6,200	6,400	U.S.A.	5,850	8,540
U.S.S.R.	13,000	6,100	France	1,550	7,400
France	3,400	2,500	United Kingdom	2,050	8,190
Poland	2,240	2,540	Canada	4,250	4,670
Western Germany	2,500	2,050	Turkey	2,300	3,300
WORLD	62,100	46,800	WORLD ..	59,000	104,700
RYE			**MILLETS AND SORGHUMS**		
U.S.S.R.	17,950	16,100	India	12,000	13,800
Poland	6,350	8,290	U.S.A.	3,900	17,100
Western Germany	3,050	2,823	Ethiopia ..	1,700	n/a
Eastern Germany	2,500	1,910	Argentina ..	250	6,600
Czechoslovakia ..	1,100	822	Nigeria	2,680	1,120
Turkey	500	775	Niger	600	1,120
WORLD	37,700	35,400	WORLD ..	46,200	51,000

Source: *U.N. Statistical Yearbook.*

BARLEY

Barley finds optimum conditions for growth in substantially the same areas as wheat. However, it is more drought-resistant than wheat, succeeds in regions of lower summer temperatures, and matures in a shorter time. Some types are also tolerant of moist conditions. Barley is therefore distributed widely over the surface of the earth, and can be found in cultivation from areas north of the Arctic Circle to the tropics, and from sea level to over 11,000 feet in the Andes.

Barley acreages have increased considerably since the Second World War because of a growing demand for a high-quality feed grain. The use of more prolific strains have also substantially reduced the cost of barley production. It is now the leading cereal in the British Isles, having surpassed both wheat and oats in sown area and output (Table 29). Four fifths of the British barley crop goes into livestock rations. An important market also exists for high-quality malting barley in Britain and other countries.

The leading producing countries are indicated in Table 28.

MILLETS AND SORGHUMS

The ability of this group of cereals to survive with a minimum of attention on land which is too dry and poor to support most other

TABLE 29

PRODUCTION AND YIELD PER ACRE OF CEREAL CROPS IN THE UNITED KINGDOM

	Production (in thousands of tons)			Yield (cwts. per acre)		
	1938	1950	1964	1938	1950	1964
Wheat ..	1,965	2,600	3,640	20·4	21·0	33·0
Barley ..	904	1,711	7,404	18·3	20·0	29·4
Oats ..	1,990	2,690	1,325	16·6	17·3	23·6
Rye.. ..	12	57	25	13·2	16·1	14·2

Source: *Annual Abstract of Statistics.*

crops has given it a particular importance in many hot, semi-arid regions. Millets are the dominant cereal in much of Africa south of the Sahara, and in India, Pakistan, and elsewhere in Monsoon Asia where the rainfall is too low for rice. In many of the under-developed countries of the Old World they are a staple food of the poorer sections of the population. On the dry plains of Texas, Oklahoma, and Kansas, and to a less extent in Australia, they are grown as a coarse grain for cattle. Little millet enters international trade.

RYE

In a sense rye is the millet of the cool temperate lands, growing where not even oats could survive, and forming the staple diet of millions of peasants who are, or who until recently were, too poor to buy wheat. The plant is extremely hardy, and is tolerant of cold, infertile soils, and wet harvests. Yields are commonly low, principally because the crop is relegated to agriculturally marginal lands. About 85 per cent. of the world's rye is grown in Russia and on the North European Plain, where a black bread is made from it. Elsewhere it is cultivated mainly as a feed grain. Whisky and vodka are also made from rye.

CHAPTER VII

AGRICULTURAL PRODUCTS
III—THE BEVERAGES, SUGAR, AND TOBACCO

COFFEE

Coffea arabica, the principal species of coffee plant in commercial cultivation to-day, is a native of the highlands of Ethiopia. Until late in the seventeenth century the production of coffee was restricted in the main to the Yemen, but with the increasing popularity of the beverage in Europe, cultivation spread to and expanded rapidly in Ceylon and the islands of the Dutch East Indies. The plant was later introduced to tropical Latin America. The Old World industry, however, was virtually destroyed by the coffee-leaf disease in the second half of the nineteenth century, and the Latin American countries were left with a near monopoly of production. In the years before the Second World War some 90 per cent. of the world-supply originated in the New World. Since then extensive plantings in some African countries have reduced the contribution of the Americas to about three-quarters of the world total.

The coffee plant is normally raised from seed. Seedlings are protected from the sun, and when about eighteen months old are put out into the field where they are to mature. In their wild state, trees attain a height of about thirty feet, but are normally pruned to about half this size on farms. The fruit, or cherry (so called because of its resemblance to an English cherry), is borne in clusters along the twigs. Each cherry contains two beans.

Harvesting is done by shaking the ripe berries on to a sheet, or by picking them off by hand. Fruiting is continuous, and several pickings are made during the course of a year. Ripe fruit is cured by allowing it to dry in the open air, and then removing the shrivelled pulp. Alternatively a "wet" process is employed on the larger estates, whereby the pulp is loosened, and washed away mechanically. Roasting and grinding are always done at the point of consumption.

Coffea arabica accounts for about three-quarters of the coffee entering world commerce. The tree is exacting in its requirements, and flourishes only at the higher elevations within the tropics and in climates having rather more than forty inches of rain per year. The plant does best when shaded from the sun for at least part of

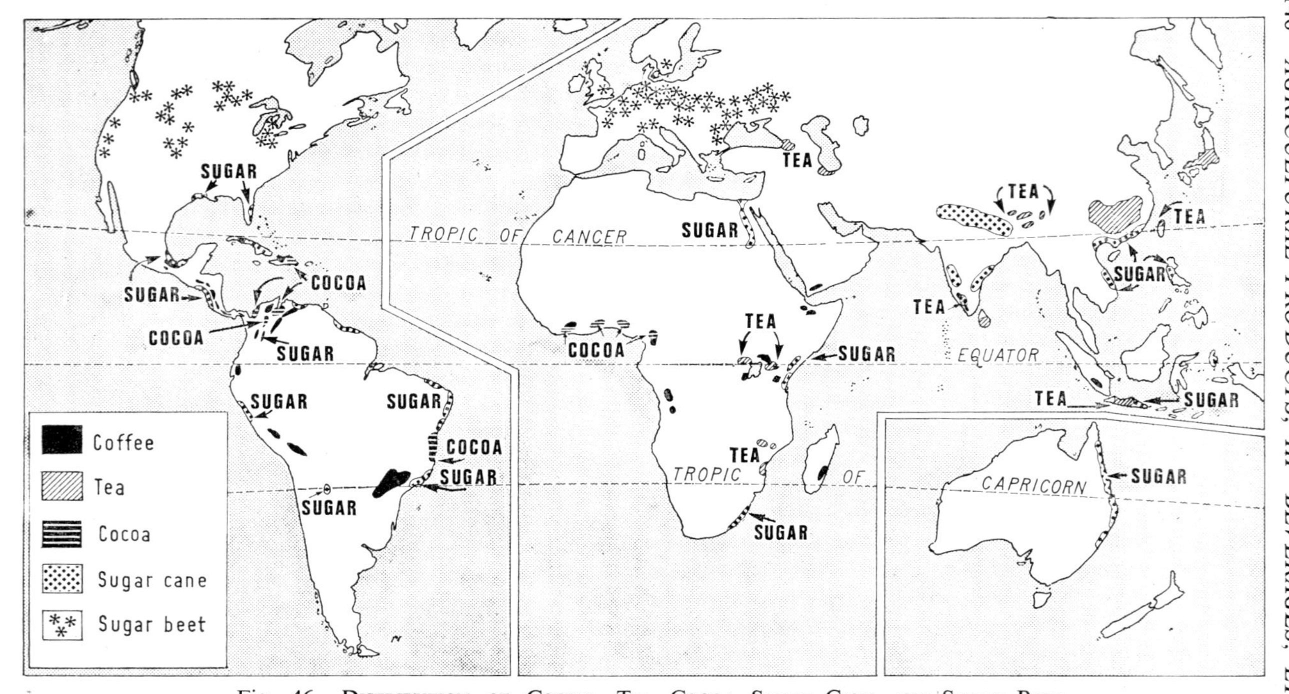

Fig. 46.—Distribution of Coffee, Tea, Cocoa, Sugar Cane, and Sugar Beet.

the day when young, and for this reason is normally grown among shade trees. The hilly, cloudy, east coast margins of the Trade Wind belt are well suited to coffee production, and some of the main regions lie within this zone. Frost is a hazard, and effectively sets an upward height limit to the areas where coffee can be safely grown.

The quality of the coffee is largely a product of altitude, and the better grades commanding the more favourable prices are grown just below the upper altitudinal limits of the plant's range. The finer grades, known in the trade as "milds", are cultivated principally in Colombia, Middle America, the West Indies, and Kenya, and the slightly inferior "brazils" in the country of that name.

Coffea robusta is much hardier than the *arabica* varieties. It thrives on low-lying ground; it is more tolerant of drought, more resistant to disease, and is more easily cultivated than *C. arabica.* Although considered to be of poorer quality, it has certain advantages in the preparation of soluble "instant" coffees, and is much used for that purpose. The chief *robusta* areas are in Africa. Liberian coffee (*C. liberica*) is grown also in limited quantities in West Africa.

Table 30

PRODUCTION OF COFFEE
(in thousands of metric tons)

	1948-52 (Average)	1958	1963	1964*	Export†
Brazil	975	1,610	1,390	600	54
Colombia	360	445	470	485	72
Ivory Coast	50	160	260	200	43
Angola	50	88	170	190	52
Mexico	65	120	140	145	9
El Salvador	75	95	115	125	53
Guatemala	58	85	105	100	63
Madagascar	33	45	50	63	27
India	22	45	70	60	1·5
Peru	6	21	50	52	4
Ecuador	21	45	43	50	15
WORLD	2,240	3,450	3,920	3,160	

*Provisional.

† As a percentage of the value of the total exports of each country in 1964.

Source: *U.N. Statistical Yearbook*, and *Yearbook of International Trade Statistics.*

The coffee region of Brazil—São Paulo state and the adjacent parts of Mineas Gerias and Parana provinces, together with a small outlying area in Espirito Santo, produce the entire Brazilian output of coffee. The crop provides the country with more than half its exports, by value. It also accounts for approximately 40 per cent. of all coffee traded internationally.

Coffee was first grown in the neighbourhood of Rio de Janeiro, but its cultivation soon spread westwards into the Paraíba Valley, and then on to the plateau of São Paulo state. At first plantings followed existing routeways, but as the value of the deep, red *terra roxa* soils became realised, the coffee areas soon became adjusted to their outcrop. Valleys were generally avoided because of their swampy floors and frost hazards, and the plantations came to occupy the upper valley slopes and watersheds. As settlement was taking place in an uninhabited frontier region, cultivation was restricted only by the availability of labour to clear the land, and to plant and harvest the crop. When the coffee frontier moved into

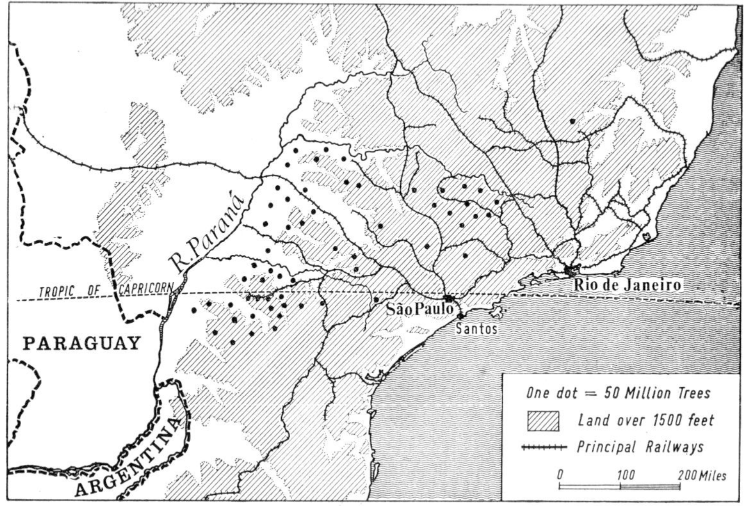

Fig. 47.—The Coffee Region of Brazil.

the interior, the older, exhausted lands were abandoned, or turned over to alternative uses. The main coffee-producing region now lies in the western parts of São Paulo state (Fig. 47).

Stimulated by a world shortage of coffee in the post-1945 period, cultivation began on an enormous scale in the northern regions of Parana province. Much of the planting was speculative, and undertaken by farmers with little real understanding of its problems. The *terra roxa* soils were occupied first, but extensive use has also been made of sandy tracts of indifferent quality. The frost risk is also much greater in Parana than further north. The high yields that growers have so far obtained are attributed to the youth of the trees, rather than to any particular skill that has gone into attending them.

The economic stability of Brazil depends to an uncomfortable extent on the foreign sales of a commodity that is particularly prone to sharp fluctuations in output and price. The periods of prosperity which followed the two world wars were in turn succeeded by depression, as production from new areas glutted the market and caused prices to tumble. The 1962 International Coffee Agreement, to which all major producers and importers subscribe, aims to bring supply and demand into equilibrium, and so prevent a repetition of the disasters of the 1930s when large, unsaleable stocks had to be destroyed. The Brazilian government for its part has introduced a subsidised "eradication scheme" to encourage growers to uproot some 200 million of the older and less productive trees, and to find alternative uses for the land.

Other Latin American producers—Coffee has come to occupy a leading position in the economies of many states of middle and tropical South America. Its importance should be gauged by the contribution it makes to the export earnings of the countries where it is produced, rather than by the volume of production, which by normal Brazilian standards is small (Table 30). Most of the exports are shipped to the United States. With a per capita consumption of sixteen pounds per year, the U.S.A. is by far the largest coffee market in the world. Imports to the value of 1,200 million dollars were received in 1964. Three-quarters of these imports originated in Latin America.

Africa—Coffee cultivation is a recent development in most of the African states. On the East African Highlands it is grown on both European and native farms. In Kenya native production is likely to exceed production from white farms in the near future. An important *robusta* industry is well established in a great crescent-shaped area round the north and north-western shores of Lake Victoria. Here a heavy rainfall ensures high yields, but the problems of drying the beans in a climate without a marked dry season are considerable. Tanzania produces both *arabica* and *robusta* varieties. Other African states with coffee growing industries include Ivory Coast, Angola, Congo, Sierra Leone, Ghana, and Nigeria.

TEA

Tea is primarily a crop of the hilly wet tropics and sub-tropics. Monsoon Asia is the main region of production, followed by the

East African states. A considerable output also comes from the Soviet Union, from the region lying to the south of the Caucasus Mountains. Negligible quantities only are produced in other areas (Table 31).

TABLE 31

PRODUCTION OF TEA
(in thousands of metric tons)

	1948-52 (Average)	1958	1964	1965
India	275	325	345	365
Ceylon	140	185	220	228
China (mainland)	65	140	not available	
Japan	40	75	80	77
Indonesia	40	48	40	89
Pakistan	22	25	25	27
Kenya	6	12	18	25
Taiwan	9	15	20	21
Malawi	7	11	12	13
WORLD	545	735	830	1,130

Source: *U.N. Statistical Yearbook* and *F.A.O. Production Yearbook.*

Yields and the quality of tea vary according to physical conditions of climate and soil, and to cultural and manufacturing practices. A rainfall of at least fifty-five inches per year is desirable, with no severe or prolonged dry season to check growth and damage foliage. In regions of marginal rainfall, a persistent cloud cover and absence of drying winds may serve to reduce evapo-transpiration rates sufficiently to save a crop that might otherwise be lost. Rainfall can rarely be too high for tea provided the soil is free-draining. On slopes, and on land where the danger of water-logging is slight, 200 inches or more are tolerable: the central mountain region of Ceylon, which produces excellent quality tea, is one of the wettest areas on earth. In Assam, on the other hand, where tea gardens occupy the level or gently rolling country of the Brahmaputra valley, artificial soil drainage is often needed although the rainfall is not excessive. High relative humidities and equable temperatures without frost or great heat are also favourable. Frost can be particularly damaging, especially if followed, as night frost generally is in the tropics, by strong sunshine and rapidly rising temperatures the following morning.

The tea plant is normally raised from seed in the nursery, and put out into the field when about six months old, and from six to nine inches in height. A tea garden comes into commercial production after about three to five years. Regular pruning is undertaken to encourage the growth of new shoots and to transform what would otherwise be a rather straggly tree into a bush of manageable size. Picking is an operation requiring skilled labour. A good picker can gather sixty pounds of leaves per day. The tea harvest is more or less continuous in equatorial regions, but is confined to the warmer seasons in the extra-tropical lands. Mechanical pickers are used successfully in the Soviet Union.

In India and Ceylon, and to a less extent in Indonesia, Kenya, and Nyasaland, tea cultivation is a plantation industry organised and managed by foreign corporations. As plantations frequently utilise land of little value to the native subsistence farmer, they are often found in thinly settled areas. Some are forced to rely on immigrant workers. The Ceylonese and Indian tea gardens, for instance, draw heavily on labour from other parts of the sub-continent.

China's tea acreage is second only to that of India. The crop is important in the hill country south of the Yangtze, where it is tended by peasant cultivators producing for the domestic market. China's leading position was lost to India before the Second World War. Internal conflict, the re-orientation of the economy following the communist revolution, and inferior methods of cultivation and leaf preparation have also contributed to the decline in exports. These are now negligible.

Approximately 70 per cent. of the recorded tea production is shipped to importing countries. The largest importers are the English-speaking countries of the Commonwealth and the United States. Consumption per head is estimated at about nine pounds annually in the United Kingdom, six pounds in Australia, three pounds in Canada, and half a pound in the United States. Tea exports are regulated by quotas under an International Tea Agreement which came into operation in 1933, and which has been renewed on a number of occasions since.

COCOA (CACAO)

The cacao tree thrives only on lowlands within the tropics. Its native home is the Amazon Basin and middle America, but the main centres of production have now become firmly established in West Africa (Table 32). Cacao is very exacting in its climatic requirements, and it succeeds only in countries where a fairly evenly distributed rainfall of 55-60 inches per year is accompanied by constantly high relative humidities, and high temperatures. A fall in temperature below 15° C. (59° F.) injures the plant. As strong direct sunlight and drying winds are also harmful to growth, forest trees are normally left in position to provide shade and shelter when a clearing is made, and tall growing food crops such as the banana planted to give protection to young trees. Finally, cacao does best on well drained soil rich in plant food, particularly iron and potash. Acid soils which are characteristic of extensive areas in the hot wet tropics are unsuitable.

Fruiting begins three or four years after planting, and the tree comes into full production when eight to twelve years old. The cocoa pods are borne directly on the main trunk and branches. After harvesting, the beans are removed from the pods, piled into heaps to ferment, and then set out in the open air to dry. Flowering

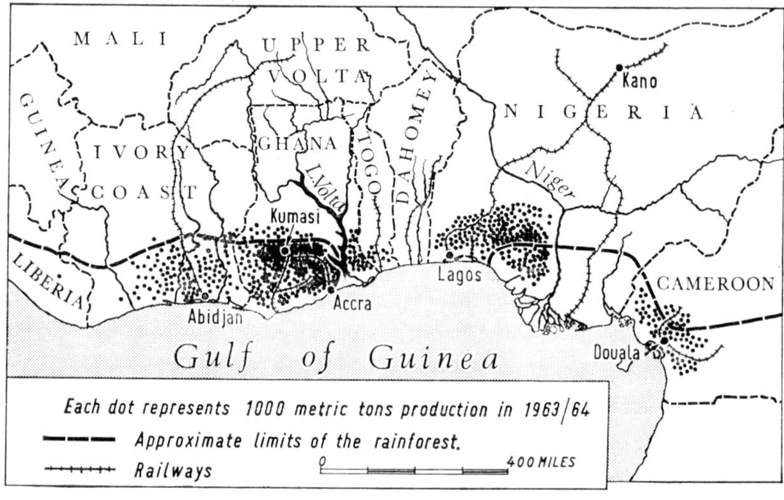

Fig. 48.—THE COCOA LANDS OF WEST AFRICA.

and fruiting are continuous, but the main harvest occurs between November and March in the northern hemisphere, with a subsidiary harvest in June. There is little consumption of cocoa or cocoa products in the main producing countries, and the crop is grown almost entirely for export. As cocoa beans do not store well in tropical conditions it is necessary to provide for their dispatch from the farms within a few weeks of gathering. Cocoa cultivation has therefore stimulated the construction of rail and road communications between the growing areas and the ports in the main regions of production.

The United States, Britain, Germany, the Netherlands, and France take 80 per cent. of all exports. The chocolate and confectionery industries are the main consumers.

Cocoa cultivation in Ghana—Cocoa was first established in the Gold Coast in 1879. The development of the industry was spectacular. Within a few years beans were being shipped abroad. By the end of the second quarter of the present century, the Gold Coast had displaced Ecuador as the leading producer, and the crop had become the colony's principal export. To-day cocoa occupies some 4 million acres of the equatorial forest belt, and extends to within ten miles of the sea. The main concentration is in Ashanti Province round Kumasi (Fig. 48). The cacao tree is grown on native family farms of between one and three acres in extent. Cocoa production is not a plantation industry in Ghana, and the role of the European is restricted to research, advice, and marketing.

West African native people were formerly shifting cultivators with a tribal system of land tenure in which land was held in common. The introduction of commercial farming has resulted in a natural desire for the population to own the land which provides the main, if not the only, source of cash. Tribal influences have therefore been weakened. The success of cocoa cultivation has also been at the expense of staple food crops, some of which now have to be imported.

Cacao is particularly susceptible to attack by disease. The spread of Witches' Broom and *Monilia* were in part responsible for the decline of Ecuador as a major producer. In Ghana, Swollen Shoot—a virus disease transmitted from tree to tree by the mealy bug—has devastated wide areas. Until recently only the drastic practice of cutting out and burning infected plants was successful in checking its spread. In spite of a government scheme to compensate farmers for losses, growers were reluctant to eradicate diseased trees, especially as they continued to bear useful crops for some years after becoming infected. Since the war disease-resistant seedlings have been brought in from the Amazon, and planted with the aid of government money. The coming into yield of these new and improved varieties has been largely responsible for the upsurge of Ghanaian cocoa production during the last few years (Table 32).

Ghana has come to depend heavily on her cocoa exports, which account for a very large, though now declining, percentage of her foreign trade. A stabilisation fund has been successful in cushioning the peasant against the worst effects of fluctuating prices to which the commodity is very prone, and at the same time has provided funds for research and for social and economic development in the country.

The bulk of Ghana's cocoa export trade passes through Accra and Tema.

Other cocoa-producing regions—Peasant cultivators are responsible for the production of substantial quantities of cocoa in the forest lands of Nigeria, Ivory Coast, and Cameroon. In the Americas, Brazil is the main producer. A finer quality cocoa is grown in Ecuador, Venezuela, and the Dominican Republic. In these states foreign owned and managed plantations are the rule rather than the small, independent farm which is characteristic of West Africa.

TABLE 32

PRODUCTION OF COCOA BEANS
(in thousands of metric tons)

	1948-52 (Average)	1958	1963	1965
Ghana	255	260	427	415
Nigeria	105	136	220	184
Ivory Coast	53	56	98	121
Brazil	120	165	140	161
Cameroon	53	66	85	71
Ecuador	28	33	36	36
Dominican Republic	30	33	45	30
WORLD	760	900	1,230	1,236

Source: *U.N. Statistical Yearbook* and *F.A.O. Production Yearbook.*

YERBA MATÉ

Yerba maté, or Paraguay tea, is obtained from the dried leaves of a small evergreen tree (*Ilex paraguayensis*) that grows wild and on plantations in Paraguay, and in the neighbouring territories of Brazil and the Argentine. It is an important beverage in the regions of production, and in much of southern South America. There is a small export to Spain and Portugal.

SUGAR CANE

All plants contain sugar, but only two are of commercial importance, *i.e.* sugar cane—a giant perennial grass of the tropics, and sugar beet—a root crop of temperate regions.

Cultivated varieties of sugar cane have been introduced to the tropical and sub-tropical lowlands of all continents where high summer temperatures, warm winters without frost, abundant sunshine, and an annual rainfall of more than fifty inches prevail. Excellent crops are also grown in drier areas by irrigation. For the highest yields, deep, well-manured soils of high fertility are essential as the plant is a heavy feeder, and in many commercial producing countries its cultivation amounts almost to monoculture. Alluvium, and weathered volcanic rock, provide the best sugar lands.

The plant is propagated from cuttings (setts) of mature cane. In a matter of days buds on the cuttings sprout, and normally between six and ten stalks grow from each cutting. The cane reaches maturity after twelve months to two years, according to climate and variety. Little cultivation is done during the growing period beyond controlling weeds while the plants are young. Before harvesting, the cane is often fired in order to remove dead foliage and to eliminate field pests. When ripe, the cane is cut by men armed with machettes. The stalk is severed as close to the ground as possible, as the base is richest in sugar. After cutting, the cane puts out new shoots or *ratoons*. An indefinite number of crops can be taken from a single planting, but as the yield from each successive ratoon deteriorates, it usually pays a grower on valuable land to pull out the old root stock after the second or third ratoon, and replant.

Raw cane is a bulky commodity. Its sugar content is between 10 per cent. and 20 per cent. Transport costs are prohibitive unless the crop is grown within a few miles of the crushing mill, where the juices are extracted from the cane and concentrated. Whether cane is produced by independent farmers as in Queensland, on company-owned estates as in Hawaii, or on land leased to peasant farmers by sugar companies as in Jamaica and other West Indian islands, the whole business of sugar production is organised round the mill or *central*. The capacity of the mill determines the area that can be planted, and the rate at which cutting can proceed. A stoppage brings work in the fields to a standstill, as cut cane must be processed within forty-eight hours if the quality of the sugar is not to be impaired. In regions where good growing conditions extend throughout the year, the harvest period can be spread over several months, thereby allowing the mill to be kept in more or less continuous operation. This produces a substantial saving in processing costs.

It must be emphasised that the crushing mill is not a refinery, but is concerned only with the initial stages of sugar manufacture. The product leaves the mill in the form of raw, brown sugar crystals for export to the refineries in the importing countries. By-products of crushing include the cane residue known as *bagasse*, which can be used as a fuel, sold as a cattle food, or used as a raw material of the paper, fibre board, and synthetic fibre industries; molasses from which rum, treacle, and many chemicals, including industrial alcohol, are produced; and filter cake—a useful fertiliser.

The largest producers of cane sugar are India and Brazil. Little of their production, however, passes into international trade. Cuba, Pakistan, Mexico, Hawaii, the Philippines, and Australia each produce more than a million tons annually (Table 33). The Australian sugar growing industry is concentrated on the coastal lowlands of Queensland, and stands as the only example of a significant farming enterprise within the tropics in which labour as well as management is provided by the white man.

SUGAR BEET

Sugar beet is an annual plant requiring a climate similar to wheat. Deep, fertile, free-working, and well drained soils are also an asset. Sugar beet is a dual-purpose plant, grown for its value as an animal feed as well as for the sugar that it contains. It successfully replaces other temperate root crops in an arable rotation, and besides giving farmers an immediate cash return, has a beneficial effect on crops that follow it.

Sugar beet cultivation has developed with government aid in most of the producing countries. The sugar beet subsidy was introduced in Britain in 1925 to assist an infant industry. Costs of production are generally higher than for cane, but have decreased in recent years owing to the use of higher yielding strains, and the mechanisation of the weeding, thinning, and harvesting processes. Large areas are under the crop in Europe and North America. The sugar beet regions of Britain are shown in Fig. 49.

World trade in sugar—Surplus production in beet sugar is insufficient to generate any significant foreign trade in the product.

TABLE 33

WORLD PRODUCTION OF CENTRIFUGAL SUGAR
(Raw value in thousands of short tons.)

Cane Sugar	1954-5	1960-1	1965-6*	Beet Sugar	1954-5	1960-1	1965-6*
Cuba	5,000	7,460	6,600	U.S.S.R.	3,025	6,600	9,350
India	2,085	4,040	4,625	U.S.A.	2,040	2,450	3,000
Brazil	2,480	3,790	4,575	France	1,815	1,870	2,575
Australia	1,435	1,500	2,125	Poland	1,270	1,650	1,925
Philippines	1,375	1,450	1,970	West Germany	1,420	1,585	1,680
Hawaii	1,140	1,090	1,200	Italy	950	1,070	1,375
U.S.A.	610	630	1,100	United Kingdom	700	925	1,030
Puerto Rico	1,160	1,100	1,000	Czechoslovakia	850	1,245	770
WORLD	25,375	33,830	41,060	WORLD	16,610	26,219	28,930

* Estimates.

Source: *F.A.O. Production Yearbook* and *Commodity Yearbook*, New York.

There is a small export, however, from France and the countries of Central Europe. About one-third of the cane sugar production enters international commerce, and of this about 90 per cent. is marketed under some form of preferential agreement. Britain thus obtains more than 60 per cent. of her requirements from Commonwealth and colonial territories on a quota basis at negotiated prices. Of the remainder, 10 per cent. is purchased on the "free" market at prevailing world prices, and 30 per cent. is produced at home. Before the dispute with the Castro government, the United States gave favoured treatment to Cuba, who was her main supplier.

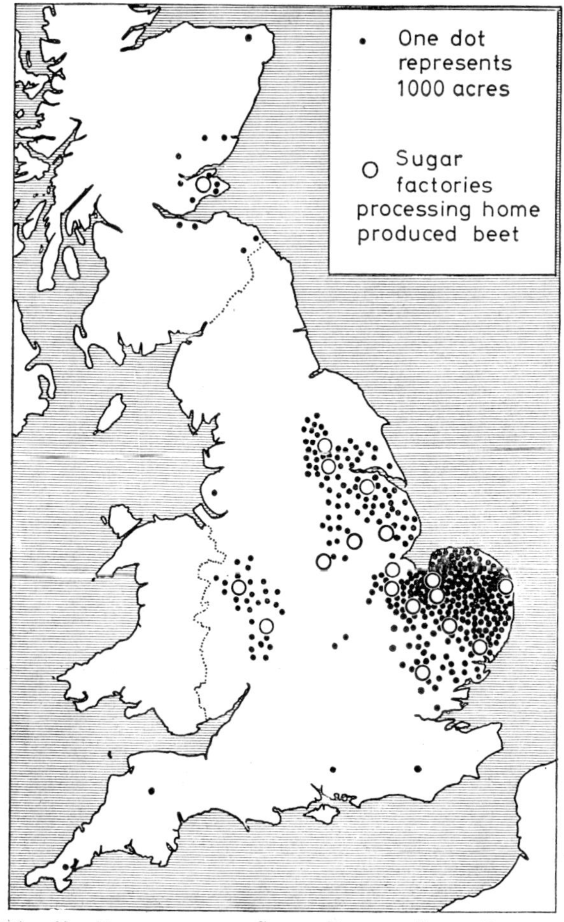

Fig. 49.—Distribution of Sugar Beet in Great Britain.

TOBACCO

The tobacco plant is an annual requiring a frost-free period of 120-180 days, moderate rainfall, and warm but not hot growing seasons. Most countries with a temperature exceeding 18° C. (66° F.) in the hottest month produce tobacco, if only for local consumption. Within the tropics it is either a crop of the uplands, or its cultivation is restricted to the cooler season.

A tobacco crop makes exceptionally heavy demands upon the soil, and sustained yields are possible only when prolific applications of manure are given. Much labour is also needed. Many more man-hours are expended on an acre of tobacco in the United States than on an acre of rice in Japan. Practically all operations are done by hand. Sowing in meticulously prepared seed beds, transplanting, thinning, hoeing, weeding, "topping" (*i.e.* the removal of the terminal growth to stimulate leaf development), harvesting the leaf, and curing, are all undertaken without the assistance of machinery. Few farmers have the resources to grow the crop on a large scale, and the acreage devoted to it on any single holding is usually small.

TABLE 34

PRODUCTION OF TOBACCO
(in thousands of metric tons.)

	1948-52 (Average)	1958	1963	1965
U.S.A.	960	790	1,060	841
India	250	240	365	369
Japan	90	140	160	193
Turkey	90	115	130	124
U.S.S.R.	160	210	155	194
Bulgaria	45	85	105	123
Greece	50	85	125	122
Rhodesia	45	80	140	126
Pakistan	70	90	100	110
WORLD	2,830	3,490	4,200	4,259

Source: *U.N. Statistical Yearbook* and *F.A.O. Production Yearbook.*

The quality and flavour of tobacco are influenced by local climate and soil conditions, to which the plant is peculiarly sensitive, as well as the variety grown, and the methods employed in its curing. Each area has its speciality, and in this respect tobacco cultivation, and viticulture are similar. Cuba, the Connecticut valley, and parts of Indonesia produce cigar tobacco; the aromatic Turkish tobaccos, noted for their excellent blending qualities, are products of the

Balkans and the eastern Mediterranean; and the "Burley" cigarette tobaccos are grown principally in Kentucky and Virginia. The quality also varies according to the part of the plant from which the leaf is taken. In order to ensure the uniformity of manufactured products, makers of cigarette and pipe tobacco normally blend leaves of different grades.

The main tobacco producing countries are the United States, India, Turkey, Japan, and the Soviet Union.

CHAPTER VIII

AGRICULTURAL PRODUCTS

IV—FRUIT AND MARKET GARDEN PRODUCE

Fruit cultivation becomes important in those regions of the world where the mean temperature of the hottest month exceeds about 15° C. (59° F.), where the frost-free period is longer than 100 days, and where, in the absence of irrigation, the rainfall is more than 15-20 inches per year.

Each type of fruit has a more restricted geographical distribution than, for example, has cotton or barley, mainly because (with a few exceptions) it is borne on perennial plants which demand appropriate climatic conditions throughout the year, and not simply during the months of active growth. Each of the main climatic zones has its specialities, although there is a considerable overlapping along the boundaries. Bananas, mangoes, pineapples, and dates are products of the hot lands; citrus fruit, peaches, apricots, and figs of the warm temperate; and apples, pears, and plums of the cool temperate regions. Untold numbers of these fruit plants are grown in their respective regions, often in ones and twos purely to supply local needs. Few gardens in rural England are without apples; the peach is grown on practically every farm and garden in the southern states of the U.S.A.; the mango is cultivated widely in India, and the orange in China; the banana is a staple of the hot wet tropics, and the date of the Old World deserts. In many of the poorer countries of the world, locally grown fruit adds variety to a diet that would otherwise be not only depressingly monotonous but also deficient in essential vitamins. Subsistence fruit cultivation, however, is often a haphazard business. Products do not have to conform to standards set by commercial markets, and the quality is frequently poor. Growers have few problems of storage and transport, and, except in the case of the staples, crop failure does not bring serious consequences in its train.

Commercial fruit production on the other hand is a highly specialised form of intensive agriculture which succeeds only within a set of closely defined physical and economic conditions. Good orchard land is less readily available than good cereal or cattle country. Few fruit trees thrive on cold, wet, or very shallow soils. Light, free draining land that warms up quickly in spring is desirable, especially if the crop is intended to mature early in the season: hence alluvial, sandy, or gravelly tracts are preferable to areas of heavy clays. Frost is perhaps the fruit grower's greatest hazard. Many of the tender, evergreen trees whose cultivation has spread into regions where a frost risk is present, are damaged by exposure to temperatures of more than a degree or two below freezing point at any time of the year. The great freezes in the winters of 1885-6, 1894-5, and 1898-9 virtually destroyed the orange-growing industry of northern Florida. By contrast, deciduous fruit trees are winter hardy, some varieties of apples tolerating a temperature of – 40° C. (– 40° F.) in their dormant stage, apricots and peaches – 23° C. (– 10° F.), and vines – 18° C. (0° F.) before damage occurs. Frost at blossom time is more serious, and occasionally a grower may lose his year's crop as a result of a single freeze, even in the best sited orchards. The risk can be minimised by planting on hill sides where air-drainage is good (even a rise of a few feet above a level plain can make all the difference, see Fig. 50), or by large bodies of water, which have the effect of raising night minimum temperatures. In certain regions it has proved worthwhile to give fruit trees artificial protection, as in Italy, where lemon groves are covered with light screens in winter, or in California, where oil burners are employed to raise temperatures in orange groves. Another method, effective but expensive, is to direct a fine spray of water on to the trees during a frost: water freezes on to the blossoms, and paradoxically prevents damage. If cold winds are a hazard, shelter may be provided by wind breaks. The practice in the "Mistral" country of the lower Rhone is to plant thick hedges of cypress and bamboo to protect apricots, peaches, and early fruit and vegetables from continental air moving down the valley.

Economic aspects of fruit cultivation

Labour is easily the highest single cost item in fruit farming. Mechanical operations are normally restricted to site preparation, ploughing and discing between trees, crop spraying, and handling after harvesting. Planting, budding and grafting, pruning, fruit thinning, and picking are done by hand, and are activities calling for considerable skill and care.[1] Labour is needed throughout the year, but the peak demand is at harvest time when additional workers are employed.

[1] Mechanical "shakers" are in use in citrus orchards in the U.S.A., but as they bruise the fruit, they are only suitable for harvesting crops destined for processing.

Fruit farming also calls for much specialised knowledge which may have application only in the area where it is acquired. Experience gained in apple cultivation in Kent, for example, has limited

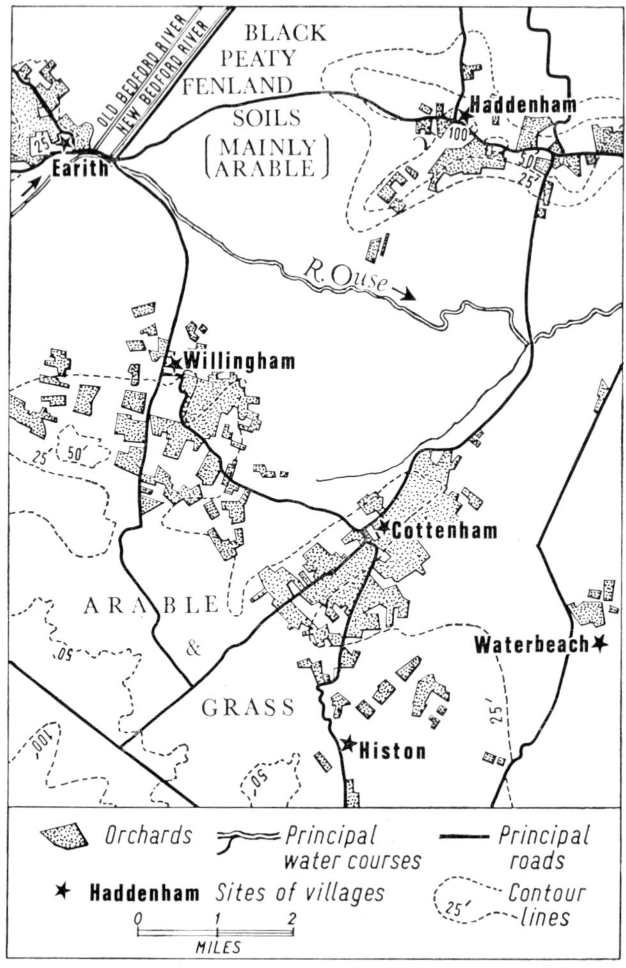

Fig. 50.—PART OF THE ORCHARD COUNTRY NORTH OF CAMBRIDGE.

value in the different conditions of the north and west of England. For this reason the development of fruit farming in new areas tends to be inhibited.

Most trees are prone to attack by pests and diseases, whose control is made all the more difficult by the monocultural practices adopted by fruit farmers. The application several times a year of poisonous sprays and dusts is now almost universal in commercial orchards. The wisdom of applying such highly toxic substances as parathion, malathion, aldrin, and D.D.T. to food crops has been questioned by many who fear for the consequences to wild life, including beneficial insects, and to man himself. It has been estimated that sufficient parathion is used annually on Californian farms to give a lethal dose to between five and ten times the present world population. Economically, spraying programmes are costly, and to some extent self-defeating, as insects have a way of developing immunity to chemicals. There are several well-documented records of pest damage actually increasing after spraying had been undertaken.[1]

Many kinds of fruit are highly perishable, and special storage and transport facilities must be provided unless the fruits are for local and almost immediate consumption. Glut, followed by shortage, is a likely consequence of a harvest being confined to a period of a few weeks in the year. The problem of shipment to distant markets has to some extent been solved by the growth of the processing industries—drying, canning, freezing, and the manufacture of juice concentrates in the areas of cultivation. The development of these market outlets has tended to increase further the competitive advantages of established areas of production, as the processing industries have become closely integrated with farm operations. Fruit is generally grown under contract, and delivered to the factory at specified times and in specified quantities. Growers at a distance from a processing plant are handicapped, especially if the fruit is destined for canning and freezing, as these operations must be carried out within a few hours of harvesting. Transport costs on fresh fruit are high, although co-operatives are often able to secure favourable rates when bulk shipments can be arranged. Processed fruit is more easily handled, and normally takes up less space in the transport vehicle, with a saving in transport costs. Concentrated fruit juice is only about one twenty-fifth as bulky as the fresh fruit from which it is derived. On the other hand, frozen products must be stored and shipped in refrigerated holds and cars, and held at freezing temperatures until consumed. The frozen food industry is thus dependent, not only on specialised bulk transport facilities, but also on the provision of retail, and even domestic refrigeration.

[1] See *Silent Spring* by Rachael Carson, Hamish Hamilton (London), p. 25 and p. 200ff.

TROPICAL FRUIT

BANANAS—The banana is the most important fruit of the tropics, and is the leading commodity, both by weight and value, of the world fresh fruit trade (Table 35). Starchy varieties (plantains) are also widely grown, and form the staple food of countless people.

TABLE 35

WORLD EXPORTS OF THE PRINCIPAL TYPES OF FRUIT AND DRIED FRUIT PRODUCTS, 1963
(in thousands of tons)

Fruit	Exports	Fruit	Exports
Bananas	4,000	Rasins	330
Oranges	2,725	Grapefruit	205
Apples	1,300	Dried prunes	95
Grapes	700	Plums	75
Lemons	460	Apricots	62
Dates	400	Pineapples	55
Pears	360	Dried figs	55
Peaches	330		

Source: Commonwealth Economic Committee—*Fruit*. H.M.S.O.

The plant thrives in deep, well-drained alluvial soils in sheltered situations. It is a crop of the lowlands. Exposure to temperatures of below 11° C. (52° F.) for more than a few hours causes serious injury. Water requirements are high, and irrigation is generally necessary unless an evenly distributed rainfall of at least sixty inches per year can be guaranteed. High winds wreak havoc among banana plantations, and few growers in the Caribbean and on the adjacent mainland have not at some time suffered from a visitation of the tropical hurricane. Fortunately the plant recovers, and only the current harvest is lost. Disease, too, has made inroads into plantings, and large areas have been wiped out by *sigatoka* and *Panama disease*. An effective treatment for *sigatoka* has been discovered, but *Panama disease* continues to spread virtually unchecked, so much so that it has become customary for growers to hold more land than is needed to supply market requirements, in order to ensure that production is not too seriously affected when disease strikes.

The first harvest is ready 12-15 months after planting. One stem only is borne on each plant. After fruiting the plant dies back, but new shoots develop from the root stock, and thereafter production is continuous. About 300 stems per acre, representing about 20,000 pounds of fruit, can be obtained annually from good land.

Bananas are harvested while green. The problem thereafter is to ship the fruit from field to market as quickly as possible, perhaps over a distance of several thousand miles. Cutting cannot be delayed, and the fruit cannot be stored. Bananas must be consumed within three weeks of gathering. Cutting schedules are arranged to fit in with the arrival of the banana boat, a specialised carrier in which the fruit is stored, according to variety, at controlled temperatures of between 10° C. and 15° C. (50° F. and 59° F.).[1] Insulated rail cars convey the bananas from the importing port to town and city distributors. As yet there has been no development of a processing industry on a scale to warrant any alternative to cutting and shipping the fruit when ripe.

The banana is produced commercially on both large company-owned plantations and on small family farms. It is a useful crop for the peasant as it yields fruit throughout the year, makes a steady demand on labour, and brings in a regular income. The small grower is however completely dependent on the specialised transport and marketing organisations, with whom he contracts for the sale of his produce.

TABLE 36

PRODUCTION OF BANANAS
(in thousands of metric tons)

	1948-53 (Average)	1963	1964	1965
Brazil	3,207	4,070	4,397	4,531
Ecuador	392	2,098	3,300	3,300
India*	2,013	2,601	2,670	2,700
Venezuela	950	1,456	1,203	1,230
Honduras	813	801	831	850
Thailand	not available	796	743	750
Philippines	462	755	685	700
Panama	345	422	485	583
Costa Rica	434	466	486	567
Dominican Republic	337	389	350	318
Mexico	252	413	421	426
Jamaica	131	281	290	327
WORLD	13,900	22,410	22,089	23,024

* Includes plantains.

Source: *F.A.O. Production Yearbook.*

More than half the bananas entering world trade originate in the six "Banana Republics" of Latin America—Colombia, Ecuador, Costa Rica, Guatemala, Honduras, and Panama (Fig. 51). The United Fruit Company of America owns or controls substantial acreages in these states, and markets some 60 per cent. of the bananas produced. The Canary Islands, Brazil, and Jamaica are also major exporters. The main markets are in North America and Western Europe.

[1] The importance of warm storage conditions is often overlooked by retailers, who keep bananas with other fruit and vegetables in an icy room at the back of the shop.

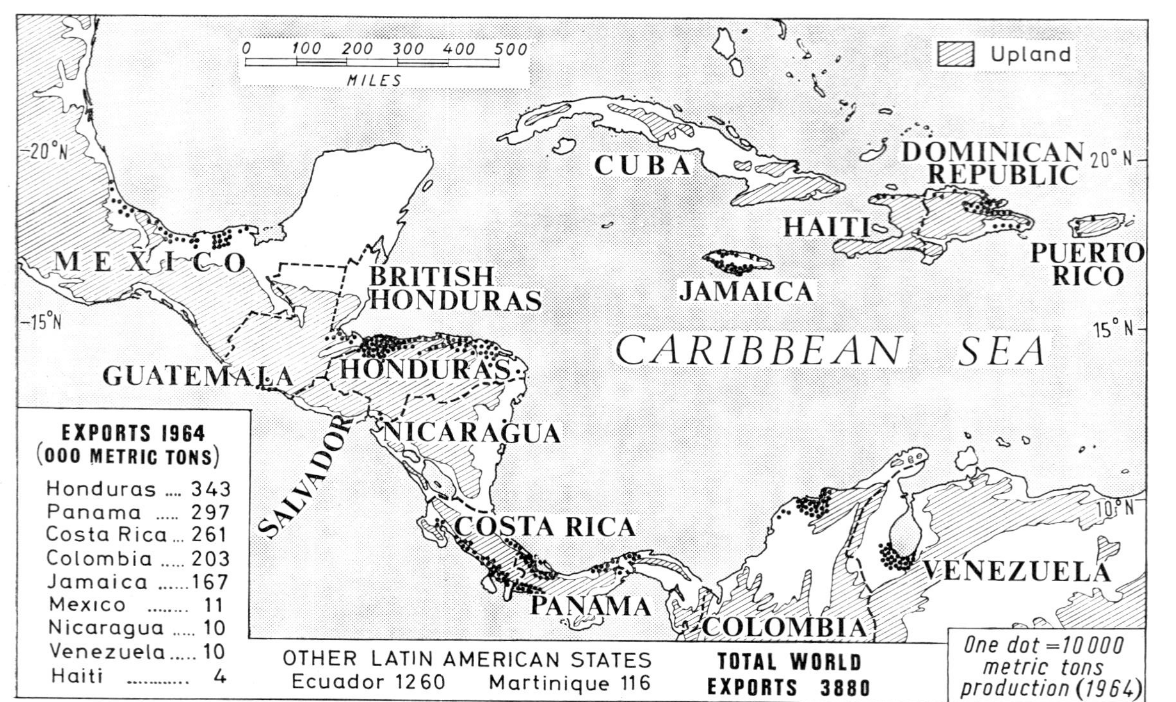

Fig. 51.—The Banana Areas of the West Indies and Central America.

PINEAPPLES—Pineapples are fruits of the trade wind climates. Their cultivation shows a remarkable concentration in the Hawaiian Islands which produce about three-quarters of the world's commercial output (Table 37). The remainder are grown in the Caribbean area, the Azores, Queensland, Mexico, and a few regions in South East Asia. As the fruit must be left on the plant until ripe, when it is very perishable, there is little scope for the export of fresh pineapples, except from regions located close to markets. The Azores are thus favoured by proximity to Europe, and the Caribbean to the North American mainland; but Hawaii, separated by several thousand miles of ocean from its major markets, must process almost the whole of her crop prior to shipment.

TABLE 37
PRODUCTION OF PINEAPPLES
(in thousands of metric tons)

	1948-9 to 1952-3 (Average)	1963	1964	1965
Hawaii	680	935	935	935
Brazil	135	274	291	292
Malaya	34	295	314	355
Mexico	125	193	198	201
Thailand	not available	303	260	300
South Africa	36	111	111	111
Cuba	120	100	100	100
WORLD	1,450	3,283	3,365	3,516

Source: *F.A.O. Production Yearbook.*

MANGOES—The mango is one of the finest flavoured fruits in cultivation, but has poor storage qualities. It is widely grown in India and other tropical countries with a pronounced dry season. Commercial mango orchards have been successfully established in Florida, where, unfortunately, the tree is subject to frost damage.

DATES—Southern Iraq is probably the native home of the date palm, but its cultivation had spread, even before historic times, to all the deserts of the Old World wherever suitable conditions prevailed. It is a tree without rival in the oases, giving shade to man and beast, and to other crops, and furnishing the desert dweller not only with a compact, durable, and easily transportable food, rich in sugar and protein, but also with many of his other wants. There are few trees so completely utilised as the date palm: from its fruit, leaves, trunk, and roots come hundreds of different products.

The tree bears fruit only in the true desert climate. Very high daytime temperatures, at least for a few months in the year, cloudless skies and low relative humidities are essential. Light winter frost however is not harmful, and for this reason the date palm cannot be considered as a truly tropical plant. Moisture, of course, must be present in the soil. In many oases, the water table lies near enough to the surface to be reached by the tree's deeply penetrating root system, but irrigation is often necessary, particularly for seedlings and young plants.

The main area of commercial date production is the valley of the Tigris-Euphrates which supplies 80 per cent. of the dates entering world commerce. The oases strung out across North Africa from El Fayoum to Marrakech are also important producers. Date gardens have been planted in the Coachella Valley, California, although their output is as yet small.

WARM TEMPERATE FRUIT

Citrus

Of the citrus fruit, the orange is by far the most important. It originated in the summer rainfall regions of sub-tropical Asia, but is now most extensively cultivated in countries enjoying a Mediterranean type of climate, where the very warm, brilliantly sunny summers and mild winters (which are nevertheless cool enough to provide the slight check to growth from which the tree benefits), offer an environment which is almost ideal. Summer drought is detrimental to growth, however, and irrigation in Mediterranean regions is essential. California, Spain, Italy, Israel, and the Republic of South Africa are the principal "Mediterranean" producers (Fig. 52). Outside this climatic zone, Florida, Eastern Brazil, the Argentine, and Mexico also produce considerable quantities (Table 38).

While varieties such as the Valencia ripen in summer, the principal orange harvest occurs between November and April in the northern hemisphere, and between May and October in the southern. The Jaffa and Washington Navel are thus on sale in British shops in winter, and the South African "Outspan" in the summer months. Ripe fruit can remain on the tree unharmed for several weeks, and hence the harvest period can be staggered, and the burden on the transport services relieved. Much of the United States' crop is converted into concentrated fruit juice, and the increase in orange production in recent years has been due to the development of this outlet (Table 39).

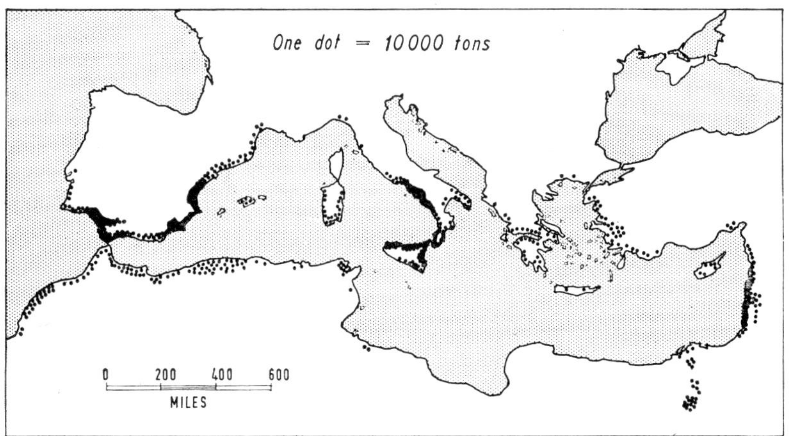

Fig. 52.—Production of Citrus Fruit in the Mediterranean Basin, 1963-4.

Table 38
Production of Citrus Fruit
(in thousands of metric tons)

	1948-9 to 1952-3 (Average)	1963	1964	1965
Oranges				
U.S.A.	4,500	3,709	4,885	5,648
Brazil	1,320	2,280	2,223	2,485
Spain	975	1,976	1,777	1,921
Japan	375	1,113	1,437	1,554
Italy	550	1,066	1,183	1,175
World	12,100	18,500	20,300	21,300
Grapefruit				
U.S.A.	1,470	1,249	1,512	1,718
Turkey	1	182	224	252
World	1,700	1,714	2,051	2,300
Lemons and Limes				
U.S.A.	440	710	551	625
Italy	315	552	621	602
Mexico	70	171	166	168
Argentina	57	79	79	70
World	1,600	2,905	2,855	2,931

Source: *F.A.O. Production Yearbook.*

Mandarin oranges, which include the tangerine, are products of Florida, South Africa, and the countries of Mediterranean Europe. The bitter orange—the *Seville*—is grown principally in southern Spain, and is used in the manufacture of marmalade.

TABLE 39
UTILISATION OF THE U.S. CITRUS CROP
(in thousands of tons, 1963)

	ORANGES	GRAPEFRUIT	LEMONS
Production	3,600	1,220	610
Processed (in total)	2,170	500	300
(i) In California	300	35	260
(ii) In Florida	1,850	440	—
(iii) In other states	20	25	40
Consumed in U.S.A. as fresh fruit	1,305	645	210
Exports	125	75	100

Source: Commonwealth Economic Committee—*Fruit.* H.M.S.O.

Lemons and limes—The lemon requires broadly similar conditions to the orange. However, it is less tolerant of frost, and desiccating heat, and finds coastal situations best suited to its growth. The northern shores of Sicily, the Bay of Naples region, and the area round Los Angeles, where cool on-shore winds reduce day-time temperatures, are of particular importance. In favourable locations the tree bears fruit throughout the year. Lemons are normally gathered when green, and allowed to ripen in conditions of controlled temperature and humidity. The lime is cultivated on a small scale in Mexico, Egypt, southern Florida, and the West Indies. Neither the lemon nor the lime are important as dessert fruits, and consequently production is small when compared with the orange. Like the orange they find use in the manufacture of juice concentrates, soft drinks, flavourings, and medicinal preparations.

Grapefruit—The only commercial grapefruit producing country of any real significance is the U.S.A. Florida and Texas are the leading states. Marketing is complicated by the fact that the crop ripens only in winter while maximum demand coincides with summer heatwaves. This particular problem has to some extent been overcome by the development of the canning industry.

The vine

The Old World Vine, *vitis vinifera*, has been cultivated for thousands of years in the lands surrounding the Mediterranean Sea. It was acclimatised in Western Europe during the early centuries of the Christian era, and introduced to the Americas in the years following the voyages of Columbus. From this species, or from hybrids developed from it, comes most of the world's production of grapes. Because of its susceptibility to disease, particularly when grown in humid climates, resistant American varieties are sometimes cultivated, or used as root stocks on to which *vinifera* species are grafted.

Viticulture is most successful in lands enjoying very warm summers and cool winters. A mean temperature of 18° C.-25° C. (65° F.-77° F.) in summer, and 0° C.-10° C. (32° F.-50° F.) in winter provide the best conditions. The vine tolerates moderate or even severe winter frost, and damage by spring frost can normally be averted by delaying pruning, and thereby the appearance of new, tender shoots until the risk has passed. More than fifteen inches of rain, falling chiefly in winter, and a dry sunny period at harvest time are also necessary for the production of the highest quality fruit. Heavy or prolonged rain, and unseasonably low temperatures late in the season, increase the acid content of the grape and impair its quality. The vintage years of the wine industry are normally years of warm, dry summers. Vines respond well to irrigation in regions of low rainfall, and most of the Californian vineyards are given a light watering in the early months of the year. Irrigation is difficult on the terraced vineyards of southern Europe, and is not generally practised.

Vines are peculiarly sensitive to local variations in temperature, rainfall, sunshine, exposure, and soil. Varieties which do well in one area may fail, or at best produce indifferent quality fruit, in another. Nearly all the raisin grapes of the U.S.A., for example, and half the raisin grapes of the world are grown within a short distance of Fresno in the San Joaquin Valley (California), where a combination of fertile permeable soils, irrigation, very high daytime temperatures and low humidities, and an almost complete absence of rain in September, the harvest month, give conditions as near perfect as the grower could wish for. Southern Greece and Turkey and the Malaga region of southern Spain also possess these advantages, if to a lesser degree, and are likewise major producers of dried grape products. The Fresno region and a small area near Lodi (California) are famous for high quality table grapes. Again, wine grapes have highly localised distributions. Regions, districts, and even specific vineyards are recognised for the individual character of their wines, some of which have attained international reputation. The outstanding wines of Europe—champagne, sherry, and port are made from grapes occupying only a few square miles of territory in their respective regions, and attempts to cultivate these grapes elsewhere have never been entirely successful.

The principal wine producing regions of the world are in southern Europe. Other regions of distinction include the Loire, Burgundy, Bordeaux, Alsace, and the Champagne regions of France; the Rhine and Moselle Valleys of Germany; the hill country of Tuscany, Italy; the valleys within the Cape Ranges of South Africa; the

Algiers Plain; the Hunter Valley of Australia; Central Chile; and the San Francisco district of California (Table 40).

TABLE 40

PRODUCTION OF WINE
(in 100 million litres)

	1948-9 to 1952-3 (Average)	1963	1964	1965
Italy	43·4	53·6	67·0	68·2
France	52·5	57·5	62·4	68·4
Spain	14·9	25·8	34·2	27·6
Argentina	11·6	20·7	19·5	18·3
U.S.S.R.	3·2	11·9	12·7	13·4
U.S.A.	9·0	13·3	11·6	15·1
Portugal	8·0	13·0	13·6	14·8
Algeria	13·5	12·6	10·5	16·3
WORLD	189·0	256·4	283·0	289·1

Source: *F.A.O. Production Yearbook.*

Peaches and apricots

Peaches and apricots find optimum conditions towards the cooler margins of the Mediterranean lands. They are also grown successfully in continental regions where the severity of winter is tempered by large bodies of open water, as along the shores of the lower Great Lakes and the Ontario Peninsula. Of the two trees, the apricot is the more drought-resistant, but the peach, because of its late flowering characteristics, is more tolerant of spring frost. The apricot is a tree of some importance in the semi-arid mountain states of the western U.S.A., and the peach in the Californian Valley. Considerable quantities of both fruits are produced in southern Europe. The canning industries absorb much of the output.

Figs

The Mediterranean lands of southern Europe supply most of the world's figs. Outside Europe, California and Texas are the only important producing regions. If the fruit is destined for the fresh fruit market or the canning industries it can be grown in humid conditions. Figs for drying are more successfully cultivated and processed in semi-arid climates.

Other fruit crops of the warm temperate zone include prunes (plums that can be dried to give a non-perishable product of high sugar content)—the Pacific states of the U.S.A. are the main producers of commercial prunes in the world; pomegranates from the dry areas of South West Asia and North Africa; and the melon. Nuts, especially walnuts and almonds, are also important. Towards the cooler margins of the zone, and also on higher ground within it, cool temperate fruits are cultivated. The olive is described in Chapter V.

COOL TEMPERATE FRUIT

The cool temperate fruits are adapted to conditions of warm, but not hot summers, differing lengths of daylight throughout the year, ample sunshine, especially late in the season, moderate rainfall, and cool or cold winters. Fruiting is absent or weak in the tropics where the length of daylight is constant, and where winters are not cold enough to enforce a period of dormancy.

APPLES—The apple is under cultivation throughout much of the temperate belt. The poleward limits of the crop are set approximately by summer 15° C. (59° F.) isotherm, and by the 100-day frost-free isopleth. The absence of cold winters checks its extension equator-wards at roughly the thirtieth parallel. A moderate rainfall of 20-30 inches is desirable, although excellent crops can be produced by irrigation.

Intensive commercial production is concentrated into many small areas of all West European countries. Italy, West Germany, France, and the United Kingdom are the main producers. The United States accounts for about one third of the commercial production outside the communist world, with Washington, New York, Virginia, Pennsylvania, and California as the leading states. The apple regions of Canada are the Okanagan Valley (British Columbia), the Annapolis Valley (Nova Scotia), and the Ontario Peninsula. Tasmania, Victoria, Central Chile, and the Argentine are important producers in the southern hemisphere (Table 41).

TABLE 41

PRODUCTION OF APPLES
(in thousands of metric tons)

	1948-9 to 1952-3 (Average)	1963	1964	1965
U.S.A.	2,400	2,737	3,031	2,962
France	3,700	2,581	3,424	4,485
Italy	740	2,336	2,381	2,185
Western Germany	1,170	1,941	1,202	1,188
Japan	380	1,155	1,090	1,132
United Kingdom	600	582	740	615
Hungary	60	503	432	379
Spain	290	481	322	450
Canada	300	470	409	455
Austria	340	436	447	222
WORLD	13,400	18,500	19,500	19,200

Source: *F.A.O. Production Yearbook.*

When correctly stored, at temperatures a little above freezing point, late maturing varieties can be kept in good condition for several months, and transported without any particular difficulty to markets remote from the areas of cultivation. Nearly 1·5 million tons of apples enter world trade each year. The fresh fruit market absorbs the bulk of the crop, although the making of cider and of unfermented apple juice is important in Europe and North America.

PEARS—The pear succeeds in broadly similar climatic and soil conditions to the apple, but prefers rather warmer springs and summers, and lower rainfall. It also resists winter frost less successfully, suffering injury if the temperature falls below −30° C. (− 22° F.). World pear production is approximately one quarter of the apple production. Dessert and cooking varieties are the most important, although the perry pear, used in the manufacture of an alcoholic beverage, is grown extensively in France, West Germany, and Switzerland. Large quantities of pears are canned for export in the United States, Australia, and South Africa.

PLUMS—Nearly all countries that produce apples and pears also produce plums. The fruit is cultivated over a wide area in Europe, North America, and Asia. Yugoslavia, Germany, Turkey, and the United States are the leading producing nations. The prune plum is grown in the Pacific states of the U.S.A.

Fruit cultivation in Britain

The rise of an important commercial fruit growing industry in Britain dates from the last century, when developments in the field of transport brought these islands within the orbit of the low-cost grain-producing lands of the Americas and Australia. In certain suitably located regions, arable land was converted to the raising of fruit crops which were relatively immune to foreign competition, and for which there was a growing home demand. Areas well served by communications and possessing suitable soils and favourable climates became important.

To-day, some 280,000 acres are under fruit in the British Isles (Fig. 53). Large commercial orchards are confined to a few parts of the country, and while each fruit growing area is responsible for a considerable range of products, there is also a marked degree of specialisation. Apples are of greatest importance in mid- and north Kent, and in the Vale of Evesham; the Vale of Evesham also leads in the output of plums; cider apples are grown principally in Devon, Somerset, and on the Hereford Plain; hops are concentrated in Kent and Worcestershire; and soft fruit is a speciality of the area round Wisbech in the Fens, and on the Carse of Gowrie. The Carse of Gowrie is the most northerly commercial fruit growing region in the British Isles and concentrates, significantly, on the raspberry—a crop that flowers late and matures early, and which is therefore well suited to a region of late frosts and cool summers.

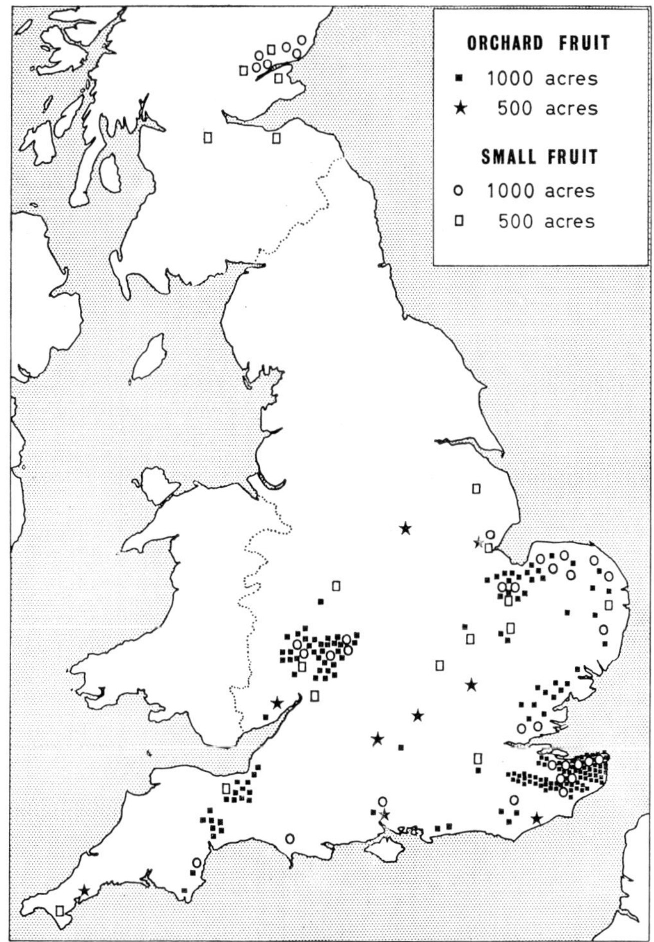

Fig. 53.—Distribution of Orchard Fruit in Great Britain.

MARKET GARDENING

The occupation of market gardening is concerned with the production of kitchen vegetables, and sometimes flowers, for sale in urban centres. It is often combined with fruit cultivation, on the one hand, and with arable farming on the other. A common practice in the Vale of Evesham, for instance, is to interplant apple and plum trees with bush fruit and vegetables, and a frequent rotation on the Plain of south-west Lancashire is winter wheat, followed by early potatoes, followed in turn by spring cabbage.

Characteristically, market gardens are small, sited on light, free-draining soils that are not necessarily of high natural fertility, but which have been heavily manured and fertilised. They are also commonly found occupying land near large centres of population, as their products tend to be bulky, and very perishable. Most of the cities of Britain are surrounded by a zone of market gardens located within, or just beyond, their outer suburbs. The truck farming areas of the sandy coastal belt of New Jersey occupy a similar position in relation to New York and Philadelphia. More remote regions have sometimes grown to importance where they have been favoured by good transport services, or have possessed outstanding environmental advantages such as mild winters and exceptionally early springs. The Penzance area, the Isles of Scilly, and the Channel Islands of Britain; the Imperial Valley and the Gulf Coast lowlands of the United States; and the coastal plains of Algeria are examples.

On market gardens in mild climates, cropping is continuous throughout the year. Extensive use is made of greenhouses, cloches, and frames to bring on seedlings prior to transplanting them in the open. A few crops are grown exclusively under glass, *e.g.* the tomato, which occupies half of the 4,000 acres under greenhouses in this country.

Market garden cultivation is very intensive. Field work is often mechanised, but a heavy demand is also made upon labour, and operating costs are high. The aim must be to produce a heavy crop as early in the season as possible when prices are favourable to the grower. High-yielding, disease-resistant, and early-maturing characteristics, however, are often rated above the quality and flavour of the fruit. Successful marketing also depends as much on appearance, form, and attractive packaging as on the eating or cooking qualities of the product, which in any case the customer finds less easy to appraise, at least until he has parted with his money. With high production costs, and present-day consumer preferences, it is often more lucrative to grow fruit and vegetables that *look* like choice strawberries, tomatoes, potatoes, etc., rather than products which *taste* like them.

CHAPTER IX

AGRICULTURAL PRODUCTS
V—ANIMALS AND ANIMAL PRODUCTS

CATTLE

Cattle of one type or other (the term, it should be noted, includes the Indian buffalo, the humped Zebu and Afrikander cattle of Asia and Africa, and the yak, as well as the common European beef and dairy breeds) are kept in almost every country of the world for milk, meat, hides, or as draught animals. They are of greatest economic importance in the temperate lands of Europe and the Americas, although the largest numbers are found in India (Fig. 54).

In the commercial cattle rearing countries European breeds predominate. The Jersey, Guernsey, and Ayrshire are common in many dairy farming regions. Of the beef types, the Hereford, Aberdeen Angus, and the Beef Shorthorn, all of which originated in Britain, have now spread across the world. The Charolais, the most important French beef breed, is being introduced into a number of countries for crossing with stock of European, and sometimes of Asian, origin. Increasing interest is now being shown in dual purpose animals such as the Friesian, Dairy Shorthorn, and Red Poll. The cows of these breeds give a high yield of milk, whilst the bull calves can be fattened to produce excellent quality beef. This development is bringing about a closer economic association between the dairying and beef growing industries than existed formerly. The two enterprises still remain geographically separated, however, each being influenced by a different set of factors. It is therefore appropriate to consider each in turn.

Characteristics of dairy farming

1. Dairy farms are engaged in the production of milk for sale in liquid form, or for processing into condensed milk, cheese, and butter. Only a few farmers combine milk and beef production, although many dairy farmers run pigs and poultry on their land.

2. A dairy herd needs to be fed liberally throughout the year. The best and cheapest food is grass, grazed either directly from permanent or temporary pastures, or harvested, stored, and consumed as hay or silage. The quality of the pastures is determined by the

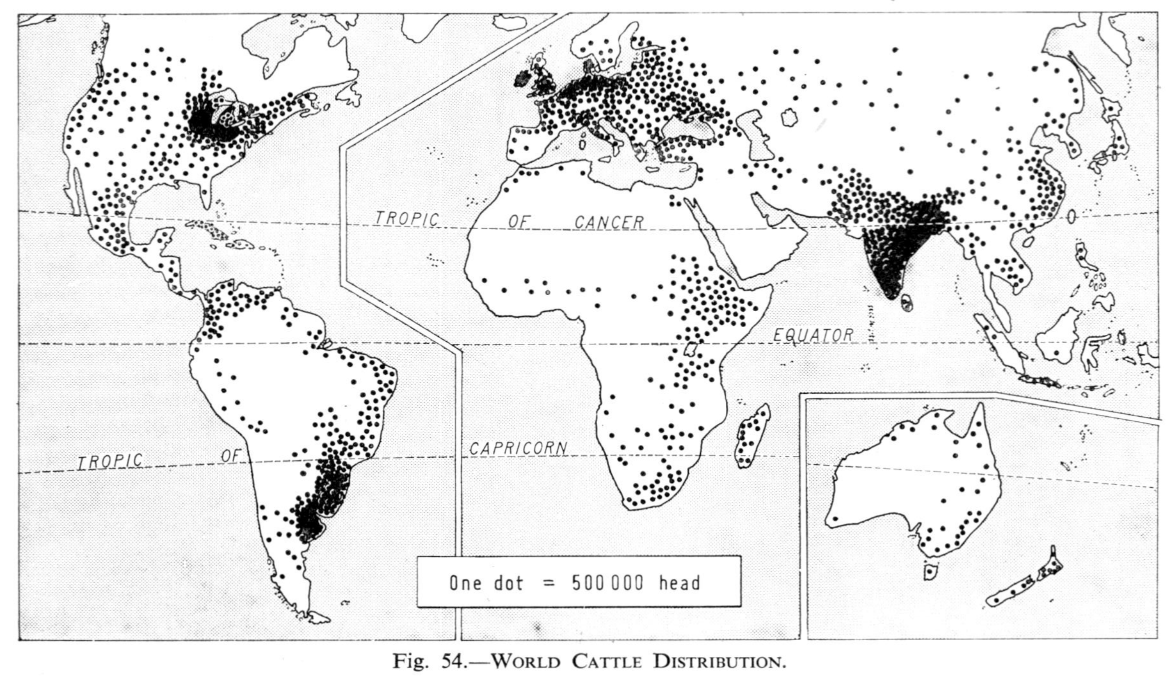

Fig. 54.—World Cattle Distribution.

grasses, herbs, and leguminous plants that comprise it, the management it receives, and upon factors of soil and climate. The best pastures are found on moisture-retentive lowland soils, in mild regions receiving a moderate or heavy rainfall distributed evenly throughout the year. Such regions were formerly forested, and the grasses have invariably been sown. Many pastures in Britain have been in position for so long that the term *permanent pasture* is appropriate. However, since the Second World War the advantages of the temporary grassland or *ley* have been realised. In predominantly arable areas, the ley takes a place as a rotation crop in a cycle of cereals, pulses, roots, and brassicas, and may occupy the land for only a few months. In pastoral regions, on the other hand, it becomes a semi-permanent feature of the farm, and is renewed perhaps every three, six, or ten years. In other words the length of the ley depends on the pattern of farm economy in which it has to fit.

3. The aim of the dairy farming industry is to produce, as far as possible, a steady yield of milk throughout the year, or, if demand fluctuates seasonally, as it does near large tourist centres, to ensure, again as far as possible, that the period of maximum yields corresponds to the season of peak demand. Output of milk unfortunately cannot be regulated like the production of a manufactured article. Unfortunately, too, liquid milk is a highly perishable commodity that cannot easily be stored. Under natural conditions in a cool temperate climate it is most plentiful in late spring when there is a vigorous growth of new grass, and scarce in winter when grazing is difficult. Winter production of milk, therefore, depends upon supplementary feeding, and as the supplementary feedstuffs—peas, beans, kale, roots, sugar beet tops, and grains—are normally produced to-day more cheaply on the farm than purchased, the majority of dairy farmers find themselves involved in cultivation as well. Autumn and winter calving also assist in maintaining a high yield of winter milk.

4. Efficient transport is essential to a prosperous dairying industry. All the major liquid milk producing regions of Britain—Ayrshire, the Solway Plain, the Fylde, the Cheshire Plain, the West Midlands, the Vale of North Wiltshire, and the Plain of Somerset, are situated within a few hours' trunk road or rail distance of a large urban market (Fig. 55). Local as well as trunk transport is important, and a farmer at the end of a narrow, rutted lane, impassable by motor truck, is likely to find his vocation in pig and poultry keeping rather than in milk production. Cheese, butter, and condensed milk products are made in factories throughout Britain during the summer

months when milk output is in excess of the volume that can be absorbed by the liquid milk market, but it is in regions which are physically suited to dairy farming, but which are handicapped by relative isolation from major centres of population, that the manufacture of such products assumes the greatest importance. Thus

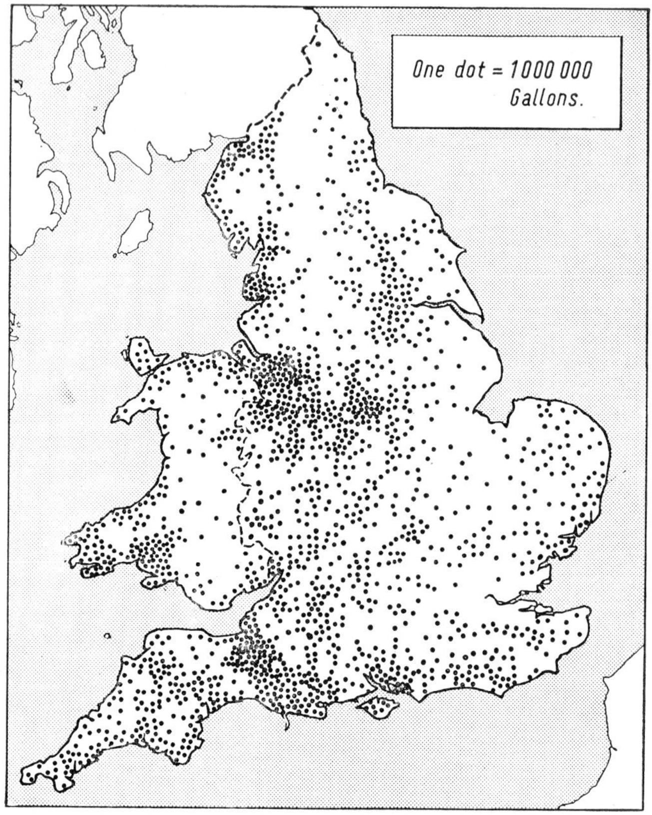

Fig. 55.—PRODUCTION OF MILK IN ENGLAND AND WALES.

Australia and New Zealand convert some 80 per cent. of their milk into non-perishable and easily transportable commodities.

5. Dairy farms are usually smaller than arable farms, and very much smaller than farms devoted to sheep and beef cattle rearing. Dairying is primarily an activity of fertile, well-watered lowlands

near towns where competition for land is great. It is an intensive type of farming, in which the viable economic unit need not be large. The practice of buying in at least some of the feedstuff ration allows

Fig. 56.—DISTRIBUTION OF CATTLE (ALL TYPES) IN THE BRITISH ISLES.

more animals to be kept than would be possible if they were supported entirely by the farm on which they were housed. The fact that dairy cattle have to be rounded up for milking twice a day also limits the area over which they can be effectively grazed.

6. In certain mountainous regions, *e.g.* the European Alps, valley pastures are restricted, but excellent summer grazings occur at heights of up to a few thousand feet above the valley floors.

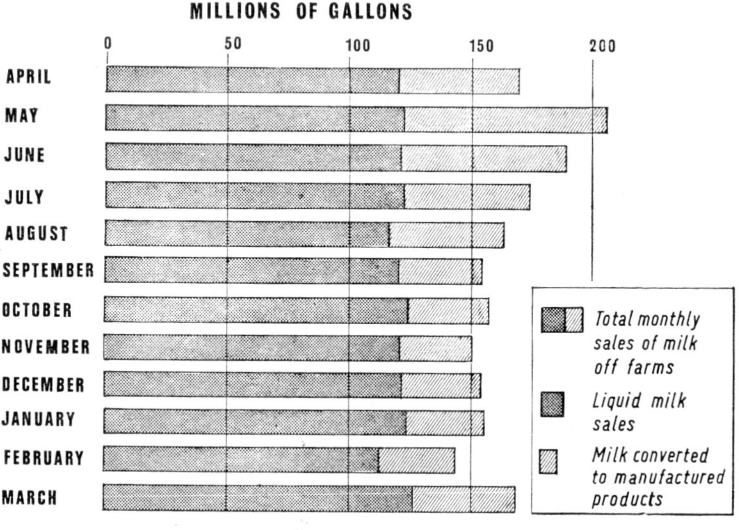

Fig. 57.—Production and Utilisation of Milk in England and Wales. (April, 1964—March, 1965.)

Total sales of milk off farms = 1,990. Converted into manufactured products 527, of which cheese, 217; butter, 68; condensed milk, 91; fresh cream 90; milk powder, 38 (all quantities in millions of gallons).

Note (i) the remarkably steady demand for liquid milk, minor fluctuations in which can be largely accounted for by variations in the length of the months (*e.g.* February), (ii) the slight fall in demand in August during the school holidays.

These conditions induce a regular migration of both animals and men to the mountain grasslands in spring, and a return to the shelter of the valleys in autumn—a practice known as *transhumance.* The difficulty of marketing fresh milk produced on inaccessible Alpine slopes is overcome by converting it into butter and cheese on the upland farm. The use of small diameter plastic pipes for transporting milk to central creameries in the valleys is a recent development with a promising future.

The main milk-producing countries are indicated in Table 42. After allowance has been made for the fact that these countries vary enormously in size, it is clear that the principal dairy farming regions lie not only in the better watered parts of the temperate belt, but also in regions where living standards are high. There is a notable absence of milk production in the monsoon countries (where land is too valuable for the pasturing of animals), in the Mediterranean Basin (where grasses are poor), and in the hot wet tropics (where indifferent pastures, disease, and the difficulty of keeping milk fresh even for a few hours are inimical to the development of dairy farming on anything but a minor scale).

TABLE 42

PRODUCTION OF COW MILK IN SELECTED COUNTRIES (1963)

	Production (000 metric tons)	Production per thousand of the population (metric tons)
Western Europe		
France	25,300	535
West Germany	20,700	375
United Kingdom	12,600	240
Netherlands	7,000	580
Northern Europe		
Denmark	5,100	1,085
Sweden	3,800	500
Finland	3,800	825
Norway	1,700	495
Mediterranean Basin		
Italy	8,500	160
Spain	2,400	78
Greece	400	47
Israel	325	130
North America		
United States	56,600	290
Canada	8,350	440
Tropical Africa		
Mali	690	140
Kenya	250	27
Ethiopia	32	1·5
Congo (Leopoldville)	12	0·8
Monsoon Asia		
India	8,500*	20
Pakistan	2,600	26
Japan	2,100	22
Malaysia	16	1·5

* 1961.

Source: *F.A.O. Production Yearbook.*

Cattle rearing for beef

The production of beef is generally undertaken in two quite distinct, but inter-related stages:

(i) The raising of store cattle.

(ii) The subsequent fattening of the stores in preparation for market.

Raising and fattening are commonly carried on in regions widely separated geographically, although sometimes they are combined under the same management on a single farm. Where the "integrated" beef farm is found, as for example in north-east Scotland and the Border counties, different kinds of pasture support the growing and fattening animals.

Cattle raising is not an economic proposition on fertile, accessible land, as growing cattle cannot utilise fully the crops, including grass, that such land is able to produce. Highly productive country is much more likely to be used for cash cropping, dairying, or beef fattening. By contrast, cattle raising is often the most profitable enterprise on land that does not repay the cost of cultivation. Uncultivable land is plentiful on the flanks of the high ground in the north and west of Britain, on the uplands of Western Europe, on the Irish Plain, and on the temperate grasslands of both hemispheres. The tropical savanas also have extensive grazing areas, but these are regions where cattle farming is beset by particular difficulties. The savanas are described below (p. 185).

Store cattle are normally raised on poor pastures until about eighteen months to two years old, and are wintered out of doors. For some reason, not fully understood, cattle reared in rough conditions fatten more readily when put on to rich land than those reared in more congenial surroundings. Grass, harvested by the animals themselves, is the most economical feedstuff, and suffices provided its growth is not too severely checked by cold or drought. Supplementary winter feed in the form of hay, silage, swedes, mangolds, etc., is generally necessary in Britain, even in the mildest areas. On the Great Plains of North America, and other regions where winters can be severe and drought is a recurring problem, the establishment of small irrigated areas throughout the range on which supplementary feed can be grown, helps to prevent loss of condition among the stock during adverse weather, and increases substantially the number of animals that can be safely kept.

Cattle-fattening regions—Movement is an outstanding feature of the beef-growing industry, and each year millions of cattle make the journey from the raising grounds to the fattening areas. In the British Isles they are shipped from the northern and western areas, and from Ireland to the rich permanent pastures of the English Midlands, and to the arable lands of East Anglia, East Yorkshire, and East Scotland. On arable cash farms cattle consume roots, rotation grasses, sugar beet tops, and other farm wastes, and provide valuable manure.

The main cattle-fattening region of the world is the Corn Belt of North America, where stores from the western ranges and animals bred and reared in the Corn Belt itself keep company with a vast number of pigs and poultry prior to dispatch to the slaughterhouses and meat factories in Chicago and other Mid-West centres. Situated in the heart of the U.S.A., and served by an excellent network of roads and railways, the Mid-West farmer has access to the greater part of the national market. From the Corn Belt, too, go exports of meat and meat products worth many million dollars to the rest of the world.

The South American counterpart of the Corn Belt is the humid Pampas. Cultivated alfalfa pastures are employed here to condition the animals. In spite of the Argentinians' liking for beef (they consume 200 lb. per head per year—nearly twice as much as the people of any other country) there remains a large surplus for shipment abroad. This leaves the country as chilled, frozen, or canned meat, or as meat extract. The principal market is the United Kingdom.

Other beef exporting countries are New Zealand, France, Denmark, Yugoslavia, Uruguay, and Ireland (Table 44).

TABLE 43

PRODUCTION OF BEEF FROM INDIGENOUS ANIMALS
(in thousands of metric tons)

	1948-52 (Average)	1963	1964	1965
U.S.A.	4,780	7,887	8,838	8,952
Argentina	1,970	2,663	2,056	2,160
France	950	1,661	1,587	1,600
Brazil	1,090	1,361	1,437	1,450
Federal Germany	520	1,101	1,058	958
United Kingdom	565	966	937	881
Australia	625	1,003	1,025	906
WORLD	20,900	32,200	32,400	32,900

Source: *F.A.O. Production Yearbook.*

The savanas—problems and prospects

The tropical savanas extend over millions of square miles of Africa, South America, and Australia, and occupy a position on the

TABLE 44

PRINCIPAL BEEF* EXPORTING COUNTRIES
(in thousands of metric tons)

	1959	1962	1965
Argentina	345	390	349
Australia	230	205	321
New Zealand	90	118	121
France	30	155	65
Denmark	60	75	63
Yugoslavia	8	64	66
Uruguay	22	55	65
Ireland	35	60	55
Netherlands	28	36	71
WORLD	975	1,340	1,450

* Fresh, chilled or frozen.

Source: *F.A.O. Trade Yearbook.*

poleward side of the rain forests. There are also extensive savana tracts in southern and South East Asia, the Caribbean and Central America, and in the basin of the Congo, where rainfall totals might lead one to expect forest. Whether these grasslands represent a climax or merely secondary plant association is not of immediate interest: it is sufficient to note that they are more extensively distributed than any other vegetation type within the tropics, and that evidence suggests that they are spreading.

Where characteristically developed, the savanas consist of tall, exceptionally coarse seasonal grasses that are palatable to stock for a few weeks during the flush of new growth, but that become parched and brittle in the dry season, which may last for as long as eight months. Trees are common, and grow singly, in clumps, or in ribbons along water courses.

For many reasons the economic development of these grasslands is retarded. Cultivation is generally rudimentary, and stock rearing —the most important activity, and the one to which the regions are best suited by nature—is practised only on an extensive basis. Nomadic herding still persists in parts of the African continent. Cattle are all too frequently under-nourished and slow-maturing. Hides are generally a more valuable product than beef. Disease is rampant over wide areas, and is proving almost impossible to eradicate because ranges are unfenced. Australia suffers least from animal diseases, partly because there were no indigenous cattle on the continent that could spread infection among introduced European breeds, and also because in recent years the import of live cattle, a possible source of fresh infection, has been prohibited. These factors, however, have not prevented tick fever, pleuro-pneumonia, and tuberculosis becoming serious problems in the north. Tick fever and foot-and-mouth disease are prevalent in South America. Almost all the illnesses that cattle are heir to afflict herds in tropical Africa. Among the most serious are rinderpest and trypanosomiasis. The latter, spread by the tsetse fly, is endemic over some 4 million square miles of forest and grassland wherever trees and bushes provide shade. European cattle are particularly subject to attack by insect-borne disease, although native cattle have acquired a degree of immunity. Hope for the future lies in the fact that zebu cattle from India, when crossed with native breeds, produce stock which are comparatively disease-resistant, and at the same time give fair-quality beef.

The up-grading of stock is made extremely difficult by the practice—almost universal on the savanas of all continents—of grazing herds on the open range. Half-wild, intractable beasts roam the grasslands, breeding indiscriminately and spreading infection. From time to time they are rounded up for dispatch to the slaughter houses. The location of the grazing grounds at great distances from important consuming centres or from exporting ports, and the inadequacy of road and rail communications, often leaves the graziers with no other alternative than to drive the animals to market on foot. On arrival, their condition rarely attracts the attention of discriminating buyers.

The problem of delivering animals in prime condition to the meat factories could be solved in two ways; first by constructing an all-weather road network to link grazing areas with markets, and secondly by increasing substantially the area of irrigated pasture on which cattle could be conditioned prior to slaughter—a development that would involve a much closer association between the rancher and the cultivator than has hitherto existed. Some progress has already been made along these lines in Venezuela, where oil revenues are being put to good use; and in West Australia where the Ord River has been dammed, and may eventually irrigate 200,000 acres of country now plagued by drought. Some fattening is also done on mixed farms in the wheat belt and on the Queensland coast. The possibility of using aircraft to lift cattle to the coast is also being explored in Australia.

Unimproved savana has a very low carrying capacity—perhaps one animal to every fifty acres on the better land. Range improvement is still in the early experimental stage. The problem of providing water can be acute, and frequently results in serious overgrazing near streams and water holes, and under-utilisation of pastures where drinking water is unobtainable. The enclosure of the range land, and the sub-division of enclosed areas into paddocks with watering points in each, would increase the area of accessible pasture, and would also permit some form of rotational grazing to be practised.

The future of the savanas as beef-producing regions depends on the extent to which capital can be made available to overcome their natural handicaps of drought, disease, and isolation. The upgrading of herds, the construction of fences, bore holes, irrigation works, all-weather roads and railways, port installations, and meat factories—all of which are measures necessary to the success of any major development project—are not undertaken cheaply, and are far beyond the means of individuals. If the savanas are ever developed to their full potential it will be through the intervention of national or international agencies. Private capital is unlikely to be attracted to schemes which by their very nature are long-term and slow to produce results. At present, the returns on investment in beef production in the temperate lands are greater than in the tropics, and progress in the savanas is likely to be slow and faltering until the problem of feeding the growing world population forces attention upon these difficult regions.

India

The fact is often overlooked that India harbours a quarter of the world's cattle. Cattle are found in every inhabited corner of the country, and as they are kept mainly for draught purposes on farms, their distribution corresponds closely to the distribution of the rural population. The humped zebu breeds are commonest in the dry regions, whilst the water buffalo predominates in the rice lands of the Ganges Delta and the south east.

To the Hindu, cattle are sacred. To the European, they appear as one of the scourges of the sub-continent that is hindering its development. Many of the creatures through age, disease, or sheer starvation are too weak to work or to produce milk. Their meat, even if the Hindu could be persuaded to eat it, would be scarcely worth preparing. It is little wonder that the cow is of more value dead than alive, for when eventually it does expire, its hide becomes a product of some commercial importance. Twenty-five million cow and buffalo hides are produced annually.

There is little permanent pasture in India, and, as almost every available acre must be devoted to the cultivation of crops for the expanding population, the peasant can hardly be expected to sense the urgency of growing feed for his animals. Hence they are obliged to forage among wayside verges, harvested wheat and rice fields, and town garbage. And yet, when given proper attention, the zebu cattle have proved themselves to be useful and adaptable animals, well suited to tropical and sub-tropical environments. They are used in parts of Africa and South America to improve native beef herds, and in the Gulf States of the U.S.A. for crossing with breeds raised elsewhere in the country, in order to produce animals better able to withstand the hot humid climate of the South. On a few government farms in India they have given promising results as milkers. India would be well rid of at least half her cattle: the survivors might then have a chance of making a worthwhile contribution to the nation's economy.

SHEEP

There are approximately 1,000 million sheep in the world to-day—one to every three human beings. Sheep are more widely distributed than any other domestic animal. Their range is obviously limited by the extent of the world's natural and artificial grasslands, but otherwise one breed or other has been introduced into almost every type of environment. Only the hot wet tropics, and the very cold lands, have proved to be unsuitable (Fig. 58). Sheep can subsist where most other animals would starve. They are found in North Africa where the rainfall is five inches per year, and in Snowdonia where it approaches 200 inches. They are equally at home in rugged mountain country and on open plains. Large areas in Australia, southern Africa, South America, western Asia, the Mediterranean lands of Europe, and even the British Isles would have little economic value if it were not for the sheep. Furthermore, wool is easily stored and transported, and the development of refrigeration has solved the problem of the shipment of mutton and lamb to distant markets. Remoteness therefore is not a limiting factor in commercial sheep farming.

Major sheep rearing countries of the world

THE UNITED KINGDOM—The sheep density in the United Kingdom is greater than in any nation in the world, with the single exception of New Zealand. Sheep are kept in every part of the country, but the greatest numbers are found in the upland regions of the north and west (Fig. 59). Over the Highlands and Uplands of Scotland, the Lake District, the northern Pennines, the plateau of Wales, and the moorlands of the South West Peninsula, a combination of heavy rainfall, steep slopes, thin, leached soils, and remoteness from major centres of population, generally preclude cropping, and the intensive pasturing of animals. These regions are the domains of the mountain breeds of sheep—the Scottish Blackface of the Highlands, the

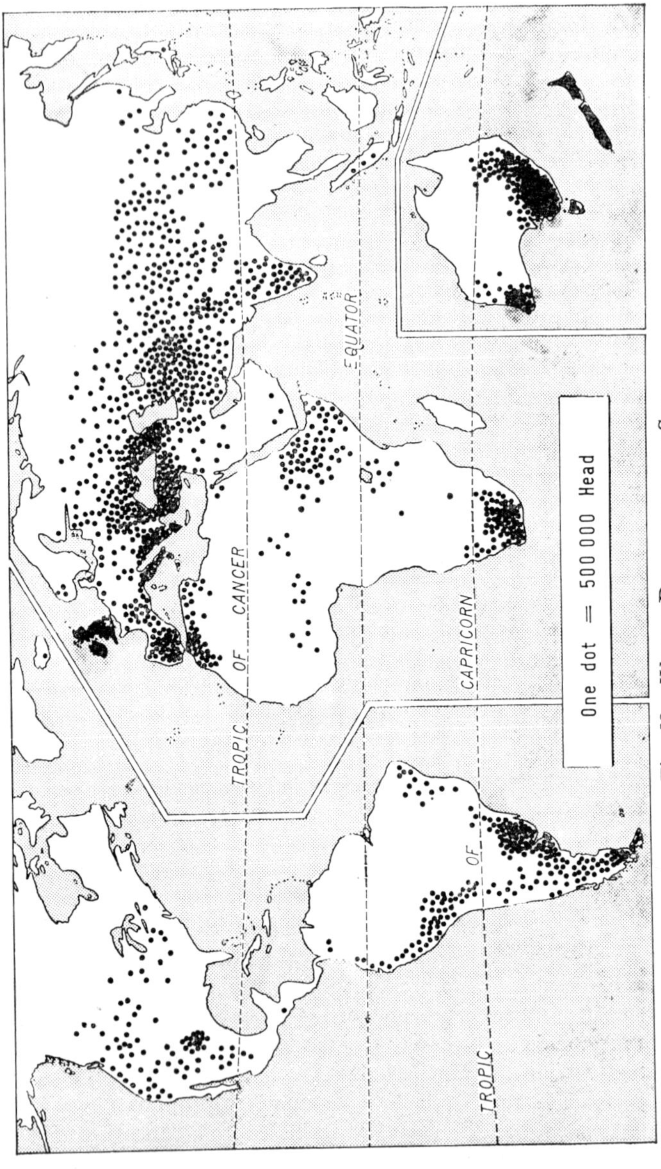

One dot = 500 000 Head

Fig. 58.—World Distribution of Sheep.

Cheviots of the Border Counties, the Herdwick of the Lake District, the Welsh Mountain of Snowdonia, and the Gritstone of the Pennines—sheep which over the centuries have become acclimatised to

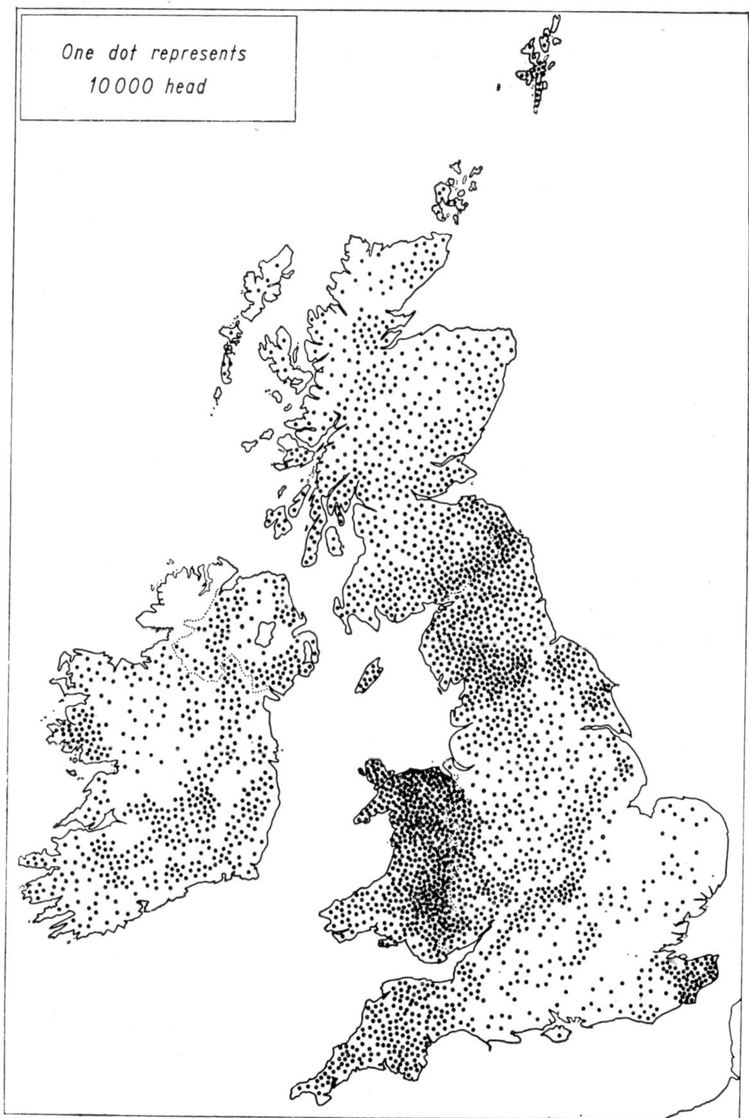

Fig. 59.—Distribution of Sheep in the British Isles.

mountain and moorland conditions, and whose hardiness and adaptability allow them not only to survive but to utilise profitably large tracts of these islands that would otherwise go unused.

Upland grazings vary considerably in quality. Limestone pastures are generally superior to those developed on sandstones, shales, or volcanic rocks. The steeper, better drained lower mountain slopes, on which sheep's fescue (*Festuca ovina*) and the bent grasses (*Agrostis tenuis* and *A. alba*) thrive, provide good sheep runs, but are inferior to the alluvial pastures of the valleys. Purple moor grass (*Molinia coerulea*) is widespread on the higher and reasonably well-drained peat areas, and is extensively grazed in spring, but is of little value for the rest of the year. Mat grass (*Nardus stricta*) is common on poorly drained slopes, but is unpalatable except when young, and is deficient in essential minerals. The cotton-grass moors are of little use, and bracken-infested slopes are worthless. There has been a considerable extension of bracken during the last century in some upland areas, following the displacement of cattle from the mountains by sheep. Cattle keep bracken in check by eating and trampling the young shoots; sheep on the other hand avoid bracken, even when it is young, and concentrate instead on the finer grasses which are thereby over-grazed and weakened. Mat grass, which is eaten infrequently by sheep, is also tending to colonise heavily-grazed *Festuca-Agrostis* pastures. Heather provides useful grazing, and in the winter it may be the only forage available.

On any mountain there is apt to be a wide gap between the amount of food available in summer and winter. Hence particular significance attaches to the alluvial pastures which provide winter feed and shelter. The importance of the valleys in the hill farm economy accounts for the objections raised by farmers to any proposals to use them as sites for reservoirs. Without the bottom land the value of the slopes is reduced. Lambs are wintered in the valleys, or on farms in the adjacent plains. The Solway Plain, the Lleyn Peninsula, and the shores of Cardigan Bay are among the regions which offer wintering facilities for sheep.

Sheep farming on the lowlands—In the hills, sheep farming may be the only enterprise. Its object is to maintain the breeding stock and to provide lambs for fattening on lowland farms. Some mutton is produced, but its importance is declining. The wool clip is generally a sideline in Britain. Both breeding and fattening are undertaken on lowland farms, but here sheep rearing has to compete directly with dairy farming and crop production. On good land the return per acre will be much lower from sheep than from cattle and crops, and sheep gain a foothold on the lowland farm only as a part of the general farm economy. They are used, for instance, to graze down cattle pastures, and to dispose of sugar beet tops and other farm wastes. The emphasis placed on milk production during the Second World War resulted in a marked decline in the importance of lowland sheep farming from which it has not recovered. On the lighter chalk lands of the south-east, the extensive sheep runs of thirty years ago have been reduced in number, and the practice of folding sheep on kale and root crops has now largely disappeared. Much of the natural grassland of the Downs has been ploughed, and an arable-dairying economy has evolved to replace in part the traditional arable-sheep economy of the region.

Australia

Australia has the largest sheep-rearing industry in the world, but in contrast to the United Kingdom conditions in that country favour the production of wool rather than fat lamb and mutton (Tables 45 and 46). Australia produces nearly two-thirds of the world's apparel wool, and normally exports 90 per cent. of her wool clip.

The basis of the wool-growing industry is the flock of 110 million merinos which grazes with a minimum of attention on the dry downlands and plains to the west of the Eastern Highlands and in Western Australia (Fig. 60). These regions experience a mean annual temperature of between 13° C. and 20° C. (55° F. and 68° F.) and a rainfall of fifteen to thirty inches per year. They support a cover of short grasses and drought-resistant shrubs and bushes of the eucalyptus family. The merino also succeeds in the mulga scrub and salt bush country of the desert margins. The carrying capacity of these lands is low, however, and the weight of the fleeces obtained (about five pounds per animal) is only about half the average from the better watered parts of the continent. The coarse, tropical grasses of the north are unsuitable. The merino has never been successfully acclimatised to moist regions, and in the higher rainfall sections of the south east, on irrigated lands, and also to some extent in the wheat zones, crossbred sheep are reared and fattened for their meat. There are few sheep of any kind on the eastern coastal strip where a heavier and more evenly distributed rainfall, and denser human settlement, induce a more intensive form of land utilisation.

Considerably more than half the Australian flocks are run on "stations" operated by graziers whose sole concern is sheep. The remainder are owned by farmers to whom sheep rearing is a complementary enterprise to cultivation, particularly wheat cultivation.

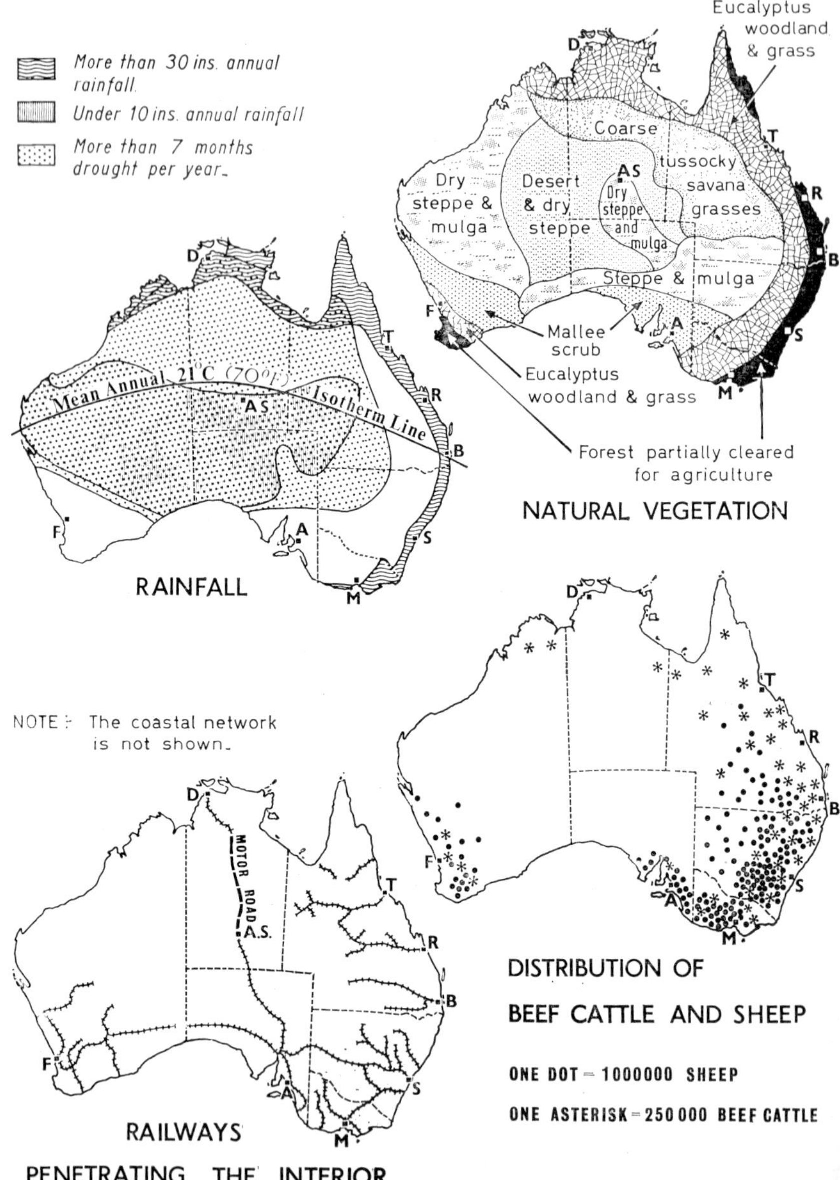

Fig. 60.—The Geographical Bases of the Australian Pastoral Industries.

Sheep stations increase in size and relative importance towards the interior where agriculture becomes more and more precarious because of low and uncertain rainfall. The interior too, is badly served by surface transport, a handicap from which wool production suffers less than most farming activities.

Sheep rearing in central Australia is beset by many problems. Two of the most serious are drought, which periodically grips the plains, and fluctuating wool prices. Over the latter the grazier has little direct control, but by wise management he can often mitigate the worst effects of a prolonged spell without rain. The first principle of sound livestock husbandry must be to restrict the number of animals to the grazing capacity of the land in poor seasons, and to resist the temptation to over-stock in good years when pastures are abundant. On the better-run sheep stations, the land is divided into paddocks (fenced enclosures of several thousand acres) which are grazed in rotation. This practice helps to prevent damage to the range grasses, and allows some of the land to be held in reserve for use when the rains fail. High labour costs generally preclude the making and storage of hay and silage, although in the few cases where it has been done it has helped to save the lives of thousands of animals during prolonged drought.

Pests, especially those which compete with sheep for the limited pastures, are another problem. Since its introduction by early settlers, the rabbit has become an unqualified nuisance, particularly in the south-east. Myxomatosis reduced the rabbit population in the early 1950s, but ten years later numbers were increasing again. Kangaroos and wallabies, also browsing animals, are a menace in some thinly settled areas.

As on cattle ranches, the effective grazing area is determined not so much by the abundance of the pastures as by the number and spacing of water holes. A sheep is unable to travel more than about three miles from drinking water, and in hot weather the distance is less than this. Perennial streams and natural water holes are uncommon, and the grazier must rely to a large degree on artesian and sub-artesian water. It does not follow, of course, that water is necessarily available at the surface because an artesian basin is indicated on a small-scale map.

New Zealand

Wool, sheep skins, mutton, and lamb together account for almost three fifths of the value of New Zealand's foreign trade. The country is the largest exporter in the world of frozen mutton and lamb. For fat lamb production, New Zealand enjoys the advantages of a moderate to heavy, well-distributed rainfall, equable temperatures, good pastures, and an arable farming economy geared to livestock fattening rather than to cash cropping. The proximity of the fattening grounds to ocean transport is an additional asset, as the bulk of the mutton and lamb production is exported to distant markets.

English breeds predominate, and hill and lowland farms are complementary units in an integrated economy, as in Britain. Mixed farms depend upon the uplands for breeding stock and lambs for fattening, and there is an annual movement of animals from the rough grazings of the interior to the lower valleys, and to the Canterbury Plains. Many hill grazings have also been improved by sowing fertilisers and clover seed from the air, and lamb fattening is now possible in the foot hills, if not in the mountains themselves.

The hill and mixed farms produce both wool and meat. The proportion of wool to meat varies from year to year according to prevailing prices. On the tussock grass country, however, the merino is the principal breed kept, and meat production is of minor importance. The tussock region, which runs the full length of South Island along the leeward slopes of the Southern Alps, affords at best poor grazing land, supporting about one sheep per four acres. It is divided into huge ranches which equal in size some of the sheep stations of central Australia. The tussock country is a problem area. Erosion is active on the steeper slopes, and the region's usefulness, which has never been great, is declining. Its potential as merino country is recognised, however, and conservation measures now being planned by the government are directed towards increasing its sheep-bearing capacity.

Southern Africa

South of the Limpopo, the savanas of southern Africa are gradually replaced, first by the temperate grassland of the High Veld, and then westwards and southwards in the direction of decreasing rainfall by drought-resistant shrubs and bushes of the karroos. Southwards again, among the drier valleys and depressions of the Cape Ranges, a similar type of karroo vegetation prevails.

These scrub lands are among the poorest, agriculturally, of the Republic of South Africa. They are characterised by extremes of temperature, a low and uncertain rainfall averaging between five and fifteen inches per year, a general absence of surface water except in some valley sections of the Cape Ranges where irrigation and intensive farming become possible, poor soils, sparse human settlement, and long and difficult lines of communication with the outside world. They are predominantly grazing regions, and support the great majority of the country's 38 million sheep. Wool breeds are reared almost exclusively, with the merino predominant. Farms are very large, and are based largely on water holes. The karroo-type vegetation affords excellent browsing for sheep, but its carrying capacity is very low. An important enterprise in the Republic and in South West Africa is the breeding of karakul lambs. These are valued for their pelts of tightly curled, hard-wearing wool which are marketed as Persian lambskins. Several million pelts are produced annually from one- to three-day-old animals.

The U.S.A.

Between the Coast Mountains of the Pacific and a line drawn from central Montana, through Nebraska into western Texas, extends a vast, physically diversified land of plains, mountains, plateaus, inter-montane depressions, and valleys. In this region exposed mountain slopes are well watered and forested, and favoured valley floors have the benefit of dependable irrigation water, and are intensively cropped. Over the greater part of the West, however, conditions of low and precarious rainfall and high evaporation rates prevail. The vegetation is at best steppe, and at worst desert scrub. Orthodox cultivation practices are difficult and dangerous, and often impossible.

Grain farmers have been tempted during periods of high prices and years of more than average rainfall to plough the grasslands, only to be driven out by drought and dust storms. In a few areas they have managed to settle, and by carefully contrived dry-farming techniques have produced crops of wheat without destroying the top soil. But over the greater part of the region, livestock ranching is the only possible activity. Sheep are kept in every state of the West. In mountainous districts, *transhumance*, or the seasonal movement of animals to summer upland pastures, is well developed. The climate is generally mild enough for outdoor grazing in winter, and the valleys are normally clear of deep snow. On many ranches, supplementary feed is provided from irrigated meadows. High-quality wool and mutton sheep are raised, and there is an annual shipment of lambs to the fattening grounds of the Maize Belt.

Southern South America

Another great region of temperate grassland extends from Rio Grande do Sul state, through Uruguay and the Argentine, to the southern tip of the continent. The most favoured sub-regions are the flat Argentine Pampas and the low rolling uplands of Uruguay.

Here rainfall exceeds thirty inches per year, drought is rare (but not unknown), and temperatures remain high enough throughout the year to permit the continuous growth of tall prairie grasses.

The increase in the area under crops and the growing popularity of sown alfalfa pastures, which sheep damage by close grazing, has resulted in a decline in the numbers of sheep on the Pampas. Sheep are still more numerous on the Pampas, however, than elsewhere in the Argentine. Large flocks are also tended on both natural and artificial pastures in Uruguay and Rio Grande do Sul. More than half the sheep in Brazil are found in Rio Grande do Sul. Patagonia and the Argentine section of Tierra del Fuego are essentially wool producing regions, their semi-arid climates and steppe vegetation favouring the merino, which is grazed extensively on enormous farms. The erection of refrigeration plants at Punta Arenas, and other ports in Patagonia, has also encouraged the development of a small trade in mutton from crossbred animals.

TABLE 45

PRODUCTION OF LAMB AND MUTTON

(in thousands of metric tons)

	1948-52 (Average)	1963	1964	1965
Australia	332	595	594	574
New Zealand	325	465	489	476
U.S.A.	285	349	324	295
United Kingdom	145	245	256	239
Argentina	195	151	135	140
Spain	78	115	128	134
WORLD	4,100	5,960	6,000	5,920

Source: *F.A.O. Production Yearbook.*

TABLE 46

PRINCIPAL WOOL EXPORTING COUNTRIES

(quantities in thousands of metric tons—"greasy", *i.e.* unscoured basis).

	1963	1964	1965		1963	1964	1965
Australia	580	627	606	Argentina	109	72	94
New Zealand	226	224	209	South Africa	103	101	112

Source: *F.A.O. Trade Yearbook.*

PIGS

Pigs are not grazing animals, and hence their range is not limited by the distribution of the world's grasslands. Pigs are kept in many countries from the tropics to the Arctic Circle, sometimes on specialist farms, but more commonly in small groups on dairy, arable, or mixed farms, or on backyard holdings. They function as scavengers, and as very efficient converters of household scraps, wastes from factory canteens, hotels, milk processing plants, and dairies, into valuable animal protein. In Europe surplus potatoes and barley, and in the United States, Brazil, and the Argentine surplus maize are also utilised as pig feed on a large scale.

Pig keeping takes up little space and is therefore an appropriate activity in densely settled and intensively cultivated regions where land is valuable and scarce. The largest pig populations are in China (180 million), Brazil (57 million), the U.S.A. (53 million), the Soviet Union (52 million), and West Germany (18 million). The highest densities occur in North West Europe, particularly in Denmark, and in the Corn Belt states of the U.S.A. Few pigs are kept in regions of extensive livestock ranching, and they are virtually absent from the Muslim lands.

The very high reproduction rate of the pig (two litters, each of six to nine young, can be expected annually from a mature sow), and the short time the animal takes to grow to marketable size, allows a herd to be built up much more quickly than is possible in the case of cattle and sheep. The short cycle of production also makes it a comparatively easy matter for a farmer to switch from pig keeping to the cultivation of grains or roots for cash, or vice versa, according to prices prevailing at any given time. Short-term fluctuations in the size of the pig population are a feature of the industry. In Britain numbers declined by a half during the Second World War, when concentrated rations were expensive, but rose by 45 per cent. between 1951 and 1952, when feeding stuffs became more readily available.

Pig meat enters international trade principally as bacon and ham. The chief exporting countries are Denmark, Poland, Ireland, and the United States (Table 47).

TABLE 47

WORLD TRADE IN BACON AND HAM
(in thousands of metric tons)

MAIN EXPORTING COUNTRIES

	1960	1965		1960	1965
Denmark	255·5	312·0	U.S.A.	23·9	9·4
Poland	50·7	51·9	TOTAL WORLD	398·4	443·9
Ireland	19·3	26·9			

More than 90 per cent. of all bacon and ham exports are shipped to the United Kingdom.

Source: *F.A.O. Trade Yearbook.*

GOATS

Goats are multi-purpose animals, supplying milk, meat, wool, and skins. They are particularly well adapted to country that is too dry or too rugged to be cultivated, or to plots of land too restricted in area, or too poor in quality to support a cow. Goats are extremely useful animals on small peasant holdings of southern Europe, sub-humid Africa, the Far East, and the Andean states of South America. In the Old World their distribution is similar to the distribution of sheep (to which they are closely related), with the following significant exceptions:

(i) There are few goats in the British Isles. In these islands the large urban demand for milk can be better satisfied by the dairy cow, and the sheep is more suited to the cooler uplands.

(ii) Goats are relatively more important than sheep in certain monsoon countries, especially India, Pakistan, and Java. India has one third of the world's goats (Table 48). They are reared in the rice lands as well as in the driest regions, but they are always grazed on the rougher hill slopes or on uncultivated strips between fields. Milk is the main product, although no objection is taken on religious grounds to eating goat meat.

The Angora and Cashmere goats are valued for their wool. The Angora requires a dry climate, and is found in greatest numbers in South Africa and the United States. More than 80 per cent. of the mohair production of the United States comes from central Texas. The Cashmere goat is not important outside its native home in northern India. Its undergrowth of short hair is used to make Cashmere shawls.

Some 65 million goat and kid skins are available annually from slaughtered animals. India, China, Italy, and South Africa are the main producers.

TABLE 48

PRINCIPAL GOAT-REARING COUNTRIES
(numbers of goats in thousands)

Country	Goats	Country	Goats
India	60,800	U.S.S.R.	7,000
Turkey	18,300	Sudan	6,300
Ethiopia	15,800	Republic of South Africa	5,100
Iran	12,500	Greece	5,000
Brazil	11,500	Peru	2,800
Pakistan	9,500	Spain	2,700
Indonesia	8,200		

POULTRY

Poultry are kept in every inhabited country. As so many birds are the property of smallholders who make no statistical returns it is impossible to be precise about world totals, or even numbers in individual countries, but it is likely that the global figure exceeds

3,000 million. More than 110 million are in the United Kingdom and 400 million in the United States.

The ordinary economic tests of profitability are rarely taken into account by the backyard producer, for whom poultry keeping is a hobby or a means of utilising spare land he has no inclination to cultivate. Because the eggs are eaten by the family, or sold privately, it is difficult to estimate the volume of production from this source, but during the Second World War it probably amounted to one quarter of the total output in the British Isles. Backyard production, however, is on the wane, and the poultry industry is becoming increasingly concentrated in commercial units. The size of the poultry farm has also grown. In Britain to-day, 30 per cent. of all hens are in flocks of 1,000 or more.

The last two decades have witnessed a significant movement towards a specialised and intensive type of poultry farming. Before 1945 commercial egg production was a supplementary enterprise on many farms and holdings to the main business of dairying or cereal production. Hens were allowed more or less free access to a part of the farm. They required feeding twice a day, otherwise they made little demand upon labour, save at Christmas time, when the preparation of table birds brought additional work that generally fell on the farmer's wife. A certain amount of food—spilt corn, hay seeds, roots, and grass could be picked up from the farmyard and fields. Simple shelter, preferably portable, was all that was needed by way of equipment. The disadvantage of the system was that production averaged no better than about 100 eggs per bird annually, and the laying season was concentrated into the spring and early summer. Autumn and winter were periods of scarcity and high egg prices.

Rising costs of feeding stuffs and intense competition in the industry is forcing a change of methods on many producers. The "free range" is being replaced by the intensive farm, organised on industrial lines. Birds are housed individually in cages, and their movement and diet rigorously controlled. Performances are carefully checked, and poor layers removed from the flock. The environment is wholly artificial. Temperatures are regulated, and electric lighting is used to extend the period of natural daylight in order to simulate spring and summer conditions throughout the year. By means of these strategems seasonal fluctuations in the output of eggs have been damped down, and overall production greatly increased. In Britain it has doubled since 1951.

The United States, the U.S.S.R., Japan, and the United Kingdom are the largest egg producers (Table 49). Like other animal products, eggs are expensive and consumption tends to be highest in the more prosperous countries. Eggs are semi-perishable, but with proper storage in temperatures below 12° C. (55° F.) they remain edible for several months, long enough for them to be shipped to distant markets. Australian and Chinese eggs are regularly exported to West European countries. There is also a substantial trade in fresh eggs from the Netherlands and Denmark to the industrial regions of continental Europe.

The intensive rearing of young table birds or "broilers" has now developed into a major industry. Several millions are produced each year in Britain alone.

TABLE 49

PRODUCTION OF EGGS IN SELECTED COUNTRIES
(in millions)

	1963	1964	1965
United States	63,800	64,400	64,600
U.S.S.R.	28,500	26,700	29,100
Japan	15,300	17,900	18,600
United Kingdom	13,200	14,600	14,400
West Germany	10,000	11,200	11,900
France	9,300	9,300	9,300
Brazil	7,300	7,800	8,300
Italy	7,400	8,400	8,300
WORLD	264,000	273,000	279,000

Source: *F.A.O. Production Yearbook.*

CHAPTER X

FORESTS AND FOREST PRODUCTS

Forests once covered 60 per cent. of the world's land area, and were the most widely distributed of the major plant communities. Throughout the ages, however—and at a pace which has accelerated as human populations have multiplied and as technologies have improved—they have been plundered, so that to-day less than one half of the original cover remains, and most of that in regions difficult of access to civilised man. In settled areas forests are now generally of insignificant extent, and exist only by the virtue of the fact that the land they occupy is of little value for agriculture or urban development (Fig. 61).

TABLE 50

FOREST AREAS IN SELECTED COUNTRIES
(in thousands of hectares*)

	Forest Area		Percentage of total land area under forest
	Total	In use	
Finland	21,900	21,900	72
Brazil	562,000	40,000	66
Burma	45,300	24,000	66
Colombia	69,400	6,800	64
Indonesia	121,000	61,400	63
Ghana	14,100	1,720	58
Paraguay	20,900	5,000	54
U.S.S.R.	1,131,000	458,500	51
Canada	417,600	186,600	45
U.S.A.	315,800	213,600	34
Belgium	601	601	20
France	11,600	11,500	19
Mexico	38,900	1,350	18
United Kingdom	1,650	1,600	7.5
Australia	48,400	17,800	6

* One hectare equals approximately two and a half acres.

Source: *F.A.O. Yearbook of Forest Product Statistics.*

DISTRIBUTION OF THE WORLD'S FOREST RESOURCES

The tropical hardwood forests

Almost half the world's forests are situated within the tropics. The true rain forest is restricted to comparatively low-lying ground where precipitation is heavy and temperatures constantly high, but dense stands of evergreen and semi-deciduous hardwoods also clothe the mountain slopes of South East Asia, the East Indies, and Central America.

The tropical forests have remained more or less intact in regions where human settlement is sparse. Elsewhere extensive areas have been cleared to make way for agriculture, especially in the monsoon lands. Commercial exploitation has been restricted in the main to the more valuable species—Brazilwood, mahogany, iron wood, and various types of "cedar" in tropical America; ebony, sapele, rosewood, and African walnut in Africa; and teak and sal in India and South East Asia. The production of the cheaper "utility" woods is increasing, however, and the bulk of the timber exports from Nigeria and Ghana are now of this type. Many tropical forests also yield enormous quantities of fuel wood. Frequently this is the most important product.

The opening of the low latitude forests to the markets of the world has been retarded by a number of factors. Isolation is a major handicap in some areas, although it is worth noting that the largest and least developed of all the forests—those of the Amazon basin—are threaded by a network of excellent waterways on which transport would not be difficult to organise. In this particular case the problem is not so much one of gaining access to the region itself, but of locating and extracting the timber. Economically valuable trees often grow deep in the jungle among worthless species, making the task of felling and transport to the river arduous in the extreme. Labour is also scarce, and having to work as it must in one of the most debilitating climates on earth, is not well disposed to undertake the heavy tasks that lumbering involves.

Isolation retards development in another way. Lumbering is becoming increasingly a mechanised industry. The power chain saw is replacing the axe, and the caterpillar tractor is replacing animal and human power. Mechanisation increases the dependence of any activity on the industries that provide equipment and spares, and thereby enhances the attraction of regions with well established lines of communication with the supply centres. The tropical forests are not always well placed in this respect. Conditions naturally vary greatly over an area that spans three continents. Significant progress has been made in introducing modern logging techniques to the Congo and some West African countries. Elsewhere methods tend to remain primitive, and are unlikely to change drastically until the demand for wood and wood products in the temperate regions grows to the point where even the remote forests can be no longer ignored.

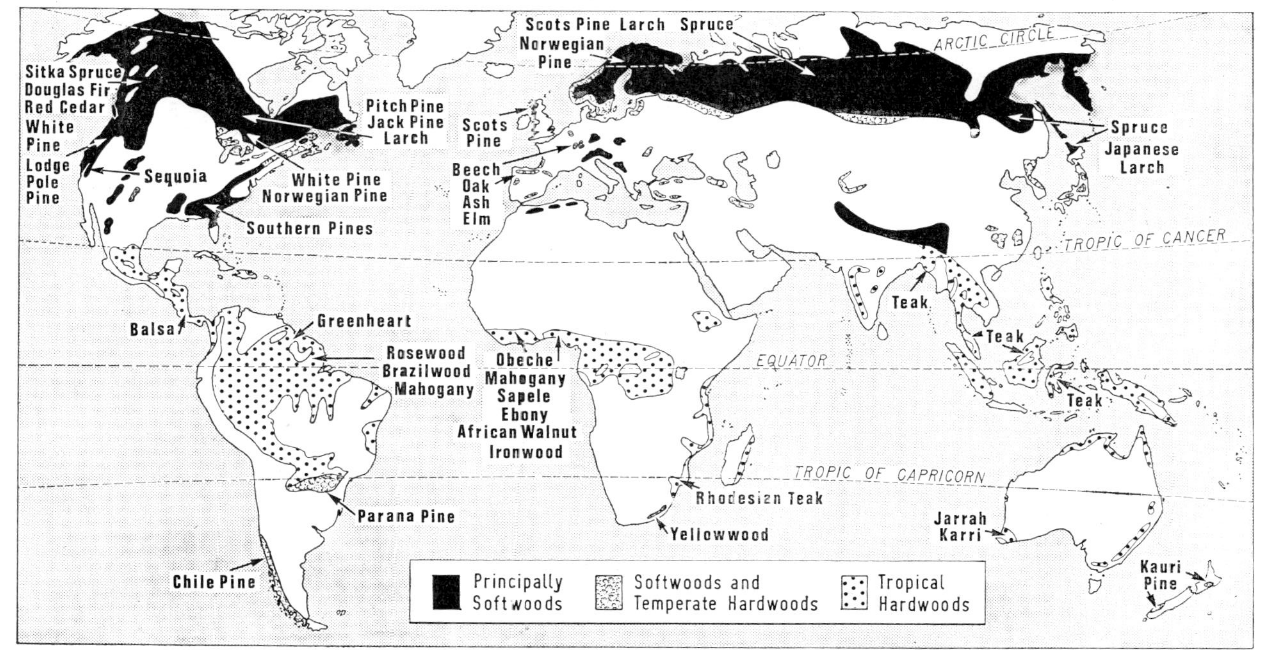

Fig. 61.—World Timber Resources.

The hardwoods of Australia—Forests cover only six per cent. of the Australian continent. Trees belong almost entirely to the drought-resistant eucalyptus family, and generally yield timber useful for fencing and other purposes for which low-grade wood suffices. The best commercial forests are in the south west. Jarrah and karri grow in fine stands in the rainier parts of Swanland. Their wood is hard, durable, and resistant to fire and salt water, and is much used as railway sleepers, telegraph poles, and in heavy constructional work such as pier and jetty building.

Reserves of indigenous softwoods are small and scattered in Australia, but more than half a million acres of conifers have been planted by the government, mainly in Victoria, New South Wales, and South Australia, in order to reduce the country's dependence on imports. Currently these plantings account for nearly one third of Australia's sawn wood production.

The temperate hardwoods

Deciduous hardwood forests constitute the climax vegetation of the lower ground in three main regions of the world:

1. West and Central Europe.
2. Northern China, Manchuria, and northern Japan.
3. The eastern United States, and southern Ontario.

Many of the deciduous hardwood forests have been extensively cleared, lying as they do in areas eminently suited to agriculture. Over millions of square miles their destruction is virtually complete. Reforestation schemes have been confined in the main to rougher country, and have concentrated upon the quick maturing conifer, so that the nature of this forest, if such it can still be called, is changing.

Hardwoods were once indispensable to many of the constructional trades, to the shipbuilding industry, and to the manufacture of certain types of machinery where strength and durability were essential requirements. Concrete, steel, aluminium, and plastics have now replaced wood over a wide range of uses. Hardwood is expensive. Logging operations are costly when stands are small and scattered. The timber itself is also difficult to work. Total production of hardwood from the temperate zone amounts to approximately 120 million cubic metres per annum, or only one sixth of the production of softwood.

Softwood forests of the northern hemisphere

The U.S.S.R.—A vast zone of coniferous forest stretches almost unbroken from Norway to northern Japan, and Kamchatka, and contains the largest reserves of virgin timber in the world (Fig. 61). Fully 90 per cent. of these forests lie within the Soviet Union. The Siberian forests are remote, uninhabited, and little exploited. Those of European Russia also offer a generally unfavourable environment for human settlement, but, because of their comparative proximity to the great consuming areas of the Soviet Union and Western Europe, they have been much more fully developed. About 30 per cent. of the total world production of roundwood, *i.e.* wood prior to initial processing, comes from the forests of European Russia, much of it from the Dvina River and Karelia regions in the hinterlands of Archangel and Leningrad.

The softwood forests of Scandinavia and Finland are much more intensively utilised than those of the Soviet Union. Practically the whole of the Finnish and Swedish forested areas are accessible and in use. The main trees are the Scots and Norwegian pines, the spruce, and the larch. The numerous rivers which facilitate the movement of logs and provide water power sites; the easy communications with important export markets in Britain and continental Europe (see Table 51); and climatic conditions which on the whole are unfavourable to the pursuit of agriculture, have helped to establish forestry as an activity of outstanding importance in these northern lands. Wood and wood products comprise no less than 85 per cent. of the exports of Finland. Finnish timber is in particularly high demand, as the slow growth-rate of trees, especially in the northern and middle sections of the country, is conducive to the production of close-grained wood of high quality.

The northern and eastern forests of Canada and the U.S.A. The northern coniferous forest belt of North America extends from Alaska to Newfoundland and New England, and sends a tongue southwards along the Appalachian ridges into West Virginia. Economically valuable species within this forest include the white pine of the New England-St Lawrence-Great Lakes region (the white pine was once one of the most important timber trees of the continent); the Norwegian pine with a range similar to the white pine; the red spruce (a valuable pulp tree); and on poorer sites in the more northerly regions the jack pine, pitch pine, larch, white and black spruce, hemlock, and the balsam fir.

Much of the good timber has been removed from the southern parts of the forest, especially from the sections lying within the United States where exploitation went on unchecked until the beginning of the present century. On the other hand some 500 million acres in Canada are awaiting development. Isolation is hampering the opening up of vast areas of timber and pulp country in Ontario

TABLE 51

ORIGIN OF WOOD AND WOOD PRODUCTS IMPORTED INTO THE UNITED KINGDOM (1964)
(in thousands of cubic metres)

DESCRIPTION	EUROPE (Total)	FINLAND	SWEDEN	NORWAY	U.S.S.R.	CANADA	U.S.A.	CENTRAL AMERICA	SOUTH AMERICA	AFRICA (Total)	GHANA	NIGERIA	ASIA	OCEANIA	TOTAL FROM ALL COUNTRIES
Coniferous logs (saw logs, veneer logs, and logs for sleepers)	12	7·1	—	0·4	1·5	6·1	—	0·4	0·6	—	—	—	—	0·1	21
Broadleaved logs (saw logs, veneer logs, and logs for sleepers)	12*	—	—	—	—	34	2·1	0·7	14	461	79	219	23	0·2	545
Pulpwood	57	46	—	—	46	209	—	—	—	—	—	—	—	—	313
Pit props	191	138	—	—	454	—	—	—	—	—	—	—	—	—	645
Coniferous sawn wood . .	4651	2019	1478	137	2336	2184	77	8·2	231	0·5	—	—	—	—	9488
Broadleaved sawn wood . .	387	31	3·5	—	—	48	39	4·0	9·3	273	151	52	283	4·6	948
Plywood	387	262	—	—	125	218	—	—	2·4	50	12	20	78	—	864
Wood pulp†	2326	616	1060	528	71	302	190	—	—	128‡	—	—			3017
Newsprint †	250	158	68	24	—	433	—	—	—	—	—	—	—	—	683

* Mainly from France. † In thousands of metric tons. ‡ Mainly from South Africa. — = Nil, or negligible quantities.

Source: *F.A.O. Yearbook of Forest Products Statistics.*

and Quebec, and in the Prairie provinces. Few man-made communications penetrate these regions, and the streams, numerous as they are, are of little value as navigable highways. Further north the rocky soils and cool summers support but small, slow-growing trees that become more and more scattered as the tundra is approached. Commercially, this sub-Arctic forest—the *taiga*—is unlikely ever to be of much significance.

The Southern coniferous forest of the United States—Nearly one third of the forest acreage in the U.S.A. is in the South. Excluding the predominantly Prairie states of Texas and Oklahoma, more than half the region is classified by the U.S. Department of Agriculture as being "under forest".

The region of Southern pines which extends from Virginia into eastern Texas is the most important. Four species predominate—the long leaf, short leaf, loblolly, and slash pine. The Southern forest was exploited early, but it was not until the timber reserves of the north and east were showing signs of exhaustion towards the end of the last century that it became the leading lumbering region of the continent. At present it contributes a little over 30 per cent. of the United States' annual crop of timber (Table 52). More than half the pulp wood and practically the entire production of naval stores (tar, pitch, turpentine, etc.) also originate in the South. The Southern pines grow very quickly. Thirty to forty years are sufficient to produce a mature tree. The rapid pace of natural regeneration, coupled with the extensive replanting programmes of the large pulp and paper companies operating in the South, have managed to maintain a rate of new growth at least equal to the forest removals, and losses by fire.

TABLE 52

PRODUCTION OF LUMBER IN THE U.S.A. 1963
(in millions of board-feet)

Division		Region	
New England	600		
Mid Atlantic	735		
East North Central	1040		
West North Central	610	North and East	2,985
Pacific	16,800		
Mountain	3,860	West	20,660
South Atlantic	4,800		
East South Central	3,050		
West South Central	3,000	South	10,850
		Total	34,595

Source: *Statistical Abstract of the United States.*

The Pacific and mountain forests

Clothing the slopes of the coast ranges from Alaska to the latitude of San Francisco is one of the finest forests in the world. It is almost entirely coniferous, and is noted for the magnificence of its species, some of which in really favourable situations attain heights of over 300 feet, and diameters of twelve to fifteen feet at their base. The main trees are the Douglas fir—the leading timber tree of the continent—the Sitka spruce, the white and sugar pines, the western hemlock, red cedar, and the redwoods, of which *Sequoia gigantea* is the largest and best known, although its range is restricted.

Oregon, California, and Washington are the leading timber producing states in the U.S.A. Fifty per cent. of Canada's annual cut comes from British Columbia. It has been estimated that half of the original Pacific forest has been felled, and although growth is rapid in a region of mild winters and heavy rainfall, drain is greatly in excess of renewal. In California it is nearly twice as great.

The mountain forest is scattered and isolated, and not extensively exploited. The trees include the Douglas fir, white pine, lodgepole pine, the western larch, and the spruces. On the whole growth is lower, the stands more open, and the trees less valuable than in the Pacific region. Timber reserves are considerable, and of necessity they will be developed in the future as the more accessible resources become depleted.

Coniferous forests of the southern hemisphere

Natural softwood forests of South Africa, Australia, and New Zealand are small, and generally of local importance only. Some fairly extensive plantings, however, have been made in the three countries in recent years. In South America softwoods are found in two areas: (i) in southern Chile where the rugged topography and heavy rainfall make logging operations extremely difficult, with the result that less than one quarter of the forest is productive, and (ii) the sub-tropical Parana pine forest of southern Brazil, and the adjoining portions of the Argentine and Paraguay. This forest is the largest and most important source of commercial timber in the continent. Brazil is the leading producer of softwood in Latin America. The greater proportion of the 6·75 million cubic metres removed annually for industrial purposes and the 12 million cubic metres cut for fuel comes from the state of Parana.

Logging and transport in the coniferous forests

The purity and density of most coniferous stands, and the general absence of interfering undergrowth makes for comparative ease of lumbering in the softwood forests. Large scale and highly organised enterprises which make the fullest use of mechanical equipment are characteristic. Owing to the remoteness of many lumber camps from the ultimate markets for timber and wood products, the transport problem assumes more than usual significance. Trimmed lumber is dragged from the cutting area to the nearest permanent highway and dispatched to the saw mill. The advantage of water transport is evident from the number of mills located on the banks of rivers and along coastal inlets, but waterways are not always superior to roads or railways. The usefulness of many rivers is reduced by shoals, rapids, sharp bends, and on some streams by power dams. No energy, of course, is required on running waterways, unless movement is against the current, as sometimes it must be. Tugs are needed on lakes and coastal fairways. Sorting points, manned by a large and expensive labour force, are necessary where waterways diverge, or where they are used by a number of companies floating timber to different destinations. Because of these handicaps, roads and railways may provide the cheaper form of transport, and in Scandinavia they have diverted to themselves some of the traffic from busy rivers. Haulage from saw mill to market is normally undertaken by established carriers. Very long rail hauls are sometimes involved, *e.g.* from the Pacific forests to the eastern cities of North America, and from Siberia into European Russia.

TABLE 53

PRODUCTION OF ROUNDWOOD (INDUSTRIAL WOOD ONLY) FROM THE CONIFEROUS FORESTS, 1964

(in thousands of cubic metres)

U.S.S.R.	233,200*
U.S.A.	216,600
Canada	85,600 (1963)
Sweden	40,300
Finland	31,300
China (mainland)	21,000*
Germany (Federated Republic)	17,600
Poland	13,300
France	13,100
Czechoslovakia	9,000
Austria	8,900
Brazil	7,100
WORLD	792,000

* Unofficial figures.

Source: *F.A.O. Yearbook of Forest Products Statistics.*

MANAGEMENT AND CONSERVATION OF FOREST RESOURCES

It has taken centuries for man to realise that the world's timber resources are not inexhaustible, and even to-day, if judged by the rate at which destruction is proceeding in some parts of the world, the fact is still not universally appreciated. The demand for wood and wood products is enormous and will increase. Future requirements can only be met if forests are managed as good farm land is managed, *i.e.* by methods that ensure a maximum output on a sustained yield basis and not, as has been the case in the past, by exploiting them as wasting assets, after the manner of coal or iron ore.

In the nature of things, the economic benefits that derive from forest conservation are long-, rather than short-term. Outside the tropics and sub-tropics, where the rates of reproduction and growth are comparatively rapid, it takes from fifty to 200 years for a tree to reach maturity. In Britain 100 to 150 years are required for an oak, and fifty to seventy years for most of the conifers. A crop of forest thinnings will, of course, be ready earlier than this. A factor which has inhibited the development of scientific forest management in the past has been the knowledge that seedling trees could not be ready for harvest during the lifetime of the person who planted them. The restocking of woodlands, if done at all, was undertaken by an enlightened few with an interest in posterity.

A feature of the present century has been the increasing degree of control exercised by national governments over the forest lands. In the U.S.S.R. public control is complete. In the United States and Europe about half are in state ownership. The effectiveness of control, however, is another matter. Many of the African forests are publicly owned, although few countries can claim even to have mapped them and surveyed them satisfactorily, to say nothing of the far more difficult task of checking the illicit cutting and burning that goes on round many of the villages. This particular problem is doubly intractable in regions where shifting cultivators are active and where there is a shortage of coal. Ninety per cent. of the trees taken from the forests of Africa are used for fuel, and the proportion in South America is only marginally less, although not all removals are unsanctioned (Fig. 62). It is nevertheless abundantly clear that the forests of Africa, Latin America, and of other regions where the problem exists, cannot be developed scientifically until the states under whose nominal control they happen to be can take more effective steps to check the depredations of the forest dwellers themselves.

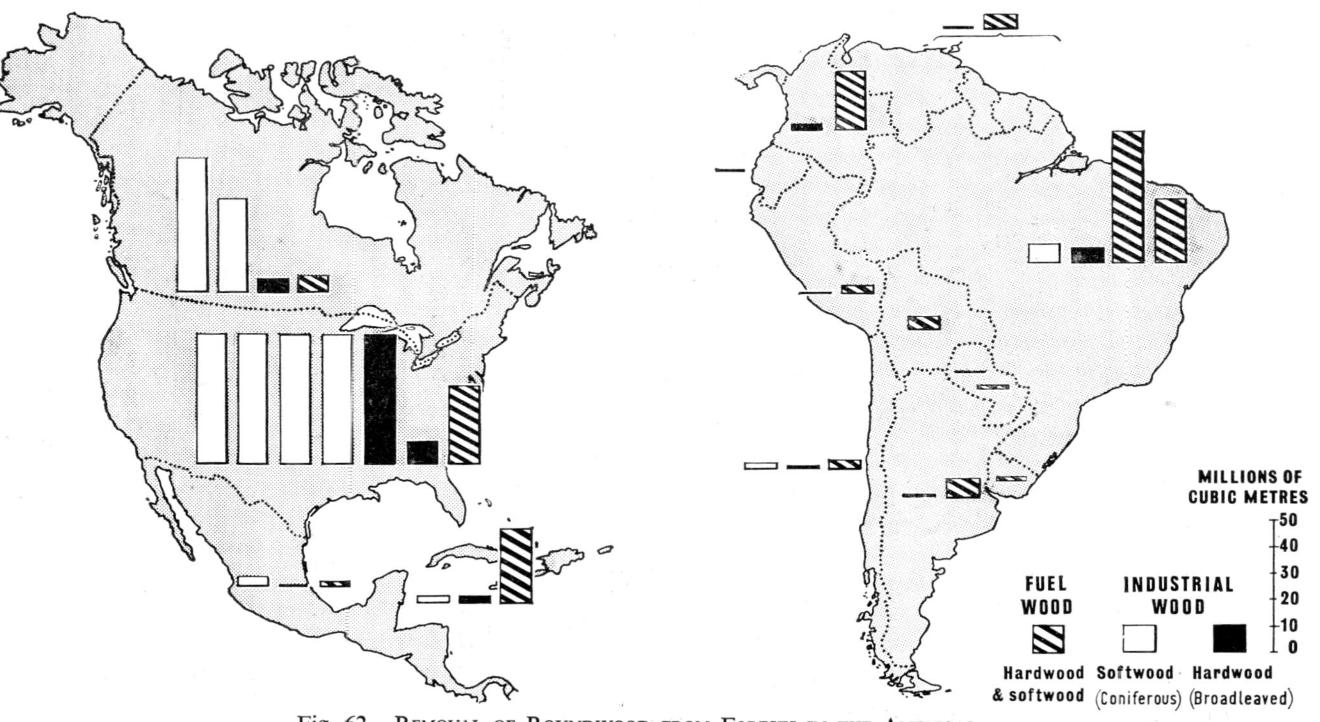

Fig. 62.—Removal of Roundwood from Forests in the Americas.

Methods and objectives of forest management

The following practices are adopted to try and ensure the maximum possible output of timber without depletion of the reserves:

1. FOREST ESTABLISHMENT—In areas carrying no forest, or on forest land so impoverished as to be worthless, growing stock can be established only by putting out trees raised in the nursery. Almost half the 4·3 million acres under forest in Britain have been planted in this way by the Forestry Commission since 1919. Millions of trees in Britain are now growing on land which at the time of planting had not carried forest within living memory. Much of this land is only marginally productive, agriculturally, and gives higher return from timber than from sheep and cattle. In these circumstances forestry represents the more intensive use of resources.

2. SELECTIVE CUTTING—In a forest consisting of trees of all ages, only the fully developed, weak, or interfering members are removed. Unripe trees are allowed to grow on to maturity. In the tropics, where useful species are found in ones and twos rather than in stands, care is taken to leave a sufficient number of quality trees for natural regeneration, otherwise the value of the forest deteriorates. Selective cutting never exposes the site to the risks of erosion, and the heavy cost of replanting totally cleared areas is avoided. On the other hand management costs are high and the timber is difficult to extract. Young trees may also be damaged when the larger ones are felled.

3. CLEAR CUTTING entails the removal of all trees, regardless of age or worth. It is cheaper than selective cutting, and is the only method applicable when the forest is of uniform age. If felling is done in swaths, preferably along the contour or across wind, erosion can be avoided and the cut areas will be re-seeded from the trees that remain. Clear cut forests are managed on a long-term rotation. A seventy-five-year rotation cycle allows four acres to be removed annually from each plot of 300 acres.

4. FOREST PROTECTION—Fire is the greatest hazard in all forests outside regions of heavy and well distributed rainfall. Coniferous forests are particularly subject to destruction by fire. Millions of acres are sometimes devastated in major outbreaks, and less extensive fires kill seedlings even if they do not harm mature trees. Dry season fires are commonplace on the savana margins of Africa where burning is a long established method of land clearance. The danger is ever present in Australia and the United States. In the U.S.A. more than 4 million acres were burnt in 1959 in over 100,000 separate incidents. Of these incidents, less than 10 per cent.

were due to natural causes: the rest were attributed to human carelessness. In Britain the fire risk is much less owing to the moister climate and the fragmented nature of the forest land. It is perhaps interesting to note in passing that more than half the outbreaks that occurred in Britain between 1928 and 1950 were started by the railways.

Much research is taking place to determine the conditions in which fires most commonly occur. Considerable progress has been made in the use of aircraft in their detection, and of chemical sprays in their suppression.

Insects are among the most serious enemies of the forest. Insects, and the diseases they transmit, are most damaging when introduced accidentally to a region where trees have little natural immunity. Dutch elm disease has wrought havoc among the elms of North America since it first appeared in New York State some thirty-five years ago, although the European elm is highly resistant to it. The gypsy moth, too, has been a troublesome immigrant in the New World. Millions of acres of forest land are sprayed at intervals to keep these and other pests in check. Blanket spraying, however, can rarely be more than an expedient, and experience is showing that biological methods of control (by, for example, the introduction of predator insects) give the best hope of lasting success.

Finally, it is necessary to protect forests against damage caused by animals. The rabbit is perhaps the greatest destroyer of young trees, particularly during severe weather. In the winter of 1946-7, twenty-year old larches were killed by rabbits gnawing and "ring barking" them a few inches above the ground. Domestic animals can also be a menace when allowed to graze forest pastures: cows, sheep, goats, and sometimes horses browse and trample young trees, and pigs uproot them. The exclusion of farm animals from woods and forests would bring little but benefit, especially as the forage value of most forest lands is very low.

Other aims of forest conservation

Whilst the prime aim of forest management must be to ensure future supplies of marketable timber, it is by no means the sole aim. Forests play an important role in watershed protection, and the prevention of soil erosion by rain and wind. The task of making trees grow on the dry steppes and Prairies is not easy, but certain species, notably the cottonwood poplar, the green ash, the Chinese elm, and bur oak have been successfully established and provide very effective wind breaks. Flood control and the safety of water supplies are often best ensured, particularly in areas of broken relief subject to convectional storms, by a cover of trees. There is further the aesthetic appeal of the forests, the opportunities they afford for sport and relaxation, the part they play in the enrichment of a nation's wild life resources—these, and other intangible benefits that the forest lands bestow, are impossible to evaluate in economic terms, but they are nevertheless important and life would be immeasurably poorer without them.

FOREST INDUSTRIES

The pulp and paper industries

Small amounts of paper have been made in the past, and to some extent still are made, from the stems of fibrous plants, from the textile fibres, and from material of non-vegetable origin. In the middle of the last century, however, a satisfactory process for making paper pulp from wood was discovered, and a seemingly endless supply of raw material was made available to the paper making industries in the form of the world's forests, particularly the softwood forests. To-day, some 90 per cent. of the world output of pulp is produced from wood. The older materials continue to be used in the manufacture of special types of paper, and also retain their importance in regions where wood is scarce and expensive, and where the demand for paper is small.

Pulp is made by two different methods. The mechanical process, in which a revolving grindstone tears the fibres from the wood, is cheap and produces little waste. The pulp, however, is suitable only for newsprint and other forms of low grade paper, and the process can only utilise non-resinous, long-fibred softwoods. Hardwoods and the pines are unsuitable: the best trees are the spruces. In the chemical process, wood chippings are "cooked" in acids or alkalies, in order to dissolve and wash out the gums and resins: the chemically inert cellulose, the basis of the pulp remains. The chemical process is the more expensive and wasteful, but produces pulp of high grade. Hardwoods and the resinous pines, *e.g.* the Southern pines, can also be utilised. Chemical processes now account for 70 per cent. of the total world pulp output.

In the conversion of pulp to paper, the pulp is further refined, beaten, rolled, coated, dyed, and sized.

Location factors in the pulp and paper industries

Many pulp and paper mills are integrated units, but pulping and paper making are in effect separate industries, with different locational requirements. The pulp industry tends to be located in relation to its principal raw material—wood—which is bulky and of low value. The main factors are:

1. Modern pulp mills are large, elaborate, and equipped with plant that is both costly and durable. Access to forests extensive enough to supply suitable wood for many years is therefore essential. Mill sites are commonly found on the coast or on navigable or "floating" rivers, as such sites permit access by cheap water transport to distant, as well as local lumbering areas. Many mills have been established on the shores and inland waters of southern Norway, southern and eastern Sweden, and on the rivers of Ontario and Quebec. In Britain, where domestic pulp resources are negligible, the pulping industry has grown up on the banks of the Thames and the Manchester Ship Canal, and at Aberdeen, and Dundee.

2. The pulping industry is a heavy consumer of electricity, and is attracted to power sites on rivers. Coal, oil, natural gas, and sometimes waste wood products are also used in large quantities for steam raising, heating, and drying purposes.

3. Much water is also consumed. Certain chemical processes require as much as 100,000 gallons for each ton of pulp produced. The water must be fresh and pure.

4. The industry is not a large employer of labour, and can therefore be located away from centres of population.

Paper mills are generally smaller than pulp mills, more highly specialised, and more widely distributed. They tend to be located with reference to the markets for their products, rather than the source of their raw materials. In Britain they often occupy inland sites, normally on soft water streams. Darwin, Chorley, the Pennine valleys north and east of Manchester, and the Kendal area are important paper making centres.

Salient features of the world pulp and paper industries are contained in Tables 54 and 55.

Forest collecting industries

RUBBER—Almost the entire world output of natural rubber is obtained from a tree of the equatorial rain forests—*Hevea brasiliensis*, and, until the beginning of the present century, the wild, scattered, and generally low yielding Hevea trees of the Amazon lowlands were the only source of commercial rubber available to man. In 1876, however, a number of Hevea seeds were smuggled out of Brazil and germinated in the hot houses at Kew. The seedlings were transferred shortly afterwards to Ceylon where they thrived. These, and subsequent plantings made in Malaya and

TABLE 54
PRODUCTION OF WOOD PULP
(in thousands of metric tons)

	1963	1964
U.S.A.	27,325	28,800
Canada	11,315	12,450
Sweden	5,675	6,360
Finland	4,825	5,330
Japan	4,575	5,020
U.S.S.R.	3,900	not available
Norway	1,595	1,800
West Germany	1,380	1,370
France	1,270	1,360
WORLD	69,600	74,700

Source: *F.A.O. Yearbook of Forest Product Statistics.*

TABLE 55
PRODUCTION OF PULP PRODUCTS, 1964
(in thousands of metric tons)

	PAPER AND PAPER BOARD				FIBRE BOARD	TOTAL
	Newsprint	Printing and writing paper	Other paper	Paper board		
U.S.A.	1,940	7,140	8,715	17,670	1,990	37,455
Canada	6,625	510	585	1,250	250	9,220
Japan	1,150	1,300	1,700	3,160	170*	7,480
United Kingdom	760	1,010	1,385	1,240	735	5,135
West Germany ..	200	1,050	1,770	1,000	280	4,300
U.S.S.R.* ..	560	805	1,500	990	350	4,205
France	460	890	1,340	440	180	3,310
Sweden	680	350	1,320	600	700	3,650
Finland	1,080	420	555	925	240	3,220
WORLD	16,100	17,150	26,500	31,650	5,780	97,180

* 1963.

Source: *F.A.O. Yearbook of Forest Product Statistics.*

other countries of South East Asia, laid the foundations of the great rubber plantation industry that was soon to develop in that region.

Indonesia, Malaysia, and Ceylon are to-day the main producers of natural rubber (Table 56). These lands are able to recruit labour that can be trained to the delicate work of rubber tapping, and they further enjoy the advantage of a tropical monsoon climate which favours the cultivation of high yielding trees. Most of the plantations are on sites near the coast, or within easy reach of all weather highways, and transport costs on exported rubber, even on rubber dispatched to distant markets, are low.

The initial processing of latex into rubber is undertaken at the plantation factory. It involves treating the latex with a coagulant, and then passing the coagulum through a series of rollers to produce a sheet of required thickness. The sheet is then dried in the smoke house. If latex as such is to be marketed, the raw product is concentrated by a centrifugal process which separates the rubber particles from the water in which they are dispersed. The concentrate is then shipped by tanker. Handling costs are less than for dry rubber.

TABLE 56

PRODUCTION OF NATURAL AND SYNTHETIC RUBBER
(in thousands of tons)

	1955	1960	1964	1966
NATURAL RUBBER				
Malaysia—				
Total	698	780	893	927
From smallholdings	286	294	347	412
Indonesia				
Total	737	610	638	704
From smallholdings	475	398	420	480
Thailand	130	168	218	204
Ceylon	94	97	110	129
Vietnam	65	75	73	48
India	22	25	44	52
Cambodia	28	36	45	51
Brazil	21	23	28	24
WORLD	1,918	1,990	2,240	2,403
SYNTHETIC RUBBER				
U.S.A.	970	1,436	1,765	1,970
Canada	104	160	198	200
United Kingdom	nil	90	153	191
Federal Germany	11	80	136	182
Japan	nil	18	120	228
France	nil	17	128	161
Italy	nil	66	110	120
WORLD	1,085	1,880	2,800	3,330

Source: *Rubber Statistical Bulletin.*

Although rubber finds innumerable uses in industry to-day, the bulk is absorbed by the motor vehicle industry. The U.S.A., with no natural rubber production of her own, is the leading importer and consumer. The U.S.A. also produces two-thirds of the world output of synthetic rubber. Synthetic rubber production increased rapidly after the outbreak of the Japanese war in 1941, and now accounts for about 55 per cent. of the total production from all sources. The declining percentage usage of natural rubber would place the economies of many of the primary producing countries in serious peril, were it not for the fact that the overall demand for rubber is increasing at the rate of almost 6 per cent. per year, so that there is room for both industries—synthetic and natural—to flourish side by side. Given political stability in South East Asia, and the success of the replanting schemes, and improved agricultural practices that have been introduced during the last decade, there is little reason to doubt that natural rubber will command a substantial market for very many years.

CHICLE is another latex product, used, in this case, in the manufacture of chewing gum. It is obtained wholly from wild trees of the forests of Central America. The trees are tapped in the cool of the morning, and the latex taken to a central collecting point where it is concentrated by boiling prior to shipment. Careless tapping threatens the industry as it threatened the wild rubber industry half a century ago, and so far little has been done to conserve the limited resources. A rival has also appeared in the form of a synthetic substitute. The future for the chicle gatherers is not very bright.

CORK is obtained from the bark of the evergreen cork oak (*Quercus suber*). The tree grows largely untended on rough ground in the countries of the western Mediterranean. Cork is gathered by peeling the bark from mature trees. So long as care is taken to avoid damage to the live tissues beneath the cork layer the tree is not harmed, and a period of eight to ten years is sufficient for a new layer two or three inches in thickness to form. Too frequent stripping is injurious, and can be fatal. Regulations are in force in most countries to restrict harvesting to once every ten years, or thereabouts.

Half the world annual production of 300,000 tons comes from Portugal, Spain, and southern France. The North African states also harvest significant quantities. Plantations have been established in California, but are not as yet in commercial production.

TANNIN EXTRACT—Tannins are used to convert raw hides and skins into leather. They are obtained from the wood, bark, and leaves of many plants, although not more than a few are important outside the areas of production. Temperate sources—the oak, hemlock, and chestnut—have been largely exhausted, and the bulk of the tannin output is now obtained from trees of tropical and subtropical origin. The quebracho of the Chaco lowlands, the mangroves of the tidal swamps of Africa and Asia, and the wattle tree of Brazil, Natal, and Ceylon furnish most of the world supply.

Extraction plants are often located in the forest, as tannin in a concentrated or dried form is readily transportable. There is still, however, a substantial export of logs or bark from the producing areas to extraction plants in the consuming countries.

It seems unlikely that present sources of tannin can last much beyond the end of the present century. Subsequent supplies will depend on the discovery of new sources, natural or synthetic; upon the extension of wattle plantations; and upon the development of tannin extraction as a joint enterprise with lumbering, so that both the heartwood and bark can be utilised as fully as possible. In the past, millions of oaks were cut for their bark alone. To-day, the western hemlock of the Pacific States is being exploited solely for its timber, while the bark, which has a fairly high tannin content, is wasted because there is no economic means of stripping the trees in the forest. Floating logs to the saw mill results in a considerable loss of tannin by leaching. The development of a simple method of removing the bark at the lumber camp would thus make a new source of tannin available to the world.

NAVAL STORES—Resin, pitch, tar, and turpentine are processed from the exudates of various species of pine. The term "naval stores" originated in the days of wooden sailing vessels when the main use for this group of products was the ship building trades. Such products are now consumed mainly by the chemical industries. The leading producers of naval stores are the Southern pine forests of the U.S.A. and the Landes region of south-western France.

DRUGS, MEDICINALS, ETC.—Throughout the ages the forests have furnished mankind with a vast range of stimulants, narcotics, tonics, purgatives, and antiseptics; treatments for burns, scalds, sprains, and fractures; specifics against colds, dyspepsia, and gout—preparations, in fact, for all the ailments man is heir to. Some drugs are still produced in parts of the world purely for local use, others are traded internationally after preliminary treatment in the areas of production, a goodly number, although of proved value, have been superseded by more effective synthetic products, and for others completely new uses have been found. From the long list of plants important to medicine it is only possible here to note a few of the better known.

Chincona.—The bark and wood of the chincona tree are the sources of the drug quinine. Chincona is native to the moist slopes of the northern Andes, and was unknown outside that region until 1865, when a few seeds of selected, high yielding Bolivian trees were smuggled to Java. Towards the end of the nineteenth century, quinine from commercial plantations began to arrive on the market, with which the lower quality, higher priced quinine from the forest was unable to compete. Only during the Second World War when the Far East plantations were over-run by the Japanese was any serious attempt made to revive the industry in South America. The war also stimulated research into synthetic anti-malarial drugs, and these are now undermining the chincona industry of Java. The parallel with the history of rubber is very close.

Cocaine.—Cocaine is derived from the leaves of the coco shrub, yet another native South American plant that has been domesticated on the plantations of Indonesia. Most of the commercial supply now comes from Java.

Camphor, distilled from the wood of the camphor laurel, is used as an ingredient in the manufacture of plastics, explosives, soaps, cosmetics, and certain medicinal preparations. Production is mainly from wild and cultivated sources in Japan and Formosa. Recently the tree has been introduced into the U.S.A. Methods of distilling oil from the foliage have been developed, which, if adopted generally, would remove the need for extensive felling, and thereby ensure future harvests. A considerable proportion of the world's camphor is now manufactured synthetically.

A number of important drugs are obtained from herbaceous plants. Among them are morphine, heroin, and codein, all of which are extracted from the seeds of the opium poppy of the Far and Middle East, and hashish or marijuana from the hemp plant. There is a small, but important legitimate trade in these commodities which is regulated by international agreement.

Eucalyptus oil is expressed from the leaves of the eucalyptus or gum tree. A native of Australia, the eucalyptus has been naturalised in many regions of the warm temperate zone.

Trapping industries of the forests

The tropical, as well as the temperate and cold regions of the world, share in the fur trade—chinchilla fur, for instance, is a product of South America, and leopard skins are exported from India and Ceylon—but it is from the forests of North America, Scandinavia, and the Soviet Union that the finest products are obtained.

Almost from the time of its discovery, North America has led in the production of furs. Profits from trapping provided man with the earliest incentive to explore the continent. While log-men and farmers were still subduing the coastal areas of eastern Canada and New England, the *coureurs de bois*, one of the most remarkable set of men the world has known, were ranging the forests and prairies on foot, by sledge, and canoe; struggling against hunger, disease and the harshness of the climate; setting their traps and trading with the Indians; and then returning for brief spells to the towns to dispose of pelts of mink, beaver, martin, Arctic fox, ermine, lynx, bear, and a dozen other animals. By their enterprise and resourcefulness, this handful of indomitable Frenchmen opened up half a continent to the influence of white commerce.

Trapping still continues in the north, but not in the old way. The Hudson Bay Company maintains some 200 stations in the forest and tundra which function as supply and collecting depots for men who set out into the wilderness at the onset of each winter. The heyday of the industry, however, has passed. Trapping is giving way to fur farming. Since its inception late in the last century, the fur-farming industry has been established in many centres on the North American continent, and in several European countries, including the British Isles. Almost one-half of the furs from Canada, one of the main producing countries, now comes from animals kept in captivity.

CHAPTER XI

THE FISHING INDUSTRY

Fish is the only food available to man in more than minimal quantities that is produced without human intervention. Man merely harvests what nature has provided by her own unaided efforts. In marked contrast to the progress that has been made over the centuries in plant and animal husbandry, the science of fish culture (pisiculture) remains in its early infancy. Even the need for conservation is only now gaining general acceptance. A modern fisherman, like his prehistoric ancestors, is still essentially a hunter. Only his techniques have changed with the passage of time.

Although there are few inhabited coast lines or extensive inland waters where fishing has not achieved the status of at least a minor industry, the major fisheries of the world are located upon the continental shelves—the seaward extensions of the coastal plains down to the 100 fathom line (Fig. 63). The continental shelves comprise only 7 per cent. of the total area of the oceans. In the deeper water beyond, the quantity of marine life is believed to be small.

The significance of the shallow epi-continental seas lies in the fact that they are rich in *plankton*. Plankton is a term applied to the myriads of microscopic organisms both of vegetable and animal nature which drift about in the sea under the influence of the wind and tides. Thriving only at depths to which sunlight can penetrate, and within the limits of land-derived mineral salts upon which they feed, plankton forms the basis of all marine life.

Most of the major commercial fishing nations are situated in the temperate and high latitudes of the northern hemisphere. Until quite recently 90 per cent. of the world's fish catch came from waters north of the equator. The countries of northern Europe, the Atlantic islands, Japan, and the maritime regions of North America are of outstanding importance. Peru and Chile have joined the ranks of the great fishing nations in the last few years. South Africa and a few countries in sub-tropical and tropical Monsoon Asia are important. The inland fisheries of the Soviet Union and parts of Asia are also well developed.

The rise of fishing industries in many countries has been influenced by factors other than mere proximity to prolific fishing grounds. Over wide areas of maritime Europe, Iceland, the Faeroes, Newfoundland, Labrador, and Japan, a combination of conditions

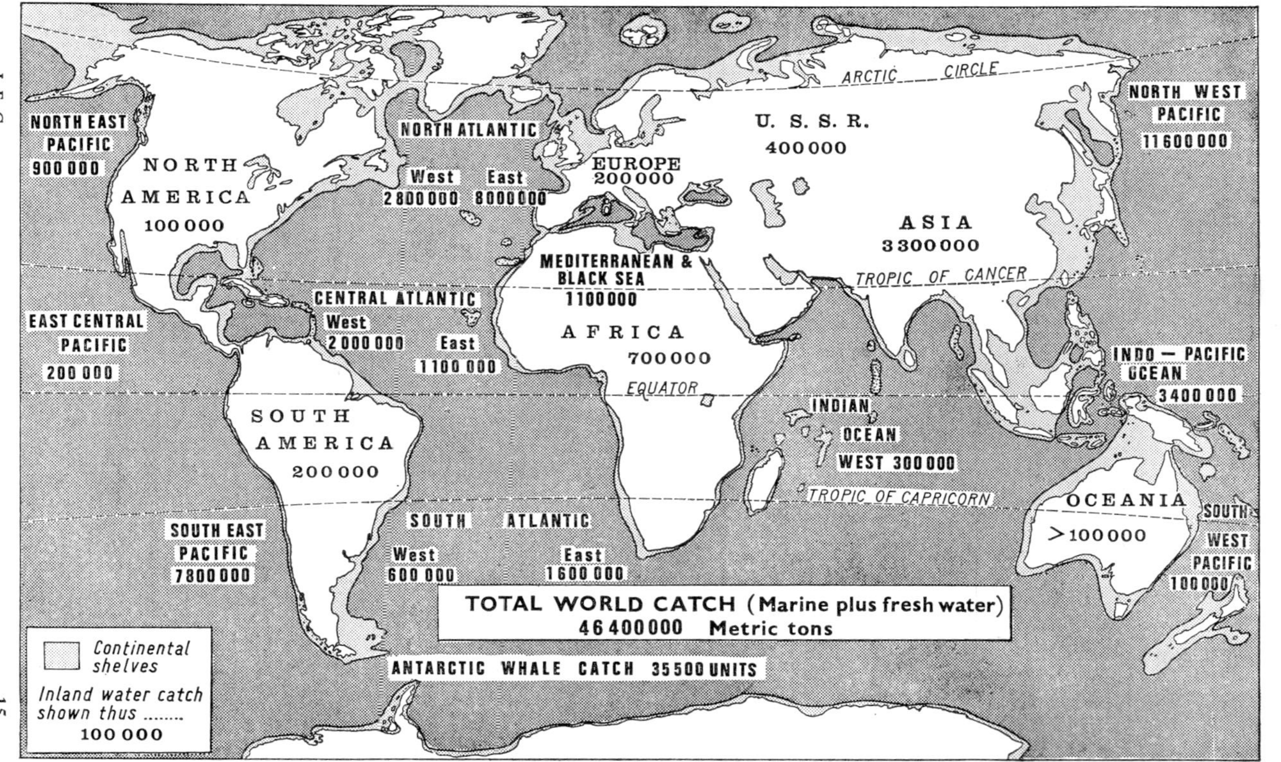

Fig. 63.—World Fish Catch.

inimical to agriculture—short growing seasons, indifferent soils, and rugged terrain—has focussed interest on the sea as a source of additional food. In the Faeroes, fishing is the leading occupation, giving direct employment to 40 per cent. of the working population, while in Japan, fish is second only to rice as a food, and supplies the bulk of protein intake. By contrast, meat is abundant and cheap in countries like Australia and the Argentine, and their populations have had less incentive to develop the fishing grounds.

TABLE 57

ANNUAL PER CAPITA CONSUMPTION OF FISH AND MEAT IN SELECTED COUNTRIES, 1965-6
(estimated edible weight in lbs.)

	FISH	MEAT
Japan	101	48
Sweden	61	142
Norway	78	112
Portugal	116	76
Denmark	88	172
Spain	52	75
Taiwan	82	48
United Kingdom ..	34	185
Canada	30	257
Australia	22	270
U.S.A.	21	273
Argentina	11	280

Source: *F.A.O. Production Yearbook.*

The nature of many coasts has also materially influenced the rise of important fishing industries. The coastlines of Europe and insular Monsoon Asia are of exceptional length. Those of Norway and Japan measure 12,000 and 16,500 miles respectively, compared with only 19,000 miles for the whole of the African continent. Estuaries penetrate far into the interior, bringing most districts within a short distance of the sea. No place in Japan lies more than seventy-five miles from the ocean. Furthermore, the relief is such that the most extensive lowlands upon which settlement is concentrated are found adjacent to the shores, so that the problems of fish distribution are greatly simplified. The countless bays, promontories, and islands also provide sheltered inshore waters and safe harbours for craft.

Methods of fishing

Fish are caught in a multitude of ways. Methods vary according to the type and habitat of the species sought, and the extent to which fishing remains a peasant activity, or has become organised along industrial lines. Equipment ranges from spears, baited hooks, traps, and fixed nets, operated from the shore or from tiny boats, by individuals and small groups, to large company owned, deep-sea, trawler fleets capitalised to the value of several tens of millions of pounds.

The importance of the small fishing enterprises that abound along the shores of many countries, especially within the tropics, should not be under-estimated. Fishing has long been a peasant occupation, often combined with farming on the coasts of West Africa, the Caribbean, India, Pakistan, and South East Asia. The precise size of the catches taken from these waters is not known, as much of the fish is consumed locally, and does not enter into commerce, but it is probably greater than official statistics suggest. Even Japan, a country with one of the most highly organised fishing industries in the world, still has tens of thousands of tiny, unpowered peasant craft operating in coastal waters. In temperate rivers and seas, salmon and shellfish are caught, also with simple gear. The bulk of the world's catch, however, is now taken in deep water by vessels employing scientific techniques for fish detection and capture. The principal methods are as follows:

1. Drifter fishing.—The drifter is used to catch pelagic fish, *i.e.* species such as the herring that inhabit surface waters. It employs a net, or more accurately a number of nets, secured end to end, and held perpendicularly in the water immediately below the surface by floats and weights. When in use the net drifts freely with the tides and currents. The drifter is a small vessel, and rarely operates more than about sixty miles from the coast, or remains at sea for more than forty-eight hours.

Herring fishing is a seasonal and often precarious occupation. Small catches are quite common, and even heavy landings bring their problems, accompanied as they often are by sharp falls in prices. Quick freeze plants have now been built in a number of ports to handle surpluses until market conditions are favourable.

2. Trawler fishing.—The trawler tows a conical shaped net measuring as much as 150 ft in length, and 80 ft across the mouth, at a depth that can be regulated. The drifter catches demersal fish, *i.e.* species that live near the sea bed. Cod, hake, haddock, plaice, sole, whiting, and halibut are the main types taken by the trawl, although herring are sometimes caught by this method during the hours of daylight when the shoals go deep. Trawling is a more highly organised activity than drifter fishing. Vessels are much larger and are designed and equipped to remain at sea for several days. Distant-water trawlers often make round voyages of 5,000 miles

from European ports to the Arctic and Newfoundland fishing grounds. In these circumstances, provision has to be made on board these vessels for preserving the catch if a dash for port is to be avoided before the holds are full, and sufficient has been earned to pay for the voyage. Crushed ice has been used since the last century, and is an adequate preservative provided the ship is not operating too far from its base. Refrigeration is now common, and freezing equipment has been installed in some of the larger trawlers. Deep-freezing, as distinct from simple refrigeration, reduces the temperature of the holds to below − 18° C. (0° F.) and brings the fish to a solid state, in which condition it can be stored safely for several months so long as the freezing is continuous. Freezing plant, however, takes up space and reduces the size of the pay-load. Such plant is also rather expensive to operate. Some trawler fleets now put to sea with attendant factory ships, which pack the catch and process the by-products ready for market when the ships dock.

3. SEINE NETTING.—The seine net is used to catch both demersal and pelagic fish. It is a large purse-shaped net, one end of which is attached to a fixed buoy, and the other to a vessel which encircles the shoal, and draws the net in. Seine netting was adopted by British deep sea fishermen after the First World War, but it has been used for a very long time by coastal fishermen working from small boats with a fixed stake ashore.

4. LINING.—Lining is less important than formerly although it is still employed to take some of the larger pelagic fish, *e.g.* tuna, and demersal fish such as the cod and halibut. The method involves the use of a series of lines with baited hooks attached. "Long liners" are trawler-like vessels which operate frequently in distant waters. They are numerous on the Grand Banks.

MAJOR FISHING GROUNDS OF THE WORLD

THE NORTH ATLANTIC.—The most highly developed fisheries in the world extend along both sides of the North Atlantic, from the White and Barents Sea to North Africa, and from Greenland to the coasts of New England. Important "outliers" occur around Iceland and the Faeroes. In these seas, activities are concentrated upon the elevated portions of the continental shelves, or *banks*, where the shallow waters are particularly rich in marine life, and where the sandy or muddy floors do not obstruct the use of the trawl net. The Dogger Bank in the North Sea, and the Grand Bank, St Pierre Bank, and George's Bank off the east coast of North

America have been important for centuries. The North Atlantic fisheries are exploited by all the maritime nations of North West Europe, Canada, and the United States. A catch exceeding 10 million tons is taken annually, representing one-quarter of the total world production of marine fish (Fig. 63).

The herring and related species which include the sprat, pilchard or sardine, and the anchovy are the most abundant of the pelagic types. Pilchard and anchovy are prolific in the warmer seas, and are caught from Portugal northwards to the coasts of Cornwall. The common herring is found in greatest numbers in the cooler waters on both sides of the Atlantic. More than 2·5 million tons are taken each year by drift and seine net, and to a less extent by the trawl. The North Sea and the Norwegian and Maine coasts are the chief herring grounds. By weight, although not by value, the herring comprises approximately 60 per cent. of the total Swedish catch, 55 per cent. of the Icelandic, and 50 per cent. of the Norwegian and Portuguese catches. The herring catch in North American waters is small, mainly because the fish has not become very popular in the United States and Canadian markets.

Herring are landed at a large number of ports along the coasts of Britain and the Continent. Some are sold and consumed fresh, but the majority are cured by salting and smoking, and marketed as bloaters and kippers. There is still a substantial export trade in cured herring from Britain to European countries, although it is much less than during the period before the First World War. In North America, the smaller herring are canned, and sold as "sardines".

Cod, haddock, plaice, whiting, skate, hake, sole, and flounder are commercially the most important of a long list of demersal fish taken in Atlantic waters. The relative size of the demersal and pelagic catches landed at United Kingdom ports by British fishermen is illustrated graphically in Fig. 64.

THE WEST CENTRAL ATLANTIC.—The fisheries of the Atlantic and Gulf Coast states have been developed mainly by the United States, and are noteworthy for the large catch of Atlantic Menhaden. This catch amounts to more than one million tons annually, or two-fifths of the United States' takings. The fish is consumed almost entirely in the manufacture of cattle and poultry meal, fertilisers, and other industrial products including margarine, linoleum, and paint. The most valuable species, however, is the shrimp. Approximately 120,000 tons are landed annually by trawlers fishing inshore waters. Oysters and crabs are also caught in considerable numbers.

The exploitation of the Caribbean fisheries is retarded by the physical conditions of the sea bed, the lack of capital in the countries of the Caribbean and the West Indies, and by the difficulties of distribution in a region of tropical climate, and poor communications. Peasant fishermen, working with crudely constructed sailing vessels, rowing boats, and dug-out canoes are responsible for most of the small catch, which is marketed in coastal settlements on the mainland and islands. The waters abound in many types of fish, and the potentialities of the grounds are believed to be considerable.

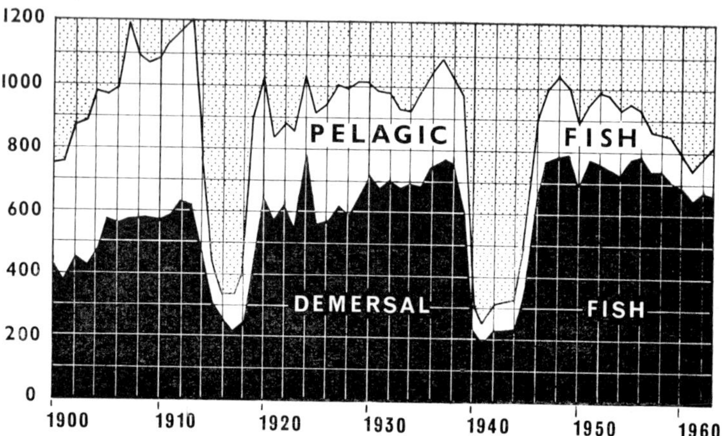

Fig. 64.—Great Britain: Landings of Fish (excluding Shell Fish) of British taking.

The East Central Atlantic.—Fishing grounds off the coasts of Mauritania and Senegal are visited by trawlers operating from European ports. A substantial catch is also taken from inshore waters along the Guinea coast by peasant fishermen. The coastal lagoons are also important.

The South West Atlantic.—Despite a long shore line, and in the south a broad continental shelf, the republics of eastern South America possess but poorly developed commercial fisheries. The pastoral industries of the Argentine, Uruguay, and southern Brazil produce an abundance of meat, and hence there is little need for the people to turn to the sea in search of food. The fishing grounds are also beyond the economic range of most North American, European, and Japanese based trawlers. Much of the catch of a little over half a million tons per year is taken in coastal waters by fishermen operating on a very small scale. Landings, however, are increasing and canneries have been established at Rio de Janeiro, Buenos Aires, Mar del Plata, and a few other ports.

THE SOUTH EAST ATLANTIC.—The principal grounds lie off the west coast of South Africa. Development has been rapid during the last quarter century, and landings at South African ports now exceed 500,000 tons annually. About the same weight is taken by fishermen operating from bases in South West Africa. Hake, crayfish, pilchards, and anchovy are the main species caught.

THE MEDITERRANEAN AND BLACK SEAS.—The fisheries of the Mediterranean are small when compared with those of the Atlantic. The sardine, anchovy, and tuna are characteristic species, and are caught along many coasts, although never on a large scale. In some ports the catch supports a canning industry. Valuable sponge fisheries are found in Egyptian waters and among some of the Greek islands. Italy is the largest fishing nation of the Mediterranean: the bulk of the very substantial Spanish catch is taken in the Atlantic. The fishing grounds of the Bosporus and the Sea of Marmara (which are exploited by Turkey), and the Black Sea and the Sea of Azov, where Russian vessels predominate, are more important than those of the Mediterranean. In addition to the Mediterranean species, the sturgeon is important, and is normally caught when it migrates towards the rivers to spawn.

THE INDIAN OCEAN.—Little in the way of commercial fishing occurs along the east coast of Africa. The fisheries of India and Pakistan are under developed, one might even say criminally neglected in view of the acute shortage of food in the two countries. India's catch amounts to about one million tons per annum, an improvement on the position of a few years ago, but still equivalent to only five pounds per head of the population. Forty per cent. of the takings consist of fresh water and estuarine species. Sea fishing is confined to waters lying within a few miles of the coast. Most of the catch is consumed in coastal villages.

A significant development in the Persian Gulf has been the discovery during the last year or two of valuable shrimp and prawn grounds off the coast of Kuwait. Their exploitation is forming the basis of a new export trade in canned products.

THE INDO-PACIFIC OCEAN.—Fishing is carried on around most of the inhabited coasts of South East Asia and the East Indian islands. Generally it is a peasant activity, and, as in many Asian regions, is confined essentially to coastal waters. Distant-water Japanese vessels, however, are active in the South China Sea. Extensive areas of shallow water, and the presence of many rivers which bring into the ocean an abundance of food have created better conditions for marine life than exist in most tropical waters. To a catch of more than 3 million tons of sea fish per year, must be added several hundred thousand tons of fish taken in rivers and lakes.

THE NORTH EAST PACIFIC.—The narrowness of the continental shelf off the west coast of North America restricts fishing grounds to the fiords and inlets, and to a belt of open water adjacent to the coastline. Salmon is the principal fish caught, and is taken by purse seine and gill net during its migratory spawning run to fresh water rivers. Some 200,000 tons are landed annually, of which Alaska contributes nearly 60 per cent. and British Columbia 25 per cent. Over-exploitation of the grounds, the erection of power dams across rivers, and to a lesser degree river pollution are a threat to the salmon industry, which has declined steadily during the last thirty years. Fishing is now regulated by a U.S.-Canadian Commission, and hatcheries have been established to increase the stock. The local market is very restricted, and most of the catch is canned for shipment to the eastern states or abroad. Herring, cod, and halibut are caught in the open sea.

THE EAST CENTRAL PACIFIC.—California has a share in the Pacific salmon fishing industry, but the greater proportion of her catch consists of true ocean species—tuna, sardines, mackerel, anchovies, barracuda, rockfish, and sole—and is taken principally in open water south of San Francisco, and in the Gulf of California.

THE SOUTH EAST PACIFIC.—The most significant episode in the long history of fishing along this coastline has been the spectacular rise of Peru to the position of leading fishing nation in the world. The inshore waters of the cold Peruvian current team with life, which until recently was little exploited. In 1947 Peru landed only 47,000 metric tons of marine fish. By 1955 the landings had increased to 213,000 metric tons, by 1960 to 3·5 million tons, and in 1964 more than 9 million tons were brought ashore. The industry is based largely on the dense shoals of anchovies in the north. This species comprises more than 95 per cent. of the total catch. More than one million tons of fish meal are processed annually.

The Chilean industry has also expanded rapidly, and landings have risen seven-fold since 1950. Tuna, sardines, and hake are the most valuable species. The cheaper types are used for fish meal production.

THE NORTH WEST PACIFIC.—Japan, China, and the Soviet Union fish the waters of the North West Pacific. The Japanese industry has grown during the course of the present century from a small-scale, though important, peasant activity into onc of the best equipped and most highly organised fishing enterprises in the world. The catch landed in Japan consistently exceeded that of other countries for many years, and in some seasons accounted for half the total world production of marine fish. In 1962, however, Japan was overtaken by Peru (Table 58).

TABLE 58
LANDINGS OF FISH IN THE PRINCIPAL FISHING COUNTRIES
(in thousands of metric tons)

	1958	1963	1966
Peru	900	6,820	8,790
Japan	5,500	6,700	6,910
U.S.A.	2,700	2,775	2,510
Norway	1,440	1,390	2,650
India	1,060	1,045	1,367
Spain	785	1,120	1,360
Canada	985	1,170	1,350
Chile	220	760	1,380
United Kingdom ..	1,140	1,060	973
Iceland	580	785	1,240
Denmark	600	850	830
West Germany ..	735	800	660

Source: *F.A.O. Yearbook of Fishery Statistics.*

The fisheries of the North West Pacific rest on a similar physical basis to those of the North Atlantic. The continental shelves are extensive, and a mingling of cool and warm currents has attracted a great abundance and variety of marine life. More than 400 species have commercial significance, the main ones being the herring, sardine, mackerel, cod, tuna, salmon, and bream, and many kinds of shellfish. Coastlines are long with many indentations, and in Japan nearly 100 million people huddle into tiny pockets of lowland by the sea. The Japanese fishing industry has received the active support of the government, which is well aware that the country's large population can only be fed by exploiting fully the resources of the oceans. From an organisational standpoint, the Japanese industry can be divided into two sectors:

(i) The coastal fisheries, worked in time honoured fashion by individuals and small groups using simple equipment. This sector is responsible for about 50 per cent. of the total catch.

(ii) The deep sea fisheries, which are exploited by some of the largest and best equipped vessels afloat to-day. Prolific grounds are situated around the coasts of Japan and Kamchatka, but trawlers and factory ships are active in waters off the coasts of Africa, North and South America, northern Australia, and in the Bay of Bengal. Japan is also the only Asian country with whaling interests in the Antarctic. The export of fish and fish products brings in £75 million worth of foreign currency each year.

THE SOUTH WEST PACIFIC.—The fishing grounds of Australia and New Zealand are incompletely explored and little developed. The abundance of meat in the two countries may explain the lack of interest in fish, as it appears to do in the Argentine and Uruguay. A little trawling takes place, and inshore oyster beds are important along the coasts of New South Wales and the Auckland Peninsula.

INLAND FISHERIES.—Fresh-water lakes, ponds, and rivers are important sources of fish in all continents. In India, Pakistan, and many of the South East Asian countries they yield almost as abundantly as the oceans (Table 59). Fish farming is also practised widely in the Far East. Among the chief inland commercial fisheries of other regions are those of the Great Lakes and the rivers of British Columbia, Washington, and Oregon; and the rivers and lakes of south-eastern Europe and the Soviet Union. The Caspian Sea and the Sea of Aral, both lakes of low salinity, produce 500,000 tons per year, notably species of sturgeon, roach, pike, perch, and bream.

TABLE 59

FRESH WATER CATCH (*a*) IN TOTAL, (*b*) AS A PERCENTAGE OF THE TOTAL FISH CATCH IN CERTAIN ASIAN COUNTRIES (1966)

	TOTAL FRESH WATER CATCH (000 metric tons)	PERCENTAGE OF TOTAL CATCH
India	477	35
Pakistan	232	56
Indonesia	281	28
Thailand	73	14
Hong Kong	31	37

Source: *F.A.O. Yearbook of Fishery Statistics.*

Conservation of the fisheries

The belief was widely held at the end of the last century, even by eminent biologists, that the resources of the sea were inexhaustible. Fish were considered to be so abundant, their breeding habits so prolific (a female cod, for instance, produces upwards of 400,000 eggs per year), and the natural hazards to which they were exposed so great, that the activities of man could have but a negligible effect on their numbers. This was in all probability a correct assessment of the position at that time, but the many developments that have taken place since have radically altered the situation, at least on the easily accessible grounds. The last eighty years have witnessed the successful application of steam power to the fishing vessel, the replacement of the beam trawl by the more efficient otter trawl, a great increase in the number, size, and economic range of ships at sea, and improved methods of fish detection and preservation. Better inland transportation has also made possible the distribution of catches to markets hitherto untapped. The net result has been a prodigious increase in the annual weight of fish landed.

Increased production, however, has been achieved mainly by extending operations into seas not formerly exploited to the full. There are undoubtedly further rich fishing grounds to be developed in the tropics and the southern hemisphere, but there is clearly a limit to what can be accomplished by opening up new grounds. The continental shelves, like the land areas that will repay cultivation, are limited in extent. In the heavily fished North Sea and North Atlantic it has been apparent for some time, both from the steady decline in the size of the daily catch taken by vessels at sea and from the smaller proportion of large fish in the catches, that the limit of fishing intensity has been reached, and even surpassed. If this is the case, then the use of more efficient gear can only serve to deplete stocks further, and so make ultimate recovery more difficult. It is interesting to note that when fishing was resumed after four years of little activity during each world war, landings increased substantially, in spite of a reduced number of vessels on the grounds.

Ideally a fishery should be managed on a sustained-yield basis. In other words, when one year is taken with another, the catch should not exceed the annual increment. If the catch is in excess of the increment, the value of the fishery will inevitably decline. On the other hand, if it is below, the grounds could with profit be more intensively exploited. The rational development of the world's fisheries, however, is made very difficult by two factors:

(i) Most of the fishing grounds lie outside the limits of territorial waters, and consequently any nation has a legal right to exploit them as it wishes. The regulation of fishing, therefore, depends on international agreement and co-operation. In view of the number of countries with interests on the grounds, agreements of value are not easily reached. A number of international conventions have been negotiated, however. One which came into force in 1954, and covered the North Atlantic, prohibited the use of nets of very small mesh. Such nets caught many small fish that should have been conserved for breeding, and which in any case were often of no economic value. The signing of the convention was a move in the right direction, but more stringent measures, designed among other things to protect breeding grounds and regulate fishing on a quota basis, will be necessary before the fisheries of the North Atlantic and other intensively exploited waters are secure for the future.

(ii) A reasonably accurate "inventory" of fish, which must be the starting point of any scientifically based programme of development, is extremely difficult to compile. The reproduction and survival rate of fish varies from year to year, and for reasons that are imperfectly understood. Predictable seasonal, and unpredictable long term migrations occur, the latter upsetting any calculations that may have been made about the potential of a fishery. The migration of herring from the Baltic in the fifteenth century, and the sudden increase in the number of cod off the coasts of Greenland and Bear Island in the 1930s, are cases in point. Most countries with commercial fishing interests are engaged in research into these and other problems, but solutions are not yet in sight. However, until it is possible to predict the nature of future seasons with some confidence, the scientific management of the fisheries will not really be possible.

WHALING

The centre of the whaling industry has shifted during the present century from the North Atlantic—where in its modern form it began—to the cooler seas of the southern hemisphere. Sixty per cent. of the whale and sperm oil production is now obtained from the catch taken in Antarctic waters. In the 1963-4 season, sixteen factory ships, seven belonging to Japan, four each to Norway and the Soviet Union, and one to the Netherlands were active in these waters. They were accompanied by 190 trawler-like vessels armed with harpoons, and known as "catchers". In addition there were several shore stations in the Antarctic. Hunting grounds also existed in the North Atlantic, South Atlantic, and off the coasts of Africa, North and South America, and Australia (Table 60).

Important turning points in the development of the whaling industry came with the invention of the heavy harpoon gun in 1865, and again in 1923 with the advent of a factory ship which could process the whale at sea. The former made possible the hunting of the largest whales, including those that sank when killed, and the latter released the whaler from close dependence on the shore station, and thereby extended its range into distant waters. The

TABLE 60

PRODUCTION OF WHALE OIL AND SPERM OIL, BY REGIONS, 1964-5
(in thousands of metric tons)

Region	
Antarctica	181
North Atlantic and Arctic	4·3
Africa	18
North Pacific	3·8
Japan and Korea	7·6
Others (including Australia, Azores, Brazil, Chile, Kamchatka, Kuriles, Madeira, New Zealand, Peru, Portugal, and Spain)	125
TOTAL	339

Source: *United Nations Statistical Abstract*, 1966.

introduction of these new techniques resulted in an increase in oil production from a few thousand barrels per year in the mid-nineteenth century to nearly 4 million barrels in 1930-1. Since then, production has declined to some 2·5 million barrels (about 500,000 tons) per season. The decline is significant. It is partly due to the increasing scarcity of whales, but also to restrictions that have been placed upon their capture by the International Whaling Commission of 1946. The Commission meets annually, and allocates on a quota basis the numbers that may be taken, and the area and season when they may be hunted. At present, the catch is limited to 4,500 "blue whale units"[1] per season, double the number that scientists regard as the maximum if stocks are not to be reduced further. At a lower level of exploitation, however, it is doubtful whether the yield would be economic. One aspect of the mounting problems facing the Antarctic whaling expeditions is illustrated by the figures in Table 61.

TABLE 61

AVERAGE PRODUCTION OF WHALE OIL PER DAY'S WORK
(in barrels)

SEASON	PER "CATCHER"	PER FACTORY SHIP
1946-7	120	1,037
1952-3	110	1,591
1959-60	87	942
1963-4	51	611

Source: *International Whaling Statistics, Oslo*, 1965.

Whale oil is by far the most important product of the whaling industry, and is used widely in the manufacture of margarine, cooking fat, and high grade soap. It has long been displaced from its position as the leading lubricant and luminant by petroleum.

[1] One "blue whale unit" equals two fin whales, two and a half humpbacks, and six sei whales. The blue whale has been for some time a totally protected and virtually extinct species.

Sperm oil from the sperm whale is a raw material of the chemical industry, and finds a use in the production of cosmetics. By-products include whale meat, whale liver oil, cattle food, and bone meal. Every part of the animal is of some economic value.

THE FUTURE OF THE FISHERIES

Most of man's fishing expeditions are directed against the marine carnivorous animals. These animals come at or near the end of a long food chain that begins with the multitude of minute vegetable organisms (plankton) that inhabit the shallow seas. Interest has been shown recently in the possibilities of harvesting some of this primary food material—estimated to be produced annually at the rate of three tons per acre over the fishing grounds—directly, rather than wait until it has been converted, stage by stage, and very wastefully into edible-size fish. If it could be done, a greatly increased supply of protein food would become available for the world's growing population. Future research may well demonstrate the economic feasibility of such a project, but at present efforts are frustrated by two factors:

(i) The immense physical difficulties of separating microscopic-sized organisms from sea water.

(ii) The rapid cycle of marine life, which results in the greater part of the potential harvest being consumed almost as soon as it is produced.

It appears more likely therefore that the prospects of increasing the production of sea food in the foreseeable future depend upon a rational exploitation of the fish resources as such. The steps that can be, and in some cases are being taken to this end are:

1. The conservation of stocks in the heavily fished grounds.

2. The development of the under-fished areas on a sustained yield basis.

3. Research into the possibilities of fish farming. Fish culture is infinitely more simple in small inland ponds and sections of rivers, where environmental control is comparatively easy, than it is in the oceans. The very size of the oceans makes it extremely unlikely that man will be able to increase significantly the stocks of useful fish by such methods as the establishment of hatcheries or the exclusion of predators from the grounds. In a few cases, however, stocks have been increased as a result of human intervention. Oysters have been cultivated for centuries on many of the warmer coasts, and salmon hatcheries have proved successful in North

America and elsewhere. The circumstances, however, are exceptional. The oyster is not a free swimming animal, and the salmon breeds naturally in fresh-water streams where local conditions can be more easily modified. Some success, too, has been achieved in "transplanting" plaice and other species from over crowded inshore waters to more favourable habitats, where they develop more rapidly, but the scale on which this work is possible is very limited. Spectacular results from this line of research should not be anticipated. It is in the extension of conservation practices that hope for the future lies.

CHAPTER XII

FUEL AND POWER

Energy consumption and living standards

One of the factors—perhaps the most important single factor—that over the years has made a rise in living standards possible, has been the progressive harnessing of the world's primary energy resources—wind and water, solid and liquid fuels, natural gas, and, during the last quarter century, atomic power.

As a community's material well-being is closely related to the value of goods and services it produces, and as most goods and many services can only be produced by consuming energy, it follows that there is likely to be at least some correlation between the value of production per head of the population and the *per capita* consumption of power. The correlation is in fact close (Fig. 65). In some circumstances, however, high living standards are not incompatable with a fairly low energy consumption, and conversely low living standards are not necessarily the result of a meagre use of power. New Zealand, Switzerland, and South Africa illustrate the point. In cases where the *per capita* income is higher or lower than the amount of power consumed might lead one to expect, it will be due to one or more of the following factors:

1. The amount of energy required to produce a given *value* of production varies from one industry to another (Table 62). A nation, therefore, which derives an unusually large proportion of its income from, for example, agriculture, or from the tourist industry, will make less demand on power resources than one in which primary metal smelting is the predominant activity.

TABLE 62

COST OF POWER AS A PERCENTAGE OF THE TOTAL VALUE ADDED BY MANUFACTURE IN SELECTED INDUSTRIES

Cost of power more than 20% of the total value added.	*Cost of power less than 10% of the total value added.*
Primary metal smelting.	Textile and leather manufacture.
Aluminium reduction.	Food canning.
Heavy chemical manufactures.	Bread and confectionery manufacture.
Brick and tile manufactures.	Motor vehicle and aircraft assembly.
Cement manufacture.	Light electrical engineering.

Activities in which power consumption is negligble: agriculture (especially live-stock rearing); the service industries (banking, commerce, wholesale and retail trades, hotel and catering).

2. Countries enjoying the benefit of cheap power tend to use it wastefully.

3. Much energy is consumed by the people of the colder countries of the world solely in order to keep warm, and such consumption makes no direct contribution to economic production.

4. In lands where distances are great, and populations scattered, the transport services consume a disproportionate amount of power.

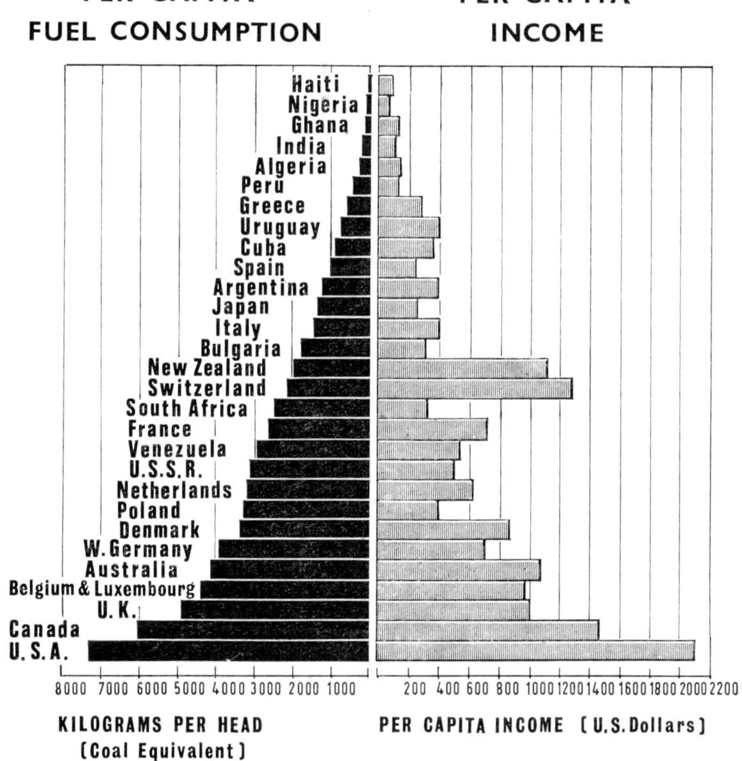

Fig. 65.—ENERGY CONSUMPTION AND LIVING STANDARDS.

World production of primary energies

The total world production of primary energies of all types is estimated to have increased from about 800 million tons, coal equivalent,[1] at the beginning of the present century to some 5,000 million tons to-day. The contribution of each of the major fuels in the years 1938, 1948, 1958, and 1963 is illustrated graphically in Fig. 66. Wood and peat for which no accurate data are available, but which are of considerable importance in many of the less developed countries, are excluded. At the present time coal satisfies about 44 per cent. of the world's energy needs, oil 39 per cent., and natural gas 15 per cent. The contribution of hydro-electricity has

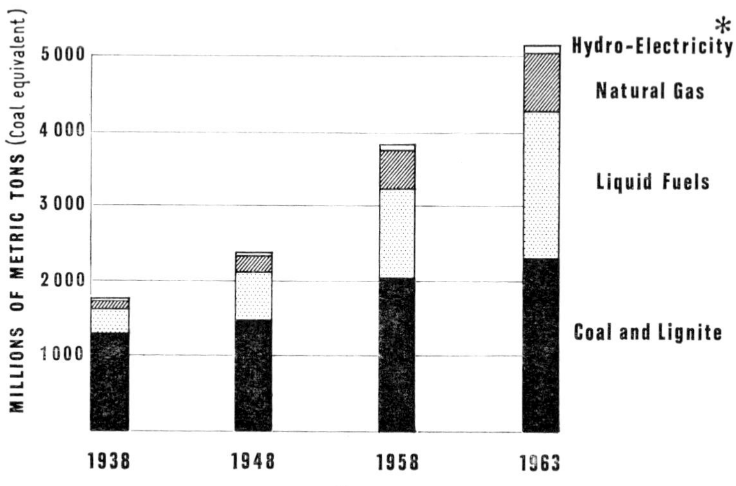

Fig. 66.—World Consumption of Primary Energy (1938-63). In millions of metric tons (coal equivalent).

remained fairly constant during the last fifty years at about 1·5 per cent. to 2 per cent. Atomic energy is of minor significance as yet, although in at least one major industrial country—the United Kingdom—it has already surpassed hydro-power in importance.

However, world figures such as these give little indication of the position in individual countries. As the demand for energy has grown, nations have developed the resources with which nature has endowed them, or have imported fuels that are most readily accessible. It is evident from Fig. 67 that coal is now a major source of power only in those countries which possess large indigenous deposits (the U.S.A., the United Kingdom, and the Soviet Union).

[1] One ton of coal is equated with $\frac{2}{3}$ tons of oil, half a ton of natural gas, 8,000 kWh. of electricity.

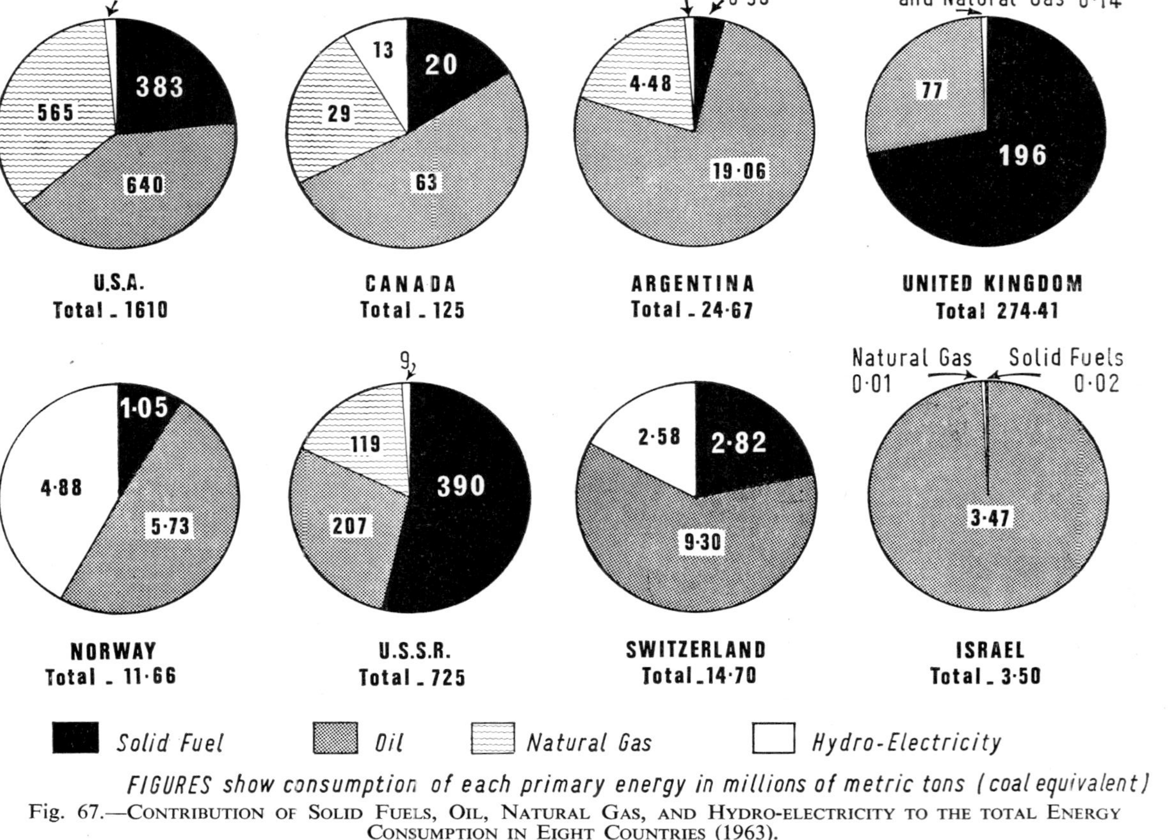

Fig. 67.—Contribution of Solid Fuels, Oil, Natural Gas, and Hydro-electricity to the total Energy Consumption in Eight Countries (1963).

Sweden, Israel, and Switzerland import oil, not coal, to supplement their own inadequate domestic fuel supplies, and it is reasonable to suppose that imports of natural gas will increase as techniques for transporting it are improved. Finally, the comparatively small role played by hydro-electricity, even in Switzerland, Sweden, and Austria where the water power potential is great, should be noted.

COAL

Methods and problems of coal mining

OPEN-CAST MINING.—Between three and seven per cent. of Britain's coal (the amount varies from year to year) is produced from open-cast or strip mines. In some countries, notably the United States and the lignite producers, the proportion is much higher. The remainder is won from underground workings.

Open-cast mining is profitable when horizontal or nearly horizontal seams are situated at not more than about 200 ft below ground level, and are covered only by a soft over-burden that can be cleared with earth-moving equipment. Surface mining is normally a highly mechanised operation in which labour productivity is high and the costs of production low. In Britain the average cost per ton of open-cast coal in 1962 was sixty-eight shillings, compared with eighty-seven shillings for deep-mined coal. Overhead costs of an open-cast working are also low, and serious losses are not incurred if a mine is closed during a period of slack demand. The present policy of the National Coal Board is, in fact, to use open-cast production as a balancing factor between supply from deep mines on the one hand, and demand for coal on the other.

Against these advantages must be set the cost of compensation to farmers and other landowners whose property is ravaged by open-cast operations. In the post-war years, when both food and coal were scarce in Britain, the practice of laying waste good agricultural land in the interests of a higher coal output raised heated controversy. Fortunately, the annoyance and inconvenience caused to the farming community need only be temporary, as with proper management the land can be restored to food production after mining has ceased.

UNDERGROUND MINING.—Access to underground mines can be gained in three ways. The commonest is by means of vertical shafts. Alternatively, a tunnel may be driven downwards at a low angle until a productive seam is reached. This method has the advantage of giving easier access to the workings for both men and equipment, and facilitating the removal of the coal. A third practice is to follow a coal outcrop into a hillside by a shaft whose slope is determined by the dip of the seam. This is the *drift* or *adit mine*. In all underground mines, unless they are very small, two or more entrances are essential to provide adequate ventilation and an alternative escape route in case of emergency.

Some modern, deep mines are beginning to achieve a degree of automatic working such as is common in manufacturing industry. Progress in this direction has gone furthest in North America, but much has been achieved in this country during the last twenty years. In 1945, 90 per cent. of the coal won from British pits was obtained by methods which involved the use of pick and shovel. To-day, 80 per cent. is produced by power loading machines which cut and load the coal in one operation, and some plant is equipped to move its own conveyors and roof supports forward as it advances into the seam. The old "cyclic" system, whereby the coalface was prepared in one shift, coal cut in the second, and removed in the third, is thus being replaced by a system in which extraction is more or less continuous. Output per man-shift has risen, and the cost of coal production stabilised. Increases in the market price of coal since 1960 have been due to higher distribution charges, rather than to higher prices at the pit head. In the near future many coal faces are likely to be completely automated and controlled by computer. The National Coal Board predicts that by 1975, 100 million tons per year will be mined by remote control from British pits. The first fully-automated British colliery—Bevercotes—went into production in 1966.

The geological structures of many fields, however, are such that automatic and automated equipment cannot be used. This is particularly the case in South Wales, North-east and North-west England, and some of the Scottish fields. The most productive pits are in Yorkshire and the East Midlands. These regions produce half of Britain's coal to-day, and given adequate investment could be made to produce much more, and at a cost at which rival fuels would find competition difficult. A complete rationalisation of the coal industry would of course involve the closure of many pits (the number has been variously estimated at between 200 and 550) in the older coalfields of the north and west, where alternative work for miners would not always be easy to find. Clearly, social as well as economic factors have to be taken into account when plans for the re-organisation of a major industry are being made.

Type and rank of coal

TABLE 63

CHARACTERISTICS OF THE MAIN TYPES OF COAL

	Percentage of Moisture	Percentage of Carbon	Heat value (B.T.U.s per lb. dry weight)	Percentage of world production
Lignite	30-60	65-70	11,000	15
Bituminous ..	20-30	75	13,000	80
Anthracite ..	5-10	90-95	13,500	5

Lignite.—In spite of the large and generally accessible reserves that exist in many countries, lignite has been of much less importance commercially than bituminous coal. It has a low calorific value and a high moisture content. It is further inclined to spontaneous combustion and crumbling when exposed to the atmosphere—characteristics which make its storage and transport difficult. Lignite is consumed by industry and domestic users situated close to the mines. Thermal electricity generating stations are major users of lignite, and advances which have been made in the transmission of electric power during the present century have increased its value as a fuel. Lignite is also an important raw material of the chemical industry. Fields situated in areas where there is a scarcity of bituminous coal have been most fully exploited. The leading producer is East Germany (Table 64).

TABLE 64

PRODUCTION OF LIGNITE

(in millions of metric tons)

	1948	1956	1960	1966
East Germany	109·9	205·9	225·5	249·0
U.S.S.R.	58·2	125·2	138·3	154·9
West Germany	65·1	95·4	96·2	98·1
Czechoslovakia	23·6	46·3	58·4	74·1
Yugoslavia	9·7	15·9	21·4	28·1
Hungary	9·4	18·2	23·7	26·0
Bulgaria	4·1	9·8	15·4	24·6
Australia	6·8	10·7	15·2	22·1

Source: *U.N. Statistical Yearbook.*

Bituminous coal.—Bituminous coal has a higher heat and lower moisture content than lignite, into which it grades. A rank intermediate between bituminous and lignite, known as *sub-bituminous*, is also recognised. Bituminous coal is the common household coal, shiny black in colour, dirty to handle, high in volatile matter, and distinguished when ignited by a smoky, yellow flame. It deteriorates little when exposed to the atmosphere, and storage and transport present no particular difficulties.

TABLE 65

PRODUCTION OF BITUMINOUS COAL AND ANTHRACITE
(in millions of metric tons)

	1948	1956	1960	1966
U.S.A.	592·9	478·0	391·5	490·7
U.S.S.R.	150·0	304·0	374·9	430·4
China (mainland)†	32·4	100·4	420·0 (?)	n/a
United Kingdom	212·8	225·6	196·7	177·4
West Germany	99·8	152·7	143·3	126·3
Poland	70·3	95·1	104·4	122·0
India	30·6	39·9	52·6	68·0
France	43·3	55·1	59·9	50·3
Japan	33·7	45·6	51·1	51·3
South Africa	24·0	33·6	38·2	53·4 *
Czechoslovakia	16·7	21·7	26·2	27·0
WORLD	1,410·7	1,687·8	1,986·1	2,052·0

* 1965 † Includes lignite.
Source: *U.N. Statistical Yearbook.*

Anthracite.—Only about 5 per cent. of the world's coal output is true anthracite. It is a hard, brittle coal, low in volatile matter, and rich in carbon. It burns slowly and without smoke. Its value as a domestic fuel is limited by the inability of many domestic grates to burn it. Its cost is greater than that of bituminous coal.

Coking coal.—Two types of coke should be distinguished, *i.e.* (i) Metallurgical coke for use in the iron smelting and foundry industries. Such coke must be as free as possible from sulphur and other undesirable impurities, and must have a crushing strength high enough to withstand the weight of the furnace charge. Not all coals make satisfactory coke, although the retort or by-product coking oven has made the utilisation of previously unsuitable coals now possible. Blending, or mixing coals from different fields, is often necessary to produce a coke of desired quality. (ii) Domestic and general purpose coke, which is a by-product of gas manufacture.

Coalfields of continental Europe

GERMANY.—The German coal industry is dominated by the great Ruhr or Westphalian field. Reserves probably exceed 100,000 million tons, and annual production is in the order of 120 million tons. All types of coal are present. The northward dip of the beds brings the oldest members of the sequence—the anthracites—to the surface along the southern flanks of the Ruhr Valley; above these occur excellent coking coals, and finally gas and long flame coals. In the northern part of the field seams are thick, and relatively undisturbed, and although lying at considerable depths, they are easy to work. The location of this field adjacent to the Rhine, and on a level plain across which communications have been easy to build has greatly enhanced its value. Upon it has developed one of the greatest industrial conurbations in the world.

The small bituminous fields of the Saar and Aachen produce respectively about one-tenth and one-twentieth of the West German output. A small field in Lower Saxony is only of local importance.

Lignite is worked in West Germany, near Cologne and near Brunswick, but the main lignite deposits lie in the Democratic Republic in the Halle-Magdeburg-Leipzig lowlands. More than 200 million tons are produced each year from this field, principally from large surface pits.

POLAND.—Second only to the Ruhr in reserves is the coalfield of Upper Silesia, which extends from Gleiwitz towards Krakow, and southwards into Czechoslovakia. This field lay in German territory until the end of the First World War when more than half was ceded to Poland. The remainder was lost to Poland in 1945. It supports the metallurgical and chemical industries of Upper Silesia, and exports some 20 million tons annually. The Lower Silesian field is small, but contains reserves of good coking coal.

FRANCE.—The largest field in the country extends in a band only a few miles in width from near Béthune to the Belgian frontier, and beyond as far as Liége. Seams are thin and badly disturbed, and mining is difficult and costly. The quality of the coal is on the whole good, although metallurgical grades are scarce. Many small, uneconomic pits on this field, on both sides of the Franco-Belgian frontier, have been closed in recent years by the European Coal and Steel Community.

The small coalfields of Le Creusot and St Etienne on the central massif are also expensive to work, but their position in the heart of the country, safe in the past from capture or destruction by invading armies, has given them a strategic importance. Iron and steel and engineering industries are located on both the fields.

BELGIUM AND HOLLAND.—Mining conditions on the Belgian portion of the Franco-Belgian coalfield are similar to those in northern France. The Campine field of the north, which is shared with Holland, was first worked after the First World War. The field is entirely concealed, and the seams, although deep, are easily exploited. It produces half of the Belgian and the whole of the Dutch output of coal, and is beginning to attract metallurgical and other industries.

SPAIN.—Three-quarters of the country's coal comes from fields in the northern foothills of the Cantabrian Mountains near Oviedo. Scattered deposits of no great importance are found in the Sierra Morena in the south. The quality of Spanish coal is generally poor.

OTHER EUROPEAN PRODUCERS.—Coal or lignite is mined in the remaining countries of Europe with the exception of Finland and Luxembourg, although in some of them, *e.g.* the Scandinavian states, Switzerland, and Albania, production is of little commercial significance. The paucity of domestic coal supplies, however, has not retarded the economic development of those lands which have access to the major fields of continental Europe or the British Isles, or which have harnessed alternative forms of energy. The relative backwardness of the Mediterranean and Balkan countries, on the other hand, can be attributed at least in part to inadequate deposits of indigenous coal.

THE SOVIET UNION.—The Soviet coalfields extend over enormous areas, especially in Siberia, where the true extent of the more remote fields is imperfectly known. Soviet industrialisation plans have been based largely on the exploitation of the country's coal resources. Production has increased from less than 30 million tons in 1914 to more than 600 million tons (including lignite) to-day. The opening up of the Siberian fields is leading to a dispersal of population, and to the growth of manufacturing industry east of the Urals. The main fields are:

1. *The Donetz Basin* (*The Donbas*).—Situated to the south of the main centres of population, this field was not developed until the end of the last century. Its importance grew rapidly, once serious mining operations had begun, and by the outbreak of war in 1914 it was producing more than 80 per cent. of all Russian coal. The existence of iron ore deposits 200 miles away at Krivoi Rog led to the establishment of large iron and steel industries in the Ukraine. It is still the most productive coalfield in the Soviet Union. Anthracite and good coking coal (which is not plentiful in the Soviet Union) are mined.

2. *The Kuznetz Basin* (*Kuzbas*) is the only Siberian field to have been worked extensively. A wide range of coal is present. The iron smelting and heavy engineering centres of Stalinsk, Novosibirsk, and Kemerovo have been based on this field. Coal is also sent westwards by rail to the Urals.

3. *The Karaganda, Irkutsk, Vladivostok, and Sakhalin fields*, also in Siberia.

4. *The Ural fields*, which are small and scattered and produce in the main low quality coal.

5. *The Tula field*, south of Moscow. This field is mainly lignitic.

6. The small Arctic field near *Pechora*.

Asia

CHINA.—Coal is mined in many parts of the country, although the greatest reserves by far are found in the north, particularly in the provinces of Shensi and Shansi, and in southern Manchuria. The Manchurian fields were developed by the Japanese between 1931 and 1945, but those of the interior of China remained isolated owing to inadequate lines of communication. Since 1950, the communist government has made strenuous efforts to build up the coal industry, and more than a ten-fold increase in output over the pre-war period is reported.

JAPAN.—The fields of Japan are small, and their thin, faulted seams present many mining problems. On the whole the quality of the coal is poor, and coking grades are very scarce. Substantial imports are necessary each year from Australia and the United States. The principal fields lie in north-west Kyushu, in the south of Honshu, and on Hokkaido.

INDIA.—Coal bearing rocks occur extensively in India. Only the fields of Bihar, Orissa, and West Bengal, however, are important, and they produce some 90 per cent. of the country's current output. These fields sustain the industrial complexes of Jamshedpur and the Damodar Valley. Total output is now about 60 million tons a year.

SOUTH EAST ASIA.—Small fields, yielding low ranking coals, are found in Malaya and Burma; and on Sumatra, the Philippine Islands, and Borneo. Their importance is little more than local. Rather better quality coal is mined in Tonkin (North Vietnam), but production is small.

North America

THE U.S.A.—Coal output in the United States has fallen steadily since the peak year of 1944, when more than 600 million tons were mined, to about 450 million tons annually at the present time. The decline is due to competition from alternative fuels, particularly oil and natural gas. Most probably, however, the present downward production trends will be reversed in the future as the country's power requirements during the remaining decades of the present century are likely to be met only by a substantial increase in the consumption of coal. The American coal industry is, in fact, planning to raise production targets to 1,000 million tons annually by A.D. 2000. The principal fields in the U.S.A. are:

1. *The Appalachian bituminous fields.*—Carboniferous rocks underlie the greater part of the Appalachian region from Pennsylvania to Alabama, although by no means the whole region contains productive coal measures. Mining is concentrated in three main areas, viz:

(i) The Northern Appalachian field of West Pennsylvania and West Virginia.

(ii) The Middle Appalachian fleld of West Virginia and Kentucky.

(iii) The Southern Appalachian or Warrior field of Alabama.

Together these regions produce 75-80 per cent. of the coal mined in the United States.

In the Northern and Middle Appalachian fields, high quality coal occurs in thick, undisturbed beds which extend with little variation over great distances. In places seams are worked by strip mining. In others they are exposed along the sides of deeply entrenched valleys, and can be followed into the hill-sides by adits. In each case the maximum utilisation of labour-saving machinery is possible, and the productivity of the American miner is consequently very high. From the mine entrances coal can often be loaded by inclined railways or chutes directly into river barges or rail-cars for distribution to Pittsburgh, Youngstown, the cities of the Lower Lake shores, and the Mid West.

The reserves of the Warrior field are much smaller than those of the Northern and Middle Appalachian fields. The quality of the coal, however, is high, and some excellent coking grades are produced. The Birmingham region consumes most of the output.

2. *The Pennsylvanian anthracite field* lies in the geologically disturbed zone of the Great Appalachian Valley. Seams are thinner and more irregular than in the bituminous region, and mining problems are greater. Production costs are high, and there has been a steady decline in the importance of the field. Output has fallen from about 50 million tons per year before the Second World War to less than 20 million tons to-day.

3. *The Interior fields.*—The Eastern Interior fields of Illinois, Indiana, and West Kentucky contain medium to good quality bituminous coal that can be mined cheaply from thick seams lying

near the surface. The coal makes a very satisfactory domestic fuel, but its high sulphur content renders it generally unsuitable for coking purposes. This factor has restricted the development of the field, which is otherwise well situated to supply the metallurgical industries of the Mid West.

The Western Interior fields of Iowa, Missouri, Oklahoma, and Arkansas, and the South-Western fields of Texas are large. Their coal, however, is of low quality, and its use is restricted to local markets. The fields are also located in regions of low population density where demand is limited. Competition from oil and natural gas is most strongly felt in this part of the United States.

4. *The Rocky Mountain fields* are small and scattered. They contain coal of varying rank from lignite to anthracite. They were developed during the last century to supply fuel to local mining companies and the trans-continental railways. Production is small.

CANADA.—The most productive Canadian field lies on Cape Breton Island, and is worked in the vicinity of Sydney. Good quality coking and bituminous grades are mined. Much of the output is used by the iron and steel industries of Sydney, and the field's coastal position gives it a price advantage over Appalachian coal in the St Lawrence Valley. It should be noted that apart from this field, and the small one on Vancouver Island, the North American coal deposits are poorly located in relation to ocean transport.

The Prairie and Mountain fields are situated in Alberta, and contain sub-bituminous coals primarily, although towards the Rockies the rank improves, and some anthracite is produced in the mountain sections. A lignite field is also worked in the vicinity of Estevan in Saskatchewan. There is also a small bituminous field on Vancouver Island.

Central America

A small field in Northern Mexico yields about 1 million tons a year, otherwise the states of Central America are either devoid of coal completely or produce quantities that have little or no economic significance.

South America

Reserves of coal in South America are smaller than in any other continent, with the exception of Africa, and good quality coking coals are very scarce indeed. The largest coal deposits are found in inaccessible locations within the Andes. Commercial exploitation is restricted to the coastal fields of Chile; to scattered areas within the

Andes of Peru and Colombia; to São Paulo and Rio Grande do Sul provinces of Brazil; and to the small fields of Rio Turbio and Mendoza in Argentina. Coal has played little part in the economic development of the continent in the past, and is unlikely to be a major factor in the future. Industrial progress will be based rather on the realisation of the very considerable water power potential of South America, the fuller exploitation of the interior oilfields, and on atomic power.

Africa

Practically all the coal reserves in Africa are found in the Transvaal and Natal. The Vryheid field of Natal produces good quality coking coal, but reserves are limited. In Rhodesia the Wankie mines are the only producers. The Enugu field of Nigeria contains the only deposits of any significance in the whole of West Africa, and the quality is generally poor. Total African production is under 2 per cent. of the world output.

Australasia

The New South Wales field, which occupies 5,000 square miles in the Sydney-Hunter Valley region, produces more than three-quarters of Australia's total production of black coal. All types are mined, including high quality metallurgical coal at Newcastle and Port Kembla. The field is well situated to supply the country's chief industrial areas and the main centres of population.

Coal is mined in the remaining states of Australia, with the exception of Northern Territory: at Ipswich, Blair Athol, and Clermont (Queensland); Collie (Western Australia); Wonthaggi (Victoria); Leigh Creek (South Australia), and at St Mary's and Hamilton (Tasmania). Considerable importance also attaches to the lignite deposits of Gippsland. Seams of great thickness are worked from open pits near Yallourn and Morwell. The lignite is used in electricity generating stations and in the production of town gas. It is also marketed as briquettes for household use in Melbourne.

NEW ZEALAND.—Coalfields in New Zealand are small and scattered, and are mainly lignitic. The chief bituminous field, which accounts for 30 per cent. of all types of coal mined in the country, is in the Westport-Greymouth district of South Island.

Coal as a factor in the location of economic activity

Coal has been used on a limited scale in Britain since the Middle Ages, but it did not become a vital factor in industry until late in the eighteenth century. Prior to this period man had depended on wood and charcoal to sustain the iron-smelting industries, and upon human and animal power, and the energy derived from wind and falling water, for the operation of such domestic and factory equipment as then existed.

During the eighteenth century two technological developments enormously enhanced the importance of coal. They were (i) the discovery of a method of making metallurgical coke from coal, and (ii) the invention of the steam engine. During the 150 to 200 years that followed these developments, the supremacy of coal was virtually unchallenged, and the immense expansion of manufacturing industry that occurred in Britain and abroad took place primarily upon the coalfields, or at points where coal procurement costs were low.

To-day the position is changing. The upward trend in world coal production continues, but increases in output are concentrated in the developing countries and the Soviet Union. In Britain, the United States, and the nations of continental Europe trends are steady, or even downwards. Over the world as a whole the percentage contribution of coal has declined at a rate of one per cent. per annum during the last fifteen years, as competing forms of primary energy have taken an increasing share of the fuel market. Coal too is losing its influence as a localising factor. The migration of population and industry to the coalfields that characterised the period of the Industrial Revolution has been halted, and in some instances reversed, and manufacturing centres are growing up in regions remote from the areas of coal production. Significantly, the areas of most rapid development in the United States are found in Florida, Texas, California, and some of the mountain states; and in Britain, in the south-east. None of these areas is on a coalfield. The reasons why the coalfields are relinquishing the grip they once held on industry are:

1. The development of alternate forms of primary energy—petroleum, natural gas, hydro-electricity, and atomic power. Factories deriving their energy requirements from one or other of these sources are in no way dependent on the distribution of coal supplies.

2. The increasing use of coal gas and electricity, and the diminishing importance of coal as a raw fuel. Gas and electricity are easily transportable, and allow a wide dispersal of industries that are adapted to consume them.

3. The greater efficiency of modern coal-burning appliances. Less coal needs to be burnt than formerly, and less therefore transported, to obtain a given output of power.

The coal-based conurbations are not, of course, on the point of extinction. They will persist for decades even though the raw material that built them is no longer the important factor it once was. Over the years they have acquired many assets—accumulated deposits of capital, labour skills, transport services, educational and training facilities, and markets for products—assets that are very attractive to many types of manufacturing industry. Migration is also a slow process, and one must keep a sense of perspective. The "drift to the south-east" which is causing concern to many planning departments in the United Kingdom is a drift and not a stampede. Manchester and Newcastle will be with us for a long time yet.

PETROLEUM

It is not known with certainty how petroleum originated, but it seems probable that it had its beginnings in the remains of countless millions of simple marine organisms which accumulated on the sea bed, there to be transformed by chemical and bacterial action, and the pressure of sediments deposited upon them into tiny droplets of oil. Because of its low specific gravity, the oil migrated upwards, and accumulated wherever suitable geological structures occurred. Oil reservoirs have only been found in sedimentary formations, and then only in commercial quantities when open-textured rocks have been sealed by a cap rock, and folded or faulted into "traps" (Fig. 68).

In the early days of the petroleum industry, prospecting was a hit and miss business in which the prospector had little to guide him, save perhaps the presence of a few oil seepages, and the success of other drillers in the area. For every productive well, dozens were dry, but the chance of a lucky strike and quick fortune brought in thousands of "wildcatters", all drilling, and if successful pumping as fast as they could, and then moving on. By the early years of the present century, however, sufficient had been learned of the sub-surface structures to allow the industry to become more scientifically based, and the modern era of oil exploration began.

To-day the search for oil is undertaken by the large petroleum companies. Aerial photography, the careful mapping of surface outcrops, and seismic, gravitational, and magnetic surveys always precede actual drilling. Certain areas of the world can be eliminated from the search, *e.g.* areas of igneous and metamorphic rocks, and rocks of pre-Cambrian age. Exploration is concentrated upon the sedimentary basins of the continents, and the continental shelves (Fig. 69). The scientist, however, can but indicate the places where oil is likely to be found. Its presence or absence can only be proved by exploratory drilling. The ratio of productive to dry wells

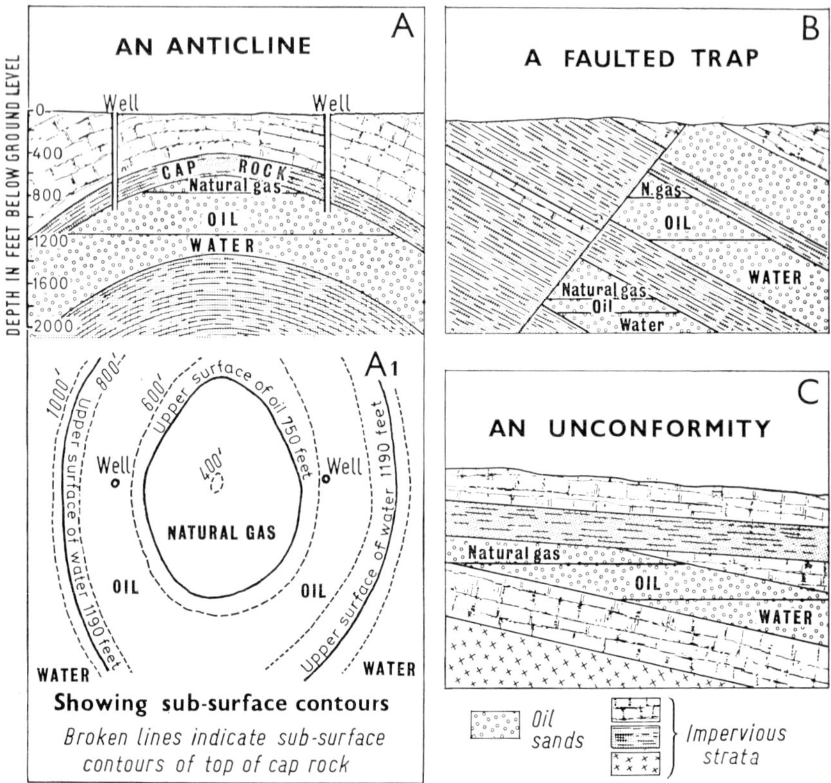

Fig. 68.—Common Types of Oiltraps.

drilled after prior investigation between 1953 and 1957 in the U.S.A. was one to nine: in Venezuela and the Middle East an even more satisfactory ratio was obtained.

Reserves of petroleum

Proven reserves are estimated at about 40,000 million tons, or about thirty-five times the present annual rate of production.

bove: A control panel at Bevercotes Colliery, Nottinghamshire. Complex coalface achinery—cutter-loader, flexible conveyor, and hydraulic roof supports are operated lectronically by remote control. (*National Coal Board*.)

elow: A thermal electricity generating station at Castle Donnington, Leicestershire, one f several such located on the rivers of the English Midlands and drawing coal from the ast Midlands. (*Aerofilms and Aero Pictorial Ltd*.)

Above: A recently developed Middle East oilfield now producing 3 million tons of cruc oil a year. Note the drilling barge in the harbour. Umm Shaif, Trucial States, Persia Gulf. (*Paul Popper.*)

Below: Aerial view of BP's Angle Bay Ocean Terminal, Pembrokeshire. (*British Petro leum Co. Ltd.*)

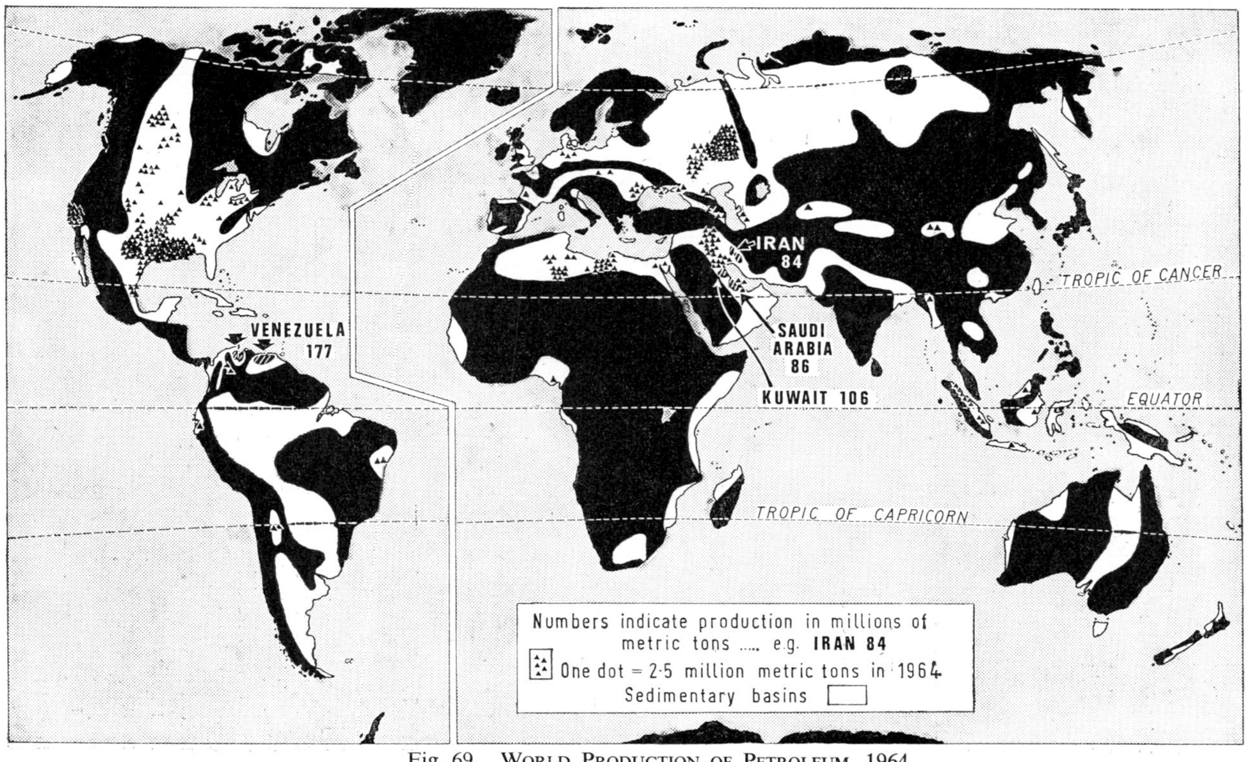

Fig. 69. World Production of Petroleum, 1964.

Proven reserves are reserves which have been shown to exist by drilling, and which are almost certainly recoverable with present-day techniques, and in present economic conditions. In a sense they can be regarded as the industry's working stock. They exclude deposits which will be discovered in the future, and the large quantities of oil in known fields that cannot as yet be brought to the surface economically. Only 30 per cent., on average, of the oil held in a given geological formation can be recovered. This percentage will increase as mining techniques improve. Deeper wells are constantly giving access to deposits which were hitherto out of reach, and secondary methods of recovery, such as the

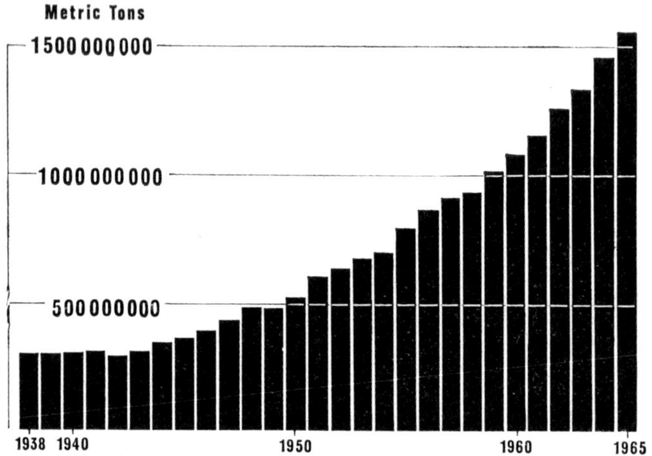

Fig. 70.—World Production of Petroleum and Natural Gas Liquids, 1938-56 (metric tons).

injection of steam into oil-bearing rocks in order to make viscous oil flow more readily are prolonging the lives of many fields. The daily yield of the off-shore South California field—the largest productive field in the United States—has been increased by nearly one-half by pumping back sea water to replace extracted oil, a measure which also reduces the surface subsidence due to the mining. A noteworthy feature of the world oil industry is that proven reserves have increased over the years, in spite of an accelerating rate of production (Figs. 70 and 71).

In addition to the conventional oilfields, enormous beds of oil bearing shale in California, Colorado, Wyoming, and elsewhere, and tar sands in Venezuela and the region of the Athabasca River in northern Canada, await only an economic method of exploitation. The tar sands are believed to contain more oil than the rest of the world's reserves added together. Ultimate reserves from all sources have been estimated at between ten and forty times as great as the proven reserves, and are sufficient to last, even if the present upward trend in production continues, for several generations. There are no grounds for fearing that the world is about to run short of oil.

Major oil producing regions of the world

THE MIDDLE EAST.—The oilfields of the Middle East occupy the great sedimentary basin of the Tigris-Euphrates-Persian Gulf

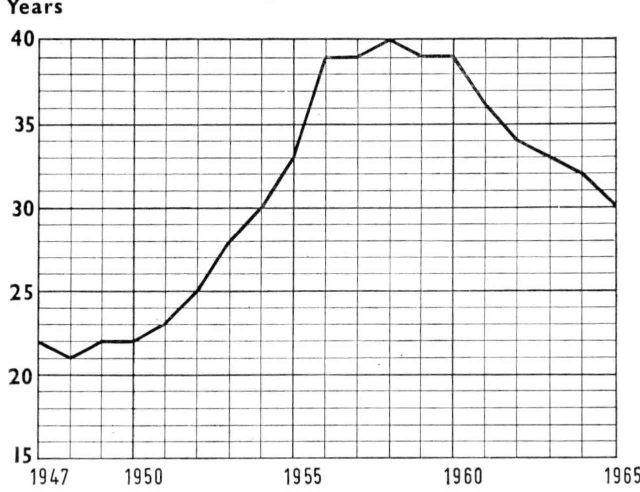

Fig. 71.—WORLD PROVEN OIL RESERVES: NUMBER OF YEARS' SUPPLY REMAINING AT YEAR'S END (1947-65).

depression. This region holds some 60 per cent. of the world's proven reserves of oil, and in 1964 accounted for more than one-quarter of the total world production (Table 66 and Fig. 72).

Oil seepages have been known for centuries in the Middle East, but the discovery of oil in commercial quantities dates only from the early years of the present century in Iran and Iraq, and from the 1930s in Saudi Arabia, Kuwait, Quatar, and Bahrain. Exploitation in Kuwait, now the fourth largest producer in the world, commenced only in 1946. Markets for oil in the Middle East are restricted because of the region's small population and limited industrial development; hence the great bulk of the output is exported to Western Europe, the Far East (notably Japan), and North America. The oilfields are connected by pipeline to terminals on the Persian Gulf and the Mediterranean (Fig. 73). Refined as well as crude oil is exported. The great refinery at Abadan, although it now suffers from competition from the more modern refineries of Western Europe and from the limitations on the size of tankers (25,000 tons)

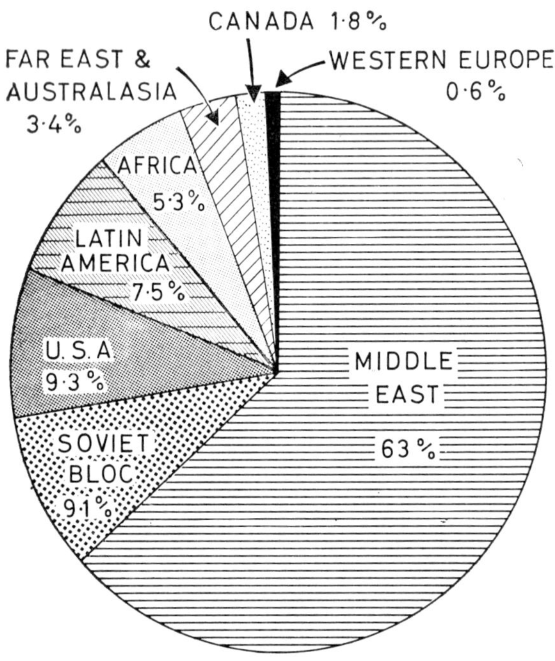

Fig. 72.—Proven Oil Reserves, 1964.

that can approach it up the Shatt el Arab, nevertheless handles one-fifth of Iran's total production. Other major refineries have been erected on Bahrain Island; at Khanaquil (Iraq); Mina al Ahmadi (Kuwait), Ras Tanura (Saudi Arabia); and at Haifa. The Haifa refinery formerly processed Iraqi oil supplied directly to it by pipeline. The pipeline was closed during the Israeli-Arab war of 1948, and has not been reopened. Another line, however, brings in Persian Gulf oil via the port of Eilat on the Gulf of Aquaba.

The importance of oil in the economies of the Middle East countries can scarcely be over-estimated. Petroleum or petroleum products account for nearly 100 per cent. of the exports of Kuwait, 99 per cent. of Saudi Arabia, 85 per cent. of Iran, and 90 per cent. of those of Iraq. Kuwait has been transformed within the last fifteen years from a poverty-stricken desert sheikdom into a country with one of the highest per capita incomes in the world. Non-producing countries have also benefited from the revenues collected on petroleum passing across their territory in pipelines.

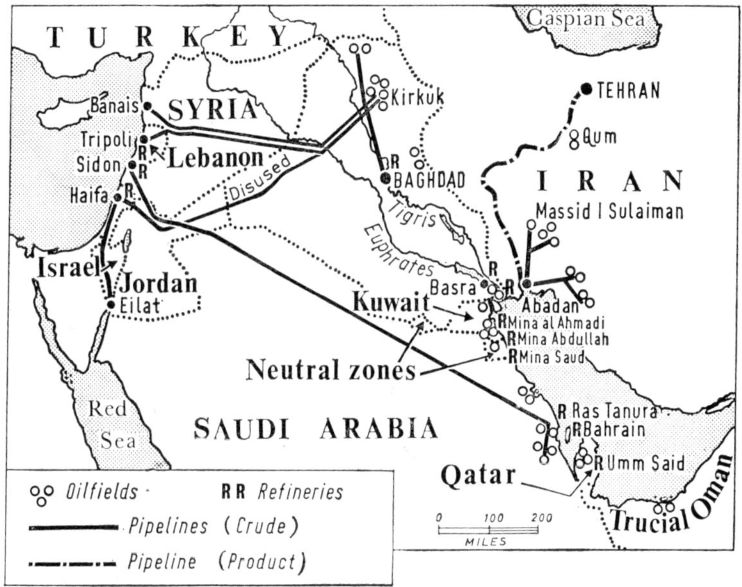

Fig. 73.—Oilfields and Pipelines of the Middle East.

Africa.—The main oilfields of the continent lie in Algeria at Hassi Messaoud and Edjele, and at Zelten, Dahra, and Beda, in Libya (Fig. 74). Oil was first discovered in Algeria as recently as 1956, and in Libya a year later, in each case after a period of feverish and costly prospecting. Success here (after eminent men had pronounced upon the impossibility of finding oil at all in the Sahara) has stimulated exploration in other African territories. New discoveries are constantly being made, and the main centres of production may well shift radically within the next few decades. Wells in Algeria and Libya are deep, and situated in inhospitable territory, and operating costs are higher than in the Middle East. On the other hand, the North African fields lie nearer to the European market, and they are probably more secure politically. Pipelines convey crude oil to terminals on the Mediterranean coast, whence it moves by tanker to refineries in West European ports. Refineries have also been built at Algiers and Hassi Messaoud, and there are plans for a third at Arzew. Besides petroleum, one of the world's largest natural gas fields has been discovered at Hassi R'Mel. The export of natural gas by tanker to Britain commenced in 1964, but the full exploitation of this and other Saharan fields awaits the construction of a submarine pipeline across the Mediterranean, as the North African market can only absorb a fraction of the potential output and transport by tanker is inadequate.

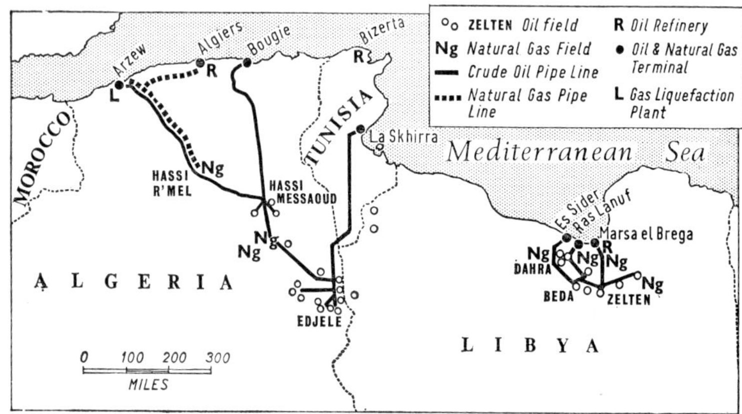

Fig. 74.—Oil and Natural Gas Fields of the Sahara.

North America.—*The U.S.A.*—For more than 100 years, except for a short period at the turn of the century when Russia produced more oil than the rest of the world combined, the U.S.A. has led both in the production and consumption of petroleum and petroleum products. It is estimated that no less than 10,000 million tons have been extracted from United States' wells between 1859 and the present day. Current production is in the order of 400 million tons, or 30 per cent. of the total world output (Table 66).

Oil is distributed widely in the U.S.A. The first fields to be exploited were in the eastern states, but these declined in importance as larger and richer strikes were made in the Mid West, the South, and California. The fields to the west of the Mississippi have played a major role in the development of Southern and Western industry, situated as most of them are in regions remote from supplies of good coal. On the other hand, their location at considerable distances from the main manufacturing centres of the continent is not an advantage, and has necessitated investment on a massive scale in transport equipment. In addition to tanker fleets and thousands of rail cars, more than 200,000 miles of crude and product pipelines carry the oil to the refineries and consuming areas.

TABLE 66

WORLD PRODUCTION OF PETROLEUM

(millions of metric tons)

	1938	1960	1966
U.S.A.	171	384	458
U.S.S.R.	30	148	265
Venezuela	28	149	176
Saudi Arabia	—	60	119
Kuwait	—	82	114
Iran	10	52	105
Libya	—	—	73
Iraq	4	48	68
Canada	1	28	48
Algeria	—	9	34
Indonesia	7	20	24
Kuwait—Saudi Arabia Neutral Zone	—	7	22
WORLD	281	1,091	1,696

PRODUCTION BY REGIONS

	1938	1960	1966
North America	172	412	507
Middle East	16	264	471
Soviet Bloc	38	167	292
Latin America	44	195	241
Africa	—	11	130
Far East and Australasia	10	27	35
Western Europe	1	15	21

Source: *World Oil Statistics*. Petroleum Information Bureau.

In spite of its enormous production, the United States is a net importer of petroleum and petroleum products. In 1963, more than 110 million tons of crude oil and refined products, a quantity equivalent to nearly double the total consumption in the British Isles, were landed at U.S. ports or entered from Canada. Exports, by contrast, amounted to a mere 10 million tons. The increase, year by year, in the volume of oil imports is due to the growing realisation in the U.S.A. that domestic reserves are shrinking, and need to be conserved (production in the U.S.A. is rising faster than new discoveries are being made); to heavy U.S. investment in the fields of Venezuela and the Middle East; and to the location around the coasts of the U.S.A. of large refineries which are as conveniently placed to handle imported oil as oil produced in the country itself.

CANADA.—The modern development of the Canadian oil industry dates from the discovery of the Leduc Field near Edmonton. Production has risen rapidly since 1947, when exploitation began, and in 1964 the output of crude oil exceeded 40 million tons. About three-quarters came from Alberta, rather less than one-quarter from Saskatchewan, and the remainder from the Ontario Peninsula and Manitoba. Marketing from the distant Prairie fields has been facilitated by the construction of pipelines to Superior, Toronto, and Vancouver.

The Athabasca tar sands are situated in northern Alberta, and constitute one of the richest reserves of oil yet discovered anywhere in the world. As yet, an economic method of oil recovery has not been found, although a process which is technically quite feasible exists.

LATIN AMERICA.—More than 75 per cent. of the oil produced in Latin America comes from Venezuela. The most productive fields lie in the Maracaibo Basin and in the east of the country behind the port of Puerto la Cruz. Both these fields are within short pipeline distance of coastal terminals and refineries. Oil has also been found in the Llanos. Until recently, most of Venezuela's oil was shipped as crude to Curaçao and Aruba in the Netherlands Antilles, where two of the world's largest refineries are situated. Since 1960, however, refining capacity in Venezuela has been increased to the point where it now exceeds that of the Dutch islands (Table 69).

Nine other Latin American countries produce oil, but none of them in more than very small quantities. Reserves are believed to be considerable, but development has been hampered by the remoteness of the interior regions. The fields that have been exploited are either readily accessible from the coast, or, as in the Argentine, lie within the hinterlands of industrial centres.

THE FAR EAST.—The oilfields of the Far East are small, and although production from the region has increased four-fold since 1940 it still accounts for little more than 2 per cent. of the total world output. The main producer is Indonesia, where wells on Java and Sumatra yield more than 20 million tons per year.

AUSTRALIA.—The long and costly search for oil in Australia has not been particularly rewarding. Only one field, producing about 500,000 tons annually, has been discovered, at Moonie, Queensland. Hopes of larger finds have not been abandoned. As regards oil, Australia is in a similar position to Britain and the countries of continental Europe, in that her industry which is becoming increasingly oil-based is forced to rely heavily on imported supplies.

EUROPE.—The output of oil from European fields falls woefully short of the continent's requirements. Production in 1963 from all European countries outside the Soviet Union amounted to approximately 34 million tons, whilst refining capacity exceeded 300 million tons, and consumption 325 million tons. The main producer is Rumania, followed by Western Germany and France. Two fields in Britain—in Nottinghamshire and Lancashire—together yield a little over 100,000 tons a year, the equivalent of eight hours' production in Kuwait. The discovery of a rich natural gas field in the Netherlands has raised hopes of finding oil beneath the North Sea, and

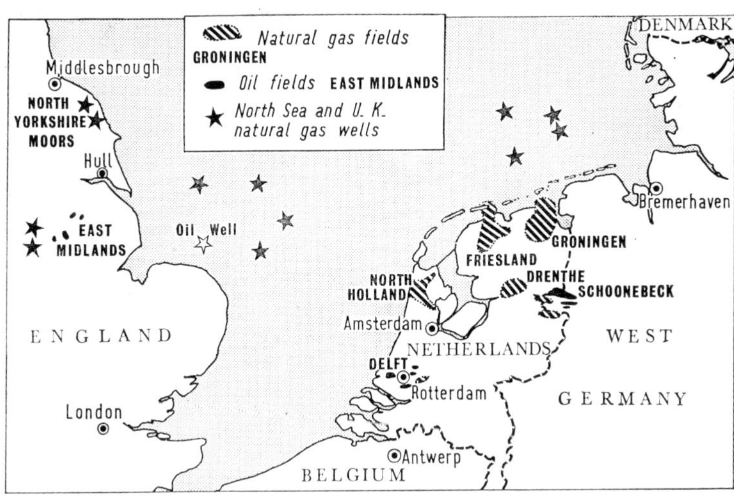

Fig. 75.—OIL AND NATURAL GAS FIELDS OF THE NORTH SEA REGION.

intensive exploration is being conducted in that area at the present time (Fig. 75).

THE SOVIET UNION.—Soviet oil reserves are enormous, and are constantly being increased by new finds in European Russia and Siberia. Until 1950, the main developed field lay in the Caucasus region, with Baku, Grozny, and Maikop as the chief centres. In 1901 this field accounted for more than half the total world output. The discovery of vast reserves between the Volga and the Urals, estimated at between 1,000 million and 2,500 million tons, points to this oil region eventually becoming one of the greatest in the world. It is being worked in the vicinity of Ufa, Perm, and Kiubyshev, and is already contributing over 70 per cent. of the Soviet production.

A pipeline links the field with industrial centres east and west of the Urals, and the "Friendship" pipeline which starts at Kuibyshev carries oil westwards to the satellite countries of Central Europe. Fields in the Western Ukraine; at Emba and Neftedag east of the Caspian; at Pechora; and on the island of Sakhalin are also important.

Petroleum and the under-developed countries

Millions of people in the undeveloped lands have good reason to be thankful that coal and oil have generally been deposited in different parts of the world. Occasionally these two vitally important fuels occur together, and a few nations are fortunate enough to possess both in abundance within their territorial boundaries. The bulk of the proven oil reserves, however, are situated in regions remote from the coalfields, often in isolated desert and jungle country. The discovery and exploitation of such reserves during the last few decades have brought to the people of many backward lands a measure of prosperity which in other circumstances would represent the progress of perhaps centuries.

The oilfields of the Middle East, Venezuela, North Africa, and other economically retarded regions, have been developed by foreign companies backed by huge capital resources. The host countries have benefited by royalties, and other payments made by the companies. Syria, Jordan, Tunisia, and other nations receive transit payments on oil passing across their territories by pipeline. Egypt levies tolls on tankers using the Suez Canal. Revenues are being spent, for the most part wisely, and often in co-operation with the oil companies, on road building programmes, irrigation works, education and health services, and the development of light industry. Sooner or later the oil reserves, however vast, will be exhausted, and it is clearly in the long-term interests of the producing countries to establish a viable economic structure against the day when oil will no longer provide the greater part of their income.

World trade in petroleum

Crude oil and refined petroleum products are the bulkiest and most valuable commodities entering international trade at the present time. More than 600 million tons are carried by tanker annually—an amount which approximates to the total of all other sea borne cargoes combined. The indispensable role played by oil in transport and modern industry, and the geographical separation of the producing and market areas, account for this vast movement. In addition, some 350 million tons are carried by internal pipeline and coastal tanker from the oilfields to the manufacturing areas of

WORLD TRADE IN CRUDE OIL
(in thousands of metric tons, 1963)

Exports from → / Exports to ↓	Venezuela	Algeria	Iran	Iraq	Kuwait	Saudi Arabia	Libya	Indonesia	North America	World
North America ..	37,400	—	5,900	—	7,150	6,680	1,150	2,600	12,300	78,100
U.S.A.	24,900	—	2,900	—	6,690	3,800	1,150	2,600	12,300	58,650
Canada	12,500	—	3,000	—	460	2,880	—	—	—	20,000
Latin America ..	62,700	—	—	—	1,620	4,875	—	120	—	
Western Europe ..	22,000	22,475	24,280	45,000	56,580	26,660	22,575	20	60	246,000
France	2,400	15,500	1,980	9,280	8,080	1,740	2,700	—	—	44,320
Fed. Germany ..	2,900	2,600	9,700	5,450	2,670	4,180	5,625	20	—	37,930
Italy	1,000	1,200	1,000	9,980	12,900	8,140	2,930	—	—	46,600
Netherlands ..	2,550	1,495	660	5,000	6,340	3,460	1,730	—	—	23,620
United Kingdom ..	7,700	280	2,980	8,840	21,850	1,970	6,240	—	60	54,500
Far East	360		14,000	4,230	26,550	12,090	—	6,440	170	71,890
India	—		4,300	580	—	1,940	—	100	—	6,360
Japan	360		7,800	2,430	22,750	9,430	—	5,200	170	51,170
Australia	15	—	1,920	550	3,360	3,160	—	3,630	—	14,860
Africa*	100	165	1,725	635	90	100	310	—	—	3,835
Middle East* ..	—	—	5,020	3,550	3,960	11,600	—	—	—	27,220
World	115,700	23,650	53,150	54,130	99,600	67,550	22,040	12,700	12,500	528,000

*Egypt, Libya, Ethiopia, and Turkey are included with the Middle East countries.
Source: "World Energy Supply." *U.N. Statistical Papers Series*, *J* No. 8, 1965.

the United States, and approximately half this quantity moves each year across the Soviet Union. The main features of the international trade in oil are given in Tables 67 and 68.

TABLE 68

INTERNATIONAL TRADE IN REFINED FUEL OILS
(in thousands of metric tons)

Principal Exporting Countries	1960	1965	Principal Importing Countries	1960	1965
Venezuela	32,500	45,450	U.S.A.	33,750	59,970
Netherlands Antilles	29,400	34,750	Sweden	10,400	15,130
U.S.S.R.	12,000	20,590	Japan	3,800	14,600
Trinidad	8,500	15,590	Fed. Germany	4,200	15,400
Iran	11,500	11,200	United Kingdom	4,600	19,760
Bahrain	8,700	7,950	Switzerland	3,800	6,660
Saudi Arabia	7,600	10,920	Denmark	5,100	7,190

Source: "World Energy Supply". *U.N. Statistical Papers, Series J No.* 10, 1966.

The oil-refining industry

Petroleum is more or less worthless in the form in which it is extracted from the well. The object of refining is to convert it into petrol, diesel, and fuel oil, etc., and into raw materials of the petro-chemical industry. As petroleum and petroleum products can be easily transported, the refining operations can be carried on near the site of the well, in the marketing areas, or at an intermediate location. Before the Second World War they were concentrated in the areas of oil production, and refined products, rather than crude petroleum, were the main cargoes of the world's tanker fleets. During the last quarter century there has been a shift in the location of the oil-refining industry from the oilfields to the market areas. The West European countries, which themselves produce only very small quantities of petroleum, increased their share of the world refining capacity from about 4·5 per cent. in 1938 to nearly 20 per cent. in 1963 (Table 69).

The following factors account for the growing attraction of market locations:

1. Improvements in oil-refining technology which have increased the range of products that can be obtained from crude oil—products which are most economically manufactured near the point of consumption.

2. The increase in the size of tankers, which has brought a sharp reduction in the cost per ton of crude oil transported in bulk.

3. The heavy capital outlay involved in the construction of a modern refinery and petro-chemical plant—an outlay which is often

beyond the means of the under-developed countries where many of the oil wells are located.

4. The political instability of many of the oil-producing countries.

TABLE 69

WORLD OIL-REFINING CAPACITY
(in thousands of metric tons)

	1938	1950	1960	1966
A. By world regions—				
North America	234,100	369,500	538,900	579,300
Western Europe	15,900	46,200	221,200	454,400
Communist bloc countries	45,200	49,200	163,500	292,850
Latin America	39,800	73,800	161,400	205,350
Far East and Australasia	13,700	14,700	70,500	184,300
Middle East	14,000	48,700	79,400	102,220
Africa	950	950	4,750	28,650
B. Principal refining countries—				
U.S.A.	225,400	350,400	492,200	522,550
U.S.S.R.	31,500	37,500	140,000	250,000
Italy	2,100	5,900	41,400	110,200
Japan	2,600	2,600	32,130	104,750
Western Germany	2,400	4,700	39,700	86,000
United Kingdom	1,900	11,500	49,200	78,200
France	7,600	15,700	40,400	80,100
Canada	8,700	19,100	46,700	56,800
Venezuela	2,700	14,200	49,200	54,100
Netherlands Antilles	21,400	33,100	36,700	36,000
WORLD	363,700	603,200	1,240,000	1,650,000

Source: Petroleum Information Bureau—*World Oil Statistics.*

Refineries processing tanker-borne oil are almost invariably situated at or very close to the oil ports (Fig. 76). The increasing size of tankers, however, is reducing the number of adequate oil port sites to a few. Cheap, flat land, and abundant water supplies are further locational requirements of modern refineries. The Fawley refinery consumes some 8 million gallons of fresh water each day for steam raising and product washing, and a further 150 million gallons of salt water for cooling purposes.

Oil as a factor in the location of economic activity

The first commercial oil well was drilled in Pennsylvania in 1859. The subsequent growth of the oil industry was steady, but by no means spectacular until the internal combustion engine created an explosive demand for petrol early in the present century. It was not until the 1920s, however, that oil entered the industrial market as a rival to coal.

As a fuel, oil is now a very attractive alternative to coal. Ton for ton it takes up less space and provides 50 per cent. more energy.

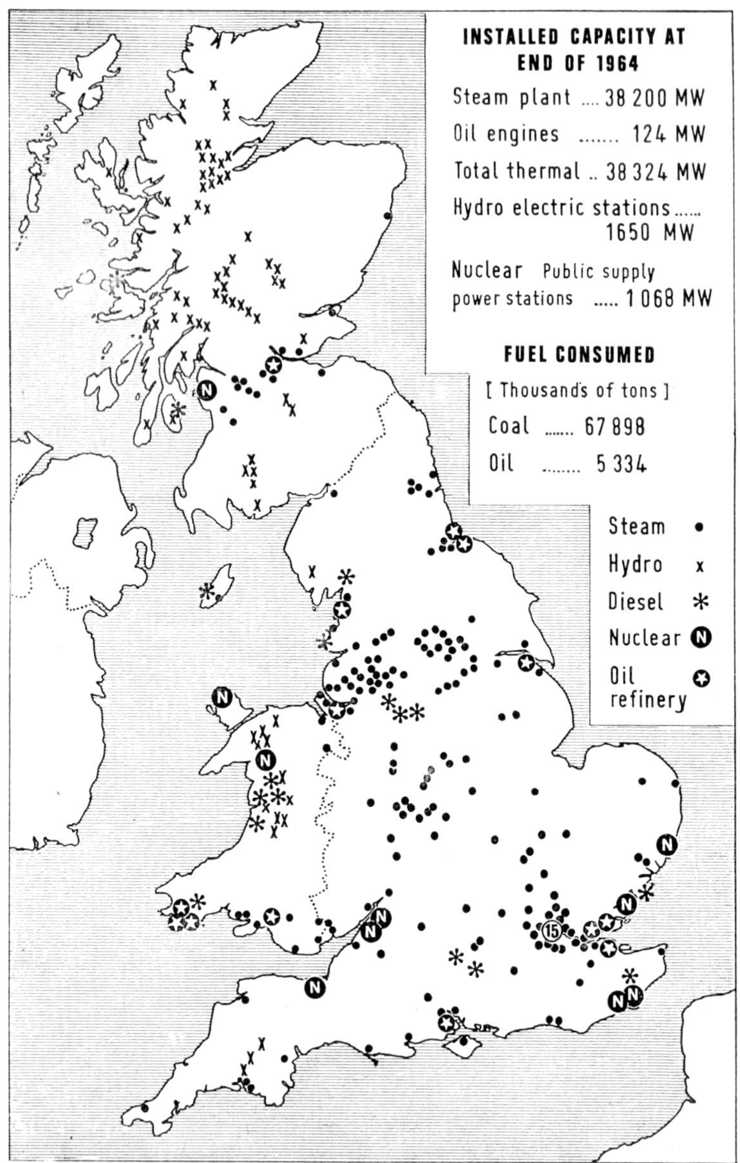

Fig. 76.—LOCATION OF ELECTRICITY GENERATING STATIONS AND OIL REFINERIES IN GREAT BRITAIN.

Installed capacity at the end of 1964: steam plant, 38,200 MW.; oil engines, 124 MW.; total thermal, 38,324 MW.; hydro-electric stations, 1,650 MW.; nuclear (public supply power stations), 1,068. Fuel consumed (thousands of tons): coal, 67,898; oil, 5,334.

It is clean in use, easy to handle and store, and creates no problems of ash disposal. Oil-burning equipment is efficient and can easily be adapted to automatic operation. These advantages are sufficient to give oil a competitive advantage over coal for steam raising, space heating, and for certain industrial processes such as metal smelting and steel-furnace operation, even when the cost of coal, on a thermal-equivalent basis, is less than oil. The consequence, inevitably, has been an increase in the consumption of the newer fuel.

So far there has not been a growth of manufacturing industry at the centres of oil production on a scale in any way comparable to that which took place on the coalfields during the eighteenth and nineteenth centuries. Where oil has attracted industry it has done so as a raw material (*e.g.* petro-chemical manufacture in the southern States and California) rather than as a fuel. The reasons for the general absence of major industrial conurbations on the oilfields are:

1. Many oilfields are in thinly populated regions where there is a shortage of labour accustomed to factory employment, and a very restricted market for manufactured products.

2. Many are also in desert regions where manufacturing costs would be increased by the need to import the greater part of the food required by an industrial population, and by the difficulty of obtaining adequate supplies of water.

3. In several instances oilfields are located in countries which are short of capital, and which would experience difficulty in attracting foreign investment, except to the oil mining enterprise itself.

4. Oil is easily and cheaply transported by tanker or pipeline. In this respect it is very different from coal, whose price increases sharply with distance from the mine. Industry had to move to the coalfields in order to avail itself of cheap fuel. There is no such compulsion for industry to migrate to the oil-producing regions. The oil companies have also a greater interest in and more to gain by transporting oil, than they have in fostering the development of industry at the point of oil production.

NATURAL GAS

Natural gas deposits occur in rock structures similar to those that bear oil. Many oilfields do, in fact, yield gas, either independently of the oil or as a by-product. The main natural gas fields, however, produce little or no commercial oil.

Natural gas is the newest of the primary energy discoveries to make a substantial impact on the world fuel situation. In 1964 it contributed some 15 per cent. of the total energy supplies. In the United States, where it is plentiful and cheap, its share was 34 per cent. In Europe, on the other hand, it was only 2 per cent. Less than twenty years ago natural gas was largely a useless product, and was burnt off at the well. Its changed status from an "oilman's nuisance" to a valuable fuel has come about mainly through improvements in the techniques of pipeline manufacture and construction—improvements which have made it possible to carry gas over long distances at high pressures. Transport at ordinary atmospheric pressure is completely uneconomic. Alternatively, it can be transported by tanker after being reduced to one-six hundredth of its original volume by liquefaction.

The composition of natural gas varies considerably from one field to another. An average sample contains about 80 per cent. methane (CH_4) and 12 per cent. ethane (C_2H_6). Much of the remainder consists of propane ($C_3 H_8$) and butane (C_4H_{10}). The first two gases can be liquefied only at very low temperatures, but propane and butane can be liquefied at ordinary temperatures by pressure alone. Liquefied propane and butane are sold in steel bottles or cylinders for domestic use.

Since for economic reasons it is necessary to use high pressures when pumping natural gas long distances, the propane and butane are separated off before pumping to avoid having liquid in the pipe. These gases are also removed before the low temperature liquefaction of methane and the subsequent transport of liquid methane by tanker. A liquefaction plant, the largest in the world, has recently been completed at Arzew, near Oran, and is now delivering Saharan natural gas by sea to the British Gas Council's terminal on Canvey Island at the rate of 700,000 tons per year. Some of the Middle East countries are also shipping liquefied natural gas to foreign markets. A natural gas pipeline from southern Iran to the Soviet Union is now under construction.

Proven reserves of natural gas are estimated as being equal to forty years' supply at the present rate of consumption. The largest deposits are in the United States and the Soviet Union. Substantial discoveries have also been made in Groningen province and near the Zuider Zee, in the Netherlands. Rich finds have recently been made beneath the bed of the North Sea. It is estimated that by the early 1970s the North Sea fields will be producing 10 per cent. of the total anticipated energy requirements of the United Kingdom.

Problems involved in the long distance transport and marketing of natural gas (which competes not only with manufactured gas but with petroleum, and the transport of petroleum is both simpler and cheaper) are likely to restrict its large scale use for the present to regions which offer a large and steady industrial market. Storage is difficult, and the under-utilisation of a pipeline during the summer months when demand is low increases the overall transport costs. In some areas, underground storage in depleted oil reservoirs is feasible, and as a method of guaranteeing domestic supplies it has proved to be cheaper, in certain circumstances, than providing additional pipeline capacity to meet conditions of peak winter demand.

FALLING WATER AND ATOMIC ENERGY

Falling water was one of the first forms of primary energy to be harnessed by man: atomic power is the most recent.

The development of hydro-electricity began towards the end of the last century. It first became important in regions having numerous swift-flowing streams, inadequate coal resources, and a substantial industrial and domestic demand for electricity in the vicinity of the water-power sites. One of the first hydro-electric plants to be brought into commission was at Niagara, and supplied power to Buffalo, twenty miles away. The use of higher voltages, in turn made possible by advances in the techniques of transmission, now permit the construction of power plants in remote areas. Transmission over distances of 1,000 miles is technically possible to-day, and in some circumstances economically feasible. However, at distances such as these, power lines normally have to cross state frontiers, and the economic benefits that might result from the development of distant sites are often lost because of the difficulties of negotiating international agreements. Even when two friendly countries share a common frontier there is sometimes a reluctance to allow one to draw upon the resources of the other. On the northern side of the Canada-U.S.A. border, for instance, there exists a large water power potential that is not being exploited by Canada, but which could usefully be developed to supply the Atlantic sea board cities of the United States. Canada, however, hesitates to see the resources of Quebec and Ontario being harnessed and exported by United States' companies, lest in the distant future she might wish to draw upon them herself.

The economics of hydro-electricity production

Ideally, a hydro-electricity station should be based upon a river having a constant discharge and a sufficient gradient to give a good head of water. For a given volume of water, the power developed at the turbines is directly proportional to the head, *i.e.* to the height of the water intake pipe above the station. On a low gradient river the head can be increased by constructing a dam. The reservoir formed behind the dam also serves to even out the flow of an erratic stream.

Hydro-electricity plants are expensive to build. The capital outlay required for preliminary survey work, dam construction, power plant and transmission line installation is normally many times greater than for thermal stations of equal capacity. On the other hand, hydro-plants are very cheap to run. There are no fuel costs, and no concern that fuel supplies may be depleted with use. Machinery is efficient, simple to operate, and possessed of a long life. Within the limits of plant capacity, the output of electricity can easily be regulated to match fluctuating demand. Provided the plant is large, is kept working to near full capacity, and is situated near to the point of power consumption, it will normally supply electricity at lower cost than a thermal plant. Unfortunately the number of suitable sites within cheap transmission distances of large centres of population is limited. Many locations meet the physical requirements admirably, but are in out of the way places—in high mountain regions, for example, or in the under-developed tropics. Africa alone is estimated to hold one-half of the world's water power potential—amounting to no less than three times all developed hydro resources on earth. Water power resources in Africa and Latin America will undoubtedly be exploited in the years that lie ahead—Kariba is perhaps a pattern of things to come—but the future of hydro-electricity in areas remote from the fossil fuels, where it could be expected to make the greatest contribution, is less certain than it was a generation ago. A new dimension has been introduced with the coming-of-age of the atomic power station, whose location is in no way influenced by the distribution of its fuel supplies, and which can, if required, be planted in the centre of the market area it is intended to serve.

Atomic energy

The technical problems associated with the harnessing of atomic energy for peaceful purposes are being overcome. It is expected that nuclear plants will be competitive with conventional thermal stations within a decade. To-day, the cost of electricity generation using the latest type of reactor is about 0·67d. per unit, compared with 0·5d. per unit for a large coal or oil fired station on a very favourable site.

It must be emphasised that these figures represent the costs of generation only. Transmission costs are very high in the case of atomic plants, which are at present usually located very unfavourably in relation to their markets. As public confidence in their safety increases, sites nearer to towns and cities are likely to become acceptable. The Central Electricity Generating Board is, in fact, basing its plans on the assumption that the next generation of nuclear reactors will be installed in areas of high power demand, in which case transmission charges could fall to the level now enjoyed by market-based thermal stations, and well below the level borne by the majority of hydro-plants. The atomic fuels are described in Chapter XV, p. 332-3

Coal, oil, and gas fired stations, and nuclear reactors are heavy consumers of cooling water, and sites on rivers or on the coast are essential.

ELECTRICITY GENERATION FROM THE FOUR MAIN PRIMARY ENERGIES—A COMPARISON

COAL	OIL AND NATURAL GAS	FALLING WATER	ATOMIC ENERGY
Capital cost of coal fired stations are comparatively low. Fuel costs increase with distance from the pit head. The cost of ash disposal has to be considered. The best locations for coal burning plants are in industrialised coalfield regions.	Capital and fuel costs are approximately the same as for coal fired stations. Fuel costs increase with distance from the refinery or natural gas fields. Oil and gas fired plants are clean in operation and create no problems of ash disposal.	Capital costs of H.E.P. plants are high. There are no fuel costs. Water is not transportable; hence hydro-plants can only be located at the water power site. Transmission costs are often very high. Hydro-stations are better adapted to intermittent working than thermal or atomic stations. There is no problem of ash disposal.	Very high capital costs, but fuel costs are negligible (the price of uranium concentrate is about £5,000 per ton (or 10/- per ton coal equivalent). When the safety of nuclear stations has been demonstrated, they will prove to be most useful when built in densely populated areas where coal and oil is expensive. Only large plants are economic.

Electricity is unique in that it is the only product that is consumed the instant it is produced. Storage is impracticable, and power must therefore be generated as required. Demand fluctuates throughout the day, rising from a night time minimum to a peak a little before midday. The midday maximum is followed by a slight fall in the afternoon, and a rise to a second peak in the early evening. The January demand is also double that of July. Electricity Boards are thus faced with the problem of under-utilisation of expensive equipment for much of the time. This they try to overcome by:

(i) The use of discriminatory tariffs.

(ii) Using the largest, most efficient stations (which are normally the stations with high-overhead but low-operating costs) to generate the base load, and the smaller stations (with low-overhead but high-

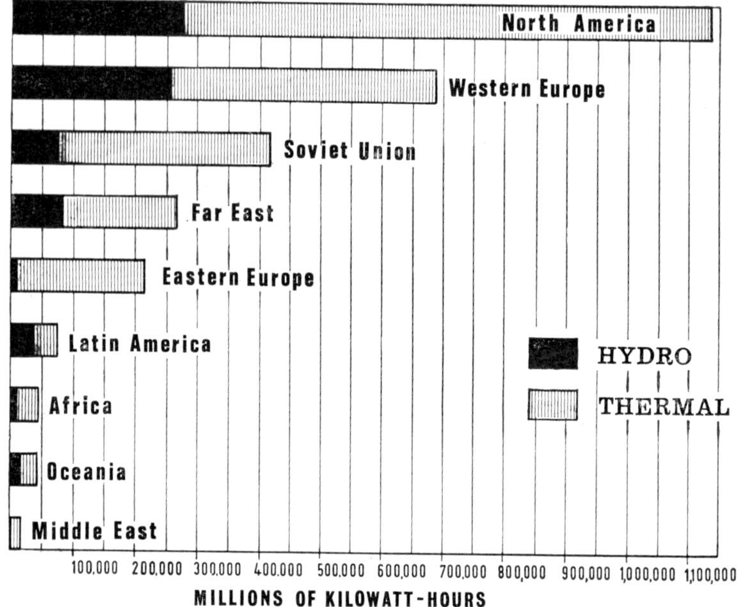

Fig. 77.—Consumption of Electrical Energy, by Major World Regions, 1963.

operating costs) as boosters during peaks. Advantage can sometimes be taken of variations in the hours of maximum demand from region to region. An exchange of electricity between France and Britain is thus possible because the peaks in each country do not coincide.

OTHER TYPES OF PRIMARY ENERGY

Wood.—The importance of wood as a fuel in the undeveloped continents must not be belittled. The Food and Agricultural Organisation estimates that some 90 per cent. of all wood removed in Africa, 80 per cent. in Latin America, and 60 per cent. in Asia is consumed as fuel by domestic users, industry, and transport. Wood, of course, is a bulky material of low calorific value, and tends therefore to be used only in the areas where it is produced.

Peat.—Peat is still important in parts of the world where it is plentiful and cheap. Millions of tons are dug annually in Ireland and the Scottish Highlands. It is also consumed extensively in the Soviet Union, on the north European plain, and locally in North America. Although normally cut by hand, mechanical methods of peat winning have been developed. The main use of peat is as a domestic fuel. Being excessive in bulk and low in heating power, and also creating considerable problems of ash disposal, it rarely competes successfully with coal in regions where the latter is readily available.

CHAPTER XIII

THE IRON, STEEL, AND ENGINEERING INDUSTRIES

1. THE IRON-SMELTING INDUSTRY

Raw-materials of the iron-smelting industry

IRON ORE.—Iron ore is the commonest, and at the same time the most useful of the metallic raw materials. It has been worked since the pre-historic period, and to-day forms the basis of the great iron, steel, and engineering industries of the world, upon which all types of modern manufacturing activity ultimately depend.

Ore bodies are widely distributed, although for various reasons not all are exploited. Among the factors which determine their economic importance are:

1. *Size.*—The extent of an ore deposit is significant, as the heavy financial outlay on mining equipment, the construction of roads, railways, and port facilities, and in remote areas on houses and social amenities for workmen and their families, cannot be justified unless a field has a life of several years before it.

2. *The metal content of the ore.*—This can range from more than 70 per cent. in pure haematite and magnetite, to less than 20 per cent. in some of the bedded Jurassic deposits of Western Europe. An ore with a metal content of below about 20 per cent. is rarely worth working, except perhaps during wartime or when a country is bent on a policy of economic self-sufficiency at no matter what cost. The value of an ore increases in more than direct proportion to its quality. Rich ores, for example, require less blast furnace capacity, and less flux and fuel to smelt them than do low grade ores. However, improvements in the techniques of concentration prior to transport or charging into the furnace are increasing the value of low-grade deposits. Concentration is effected by *screening* and *washing* to remove earthy material; *calcining* to drive off surplus moisture, sulphur, and carbon dioxide, and to make the ore more permeable to blast furnace gases; *sintering*, a process which fuses fine mineral particles into a more easily smelted clinker; and the *magnetic separation* of the iron from impurities in magnetite and ores that can be made magnetic by roasting.

3. *The cost of mining.*—Much of the world's ore is won from open quarries which lend themselves to large scale mechanical working. In these conditions the cost of mining is low. Costs increase when

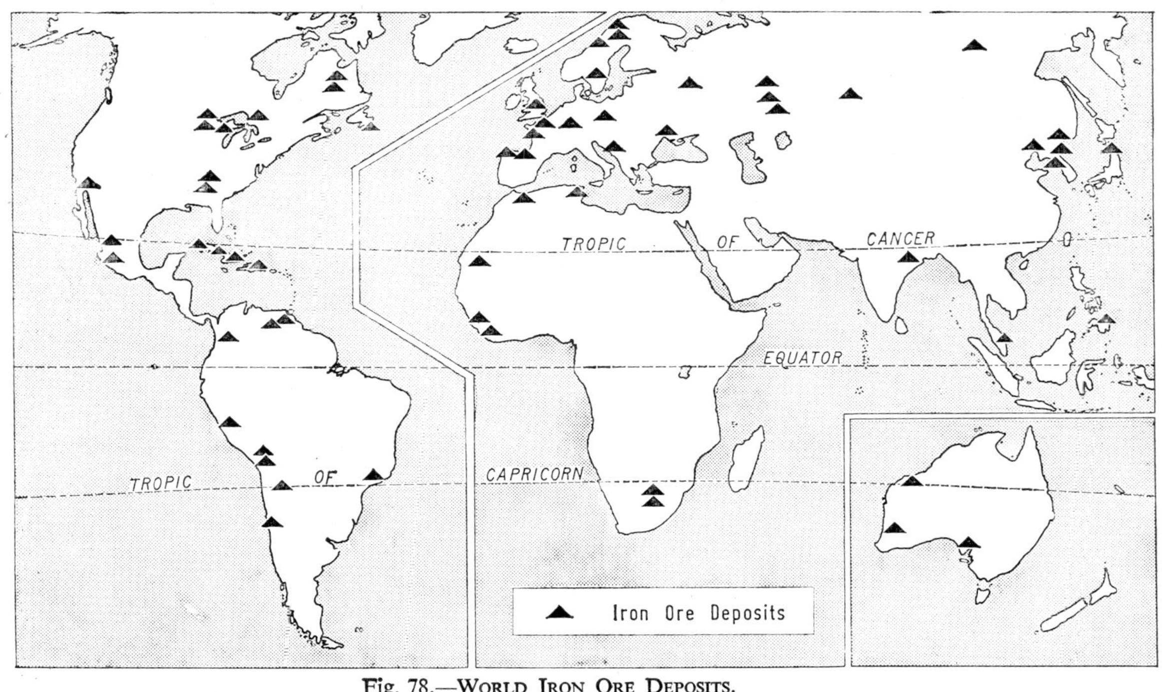

Fig. 78.—World Iron Ore Deposits.

the size of the workings or the thickness of the beds do not permit the efficient use of labour-saving machinery, or when deposits lie at some distance below ground and have to be reached by deep shafts or adits. The cost of producing each ton of ore from the thick surface deposits in the Mesabi Range is very much lower than in Northamptonshire, where the beds also lie close to the surface but are much thinner. Northamptonshire in turn has lower mining costs than Cleveland (Yorkshire), where the deposits are overlain by an overburden too thick to be removed, and consequently have to be followed into the scarp face by shafts and tunnels. High mining costs have, in fact, recently forced the Cleveland mines to close.

4. *The cost of transport.*—If ore has to be carried for long distances from mine to smelter, transport charges may well exceed the cost of mining. Lean ores are expensive to ship by any medium, and are normally worked only when they are situated near established centres of iron-smelting, or where economically viable blast furnaces can be erected upon them. The low grade deposits of the East Midlands, Lorraine, and the Harz Mountains, have thus succeeded in attracting important smelting industries. High grade ores move cheaply enough by water, but long rail hauls can be expensive, and tend to be avoided wherever possible (Table 70, p. 283). The comparative cheapness of ocean transport enhances the value of ore fields having a coastal or near coastal location, particularly now that the major consumers in Europe, North America, and the Far East are coming to depend increasingly on supplies from distant sources. The average distance that ore now travels to blast furnaces in Britain is 2,100 miles, and to Japan more than 5,000 miles, compared with 1,500 and 2,200 miles respectively little more than ten years ago. When journeys of this nature are involved, low freight charges are of more than usual significance, and the factor of low cost transport helps to explain why the ore deposits of Venezuela, Chile, and Newfoundland, which lie close to navigable water, are of more importance to Britain, Japan, and other importing countries than those situated in the interior of Brazil and Bolivia.

5. *The chemical composition of the ore* is of less importance to-day than it was in the past. Advances in smelting and steel-making techniques have made possible the use of ores once unsuitable. Before the discovery of the basic steel process towards the end of the last century, only ores having a low phosphorus content had value in the steel industry. They could be, and of course were, used in the production of iron. With the perfection of a steel converter which removed unwanted phosphorus, the highly phosphoric deposits of

Cleveland, Northamptonshire, Lorraine, and northern Sweden, as well as some of the Lake Superior ores acquired a new significance, and their massive development really dates from that event. Phosphoric ore ultimately produces a soft steel that rolls well into sheets. Acid pig, made from non-phosphoric ores, is still essential, however, if a very hard steel is required.

Frequently iron ores have to be mixed to obtain the correct smelting properties, and a cross-haul between fields or between different parts of the same field becomes necessary. Frodingham ores are thus mixed into the ratio of about 2 : 1 with ores from Northampton because the former are too limy to be smelted by themselves. A similar ore exchange takes place between Briey (Lorraine) on the one hand and Nancy and Longwy on the other.

The future of ore supplies

More than 500 million tons of iron ore are extracted annually from mines in the world—an amount that has doubled during the past decade and a half (Table 71, p. 283). Such a drain on resources has become a matter of some concern to the leading consumers, many of whom are having to face the fact that their richest and most easily accessible deposits may be exhausted by the end of the present century. Not surprisingly, the fear of a general shortage of one of the most basic of all raw materials has stimulated the exploration for new reserves, and research into methods of utilising low grade ores that hitherto have been unprofitable to work. The result of surveys undertaken since the Second World War has been to increase the estimated world reserves of iron ore of all grades from 100,000 million tons to nearly three times that amount. By no means all the newly discovered fields are conveniently distributed, and not all can be worked economically by present techniques. But suitable ore reserves are now known to be large enough to remove the spectre of an ore famine for several generations.

FUEL.—Until the 1700s the only important fuel consumed by the iron-smelting industry was charcoal. A few charcoal furnaces are still in operation in areas where there is inadequate coking coal, and where a high quality pig iron is required for special purposes. A few are in blast in Sweden and Brazil. They are, however, rarely of more than local or minor importance at the present time.

Prime metallurgical coals are restricted to a comparatively small number of fields. Britain's main reserves are in Durham and South Wales, but they are not large, and need to be conserved (Fig. 79). Abroad, the Ruhr and the Connellsville district of the Appalachian field contain some of the most extensive deposits of good coking coal in the world.

Metallurgical coke is produced from bituminous coal of low sulphur, phosphorus, and ash content. It must have a crushing

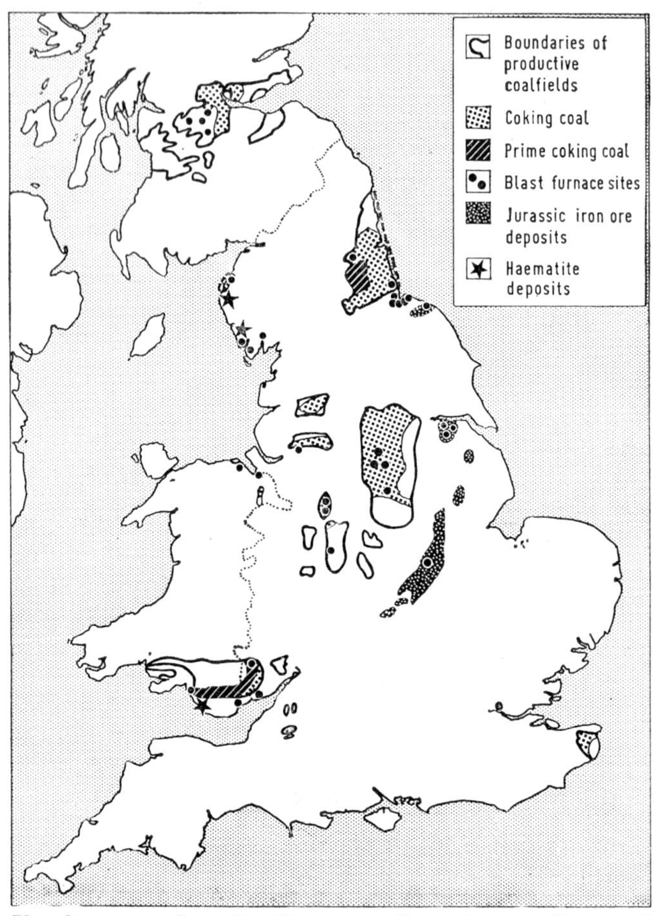

Fig. 79.—Coalfields, Iron Ore Fields, and Blast Furnace Sites in Great Britain (1965).

strength able to withstand the great weight of material fed into a large furnace, and must not fuse on heating and so prevent the free movement of furnace gases through the charge. Coke of roughly equal quality can be made in either the beehive or the retort oven. The retort oven is now in general use, as it permits the recovery of gases and other by-products released during the coking operations. One consequence of its widespread adoption has been a shift in the location of the coking industry itself, from the coalfields to the centres of iron and steel production where a market for the by-products exists.

TABLE 70

FREIGHT CHARGES ON U.S. IRON ORE, 1964
(in dollars per ton)

From Minnesota Ranges to Duluth-Superior by rail	1·28
Handling charges at Duluth-Superior	0·19
Duluth-Superior to Lower Lake ports	1·90
Trans-shipment charges at Lower Lake ports (vessel to rail car)	0·50
Lower Lake ports to Pittsburgh by rail	2·73
Total	6·60
All-rail charge from Minnesota Ranges to Pittsburgh	10·23

Note (i) transport charges to Cleveland are only half of what they are to Pittsburgh.

(ii) the use of the all-rail route during the winter when the Great Lakes are closed to shipping avoids expensive stockpiling of ore at the blast furnace sites.

Source: *Minerals Yearbook*, Bureau of Mines, Washington, D.C.

TABLE 71

PRODUCTION OF IRON ORE
(millions of tons)

	1952	1958	1966	Average iron content in 1966
WORLD	293	399	n/a	55%
U.S.S.R.	49	87	160	60%
U.S.A.	98	67	82	65%
France	40	58	55	35%
China (mainland)	4	29	n/a	—
Canada	5	14	37	70%
Sweden	17	18	28	65%
United Kingdom	16	15	13	30%
India	4	6	26	70%
Brazil	3	5	13	65%
West Germany*	16	18	7	20%
Venezuela	2	15	17	70%
Chile	2	4	12	70%
Australia	3	4	12	60%
Luxembourg	7	6	6	27%
Spain	3	5	5	50%
Austria	2	4	4	22%

* The figures for 1952 include East Germany. n/a—not available.

Source: *Commodity Yearbook* and *U.N. Monthly Bulletin of Statistics.*

LIMESTONE.—The smelting process requires a flux that will mix readily with the ore impurities. Some ores are self-fluxing, but otherwise limestone must be added with the coke and ore. Some 2 million tons of limestone are consumed annually by blast furnaces in Britain. Limestone, however, is a common and widely distributed rock, and only rarely does its occurrence become a localising factor in the smelting industry.

The techniques of iron-smelting

Iron ore is smelted in the blast furnace—a steel cylinder lined with fire bricks, and equipped with devices for receiving the burden of ore, coke, and limestone at the top, and for withdrawing the liquid iron and slag at the base. At the base, too, are nozzles or tuyères through which a pre-heated blast is forced. The high temperatures within the furnace bring about a separation of the iron from its ore, and at the same time melt the iron which trickles to the bottom of the charge. The impurities in the iron ore react with the limestone to produce a liquid slag which floats on top of the molten iron. The slag can be drawn off from above the iron, thus allowing the process to be operated continuously. The furnace is tapped periodically, and the iron run off into pigs, or in the case of an integrated plant, conveyed directly to the steel furnaces.

A single large blast furnace producing 400,000 tons of pig iron annually will consume each year some 1 million tons of ore, 400,000 tons of coke and limestone, 2 million tons of air, and more than 2,000 million gallons of water, the last mainly for cooling purposes. In addition to pig iron it will produce 200,000 tons of slag, and 2·5 million tons of low grade gas. For efficient working the furnace must be operated continuously: it goes out of blast only to have its lining replaced. It is essential, therefore, that adequate provision be made for the storage, preparation, and uninterrupted flow of this enormous quantity of material to the furnace, and for the removal of the pig iron and by-products. Marshalling yards, coal, ore, and limestone dumps, coal blending plant, coking ovens, power stations, blowing engines, loading and charging gear, cooling towers, and gas holders are consequently standard accessories on most blast furnace sites. The space they occupy is considerable. A group of three or four large furnaces, together with their auxiliary equipment will require an area of several hundred acres on more or less level ground. An integrated iron and steel works may spread over one or two square miles.

The iron-smelting industry of Britain. Historical changes in techniques and geographical location

Iron has been smelted in Britain since about 450 B.C. For some 2,000 years down to about A.D. 1500 the principle of smelting changed very little. Ore was selected from an outcrop in the neighbourhood, crushed, cleaned as far as possible of earthy material, mixed with lime and charcoal, and then heaped into a furnace or *hearth*. At first the blast was obtained by siting the furnace on a windy hill-side, but later water bellows were used. The smelting process took about twenty-four hours, at the end of which time the ore had been reduced to a spongy mass, or *bloom*. The bloom was then consolidated into usable iron by re-heating and hammering. The process was known as the direct method of iron making, and the product was wrought iron.

During this period the iron-smelting industry had become fairly widely distributed throughout the populated parts of these islands. The output, both from individual furnaces and in aggregate was, of course, small. Furnaces were located wherever wind or water could be relied upon to operate the bellows and forges. The nature of communications precluded the movement of raw materials for more than a few miles, except in coastal areas, where imported ores could be landed. Small quantities of iron ore began to arrive at the Channel ports and Bristol from France and Spain during the thirteenth century, and a little later at Hull from Scandinavia. Foreign ores were used in the manufacture of superior quality iron, as, for example, at Sheffield.

The development of the blast furnace at the end of the fourteenth century was a landmark in the history of the industry. The longer period of heating and the higher temperatures obtainable in the blast furnace made it possible actually to melt the iron, and thus free it from the mineral impurities contained in the ore. The product obtained was pig iron. Pig iron, however, contained carbon absorbed from the charcoal, and was too brittle for direct use. It was therefore necessary to re-heat and refine it in the forge to make it malleable enough for working.

The migration to the coalfields

The discovery of coke as a medium of ore reduction solved a fuel problem that was becoming yearly more acute. In the Middle Ages no less than one acre of forest had to be cut to provide sufficient charcoal to make five tons of iron, and while the blast furnace was more economical in the use of fuel than the hearth it replaced, it stimulated the production of iron to such an extent that the total quantity of fuel required was increased substantially. The result was that many centres were forced into decline, and even extinction, not because their ore deposits ceased to be adequate but because the timber reserves became so badly depleted. In fact, only those regions possessing extensive tracts of forest land, *e.g.*

the Weald, the Forest of Dean, and parts of the West Riding, were able to sustain an industry of any size for any length of time.

The transition from charcoal to coke was gradual. Initially, iron made in the coke furnace was unsuitable for many purposes, including the manufacture of wrought iron, the product in greatest demand in the metal working trades. Slowly, however, the problems were overcome, and by 1750 the coke furnace had spread to most smelting regions of the British Isles, and fifty years later the charcoal furnace had virtually disappeared.

The introduction of coke resulted in a geographical re-location of the iron-smelting industry. Gradually the forests ceased to be important, and the attraction of the coalfields grew. In addition to providing an abundance of fuel, the coalfields had other advantages, viz.

1. Many had already well-established traditions of iron working. Although charcoal had formerly been indispensable to the smelting process, coal had acquired considerable importance in the finishing trades of the iron industry. Either coal or charcoal could be used in the smithy, where bar iron from the furnaces was re-heated, and fashioned into usable products—nails, locks, bolts, agricultural implements, chains, and domestic hardware. Coal was therefore a raw material equally with charcoal in the production of iron articles, and this branch of the industry had become located in the coalfield as well as the forest areas.

2. The occurrence in the coal measures of fair-quality ore in quantities sufficient for the smelting industry of the day. The clay-band and black-band ores were often found intercalated with shales immediately above or below the coal seams, and both coal and ore were frequently brought to the surface up the same shaft. Many coal companies also became iron companies, and smelting at the site of the mine became common. By the middle of the nineteenth century, 95 per cent. of Britain's ore was obtained from the coal measures. The large quantity of fuel needed in the early blast furnaces also very effectively tied the smelting industry to the coalfields. At a time when coke and ore were charged in the ratio of 8 : 1, it was clearly less costly, if one of the raw materials had to be transported, to move the ore to the coke, rather than the other way about.

The great expansion of the iron industry from the mid-eighteenth century onwards was both a cause and a consequence of the spate of technical inventions of the period. Developments which made greater and more efficient production possible, such as improved methods of coking, larger furnaces, and the introduction of a hot furnace blast, were matched by an increasing demand for iron in almost every branch of a rapidly growing engineering industry. Regions which shared in this expansion were South Wales, where a string of iron-smelting towns grew up along the northern outcrop of the coalfield; the Black Country, where metal working was already well established and where there occurred the thickest, richest, and most easily worked coal seam in the country—the "Ten Yard Seam"; Central Scotland, which used a hard splint coal rather than coke to smelt the local ores; and Sheffield, an iron working centre since the Middle Ages, with access to the good quality coking coal of the Silkstone seam that could be mined in the centre of the town. The North West and the North East developed later, partly because of a lack of suitable coking coal in the former, and the paucity of good coal measure ores in the latter. Lancashire and the northern areas of the West Riding were occupied with their expanding textile industries and had little capital to spare for heavy investment in primary smelting.

The migration to the orefields and ports

As the nineteenth century wore on and the demand for iron increased, the smelting industry became increasingly dependent upon, and influenced in its location by, the distribution of bulk supplies of raw materials. Coal was available in abundance, but the coal measure ores were beginning to show signs of exhaustion. Large quantities of ore, however, could be obtained from three sources, none of which had any physical connection with the coalfields, and the industry was gradually pulled towards them. They were:

1. The haematite field of Cumberland.

2. The newly discovered Jurassic fields of the Cleveland Hills, the East Midlands, and Oxfordshire.

3. Foreign sources, particularly the rich, non-phosphoric deposits of northern Spain.

The migration of the smelting centres in the direction of the iron orefields was also facilitated by a steady increase in blast furnace efficiency, and a decline in the amount of coal required to produce a given amount of pig iron. In Britain to-day, coke and ore are charged into the furnace in the ratio of 1 : 2 on average, and there is generally a substantial saving in raw material procurement costs when coal is moved to the ore (Fig. 80).

The dependence on foreign ore has steadily increased in Britain over the years; 45 per cent. of the raw ore consumed in British blast furnaces and sinter plants is now imported, although the proportion varies considerably from one district to another (Fig. 81). In terms of iron content, 70 per cent. of current consumption comprises ore mined abroad. Prices have also moved in favour of foreign ore owing to the low freight rates that can be secured on bulk shipments in large carriers. Falling ocean freight rates are further enhancing

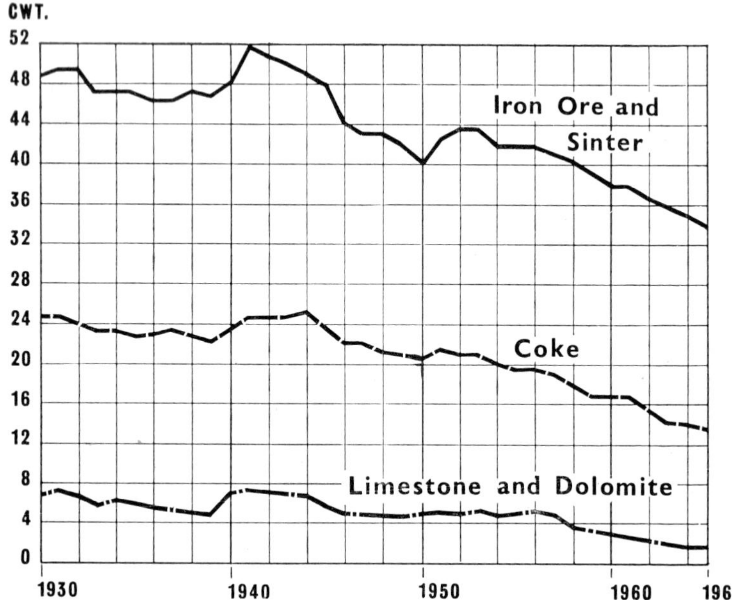

Fig. 80.—Materials Consumed in U.K. Blast Furnaces per Ton of Pig Iron Produced, 1930-65.

the already considerable advantages enjoyed by coastal sites, especially those that can offer berthing facilities for the largest vessels (Table 72, p. 290).

The influence of the market

Although the attraction of the orefields is increasing, iron-smelting still remains essentially a market-orientated industry. The main advantage to be gained from placing blast furnaces on the site of the ore deposits is that the costs incurred in assembling *raw materials* are kept to a minimum. But, of course, assembly costs are not the only costs involved. The end product of iron-smelting—namely pig iron—has to be distributed to steel works and iron foundries, and transport charges on pig iron will also be substantial if great distances are involved. It so happens that many of the more important orefields are in regions remote from coal, and outside the main spheres of industrial development. Those of northern

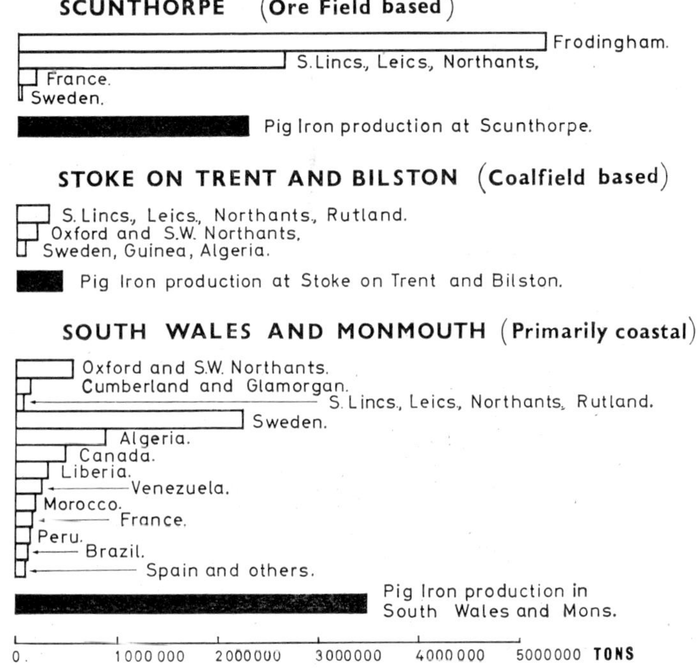

Fig. 81.—Sources and Quantities of Iron Ore Consumed Annually in Blast Furnaces and Sinter Plants, and Output of Pig Iron, in Three Iron Smelting Regions in Britain.

Sweden, Labrador, Venezuela, Sierra Leone, Mauritania, and West Australia are situated in thinly populated territories where markets for metallurgical products are very restricted indeed. To erect smelters on these fields would entail much unnecessary haulage. There would be little economic advantage to be derived, for instance, in establishing blast furnaces on the Schefferville field, feeding them with Pittsburgh coal, and then carrying pig iron back along the same route taken by the coal to steel works on the Great Lakes.

TABLE 72

BLAST FURNACE PRODUCTION IN BRITAIN, BY REGIONS
(in thousands of tons)

REGION	1938	1960	1965
1. Derby, Leics, Notts, Northants, and Essex	1,598	2,633	1,970
2. Lancs (excluding 10), Denbighshire, Flintshire, and Cheshire	277	1,236	1,448
3. Yorkshire (excluding 5 and 9)	nil	nil	nil
4. Lincolnshire	868	2,290	2,697
5. North-east Coast	1,833	3,412	3,434
6. Scotland	409	1,299	1,675
7. Staffs, Salop, Worcs, and Warwicks ..	317	553	585
8. South Wales and Monmouthshire ..	667	3,141	4,718
9. Sheffield	123	172	238
10. North-west Coast	722	1,028	695

Source: *Annual Statistics, British Iron and Steel Federation.*

In Britain, as already noted, there has been a tendency for the iron-smelting industry to migrate to the coast, where imported ore is cheaper than at points inland. But it has not migrated to Falmouth or Aberdeen. Blast furnaces still occupy sites within easy haulage distance of the major steel and engineering centres of the country. Market locations also predominate on the continent of Europe and in the United States. The persistence of the great iron-smelting centres on the Ruhr is due at least as much to the presence there of a large industrial market, as it is to the existence of the coalfield, or to the availability of cheap water transport on the Rhine (Fig. 82). The United States' iron-smelting industry is still concentrated on Pittsburgh, although there has been a dispersal to towns lying nearer the orefields, for example, to Chicago, Sparrow's Point, and Fairless on the Delaware. These centres, however, are situated well within the limits of the main manufacturing belt of the country (Fig. 83). Duluth, on the other hand, remains a comparatively minor iron and steel town, in spite of its many assets. It possesses a good deep water harbour, benefits from proximity to the Superior orefields and from the low rates on coal carried from the Erie ports as a return cargo on the ore boats, and has the resources of the United States Steel Corporation behind it. These assets, however, have not been sufficient to compensate for the lack of a mass market. To the north of Duluth lies a thinly populated hinterland, and to the south and east the market is dominated by Chicago. Even the New England market is not considered to be substantial enough to absorb production from a large integrated iron and steel plant, and proposals to construct one in the region have been abandoned.

The position in the Soviet Union is somewhat different. Prompted to some extent by military and strategic consideration, but also by the desire to save on the heavy freight charges incurred in hauling raw materials from the east to the older manufacturing centres in European Russia, the government has actively encouraged the migration of population and industry to the coal and orefields of Siberia. During the last half century, blast furnaces, steel mills, and metallurgical works have been developed rapidly, at Magnitogorsk, Chelyabinsk, Stalinsk, and other towns in the Urals, and

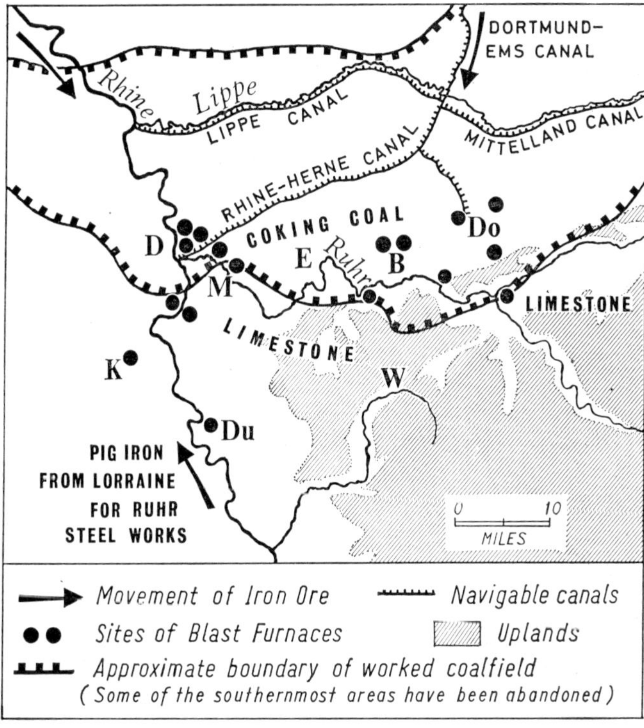

Fig. 82.—Iron-smelting Centres of the Ruhr.

on the open steppe. Some of these Siberian centres are beginning to rival in importance many of the old established industrial cities of the Ukraine (Fig. 84).

The by-product industries

The by-products of coking and smelting are consumed by other industries. Coal tar, a by-product of the retort coke oven, is the

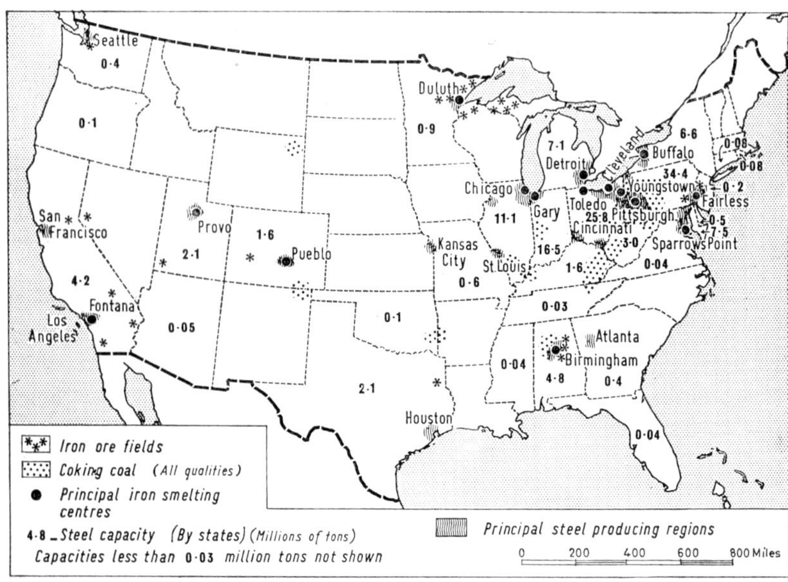

Fig. 83.—Location of Iron and Steel Industry of the United States.

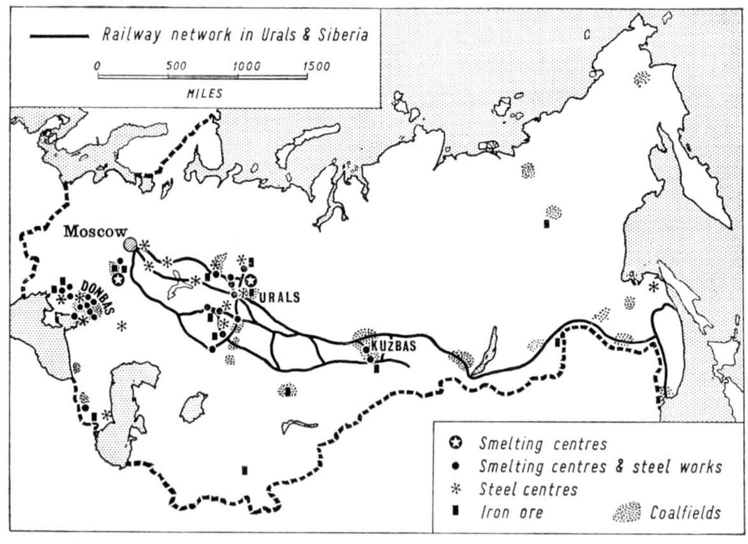

Fig. 84.—Location of Iron and Steel Industry of the U.S.S.R.

starting point for a wide range of chemicals, including dyes, fertilisers, synthetic rubber, plastics, and insecticides. Coke oven and blast furnace gases are sold as fuel to manufacturing firms and to municipal gas undertakings. Blast furnace slag is used in the production of cement. Industries utilising these and other by-products are thereby attracted to iron-smelting districts, and once established, operate as a further factor which prevents the ready migration of the iron-smelting industry itself to other regions.

TABLE 73
PRODUCTION OF PIG IRON
(in millions of short tons†)

	1962	1963	1966
WORLD	292	309	392
U.S.A.	68	74	84
U.S.S.R.	61	65	70
West Germany	27	25	25
Japan	20	22	33
China	16	19	n/a
United Kingdom	15	16	16
France	16	16	16
Belgium	7	8	8
India	6	7	7
Czechoslovakia	6	6	6
Australia	4	4	5
Luxembourg	4	4	4

† A short ton = 2,000 lbs. n/a—not available.
Source: *Commodity Yearbook* and *U.N. Monthly Bulletin of Statistics.*

2. THE STEEL INDUSTRY

Techniques of steel production

The essential difference between iron and steel lies in the amount of carbon present in the two products. Pig iron contains between three and four per cent. carbon: steel, according to type, between 0·15 and 1·4 per cent. The aim in steel making, therefore, is to remove or reduce the carbon content of the metal. This is done in a converter. In the production of steels with special qualities of hardness, toughness, and resistance to corrosion, traces of alloy metal—manganese, nickel, tungsten, chromium, molybdenum, and vanadium are added to the charge before it is run off.

The Bessemer converter

The first successful method of making substantial amounts of steel was developed by Bessemer in 1856. His "converter" is a steel container, shaped rather like a concrete mixer which is lined inside with refractory bricks, and fitted with a removable, perforated base. When in operation it is filled with molten pig iron, and a blast of cold air forced through the holes in the base. No external heat is applied, the oxygen in the air blast being sufficient when directed under pressure through the charge to set up reactions which burn out the carbon, and most of the manganese and silicon present. One "blow", producing from ten to twenty tons of steel, takes from twenty minutes to half an hour. Before the steel is drawn off, a small quantity of carbon is returned to the charge—the precise amount depending on the type of steel being made.

Early converters were given a gannister or *acid* lining. They removed most of the unwanted impurities from the pig iron, but left the sulphur and phosphorus unaffected. Pig iron could only be used, therefore, which contained sulphur and phosphorus in amounts permissible in the finished steel. It was later discovered that by lining the converter with crushed dolomite, and by adding a quantity of burnt lime to the charge, these two unwanted elements could also be eliminated. Conversion in the dolomite-lined converter became known as the *basic* or *Thomas process* (after its inventor Gilchrist-Thomas). It was an invention only slightly less important to the steel industry than the discovery of the acid Bessemer process of twenty years earlier. The acid converter was dependent on supplies of haematite pig iron, but the basic converter could utilise pig made from the highly phosphoric ores of Western Europe. Its development constituted a technological advance that laid the foundations of the steel industries of France, Luxembourg, Western Germany, and North East England.

The open hearth process

The open hearth furnace is basically a shallow, enclosed bath upon which a powerful flame of pre-heated air and gas is directed from above. The burnt gases escape by way of flues to regenerators situated beneath the furnace at each end. Periodically the direction of air and gas flow is reversed so that each regenerator in turn gives out and stores heat. In an integrated iron and steel works gas is provided by the coking ovens and blast furnaces. Elsewhere it is obtained from coal directly, or from natural gas in centres where this is cheap.

Both acid and basic open hearth furnaces are in use. The basic open hearth, like the basic Bessemer is lined with dolomite to eliminate phosphorus from the pig iron.

Most of the world's steel is now made in the open hearth furnace. The basic method predominates. The economic advantages that derive from the use of the open hearth furnace are:

1. It employs waste heat from its own burnt gases to pre-heat the air needed for the combustion of the fuel. Higher temperatures can thus be obtained, which in turn permit pig iron to be charged cold if necessary, either alone, or mixed with scrap. The open hearth furnace, therefore, need not be tied to the site of the blast furnace as it does not depend, as does the Bessemer converter, on a molten charge. Its ability to consume scrap iron and steel also economises in blast furnace capacity, and in the cost of blast furnace operation.

2. The open hearth process takes from ten to twelve hours, compared with twenty minutes for a "blow" in the Bessemer converter. The longer period allows a close watch to be kept on the steel as it is being made, and a product nearer to precise specification can be obtained.

Oxygen steel-making processes

Steel makers in the more technologically advanced countries, however, are showing a renewed interest in the "converter" principle of steel production, and are using the L.D., the Kaldo, and the Rotor converters for the purpose. These converters are akin to the Bessemer, but instead of forcing a blast of air through the charge from below, they inject oxygen at high speed on to the surface of the liquid iron from above. Steel of very high quality can be obtained by this method.

Electric processes

Electric arc and induction furnaces are used in the production of high quality alloy steels. Significantly, more than half the electric furnaces in Britain are in the Sheffield area. Electric processes, however, are expensive—the factor which alone prevents their more general adoption.

Continuous casting

This process, which has the merit of by-passing the ingot stage of steel production, is beginning to pass into general use. Molten steel from the furnace is cast directly into billets, blooms, and slabs. The need for primary and intermediate rolling mills, ingot moulds, and reheating furnaces is thus eliminated. Continuous casting plants with a capacity of more than a quarter of a million tons of steel per year are in operation in a number of steel works in Britain.

Locational factors in the steel industry

Steel making is a process lying between the production of pig iron from primary raw materials on the one hand, and the manufacture of finished articles made wholly or partly from steel on the other. The steel industry uses as its raw materials pig iron from the blast furnace, and scrap. Scrap arises from the steel works themselves in the form of ingot trimmings, and from sources external to the works. The consumption of scrap is highest in regions of heavy engineering, where it may, in the case of individual works, account for the whole of the furnace charge (Table 74).

Steel works are more widely dispersed than blast furnaces, and bear a closer relationship to the general distribution of population. They tend to be sited in the direction of the markets for their products, *i.e.* the engineering workshops, rather than backwards to the sources of their raw materials. That this is so is a consequence of (i) the somewhat higher freight rates on steel than pig iron, and (ii) the commercial advantages that are to be reaped by carrying out the intermediate and final stages of manufacture as close as possible to the consumers of the finished article. Engineering workshops are even more strongly market-orientated than steel plants.

Integrated iron and steel plants

Processing economies accrue from the geographical integration of all stages of production in the iron and steel industry. By placing coking ovens, sinter plants, blast furnaces, steel furnaces, and rolling mills adjacent to each other on the same site an uninterrupted flow of materials from one unit to the next becomes possible.

TABLE 74

PIG IRON AND SCRAP CONSUMED PER 100 TONS OF STEEL PRODUCED IN 1965.

REGION	PIG IRON	SCRAP
1. Derby, Leics, Notts, Northants, and Essex ..	77·9	33·9
2. Lancs (excluding 10), Denbighshire, Flintshire, and Cheshire	55·8	53·1
3. Yorkshire (excluding 5 and 9)	1·7	98·9
4. Lincolnshire	87·9	23·2
5. North-east Coast	69·1	41·1
6. Scotland	49·4	60·7
7. Staffs, Salop, Worcs, and Warwicks	33·3	77·5
8. South Wales and Mons	70·1	44·4
9. Sheffield	16·0	91·8
10. North-west Coast	74·7	32·3
Average	59·4	51·6

Source: *Annual Statistics, British Iron and Steel Federation.*

There is also a saving on fuel costs in an integrated plant. Waste gases from the coking ovens can be used to heat the furnace blast, and the expense of re-heating the iron or steel as it passes between the blast furnace, steel works, and rolling mills is also avoided. Economic, as distinct from geographical integration is also fairly common in the industry. Some large steel companies, such as Krupps of Germany and the Bethlehem Steel Corporation of the U.S.A., have acquired interests in ore and coal mines, transportation, and the engineering and fabricating industries, and have thus secured a measure of control over their raw material supplies (a matter of some importance during a period of scarcity and high prices) and over the markets for their manufactured products.

The advantages of large-scale operation

Capital and operating costs in the iron and steel industry are lower in the case of large plants than small ones, provided the large plants can be kept working to full or near full capacity.

Steel, of course, is not a homogeneous commodity, and there will always be room in any advanced society for the small works turning out goods for a specialised and restricted market, but the trend is undoubtedly towards the larger plant. That this is so, is apparent from post-war developments in most of the major iron and steel producing countries. In Britain 93 per cent. of the steel works in 1946 had a capacity of less than 1 million tons per annum. To-day only 35 per cent. are in this category, and 10 per cent. have a capacity exceeding 3 million tons. One-third of the steel works in the United States (where the domestic market is huge) can produce upwards of 3 million tons per year, and one—the Bethlehem Steel Corporation's plant at Sparrow's Point—no less than 7·5 million tons.

Some integrated works produce standardised finished products for which there is a large and steady demand, and in which the economies of large scale mass production can be realised. Plates for use in the shipbuilding industry, girders for constructional work, and steel rails for railway track are examples of such products. The bulk of the output, however, consists of semi-finished goods—sheets, plates, billets, blooms and slabs, heavy sections and bars, and wire rods—which are passed on to re-rolling mills and engineering shops for final processing.

The factor of inertia in the iron and steel industry

The tendency for the iron and steel industry to persist in areas where it originally became established, even though the factors which were responsible for its initial development no longer operate, is strong. Many iron and steel centres of the English Midlands and the North have survived from an earlier period, and are not located as they would be if they were being created at the present time. Sheffield illustrates the position well.

Metal working has been important in Sheffield for at least six centuries. In the early years the town had every possible advantage for the successful development of this activity. Ironstone was worked within a mile or two of the town centre; charcoal was available from the forests of the Don Valley; the Don and its tributaries provided water power for the bellows and forges and for turning the excellent grindstones brought from the gritstone formations of the southern Pennines; refractory materials were found in abundance in the coal measures; limestone deposits lay fifteen miles away in Derbyshire; and coal, when it eventually replaced charcoal, could be dug within the boundaries of the town itself. The site was as ideal as any in Britain, and Sheffield fast became one of the major metal working centres of the country.

As time went on, however, Sheffield began to lose, one by one, the assets upon which its early prosperity had been built. The iron ore deposits became exhausted, and the iron-smelting industry disappeared. By the early eighteenth century the charcoal resources were more or less spent, and a hundred years later the last coal mine in the town closed. In the meantime the growth of population and industry had so congested the narrow, cramped valley that there was little room for further expansion on level land, except downstream towards Rotherham. Sheffield's isolated, foothill position also hampered the growth of communications. It was not until 1819 that a canal reached the city, and there was no direct rail link with London until 1870. But in spite of these disadvantages, the centre continued to grow. To-day it is the seventh largest city in the United Kingdom, and possesses one-twelfth of the country's steel making capacity. The concentration of steel and engineering works in Sheffield is also greater than in any other region in the country, and probably greater than in any part of the world, including Pittsburgh and the Ruhr.

The reasons why Sheffield has maintained its position as a leading steel and metallurgical centre, despite the growing attractions of more open sites on the coast and orefields, are:

1. The city has adapted itself to changing geographical conditions. Iron-smelting was given up long ago (although the nearest blast furnaces are at Rotherham, just beyond the city boundaries), and to-day Sheffield concentrates on the manufacture of special, high quality steels for which its position is no great handicap. Two-thirds of Britain's alloy steel is now made in the region. Sheffield too has been at the forefront of technological developments

in steel making techniques. It is no accident that both Huntsman—the inventor of crucible steel—and Bessemer did much of their work in the city. It must also be stressed that the term "inertia" in the sense used by economists, is not synonymous with shiftlessness. "Inert" industries are among the most progressive, technologically, otherwise they would not survive.

2. Capital investment in Sheffield steel is enormous. Equipment in a steel mill or engineering workshop is not only expensive, but also durable, and to a large extent indivisible. A firm cannot, except at a cost which is likely to be prohibitive, transfer its operations piecemeal to another area. Either the plant as a whole is moved, or the plant as a whole stays where it is. The best time for a move, if one were contemplated, would be when equipment had worn out, and needed replacement. But equipment does not all wear out at the same time. Faced with the alternatives of (i) a wholesale transfer of operations, involving very high initial costs, but lower manufacturing costs once the transfer were complete, (ii) a piecemeal transfer, entailing considerable interference with production for a number of years, (iii) staying put, and trying to improve its competitive position by raising efficiency—given these choices, most firms choose the last. Raising efficiency, however, necessitates further investment, which in turn makes a future move even more unlikely.

3. A very high proportion of the furnace charge in Sheffield is scrap which originates within the city itself. Much of the steel output is also absorbed by the engineering trades of Sheffield. The steel industry is thus much better located *vis à vis* its raw material sources and markets than is commonly realised.

Sheffield's great deposit of skilled labour has been an important element militating against a migration of the industry in the past. The significance of labour skill is now declining, however, as manufacturing processes become more and more automatically controlled.

Major steel regions of the world

North America, the countries of Western Europe, the Soviet Union, and Japan together account for over 90 per cent. of the steel production of the world (Table 75).

Other countries in which production is significant include China (Southern Manchuria and Shantung), India (at Jamshedpur, using coking coal from Damodar and iron ore from Orissa); Australia (at Newcastle and Whyalla); South Africa (at Vereeniging, Johannesburg, Pretoria, and Newcastle); and Brazil (at Rio de Janeiro, São Paulo, and the Volta Redonda works in the Paraiba Valley).

TABLE 75

PRODUCTION OF STEEL INGOTS AND CASTINGS
(in millions of short tons*)

	1962	1963	1964
WORLD	397	425	453
U.S.A.	98	109	126
U.S.S.R.	84	88	n/a
Japan	30	35	42
West Germany	36	35	41
United Kingdom	23	25	28
France	19	19	21
China	11	13	n/a
Italy	11	11	n/a
Czechoslovakia	8	8	n/a
Belgium	8	8	n/a
Canada	7	8	n/a
Luxembourg	4	4	n/a
Sweden	4	4	n/a

* A short ton = 2,000 lbs. n/a—not available.

Source: American Iron and Steel Institute.

ENGINEERING

Engineering, in the more restricted sense in which the term is used here, embraces those industries which are concerned with the production of all kinds of machines or machine parts, mechanical and electrical, made wholly or in part from metal. Of the metals employed, steel is by far the most important, although some non-ferrous metals, especially aluminium and copper, play an essential role in certain industries.

The branches of the engineering industry are so numerous and diverse that it is possible only to mention some of the more important groups here. They include the manufacture of all kinds of electrical equipment; machines tools; textile, mining, and excavating machinery; marine engines and ships; locomotives, aircraft, motor vehicles, and cycles; agricultural machinery; and many kinds of domestic appliances. A selection is described in some detail below, although the following general characteristics apply to all.

1. They represent the final stage in a sequence of manufacturing operations that begins with primary metal smelting.

2. All must have access to supplies of steel, and frequently to other raw materials as well, although the quantities required vary from one industry to another. More steel is obviously needed to build a ship than to make a watch, and the distribution of steel supplies exerts a greater influence on the location of the ship-building industry than it does on watch making.

3. The value added during the process of manufacture is high, sometimes very high. This is evident if one compares the value of the metal in an aircraft, motor vehicle, or typewriter, with the value of the machines themselves.

4. The proportion of total manufacturing costs attributable to power is low. To-day electricity, drawn from public supplies which are available at prices that do not vary appreciably from one part of a country to another, is commonly used in engineering workshops. As far as power requirements are concerned, therefore, engineering industries have a wide choice of sites available to them.

5. Nearly all products of the engineering industries suffer an increase in bulk during manufacture, and some are fragile and require careful handling. They are therefore more difficult and costly to transport than the materials and components from which they are made.

6. Many are to a greater or lesser degree assembly industries which use bought-in components supplied by other firms.

7. Because engineering industries are relatively footloose as far as their raw material requirements and power supplies are concerned, and because transport charges are often higher on finished than on partly-finished articles, engineering workshops are generally situated near the markets they serve. The advantages of a close liaison between engineering firms and the consumers of their products are also considerable, and tend further to enhance the attractions of a market location.

Some examples of engineering industries

THE MACHINE-TOOL INDUSTRY.—The machine-tool industry is small, but it is basic to the engineering trades generally. It is concerned with the manufacture of equipment needed to produce the accurately machined, interchangeable parts that are now fundamental to all forms of mass production. The machine-tool industry uses high quality steel, but as the quantity required is small, and its value very high, the distribution of steel supplies has little influence on the location of the industry. Machine-tool production is concentrated in the older manufacturing regions of the world—the English Midlands, South Lancashire, the West Riding, the Ruhr and Rhinelands, New England, the Great Lakes region, the Moscow region, and the Ukraine. A high degree of technical skill is required on the part of the workmen—although flow production techniques are now being introduced—and for this reason the industry is slow to develop in countries where a tradition in precision engineering is weak or absent.

The machine-tool industry has had a profound effect on the geography of manufacturing during the present century. It has made possible the production of reliable components in vastly greater numbers than could ever be made by craftsmen. It has allowed industry to function with a large, predominantly untrained labour force, and has thus permitted the spread of manufacturing into regions having little previous skill in engineering. It has also made it comparatively easy for a person to transfer from one occupation to another without undergoing a long period of re-training. The industry has thus helped to increase the mobility of labour.

THE MOTOR VEHICLE INDUSTRY.—The production of motor vehicles entails the following operations:

1. The manufacture of the body and the several thousands of component parts that go into a completed vehicle. The components are so numerous, diverse, and specialised, and involve so many different products—iron, steel, non-ferrous metals, glass, plastics, rubber, leather, textiles, paint, etc.—that they could not possibly all be produced in one factory or by a single firm. The motor manufacturers are therefore, to a greater extent than most people, consumers of the products of other industries.

2. The assembly of individual components into units or "sub-assemblies".

3. The final assembly of the vehicle.

The motor vehicle industry in Britain.—Easy access to raw material supplies, particularly sheet steel, and component parts, and a location within reach of a prosperous, mass market, are two essential conditions for the successful establishment of a motor vehicle assembly plant. Raw materials must flow without interruption to the assembly lines, and this requirement can be best fulfilled if the plant is situated within the region producing most of the components. Such a region is the West Midlands—the traditional centre in Britain for the production of small and varied metal goods. It was in the Midlands that the cycle industry first developed, and it was out of the cycle industry that the motor vehicle industry was born. The Midlands, too, had accumulated a pool of labour skilled in mechanical engineering, which was to give the region a particular advantage until motor vehicle construction ceased to be the work of craftsmen. At first the car was an expensive luxury, as often as not built to suit the requirements of individual customers. It is not surprising therefore that London, the largest centre of purchasing power in the country, should also be attractive to vehicle manufacturers, and the car industry expanded there as well as at Birmingham and Coventry.

To-day, the industry has spread beyond its original centres, but it is still found concentrated within a coffin shaped zone extending from the South-East into Lancashire (Fig. 85). The importance of

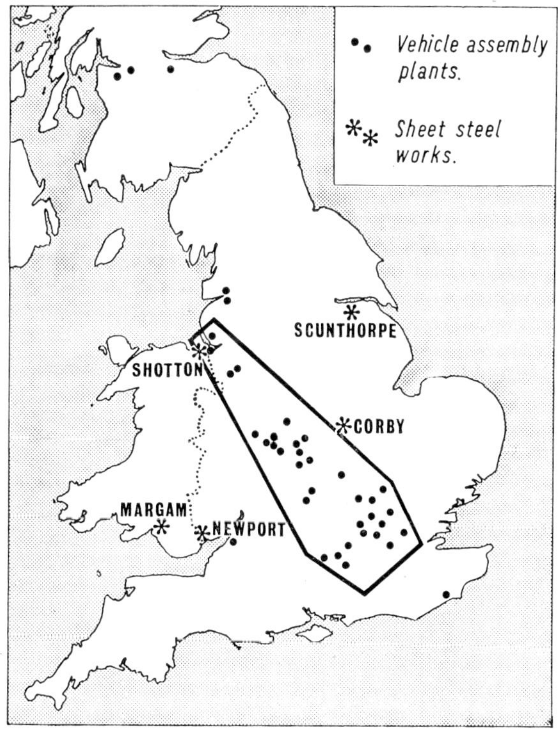

Fig. 85.—Location of Motor Vehicle Plants in the British Isles and the Midland "Coffin".

the export trade is reflected in the development of vehicle assembly plants at Dagenham, on Merseyside, and in the Glasgow region.

The motor vehicle industry of the U.S.A.—During the early experimental phase of the industry, motor vehicle manufacturing was carried on in the north-east states, and the Mid West. The geographical advantages of the Mid West, however, soon became evident, and by 1910 the Lower Great Lakes region, with its centre at Detroit was producing more than three-quarters of the country's output. At present, the vehicle component industries, and sub-assembly plants are concentrated almost entirely in this region, although for various reasons the assembly plants are more widely dispersed. The predominance of the Mid West can be ascribed to the following factors:

1. There existed near the Lake shores a thriving wagon- and carriage-making industry at the end of the last century, which was based on the region's hardwood resources. Flint, Lansing, and Pontiac are important present day centres which in 1880 were making horse-drawn vehicles, and were employing the same steel components—axles, springs, bolts, etc., that were used in the manufacture of the earliest cars. These cars were in fact simply carriages with an engine attached.

2. The vast areas to be covered, the comparatively thin rail network, and the infrequency of rail services stimulated a demand for private transport. The flat terrain was also an important factor in the days when vehicles had little power.

3. The Great Lakes waterway gave access to supplies of steel and assisted the distribution of vehicles to their markets.

4. Once the industry had become established, the region became attractive to motor firms which had attempted, although without much success, to develop enterprises in other parts of the country.

Economies of scale in the motor vehicle industry

With the exception of a few luxury cars, most motor vehicles are to-day mass produced. The flow-production technique was adapted to vehicle assembly by Henry Ford in Detroit in 1909, and has since been adopted by all the major manufacturers in the world. It depends for its success on the supply of accurately engineered, standardised, interchangeable parts, produced by the aid of elaborate and expensive machine tools. Tooling-up operations are very costly, and can be justified economically only when the demand for a model is extremely large. The importance of spreading the high initial cost over as many units as possible has led to the amalgamation of many small firms into a handful of large ones, and to the practice of using the same basic components in different makes of vehicle. The high overhead charges of motor vehicle production also explain why British and Continental manufacturers must turn out what is fundamentally the same car for several years, while American firms with a much larger market at their disposal can afford to re-tool annually.

Above: Atomic Power Station, Berkeley, Gloucestershire. Note the river-side location (bottom left), the absence of fuel dumps, and the narrowness of the approach road. (*Aerofilms and Aero Pictorial Ltd.*)

Below: The Port Talbot-Margam Abbey iron and steel works. A fully integrated works on a coastal site. Blast furnaces, steel mills, rolling mills, and much of the auxiliary plant are clearly visible. (*Aerofilms and Aero Pictorial Ltd.*)

Above: A coal-chemical plant at Rotherham, Yorkshire. (*Aerofilms and Aero Pictorial Ltd.*)

Below: Motor vehicle manufacture. A view of the FIAT works on the outskirts of Turin. (*Paul Popper.*)

Motor vehicles differ from most manufactured products in that they can travel to their markets under their own power. Many firms prefer, however, to have them transported in an unassembled or "knocked down" state, and to undertake the final assembly in the market area. Thus in the United States, whilst production capacity is concentrated in the Great Lakes region, assembly plants are much more widely scattered, and are to be found in California, Texas, Georgia, and other outlying states. On the other hand, Canada's small domestic market has not warranted the dispersal of assembly plants, and both the production and assembly branches are concentrated in Ontario.

SHIPBUILDING—Shipbuilding is an assembly industry, and like motor vehicle manufacturing, it uses components and products of other industries. Ships differ from motor vehicles in the greater size of the completed unit, and in the techniques of production. Ships are normally produced only in small numbers, and generally to individual design. Hence the mass production methods which characterise the motor vehicle industry are not so applicable to shipbuilding, although the Japanese have recently introduced them with considerable success.

Shipbuilding is perforce restricted to sites on sheltered, navigable waters. As many of the components used are heavy and bulky, the industry flourishes only where there are centres of heavy engineering at hand, or where access by cheap water transport to such centres is easy. On the other hand, many components are specialised and valuable in relation to weight and bulk and are obtained from a distance. Sheffield and the English Midlands are major suppliers

TABLE 76

PRODUCTION OF MOTOR VEHICLES
(in thousands)

A—Private cars. B—Commercial vehicles.

	1948		1960		1965	
	A	B	A	B	A	B
U.S.A.	3,909·3	1,376·3	6,674·8	1,194·5	9,305·6	1,751·8
West Germany	911·0	164·1	1,816·8	237·8	2,733·7	237·7
United Kingdom	334·8	173·3	1,352·7	458·0	1,722·0	455·2
Japan	0·4	36·8	165·1	595·2	696.2	1,222·4
France	101·1	98·3	1,115·6	233·6	1,374·0	241·2
Italy	44·4	15·0	595·9	48·9	1,103·9	71·6
Canada	166·8	96·9	325·8	72·0	710·1	144·8
U.S.S.R.	20·2	176·9	138·8	501·3	201·2	612·6
WORLD	4,640	2,030	12,790	3,690	19,090	5,210

Source: *U.N. Statistical Yearbook.*

of such components. Even Switzerland has a small, but important, marine engineering industry. Port facilities are necessary if constructional materials have to be brought from overseas. The British yards, for example, must import timber, and those of Denmark and the Netherlands, steel. Finally, shipbuilding depends upon a labour force skilled in many trades. Skilled men, however, are apt to drift into other work during depression periods (and shipbuilding is particularly susceptible to fluctuations in the trade cycle), and once lost they are not easily recovered, and fresh labour is not easily trained.

In Britain, the centres of shipbuilding have shifted with the growth in the size of vessels, and with the substitution of steel for wood. In the days of the small wooden sailing ship the industry was widely dispersed along coasts within reach of forest land: the Thames with access to the hardwoods of the Weald was the most important region. The steel built, steam driven vessel, however, could be most cheaply built near the steel towns of the north, and there was a gradual migration of the industry to the estuaries of the Clyde, Tyne, Mersey, Tees, and Wear, and to the Belfast and Barrow-in-Furness districts. To-day the Clyde and Tyne are responsible for three-quarters of the total British tonnage launched.

TABLE 77

SHIPBUILDING: MERCHANT VESSELS LAUNCHED
(in thousands of metric tons)

	1954	1959	1966	Per cent. of World total in 1966
WORLD TOTAL	5,250	8,750	14,068	100
Japan	413	1,620	7,740	55
West Germany	960	1,200	1,200	8·5
Sweden	540	850	1,180	8·4
United Kingdom	1,400	1,370	1,084	7·7
Norway	100	320	537	3·8
France	260	410	430	3·1
Netherlands	410	600	274	1·9

Source: *U.N. Monthly Bulletin of Statistics*, September, 1967.

The United States.—During the middle decades of the last century, before the supremacy of the wooden sailing vessel was seriously challenged, the north-east coast of the U.S.A. was the greatest shipbuilding region in the world. With the development of the iron, and later the steel built, steam propelled ship, the locational advantages passed to Britain where raw materials were cheaper, and where greater experience had been gained in the practical application of steam power to transport. There was also a shift within the U.S.A. from the forested coasts of New England to centres on the mid-Atlantic seaboard, particularly to Philadelphia and Baltimore, and later, with the opening up of the West, to the

Great Lakes shores. The United States is not a major shipbuilding nation in peace time, but during the two World Wars, and more especially during the Second, she increased her capacity enormously. In 1945 she was capable of launching no less than 25 million tons of shipping a year—about fifty times her normal peace time requirements. Most of this surplus capacity has now been scrapped.

Japan.—The Japanese shipbuiding industry has risen out of conditions of wartime destruction and disorganisation to become, within a period of less than twenty years, the largest in the world. Access to comparatively cheap supplies of steel; and a rapid rate of construction, coupled with very efficient design, have resulted in a fall in building costs, so that Japan is now outstripping her competitors. Forty per cent. of the world's shipping tonnage is now launched from Japanese yards. The industry is concentrated along the southern shores of Honshu, especially at Hiroshima, Osaka, and Yokohama.

CHAPTER XIV

THE CHEMICAL INDUSTRY

The chemical industry is of fairly recent origin. It is true that the making of dyes, soap, tanning materials, medicinal preparations, glass, and metal alloys—all products whose manufacture involves chemical processes—has been carried on since ancient times, but the industry in its present form, in which the principles of chemistry are consciously applied to the manufacture of economically useful goods, is a development of the last two centuries.

The chemical industry is concerned with the breaking down of raw materials (often very common raw materials such as coal, petroleum, limestone, salt, wood, and air) into their constituent elements, and then re-combining and re-grouping those elements in order to form new substances. The number of possible combinations is almost infinite, and the chance of discovering something new and of value has stimulated research to a degree found in few other major industries. As a consequence, the chemical industry has grown in a comparatively short space of time into an enterprise of bewildering complexity, turning out a vast range of products. A few of these products reach the consuming public in a form that leaves their chemical origin in little doubt—washing soda, bicarbonate of soda, vinegar, aspirin, agricultural lime, etc.; many others are employed as ingredients in such goods as plastics, synthetic fibres, dyestuffs, glass, soap, and detergents; and yet others are utilised as processing agents in the production of steel, paper, and rubber articles, and in the scouring of wool and the cleaning of cotton. There are, in fact, few industries that could function to-day without the use of chemicals for one purpose or another, and as a result the industry has become one of the foundations upon which twentieth-century manufacturing economies are built.

The heavy chemical industry

This branch of the industry is engaged in the manufacture of products which are normally cheap to produce, required in bulk, and which are consumed by other sections of the chemical industry and by industries not directly related to it. The principal heavy chemicals are the acids—particularly sulphuric acid—and the alkalies—soda ash, caustic soda, and chlorine.

SULPHURIC ACID—The use of sulphuric acid in the field of manufacturing is so widespread and essential that its consumption has come to be regarded as a reliable barometer of industrial activity generally. Sulphuric acid can be produced from:

1. Sulphur, or minerals containing sulphur such as iron and copper pyrites and anhydrite.

2. By-product gases of coke ovens, gas plants, and zinc and petroleum refineries.

Sixty per cent. of the annual production of sulphuric acid in the United Kingdom (approximately 3 million tons) is obtained from elemental sulphur imported from the Gulf States of the U.S.A., from France, and from Mexico; 15 per cent. from domestic supplies of anhydrite; 10 per cent. from pyrites imported principally from Spain; and the remainder from spent oxides from metal smelters and oil refineries. Sulphuric acid is bulky, of low value, and highly corrosive. It demands careful handling, and must be transported in special containers. It tends therefore, to be produced near the point of consumption, and many firms find it convenient to manufacture their own supplies.

TABLE 78

PRODUCTION OF SULPHURIC ACID
(IN TERMS OF 100 PER CENT H_2SO_4)
(in thousands of metric tons)

	1948	1960	1964*
U.S.A.	10,390	16,220	20,790
U.S.S.R.	n/a	5,400	7,650
Japan	1,220	4,450	5,370
West Germany	810†	3,170	3,315 (1963)
United Kingdom	1,580	2,745	3,185
Italy	975	2,300	2,870
France	1,275	2,045	2,700
Canada	615	1,520	1,775

n/a—not available. * Estimated or provisional figures for 1964.
† Excludes Saar.
Source: *U.N. Statistical Yearbook.*

TABLE 79

CONSUMPTION OF SULPHURIC ACID IN THE UNITED KINGDOM 1965
(in thousands of tons)

Phosphatic fertilisers	913·8
Titanium dioxide	500·3
Detergents	328·1
Rayon and other textiles	274·3
Ammonium sulphate	249·5
Other uses	1,075·0
Total	3,341·0

Source: British Sulphur Corporation, London.

SODA ASH (Na_2CO_3)—Soda ash is the cheapest and most important of the alkalies. Before the Industrial Revolution it was obtained in small amounts from seaweed, and other salt loving plants, and to-day dried salt-lake beds in Kenya and California are the source of minor natural deposits. Soda ash was produced synthetically for the first time at the end of the eighteenth century. The discovery that it could be made commercially by treating salt with sulphuric acid, and by roasting the sodium sulphate thus obtained with coke and limestone was made by Leblanc. The *Leblanc* process quickly established itself in all the major manufacturing nations of the world, and was not seriously challenged for almost a century. It was eventually replaced by the *Solvay* or *ammonia-soda* process which yields a cheaper and purer product. The ammonia-soda process now accounts for practically the entire world production of soda ash.

The manufacture of soda ash requires the assembly of salt and limestone, both fairly common and widely distributed minerals. Each is needed in bulk, and in roughly equal proportions. Limestone is generally more readily transportable than salt in the form in which the latter is produced (brine), and the industry therefore tends to be drawn towards the salt fields. Even so, it is only where the two raw materials occur close together, or are linked by navigable water that soda ash plants have been erected. The ammonia-soda process is also extravagant in the use of fuel for heat generation, and steam raising, and a coalfield or near-coalfield site, or alternatively a location where fuel oil or natural gas is cheap, is a further requirement for economic operation. In the United Kingdom the centre of the soda ash industry is Northwich. The town is situated on the Cheshire salt field less than thirty miles from the Carboniferous Limestone outcrops of Derbyshire and North Wales, and within a short rail haul distance of the South Lancashire coalfield. The

TABLE 80

PRODUCTION OF SODA ASH
(in thousands of metric tons)

	1948	1960	1964*
U.S.A.	4,150	4,135	4,490
U.S.S.R.	480	1,890	2,740
West Germany	n/a	1,120	1,130
Japan	220	1,300	n/a
France	715	850	1,020
East Germany	n/a	595	670
Poland	98	530	595

* Estimated or provisional figures for 1964. n/a—not available.
Source: *U.N. Statistical Yearbook.*

canalised Weaver, and the northern section of the Trent and Mersey Canal still carry a substantial traffic in coal and chemicals, although the St Helens Canal, which was a factor in the rise of the industry, is now abandoned (Fig. 86). Abroad, the great soda ash plant at Rheinberg is located with reference to navigable water and the coal

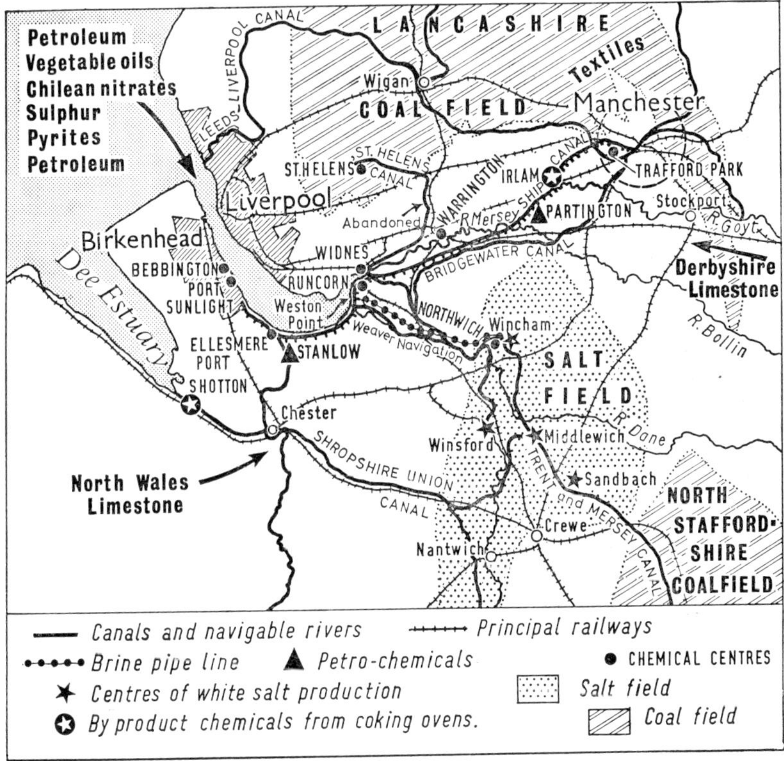

Fig. 86.—The Geographical Basis of the Cheshire and Mid-Mersey Chemical Industries.

of the Ruhr. In the United States soda ash plants are found in Detroit, Syracuse, Saltville, Baton Rouge, and near Akron.

Caustic soda (NaOH) is produced electrolytically from brine. Important centres of caustic soda production in Britain are Widnes and Runcorn. Weston Point, near Runcorn, is connected to the Cheshire salt field by a brine pipeline. Chlorine is obtained as a by-product of caustic soda manufacture.

The alkalies, like sulphuric acid, enter at some stage into the production of nearly every manufactured article. Soda ash is bulky and expensive to transport. Special precautions need to be taken when handling both caustic soda and chlorine. Industries utilising these chemicals in substantial quantities, therefore, tend to be attracted towards centres where they are produced. Thus the glass, soap, rayon, and paper industries of North West England owe their existence (among, of course, other factors) to the presence of the alkali industry in the Middle Mersey region, and the Weaver Valley.

Coal chemicals

Coal is an important raw material of the chemical industry, as well as the world's leading fuel.

Coal chemicals are recovered during the carbonisation or coking of bituminous coal and lignite. The primary object of coking in any particular instance may be (*a*) the production of metallurgical coke, in which case by-product gases released during the coking operation are collected and condensed into tar, and made to yield ammonia and light oils; (*b*) to gasify the coal as completely as possible, and to sell the gas thus produced to industrial and domestic consumers, or to process it further into the groups of chemicals named in (*a*) above.

These chemicals are starting off points for a host of products as diverse as sulphuric acid, road tar, agricultural fertilisers, insecticides, synthetic fibres, plastics, dyestuffs, detergents, explosives, and pharmaceutical drugs. Some of these products can be manufactured economically only in the neighbourhood of the coking oven and gas plant. There is a close physical association, for example, between the location of sulphuric acid works that utilise by-product gases, and the iron-smelting industry. Other products which come at the end of a long chain of processes, and whose manufacture involves the consumption of raw materials in only small quantities, and which further are of very high value in relation to their weight and bulk, can be made in almost any centre where normal urban services exist, and where appropriate labour and research facilities are available. The pharmaceutical drug industry has thus become important in cities like Basle and Boston, in areas remote from centres of basic coal-chemical production.

Petro-chemicals

Coal and petroleum are chemically similar, since they both consist essentially of a mixture of hydrocarbons. In the case of petroleum, the hydrocarbons are separated into petrol, diesel oil, paraffin, and other familiar petroleum products by the fractional distillation and cracking of crude oil in the refinery. The gases released during the refining processes were formerly burnt or discharged into the atmosphere as useless. Technological advances during the last few decades, however, have made their recovery and conversion into chemical raw materials possible. So rapid has progress been that the petro-chemical industry has grown during the last quarter century from an activity of trivial importance to one of the largest and fastest developing enterprises in the field of organic chemistry. In Britain, some 75 per cent. and in the U.S.A. some 85 per cent. of all organic chemicals are now derived from petroleum.

The growth of petro-chemicals has been partly at the expense of the coal chemical industry. The end products of each are similar, and in many cases identical. Competition between them, therefore, resolves itself into one of cost. Practically the entire output of crude oil, however, passes through the refinery, whilst the bulk of the coal mined is burnt as a fuel. The petro-chemical industry thus enjoys economies of scale not available to the coal chemical industry. The cost advantage is steadily moving in favour of petro-chemicals, especially in countries where oil is plentiful and cheap. The outlook for coal chemicals is not particularly promising.

The chemical fertilisers

The great increase in crop yields that has occurred during the last century, and especially in the years following the Second World War, could not have taken place without the widespread and intensive use of chemical fertilisers. Inorganic manures have been especially beneficial on land deficient in essential plant nutrients, and in regions where natural manures are scarce, as, for example, in predominantly arable country. The three main plant foods that are normally needed in greater quantities than many soils are able to supply are nitrogen (in soluble form as nitrate or ammonium salt), phosphorus (as phosphate), and potassium (as potassium salts). The output of nitrogenous fertilisers has more than doubled during the last ten years (Table 81).

NITRATES.—Natural deposits of sodium nitrate (Chilean saltpetre) occur as shallow beds in the longitudinal valley of northern Chile. For a century after their discovery in 1813, these deposits supplied the greater part of the world's requirements of inorganic nitrogenous fertilisers, and were the main source of nitric acid from which explosives were manufactured. Their location in one of the most arid and inhospitable regions on earth, into which labour, fuel, food, and fresh water all have to be imported, has always made their exploitation difficult and costly, and only the introduction of advanced mining and processing techniques has saved the industry from collapse. Chile's main competitors are now the industrial nations themselves, who, fearful of a shortage of saltpetre during the First World War, perfected methods of fixing nitrogen from the atmosphere. Soluble nitrogen in the form of ammonium sulphate is also manufactured from coke oven gases.

PHOSPHATES.—The ultimate source of all phosphates on earth is the mineral apatite, a constituent of certain igneous rocks. Primary phosphate beds are worked in Arctic European Russia, but

TABLE 81

PRODUCTION OF NITROGENOUS FERTILISERS
(in thousands of metric tons)

	1948-52 (average)	1960	1964*
U.S.A.	1,080	2,740	4,430
U.S.S.R.	n/a	1,004	2,100
Japan	406	1,030	1,390
West Germany	475	1,180	1,290
Italy	165	660	840
United Kingdom	275	450	595
Netherlands	172	420	525
Poland	74	270	360
Belgium	180	278	345
East Germany	245	335	335
Norway	150	275	320
Canada	160	285	315
WORLD TOTAL	—	10,900	16,500

n/a—not available. * Estimated or provisional.
Source: *U.N. Statistical Yearbook.*

TABLE 82

PRODUCTION OF PHOSPHATE ROCK
(in thousands of tons)

	1955-9 (average)	1960	1964*
U.S.A.	14,540	17,510	22,960
U.S.S.R.—			
apatite	3,810	4,630	7,870
phosphate rock	1,730	2,260	4,920
Morocco	5,890	7,350	9,940
Tunisia	2,130	2,060	2,710
Pacific Islands	1,880	2,080	2,510
North Vietnam—			
apatite	100	480	980
phosphate rock	32	50	50
Peru—guano	n/a	n/a	200

* Estimated or provisional. n/a—not available.
Source: *Minerals Yearbook.* Bureau of Mines, Washington, D.C.

they are of less importance, commercially, than the marine sedimentary deposits known as phosphate rock, from which more than half the world's phosphate production is now obtained. Other valuable sources include guano (the accumulated droppings of sea birds) from the coasts of Peru and Chile, and basic slag, a product of the basic steel-making processes.

The largest reserves of phosphate rock occur in North Africa, particularly in Morocco. Extensive deposits are also found in the U.S.A. in Florida, Tennessee, and the Mountain states; in the Soviet Union; in Brazil; and on some of the Pacific Islands.

POTASH.—Sources of commercial potash include wood ash, saline water, and the soluble potash minerals—carnallite, sylvite, and kainite. Potash minerals, now occurring as sediments, formed in inland lakes or marine lagoons during past geological periods when arid climates prevailed. They account for the greater proportion of the world supply at the present time. World reserves are large, and only the higher grade deposits are worked. The main producers are the two Germanys, the U.S.A., France, and the Soviet Union.

TABLE 83

PRODUCTION OF MARKETABLE POTASH
(in thousands of short tons, K_2O equivalent)

	1955-9 (average)	1960	1964
U.S.A.	2,200	2,640	2,900
West Germany	1,890	2,180	2,430
East Germany	1,660	1,840	2,140*
France	1,510	1,690	1,990
U.S.S.R.*	1,030	1,210	1,750
Israel..	50	90	330
Spain	260	290	320

* Estimated.

Source: *Minerals Yearbook*. Bureau of Mines, Washington, D.C.

The chemical industry of the United States

Judged from the standpoint of value added during the process of manufacture, the chemical industry of the United States ranks second only to the primary metal industries. Chemical plants are found in every state, although the main concentrations occur within the manufacturing belt of the north and east; along the Gulf Coast; and in California.

A distinction must be made between the basic, heavy chemical industries which tend to be drawn towards navigable water, coal and salt, and which are also closely associated with the large iron, steel, and engineering districts; and the light chemical trades, which are located with reference to the major centres of population and purchasing power rather than to manufacturing regions as such. Chicago-Gary, the Lower Lake shores, Pittsburgh-Youngstown, Chesapeake Bay-Delaware, and the Great Kanawha Valley (West Virginia) are examples of chemical regions in the heavy, raw-material orientated sector. The Gulf Coast chemical region is also raw-material orientated. Development in the South, which has been particularly rapid since the Second World War, has been stimulated by the local abundance of petroleum, natural gas, sulphur,

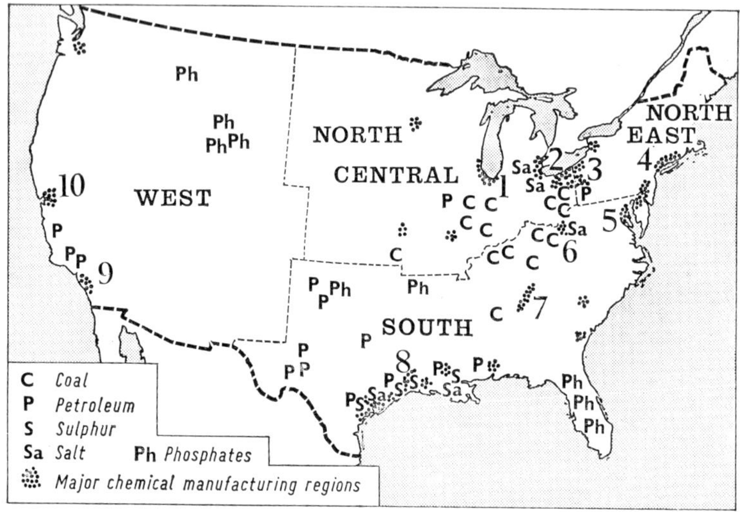

Fig. 87.—Chemical Raw Materials, and the Major Chemical Manufacturing Regions of the U.S.A.

phosphate rock, limestone, and salt, as well as wood pulp from the Southern forests (Fig. 87). The manufacture of petro-chemicals and synthetic fertilisers is of outstanding importance in the South. Large petro-chemical plants have also been constructed near to refineries on the Atlantic seaboard, the Lake shores, at inland pipe-line terminals, and in California.

Southern New England leads in the production of light chemicals (Fig. 88). Drugs, medicinals, photographic chemicals, and plastics are typical products of this branch of the industry. Characteristically they are products of very high value-weight ratio, and the outcome of long, costly, and intensive research. Light chemicals are also manufactured on an important scale in New York and Philadelphia, and indeed in most of the major cities of the country.

The chemical industry of Germany

One branch or other of the German chemical industry is represented in all the major urban centres. As in the United Kingdom and the United States, the production of heavy chemicals has

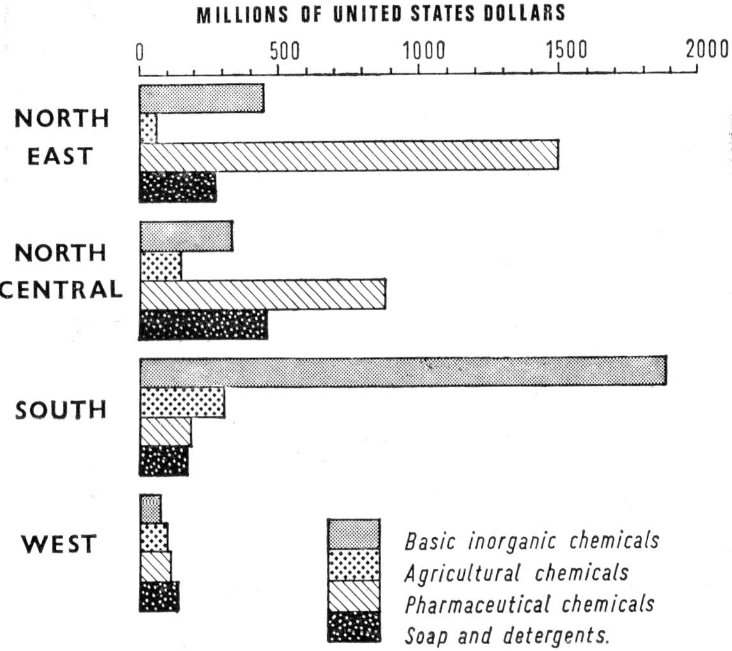

Fig. 88.—Value added by Manufacture in Selected Chemical Products Groups (by Major Regions) in the U.S.A.

gravitated towards navigable water and deposits of chemical raw materials, whilst the light chemical trades remain widely dispersed.

Before the division of the country in 1945, Upper Saxony was the leading chemical region, turning out, among a long and varied list of products, large quantities of acids, alkalies, and synthetic fertilisers. The basis of these industries was—and still is—provided by the extensive beds of lignite and of potash in the Magdeburg-Halle-Leipzig lowlands (Fig. 89). In West Germany the heavy chemical industry is concentrated in the Rhinelands and the Ruhr.

The petro-chemical industry has made rapid strides during the last twenty years, and has been based on imported and domestic supplies of oil and natural gas.

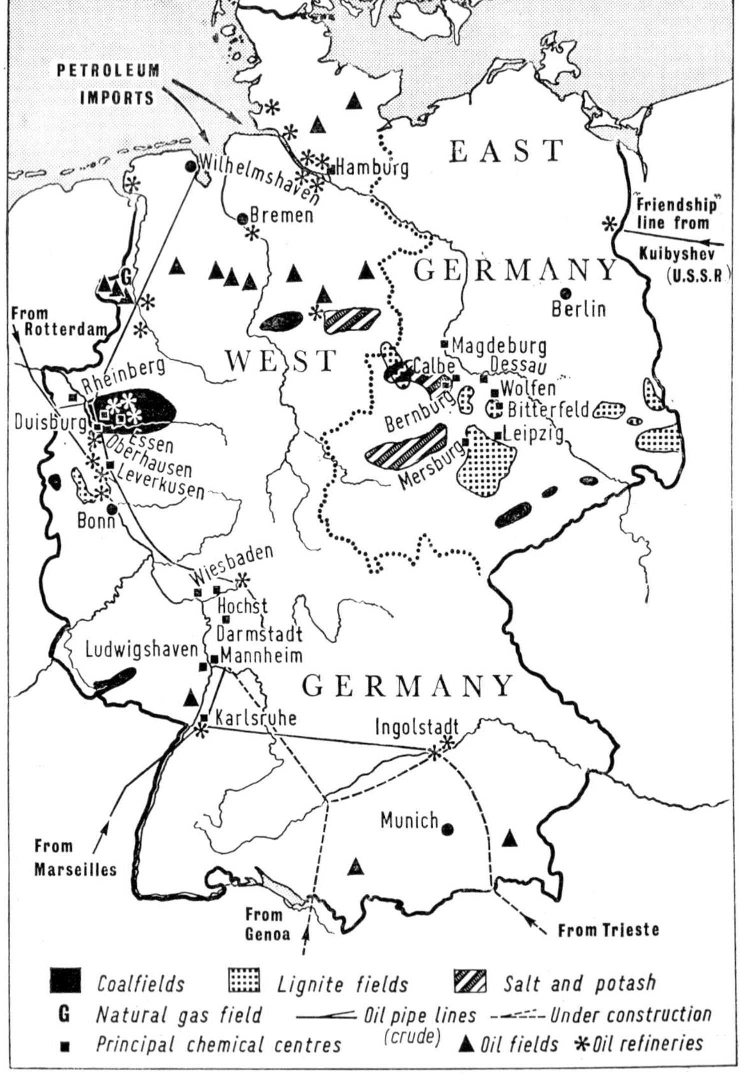

Fig. 89.—The Geographical Basis of the German Chemical Industries.

CHAPTER XV

OTHER MINING AND ASSOCIATED MANUFACTURING INDUSTRIES

THE NON-FERROUS METALS

Copper

Copper ranks after iron and aluminium as the most important metal of the present age. Production of refined copper has increased from a mere 50,000 tons per year a century ago, to more than 4·6 million tons to-day. The steady growth in output has been due to developments in mining technology, improvements in communications, the discovery of more successful methods of ore concentration, and to the opening up of new markets, particularly in the expanding electrical manufacturing and electricity supply industries. The toughness, durability, and resistance to corrosion of copper also make it a highly suitable material for the manufacture of pumps, radiators, boilers, and water pipes, and when combined with nickel, tin, lead, and zinc it makes excellent alloys.

The occurrence and processing of copper ores

In common with many metals, copper is associated with regions of igneous activity, and probably originated as a deposit from chemically rich magmatic solutions and gases injected into joints and fissures. Regions of recent, undisturbed sedimentary rocks are unlikely to contain copper. The metal sometimes occurs in a "native" or metallic state (it was for this reason that it was known and used before the art of smelting was discovercd), but more commonly it is combined chemically with other elements. Vein deposits are common, but the largest ore bodies are porphyries, in which the copper is mixed with worthless rock from which it has to be separated by mechanical methods before it can be smelted.

Copper ore is low grade, rarely of more than 5 per cent. metal content, and commonly less than 2 per cent. Ores of less than 1 per cent. metal content can be utilised provided that power and adequate transport facilities are readily available. The first stage in copper production entails the separation by a flotation process of the metallic compound from the rock in which it is held. The concentrates thus produced are then roasted to drive off the sulphur present. Roasting makes a heavy demand on coal,

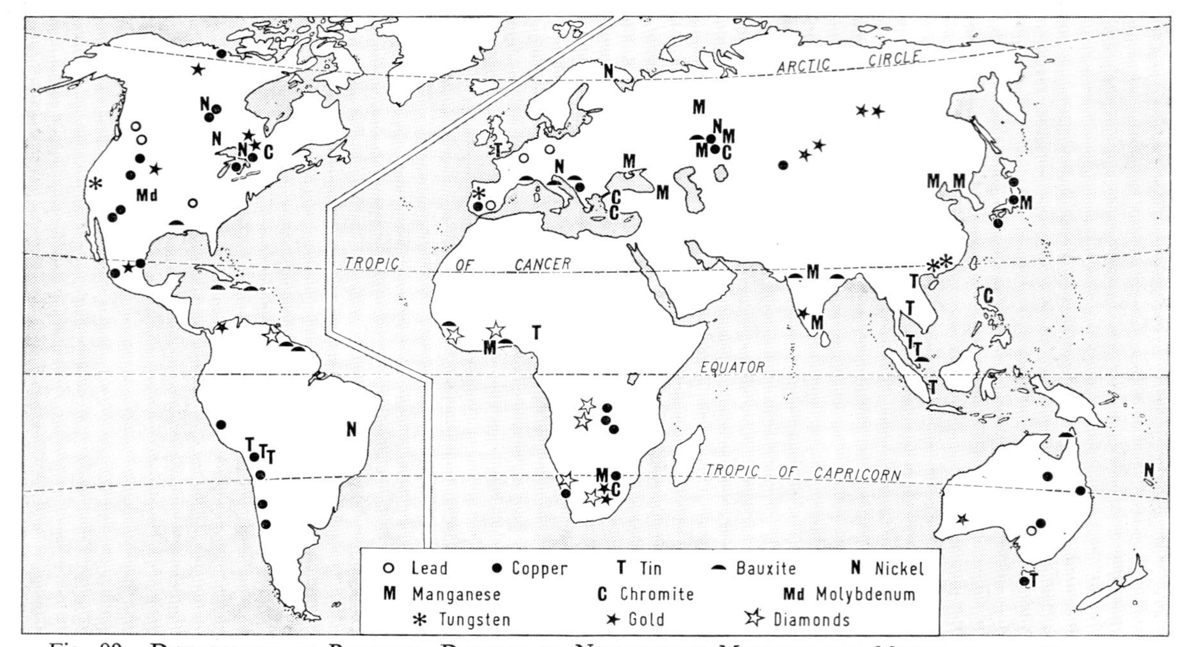

Fig. 90.—DISTRIBUTION OF PRINCIPAL DEPOSITS OF NON-FERROUS MINERALS AND METALS AND OF DIAMONDS.

bove: An automated cotton spinning mill. (*International Society for Educational Infor-ation, Tokyo.*)

elow: A view of the weaving section of a jute mill in East Pakistan. (*High Commis-oner for Pakistan.*)

Above: Brickworks, near Peterborough, on the outcrop of Oxford clay. Note (i) th location of the works astride the London-Peterborough-York railway; (ii) the clay pit some now disused and flooded. There are proposals to utilise some of the abandone clay pits near Bedford as reservoirs for town water supplies. The reservoirs would b supplied by pumping water from the River Ouse. (*Aerofilms and Aero Pictorial Ltd.*)

Below: A pulp and paper mill in the State of Maine, U.S.A. (*USIS.*)

although some ores are self-roasting once sufficient heat has been generated in the furnace. The next step is to smelt the roasted copper (or sometimes the concentrates without prior roasting) to produce blister copper. Blister copper is about 99 per cent. pure, but contains traces of other metals (often gold and silver, which are recoverable as by-products) which render it unsuitable for most purposes. The final stage, then, is to refine the blister copper. To-day this is generally done electrolytically.

Each stage of production is thus marked by a decrease in bulk, and an increase in the value of the product. Crushing, and the separation of the ore from the rock, can only be done at the site of the mine: transport charges would make any other course completely uneconomic. Roasting and smelting are also frequently carried out at the mine head, but these operations are free to be located at some distance from it. The smelters serving Butte, for instance, are thirty miles away at Anaconda, and during the last century the main smelting centre in the world was Swansea, remote from the copper mines, save the small ones of Cornwall. Copper refining tends to be an industry of the major manufacturing regions, notably of Western Europe, and the north-eastern states of the U.S.A. However, in recent years the production of refined copper has been increasing in the mining countries themselves. It grew three-fold in Zambia between 1954 and 1963, whilst during the same period, the increase in the European countries amounted to little more than one-third.

Copper ore is produced in more than forty countries. The following regions are responsible for most of the total world output:

The Mountain states of the U.S.A.—Mining occurs in southern Arizona at Bisbee, Jerome, and Morenci; and at Bingham and Tintic in Utah. At these centres ore is extracted from deep, open terraced pits. At Butte (Montana), on the other hand, the workings are underground, and the hill on which the town stands has been honeycombed by hundreds of miles of shafts and tunnels excavated during the mining operations. The metal content of the western ores is very low—less than 1·5 per cent.

The Keweenaw Peninsula of northern Michigan was one of the first copper regions of the North American continent to be developed. Mines are now at great depth, production costs are high and are increasing, and the region is declining in importance. The Great Lakes waterway, and the access it gives to the industrial markets of the continent, has always been a major factor in the exploitation of these resources.

Canada.—Copper deposits are scattered widely over the pre-Cambrian shield area of the north. They are for the most part complex, and the ores are either copper-nickel or copper-lead-zinc. The principal mines are at Sudbury, Porcupine, and Chibougamau (Ontario); Flin Flon, Sheridon and Lynn Lake (Manitoba); and Coppermine (North West Territories).

Chile.—Chile led the world in the production of copper until the end of the last century, when output fell as a result of out-dated mining techniques rather than because of depletion of the reserves. The industry has since been revitalised by the injection of North American capital. The largest mines are at Chuquicamata, Pontrerillos, and Braden south-east of Santiago. The first two centres are in rainless desert into which water, food, fuel, equipment, and labour have to be imported. Smelters are located at each of them.

The Katanga (Congo) and the Copper Belt of Zambia.—A zone rich in non-ferrous metals extends from Jadotville, in the Congo, to Broken Hill, in Zambia. It contains the largest known copper reserves in the world. Isolation retarded its commercial development until the railway reached Broken Hill in 1905, and Elisabethville a few years later, and gave access to the coast at Beira and Cape Town. In 1933, the completion of the Benguella railway shortened the journey to Europe by more than 3,000 miles. Power for the mines is available from the Wankie colliery, from hydro-electricity stations in the Congo, and from Kariba. Until 1955, the greater

TABLE 84

PRODUCTION OF COPPER
(in thousands of tons)

MINE PRODUCTION (copper content)	1961	1965	REFINED PRODUCTION	1961	1965
U.S.A.	1,040·3	1,206·9	U.S.A.	1,635·6	1,925·9
U.S.S.R.*	531·5	688·9	U.S.S.R.*	639·7	807·0
Zambia	565·7	684·8	Zambia	412·3	514·0
Chile	539·1	573·3	Canada	362·8	387·5
Canada	392·0	455·2	Japan	272·6	359·9
Congo (Leopoldville)	290·6	284·0	Germany F.R.	309·9	351·7
Peru	195·0	174·6	Chile	222·7	284·2
Japan	94·9	105·4	Belgium	199·6	275·6
Australia	95·6	89·8	United Kingdom	234·3	252·0
WORLD TOTAL	4,298·5	4,921·6	Congo (Leopoldville)	148·5	150·1
			China (mainland)*	98·4	98·4
			Australia	77·4	97·2
			WORLD TOTAL	5,044·8	6,047·3

* Estimated.

Source: *The British Bureau of World Non-ferrous Metal Statistics*, Birmingham.

part of the exports both from the Congo and Zambia took the form of blister copper, but during the last ten years production and trade in electrolytically refined copper has increased.

The Soviet Union.—An annual production in the order of 690,000 tons is obtained from mines in Transcaucasia, the Urals, and Kazakstan. Reserves are considerable, but significantly less than those of Africa and North America.

Tin

Primary deposits of tin ore (cassiterite) occur in veins in granite and granite-type rocks. The ores of Bolivia and Cornwall are of this type. Of much greater commercial importance, however, are the secondary or alluvial deposits. These are formed when cassiterite is washed from the parent veins, and deposited along with sands and gravels as sediments. Cassiterite is a dense mineral (specific gravity 6·8); hence secondary ores are commonly found in foothill zones adjacent to the metalliferous region, where changes in gradient compel the release of the heavier components of the stream load. The ores of Malaysia and Indonesia are mainly alluvial. The main tin-producing areas are indicated below.

South East Asia.—Nearly one-third of the world production of tin is obtained from Malaysia. From open pits situated along the western foothills of the Central Mountains, ore bearing rock is dug out by mechanical shovels, washed out by powerful jets of water, or, in the case of the larger, highly capitalised workings, scooped up from the bottoms, and sides of ponds by huge dredgers. Concentration is necessary before the tin leaves the mine for smelters in Singapore and Penang.

The Singapore and Penang smelters also formerly served the Indonesian tin mining industry, which is concentrated on the island of Banka. The Indonesian deposits are also alluvials, and are worked in a manner similar to those of Malaysia. Since the disruption of normal relations between the two countries, Indonesia has diverted most of her tin concentrates to smelters in the Netherlands, and has made preparations to erect her own smelter at Muntok on the north-east coast of Banka.

Bolivia.—In Bolivia tin and silver occur in association, and whilst it was silver that lured the Spanish *conquistadors* to the country in the sixteenth century, it is the tin deposits that keep the mines working today. Some silver is still produced, but largely as a by-product of tin mining. The chief centres are at Potosi, Oruro, and La Paz. Workings are deep and difficult. Labour is scarce, and at the great heights at which the mines are situated (14,000-16,000 ft above sea level) it is inevitably inefficient. Lines of communication are long and difficult, and some mines depend upon pack animals for their link with the rail head. There is no fuel in the region—hence no smelting: exports are in the form of concentrates. Bolivia is a high-cost producer, and finds competition with Malaysia very difficult.

Nigeria.—Tin ore has been produced on the Bauchi Plateau near Jos and Bukuru since the beginning of the century. Both vein and alluvial deposits occur. Ore concentrates are exported via Port Harcourt, on the Niger delta, to Britain, although increasing quantities are being handled by smelters erected in Nigeria itself.

The United Kingdom.—Tin has been worked in Cornwall since the Bronze Age, and during the eighteenth and nineteenth centuries the mines in the Camborne-Redruth district were among the most important in the world. Production has declined, however, and only about 1,000 tons are now produced annually. Two mines—at Geevor and South Crofty account for three-quarters of the Cornish output, and the remainder is obtained from alluvial workings, or from the treatment of old mine dumps. In 1965, an operation to dredge 100,000 tons of tin bearing sand annually from the sea at St Ives began. Smelting was also established at an early date at Redruth, but was later transferred to Merseyside. The Bootle plant, which treats concentrates brought in from Bolivia, now accounts for the bulk of Britain's smelter production.

TABLE 85

MINE PRODUCTION OF TIN

(metal content, in thousands of metric tons)

	1955	1960	1966		1955	1960	1966
Malaysia ..	62·2	52·8	70·0	Indonesia ..	33·9	23·0	12·7
China				Nigeria	8·3	7·8	9·7
(mainland)*	20·5	30·0	30·0	Congo			
Bolivia ..	28·4	19·7	25·9	(Leopoldville)	15·8	9·1	*7·1
U.S.S.R. ..	1·5	20·0	23·0*	South Africa ..	1·3	1·3	1·8
Thailand ..	11·2	12·3	22·9	United Kingdom	1·1	1·2	1·3
				WORLD TOTAL ..	194·0	188·9	210 *

*Estimated

Source: *U.N. Monthly Bulletin of Statistics.*

THE TIN-PLATE INDUSTRY.—Approximately half the world output of refined tin, at present a little more than 200,000 tons per year, is absorbed by the tin-plate industry. The remainder goes into the production of tin alloys, especially terne plate (sheet steel, coated with a tin-lead alloy, and used in the manufacture of petrol tanks, oil and paint cans, etc., where the inclusion of lead is not objectionable), tin foil wrappings, and toothpaste tubes.

Tin plate is made by rolling a sheet of mild steel to a thickness of about $\frac{1}{50}$th to $\frac{1}{100}$th of an inch, and then after a sequence of processes designed to impart the necessary degree of hardness and smoothness to the steel, dipping the sheet in a bath of molten tin. Before the Second World War an electrolytic method of tin plating was perfected, and has largely superseded the older bath method. Eighty per cent. of the British production is now made electrolytically.

The location of the tin-plate industry is governed primarily by the availability of suitable quality, low carbon steel; abundant power,

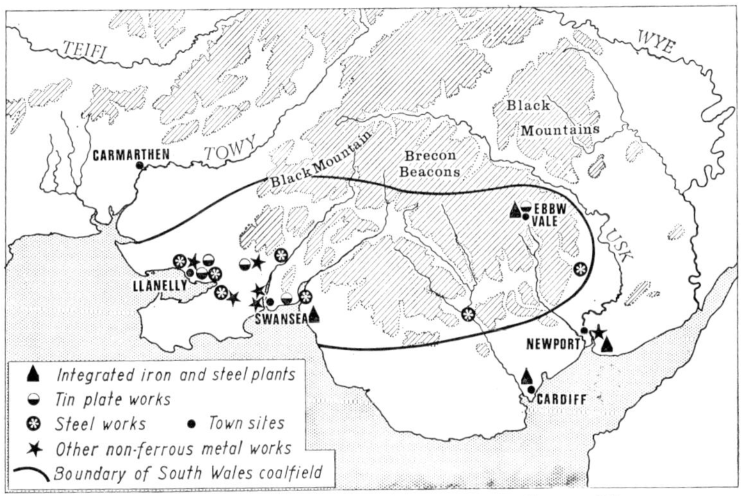

Fig. 91.—LOCATION OF METAL INDUSTRIES IN SOUTH WALES.

either thermal or electric; and ample supplies of water. The principal tin-plate centres are in the steel regions of Europe, North America, and Australia. The South Wales region is the most important in the world (Fig. 91). The distribution of the tin ore deposits is not, and never has been, of much consequence in determining the sites of tin-plate mills. There are no mills, for example, in Cornwall, Nigeria, Malaya, or Bolivia. The reasons are, first, that the ores are either smelted in the country of origin or are shipped as concentrates, and secondly that the quantity of refined tin consumed by the industry is so small, and its price so high, that transport costs form but a small fraction of the total costs of manufacture. In 1964, South Wales used only about 10,000 tons of refined tin at a little under £1,000 per ton. The importance of labour skills, which had much to do with the early growth and prosperity of the industry, has declined now that the old hand mills have been replaced by modern factories in which most of the operations are performed automatically by machinery.

The tinned food industry

Eight million tons of tin-plate are now used annually by the manufacturers of cans and boxes, and by comparison other consumers are insignificant. Tin can factories are for the most part situated in the fruit and market gardening regions of the world; in areas of livestock fattening; and in urban centres where the manufacture of biscuits, confectionery, and tobacco is important. About one-third of Britain's output of tin-plate is exported, the main buyers being the U.S.A., the Argentine, South Africa, Italy, and Spain—all countries having a significant production of fruit or meat. The canned food industry has boomed since 1945. Some 25 per cent. of all fruit and fruit juices, and 15 per cent. of all vegetables consumed by the people of the U.S.A. come out of tins. The proportion in Britain is rather smaller, but even so the consumption of tinned products amounts to seventy pounds per person per year. The growing preference for canned foods reflects the rise in living standards, and the changes in social and working habits that have occurred since the Second World War—changes which have left the housewife with more money to spend, but with less time and inclination for food preparation than she had formerly.

Aluminium

Aluminium is one of the commonest elements of the earth's crust, and is present in nearly all rocks. It never occurs, however, in metallic form, or otherwise than in combination with oxygen and other elements. The only ore from which it can be economically extracted is bauxite.

Bauxite is a clay-like deposit formed by the chemical decomposition of many types of rock in hot climates having a seasonal rainfall. In some respects it resembles laterite into which it grades. Bauxite is found in many parts of the world, especially in tropical and sub-tropical regions (Table 86). Production is generally from open, mechanised pits.

The aluminium industry

The production of aluminium from bauxite involves two distinct processes which are often widely separated, geographically, viz.

1. The concentration and chemical treatment of raw bauxite to yield pure aluminium oxide (alumina).

2. The electrolytic reduction of alumina to produce aluminium metal.

The aluminium manufacturing countries are not, in the main, significant bauxite producers. France, which is self sufficient, and has a surplus for export is a notable exception. Australia, too, mines more than she can consume at home now that the recently discovered deposits on the York Peninsula are in full production. On the other hand, the United States must import some three-quarters of her requirements, in spite of the large output from mines in Arkansas. No bauxite is produced at all in Britain, West Germany, Japan, and Canada. The main channels of world trade in bauxite run from Latin America to the U.S.A. and Canada, and from France, Greece, and West Africa to Britain and Western Europe. Hungary and Yugoslavia supplement the inadequate domestic production of the Soviet Union.

TABLE 86

PRODUCTION OF BAUXITE
(in thousands of metric tons)

	1955	1960	1966
Jamaica	2,680	5,840	9,228
Surinam	3,060	3,455	4,356
France	1,490	2,070	2,796
Guyana	2,475	2,510	3,348
U.S.A.	1,820	2,030	1,824
Hungary	1,240	1,190	1,128
Guinea	493	1,375	1,872
Yugoslavia	790	1,025	1,884
Greece	500	885	1,244
Australia	7·7	70	1,813
WORLD TOTAL	17,760	27,654	38,000 *

Source: *U.N. Monthly Bulletin of Statistics.*

Bauxite is a low grade commodity which moves economically over long distances only by water. Alumina plants built to consume imported ore tend therefore to be sited on the coast, or on a navigable river. Burntisland on the Firth of Forth, Mobile (Alabama), Baton Rouge (Louisiana), East St. Louis (Illinois), Arvida, twenty miles above the head of navigation on the Saguenay (Quebec), and Bell Island, at the mouth of the Tamar (Tasmania), are examples of such sites. On the other hand, bauxite deposits situated inland tend to pull the alumina plants towards them, as, for example, at Hurricane Creek (Arkansas).

The over-riding consideration in the location of alumina reduction mills is the availability of enormous supplies of cheap electrical energy. The conversion of one ton of alumina to aluminium requires in the order of 10,000 kWh. of electricity. The significance of water power sites is evident from the presence of major reduction plants in Norway; at Kinlochleven and Fort William (Scotland); at Alcoa, on the Little Tennessee; Arvida, on the Saguenay; Kitimat, at the head of the Douglas Channel (British Columbia); and at sites on the Columbia River in Washington and Oregon. Recently, a number of mills have been established in Texas, where cheap power is generated from oil and natural gas. Reduction plants are often situated at great distances from the alumina works that serve them, and from their markets. Fortunately, the lightness of the metal allows transport costs to be kept within bounds, even on very long hauls.

Aluminium combines the properties of strength and lightness in a way that no other metal does—properties which have made it an invaluable material in the aircraft and other transport construction industries. It is ductile, *i.e.* it can be drawn out into wires or pressed into thin sheets, a good conductor of electricity and heat, non-corrosive, and of pleasing appearance. Its uses in the fabrication, electrical, and domestic appliances industries are increasing as the price of aluminium, relative to other metals, falls. World consumption has grown from a yearly average of only 17,000 tons between 1901 and 1910, to nearly 6 million tons to-day. The leading producing and consuming countries are the United States and the Soviet Union (Table 87).

TABLE 87

PRODUCTION AND CONSUMPTION OF ALUMINIUM IN 1964
(in thousands of metric tons)

PRODUCTION		CONSUMPTION	
U.S.A.	2,316	U.S.A.	2,535
U.S.S.R.	1,000*	U.S.S.R.	850
Canada	765	West Germany	386
France	319	United Kingdom	359
Japan	265	Japan	262
Norway	261	France	250
West Germany	220	Italy	120
WORLD	6,085	WORLD	5,997

* Estimated.

Source: *Metal Statistics*, Frankfurt-am-Main.

The production of secondary, *i e.* re-smelted, aluminium is increasing rapidly as supplies of scrap come on to the market. Most of the secondary smelters are situated in the metal using regions, where most of the scrap originates. In Britain, they are concentrated in an area extending from London through the West Midlands into South Lancashire.

Lead

The chief lead mineral is galena. Galena occurs in vein deposits in igneous, metamorphic, and sedimentary rocks, and is often found in association with zinc, silver, copper, and gold (which are recoverable in a modern smelter), and with more or less useless *gangue* minerals such as calcite, fluorspar, and barytes. The occurence of this ore in a pure or nearly pure form, its easily recognisable appearance, and the ease with which the metal could be separated from it (wood or charcoal, and a hearth or *bole* on the windward side of a hill were all that was necessary—the remains of some of these early smelters can still be seen in Derbyshire, once one of the chief mining areas of the world) led to its early utilisation. To-day lead is smelted in a blast furnace, as the non-complex ores that can be handled by simple smelters are no longer available in accessible localities.

World mine production of lead is about 2.5 million tons at the present time. The leading producers are the U.S.S.R., the U.S.A., Mexico, Canada, and Australia (Table 88). Together they account for about 45 per cent. of the total world output. In addition to primary lead production, substantial quantities of secondary lead become available each year from scrap supplies.

The main uses of lead are in the manufacture of electric storage batteries, shields for nuclear reactors, protective sheaths for electric cables, glazings in the pottery industry, and, although to a less extent than formerly, in the plumbing trades and the manufacture of paint.

Zinc

The main ore of zinc is zincblende which nearly always occurs with lead, and often with silver, copper, and other useful metallic ores. Processes in the production of zinc are costly and complex. The first step is to separate the ore from impurities by a flotation process. The concentrates containing at least 50 per cent. zinc are then shipped to the reduction plants. Because of the heavy demands such plants make upon fuel and power, they are normally placed where coal and electricity are cheap, rather than in the zinc mining areas. Britain and Belgium, for example, which have but negligible deposits of zinc but ample coal, have become important smelting countries (Table 88). There then follows the roasting of the concentrates in order to eliminate the sulphur content, and to produce zinc oxide. Finally the zinc oxide is heated, usually with anthracite, and the zinc which is given off as a gas is collected and condensed into metal. Electrolytic methods of zinc production are also employed, and are gaining in importance.

TABLE 88

SMELTER PRODUCTION OF LEAD AND ZINC, 1966
(in thousands of short tons)

LEAD		ZINC	
U.S.A.	415	U.S.A.	942
U.S.S.R.	390*	U.S.S.R.	510
Australia	192	Japan	431
Mexico	179	Canada	347
Canada	168	Belgium	252
West Germany	109	West Germany	242
Belgium	93	Australia	198
WORLD	2,440	France	196
		Poland	193
		United Kingdom	101
		WORLD	3,880

* Estimated

Source: *U.N. Monthly Bulletin of Statistics.*

Commercial quantities of zinc ore are mined in over forty countries. The total world production slightly exceeds 3.5 million tons per year, of which the U.S.A. and the U.S.S.R. account for a quarter. The U.S.A., Australia, Mexico, Japan, Peru, Poland, Spain, Western Germany, and Italy each produce more than 100,000 tons annually,

The main use of zinc is as a protective covering for steel. Corrugated zinc covered sheets are employed the world over as a roofing material. When alloyed with copper, brass is produced. Zinc, aluminium, and magnesium alloys make excellent die castings for the manufacture of complicated components for the electrical and motor vehicle industry as well as for many articles in common use.

Mercury

Mercury is the only metal which exists in liquid form at normal temperatures. It is obtained from the mineral cinnabar, or mercury sulphide (HgS). When cinnabar is heated with a suitable supply of air, the sulphur is converted into the gas, sulphur dioxide, and the metallic mercury liberated vaporises and is condensed to the liquid form by cooling in suitable condensers. The most common use of mercury is in the making of thermometers and barometers. It is also used as a catalyst in the chemical industry. Mercury and its compounds enter into the manufacture of agricultural fungicides, explosives, and vapour lamps. The chief producers are Spain, Italy, the U.S.S.R., the U.S.A., and Yugoslavia.

The alloy metals

An alloy is a mixture of two or more metals. Many metals will alloy with each other. Bronze for example, is a well known alloy of copper and tin. The special interest and importance of the metals described below is that while they have only a limited use in their pure form, they have become essential elements in the manufacture of many kinds of modern steels, because of the particular qualities of hardness, toughness, ductility, and resistance to heat, rust, and corrosion that they impart. None of the alloy metals is used in great quantities (the annual consumption of manganese ore, the most important in terms of tonnage, is less than 3 per cent. of the consumption of iron ore), and many are for most purposes substitutes for each other. Nickel, chromium, and manganese can be used in the preparation of stainless steels, and tungsten and molybdenum are both suitable alloys in the manufacture of steels for high speed cutting tools. Owing to the small amounts needed, the acquisition of the alloy metals presents no particular problems to the manufacturing nations, except in war time, even though they may need to be transported for great distances. Finally all are comparatively "new" metals, none having been used commercially before the middle of the last century.

MANGANESE.—Ninety per cent. of the world production of manganese is consumed by the steel industry. Manganese is added in small quantities to all steels to remove sulphur from the furnace charge. As an alloy it imparts hardness and strength, and is used in the production of stainless steels. It is found in many countries, and as a general rule only high grade ores in easily accessible locations have been worked. The U.S.S.R., South Africa, Brazil, and India are the main producers,

NICKEL.—Nickel ores of sufficient concentration to make exploitation worthwhile are restricted. The principal producers are Canada (from the Sudbury and Lynn Lake mines of Ontario and Manitoba), and the Soviet Union (from the Petsamo region which was annexed by Russia after the war with Finland in 1939-40).

Pure nickel is used by the chemical and radio industries, but more than half is consumed by the steel industry. Nickel steels are particularly tough and hard, and are used in the manufacture of the cutting edges of machine tools, and the moving parts of transport equipment. Cupro-nickel, an alloy of nickel and copper, has been used since 1947 to make British "silver" coins. Nickel-silver, employed in cutlery manufacture, is an alloy of nickel, copper, and tin.

CHROMIUM.—Chromium is extracted from chrome ore or chromite. Compared with most non-ferrous-metal ores, chromite is rich and can be shipped to metallurgical regions without prior concentration. The main use of chromium is in the manufacture of stainless

TABLE 89

PRODUCTION OF THE ALLOY METALS, 1963

MANGANESE ORE (in thousands of short tons)		NICKEL (in thousands of short tons of contained nickel)	
U.S.S.R.	7,385	Canada	219·9
South Africa	1,442	U.S.S.R.	90·0
Brazil	1,320	New Caledonia	32·2
India	1,185	Cuba	18·4
Ghana	434	U.S.A.	11·4
WORLD	16,090	Finland	3·4
		WORLD	384·0

CHROMITE (in thousands of short tons)		TUNGSTEN ORE (in thousands of short tons)	
U.S.S.R.	1,355	China	24·9
South Africa	873	U.S.S.R.	12·1
Philippines	503	South Korea	6·7
Turkey	445	U.S.A.	5·6
Rhodesia	412	Bolivia	2·5
Albania	310	WORLD	64·7
WORLD	4,475		

MOLYBDENUM (in thousands of short tons)		VANADIUM ORE (in thousands of short tons)	
U.S.A.	32·5	U.S.A.	3·9
U.S.S.R.	6·3	South Africa	1·4
Chile	3·4	South West Africa	1·1
China	1·6	Finland	0·6
WORLD	45·8	WORLD	70·0

Source: *Commodity Year Book*. New York, 1965.

steels. Chromium plating, when applied as a coating to steel, gives a bright, rust-proof finish. The main producing countries are Rhodesia, South Africa, Turkey, and the Soviet Union.

TUNGSTEN.—Low grade tungsten ores are worked in China, the U.S.S.R., North Korea, the United States, and Bolivia. Nearly two thirds of the world production at the present time comes from communist sources. Tungsten is used in the manufacture of high speed cutting tools, lamp filaments, and in tubes for fluorescent lighting.

MOLYBDENUM.—Molybdenum ore production is concentrated in the U.S.A., where mines in Colorado yield 90 per cent. of the world output. Molybdenum is an important alloying element in the manufacture of special steels and certain non-ferrous metals.

VANADIUM.—This metal is used in small quantities to improve the strength and hardness of steel, and to increase its resistance to heat. It often occurs in association with commoner minerals, such as coal, petroleum, and phosphates, but only in a few areas are deposits sufficiently concentrated to make mining worth while commercially. Production is very small, and is confined essentially to the U.S.A., South and South West Africa.

Radio active metals

URANIUM.—Uranium is one of the less common elements of the earth's crust, but is widely distributed geographically. More than 100 minerals contain uranium, but only a handful are plentiful enough to be regarded as ores. Unaninite, an oxide of uranium, is the most important.

Until the middle nineteen fifties, most of the world's uranium was obtained from the veins of pitchblende in the Belgian Congo and northern Canada. These pitchblende deposits were rich, and easily worked, but existed on too small a scale to satisfy the growing demands for nuclear fuels. Technical advances have since made possible the extraction of uranium from very low grade ores which are worked on a large scale by conventional mining methods.

Production of uranium oxide in 1964 was estimated at about 40,000 tons. Of this total, more than 11,000 tons were produced in the United States, 6,000 tons in Canada, 4,500 in the Union of South Africa (largely as a by-product of gold mining), and 2,000 tons in France. Minor quantities were also produced in Australia, Argentina, Spain, and Sweden. Output from communist countries was estimated at between 10,000 and 20,000 tons. The largest uranium reserves are found on the Canadian shield; in the Mountain and Appalachain states of the U.S.A.; the Witwatersrand of South Africa; the U.S.S.R.; Czechoslovakia; and Australia.

THORIUM.—The chief source of thorium is the mineral monazite which occurs widely as minute crystals in igneous rocks. The main commercial deposits are found in Travancore (India), Brazil, New South Wales, Queensland, Ceylon, South Africa, Quebec, and North Carolina. The main use of thorium is as a "breeder" material in the production of atomic energy. Thorium was formerly employed on a large scale in the manufacture of gas mantles.

The precious metals

GOLD.—Throughout the ages, gold has been the most sought after of all the metals. For as long as there have been records, it has been prized as a symbol of wealth and accepted as a medium of exchange. That this is so, has been due to the softness of gold, which makes it easy to work, to its high lustre, and its extreme durability.

Of equal importance is its scarcity—exactly how scarce may be judged from the fact that all the gold mined since time began could be stored within the walls of ten or a dozen medium sized houses. The quantity of new gold coming on to the market each year, about 50 million fine ounces, would stack into a thirteen-foot cube.

Paradoxically, the earth's most precious metal is almost worthless industrially. During the Second World War, when the production of nearly every other metal increased, the output of gold was allowed to fall. Gold is used on a very restricted scale by the chemical industries, otherwise its value as a raw material is limited to the jewellery trades, to the manufacture of paints for pottery and other decoration, fountain pen nibs, and fillings for teeth. It does not even begin to compare in importance with iron, tin, or even manganese. It has even ceased to be used as an internal currency, although international transactions can be settled in gold. It is a sad commentary on the manner in which we conduct our affairs, when nearly half the population of South Africa, the main gold producing country, has to depend for its livelihood, directly or indirectly, wholly or in part, upon a metal that is extracted at great expense from the bottom of 10,000 foot shafts, brought to the surface, crushed, concentrated, and refined, only to be shipped across the Atlantic to be buried again in government vaults in the United States, the United Kingdom, and the countries of Western Europe.

Gold is produced from two types of mine. Shafts and tunnels are necessary to reach ores deep beneath the surface, while "placer" mining is possible where the metal occurs in stream gravels or in soft sedimentary strata outcropping at ground level. Most mines to-day are operated by highly capitalised companies employing a sizeable labour force, and utilising elaborate machinery. The low grade deposits which are now being worked would permit of no other type of exploitation. The days of easy mining, when a lucky prospector, armed with pick or hand pan could amass a fortune in a few weeks, or even days, are gone.

Concentration of the ore at the minehead is more essential in the case of gold than most other metals. Gravity separation techniques are still employed, but the cyanide process, which allows extremely low grade ores to be utilised, is becoming increasingly common.

The transport of refined gold, even from the remotest area, presents few problems. Its value is so great that if need be a man could carry it for long distances on his back, and still sell it at a profit. The problems that mining companies face in areas of poor communication arise out of the difficulties of obtaining machinery, fuel, and labour rather than from the task of disposing of the refined metal.

TABLE 90

WORLD PRODUCTION OF GOLD 1963
(in thousands of fine ounces)

South Africa	28,900	Ghana	920
U.S.S.R.	12,500	Rhodesia	566
Canada	4,010	Colombia	325
U.S.A.	1,470	WORLD TOTAL	52,800
Australia	1,023		

Source: *Commodity Yearbook*. New York, 1965.

Silver

Silver occurs in nature as a sulphide, and nearly all the naturally-occuring sulphides of lead (galena) copper (copper pyrites), and zinc (zinc blende) contain some silver. More than half of the silver coming on to the market to-day is in fact obtained as a by-product of lead, copper, and zinc smelting, and its output therefore depends to a considerable extent on the demand for these other metals.

About 200 million ounces of new silver become available annually, principally from Mexico, Peru, the U.S.A., Canada, the U.S.S.R., and Australia. The high price of silver restricts its industrial uses to the preparation of certain medicinal chemicals, and to the manufacture of special components for the electrical industries, *e.g.* contact points. The jewellery trades absorb considerable quantities, and large stocks are held in government vaults. About two-fifths of the annual production of the metal is still used in the minting of coins.

Platinum

Platinum is a rare, dense, white metal, or more accurately one of a group of similar metals, which are indispensable to the chemical industries because of their value as catalysts, and their resistance to attack by most chemical substances. Their high melting points (between 1550° C. and 2700° C.) also makes them uniquely suitable in the electrical industries. Their high price, however, excludes them from all but the most essential roles in industry, and substitutes are used wherever possible.

Diamonds

Diamond production is concentrated to a remarkable degree in Africa. The Congo mines account for nearly two-thirds of the world output by quantity, although not by value, as more than 90 per cent. of the stones are of industrial rather than gem quality. The mines are situated in the Upper Kasai region, and extend across the border into Angola. South Africa, Ghana, South West Africa, and Sierra

Leone are also major producers. In the Americas, Brazil, Venezuela, and British Guiana have a small output. India, although of great importance in the past, to-day mines only a very small quantity.

The main stages in the production of marketable stones are:

1. The separation of the stones from the rock that contains them.

2. The hand sorting of diamonds into stones of gem and industrial quality.

3. The cutting and polishing of the gem stones. This is a highly skilled industry which is localised in a few centres.

Industrial uses of diamonds

Eighty per cent. of the stones produced each year are consumed by industry. Their value derives from their extreme hardness. They are used to produce the grinding and polishing machines which in turn are used in the production of hard metal cutting tools. Diamonds are also employed as machine bearings, and in the manufacture of saws and drills, glass cutters, abrasive powders, and many other products in which hardness is an essential quality. While the larger and more perfect stones are taken to Antwerp, Amsterdam, Johannesburg, New York, and Tel Aviv—there to be cut and polished with infinite care and patience before being passed on to the fashion markets of the world—the smaller, humbler industrial stones find their way to Sheffield, Birmingham, and other metallurgical centres, where they fill a vital, in fact indispensable, role in many branches of engineering—a role for which no substitute (except synthetic diamonds, which are now in production) has been found.

THE NON-METALLIC MINERALS

Kaolin

Kaolin, or china clay, is a soft, white, pure clay formed by the chemical decomposition of the felspar component in granite. Only to a very minor extent has this decomposition been due to normal atmospheric processes: the Scottish granites, for example, and many other granite masses in the world, contain no kaolin. Kaolin deposits of any size are known only to occur where granites have been subjected to a process known as *pneumatolysis*, *i.e.* to the alteration of rocks by the action of chemically active solutions and gases migrating upwards from great depths.

China clay is found in many countries. Substantial deposits occur in the eastern states of the U.S.A., particularly in Georgia, and in Brittany, Saxony, New South Wales, and elsewhere. The most important china clay region of the world lies near the Cornish town of St Austell. Production from Cornish mines exceeds 1·3 million tons per year. There is also a small output from workings on the south western flank of Dartmoor.

China clay is washed from the faces of open pits by powerful jets of water, and the kaolinite (the desirable mineral in the clay) is separated from the quartz, mica, and other impurities in settling tanks. After drying it is ready for transport to the consuming centres.

Sedimentary beds of kaolin occur where there has been re-deposition of the primary deposits. Sedimentary kaolin possessing a high degree of plasticity is known as *ball clay*. Ball clay is mined near Poole, in Dorset.

Uses of kaolin

The paper industries consume about half the world production of kaolin for one purpose or another, but mainly as a filler or coating medium. Kaolin is used as a filler and reinforcing agent in rubber, plastics, and paint. The pharmaceutical industries use it in cosmetic preparations, and as a carrier for active ingredients in pills and tablets. Kaolin also acts as a carrier for the poisonous components in agricultural sprays and dusts. It finds use as an ingredient in inks, dyes, and soaps, and is employed in the production of leather and textiles. The industries which consume kaolin are, in fact, numbered in hundreds.

Kaolin and the pottery industry

The ceramics industries absorb about one quarter of all the china clay produced. The manufacture of pottery is carried on in a number of places, of which Trenton (New Jersey); Sèvres, Meissen, Copenhagen, and Limoges, on the continent of Europe; and Worcester and Derby, in Britain, are important enough to be recognised internationally. No centre, however, compares in scale and importance with North Staffordshire, where the six towns that now comprise the city of Stoke-on-Trent (Tunstall, Burslem, Hanley, Stoke, Fenton, and Longton) are known throughout the world simply as "The Potteries".

The pottery industry of North Staffordshire

Pottery manufacture in Britain is curiously localised. No major industry is as concentrated as this, with 90 per cent. of its labour force of 19,000 men and 26,000 women contained within the confines of a single urban area. The degree of concentration appears all the more remarkable when it is remembered that until the late eighteenth century pottery making was a widely dispersed domestic craft, practised wherever there was clay to be dug and fuel available for firing the kilns.

The area of the Potteries coalfield where the North Staffordshire industry became established is agriculturally marginal. It is an area where in former times farmers were forced by the difficult circumstances of their environment to eke out a living by making pottery as a side line, just as the country folk of Lancashire and the West Riding found it necessary to turn their hands to the production of simple textiles as a means of supplementing an inadequate income from cultivation and stock rearing. Only in this way could they provide for themselves a reasonable standard of material comfort.

The growth of the North Staffordshire industry was aided by the fortunate coincidence of suitable clay and coal outcropping in the same geological formation—the Black Band group of the Upper Coal Measures (Fig 92). Along the outcrop, these two essential commodities could be dug from shallow open pits. Refractory bricks could also be made from equally accessible fire clay deposits. These locational advantages were not, of course, enjoyed only by North Staffordshire. They were possessed in varying degrees by all the coalfields in Britain. On the other hand, the coal mining areas of the North East, Scotland, Yorkshire, Lancashire, the Midlands, and South Wales were better placed for the development of other kinds of industry. North Staffordshire was isolated and lacking in water power, and failed to attract the iron-smelting, metallurgical, and textile industries that began to flourish elsewhere.[1] The young pottery industry, therefore did not have to compete with other developing enterprises for labour and capital.

Until the early eighteenth century, the industry was small, and essentially of local significance. It was also based primarily on local raw materials. After about 1700, however, its character began to change. The butter pots, ale mugs, and coarse plates and dishes that had been the staples of the trade until this time began to be replaced, as changing fashions dictated, by light, delicate tableware. But this type of pottery could not be made from the North Staffordshire clays. New raw materials had to be acquired from distant places—china clay and china stone from Cornwall, ball clay from Dorset, flints from the south coast and from France, felspar from Norway, and bones from the slaughterhouses of Merseyside—and carried laboriously over land by pack horse. However, the remote-

[1] The Shelton iron and steel plant at Etruria is a development of the nineteenth century.

ness of the Potteries from the sources of these materials did not prevent the expansion of the industry for two main reasons. Such materials were needed only in small quantities: even to-day one of the largest firms in the area consumes a total of no more than sixty

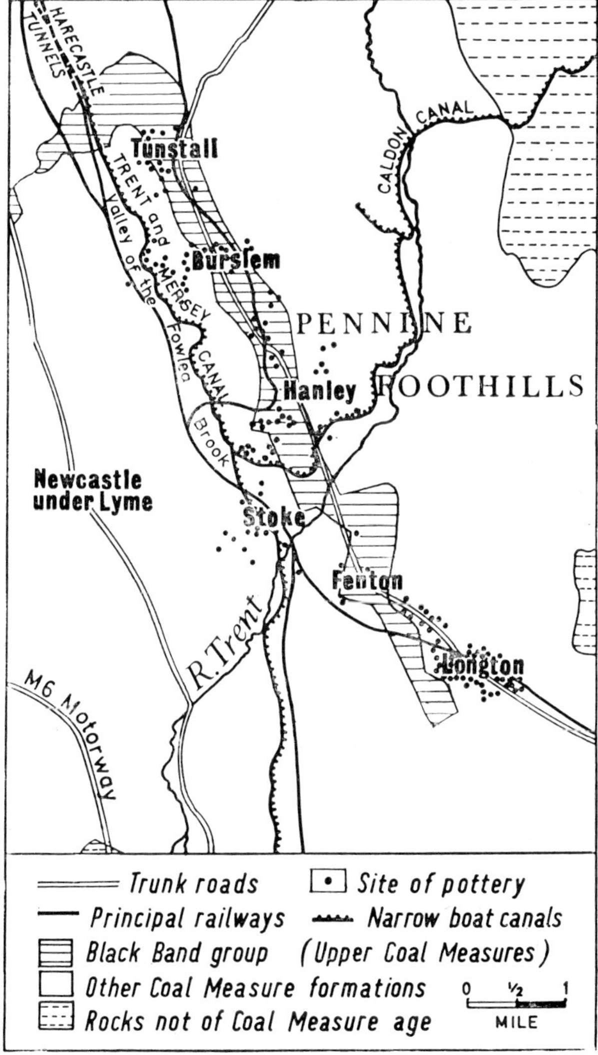

Fig. 92.—The Geographical Basis of the North Staffordshire Pottery Industry.

tons per week, or about one hundred weight per factory operative, exclusive of fuel and power. And the commodity that was required in the largest volume, namely the long flame coal for kiln firing, was mined locally, and its acquisition presented no problem. There had also by this time appeared on the scene a number of skilled potters, among whom were men—like Spode and Wedgwood—possessed of very considerable enterprise, foresight, and wealth. Within half a century such men had transformed the art of pottery making, and had made the name of North Staffordshire famous throughout the world. Not the least among Wedgwood's achievements was the part he played in the promotion of the Trent and Mersey Canal. This canal, engineered by Brindley and completed in 1777, gave the coalfield a water link with regions that were supplying raw materials to its pot banks, and at the same time cut the cost of transport to one sixth of what it had been previously.

It is evident, then, that the North Staffordshire pottery industry cannot be accounted for simply in terms of physical and economic geography. The human element is of immense importance. It is interesting to speculate on whether or not Swansea or Cardiff would now be shipping fine china to the markets of the world had Wedgwood and Spode been born on the South Wales coalfield. That region, too, possessed long flame coals, clays, and refractories, and had easier access to the Cornish china clay mines than had Stoke. South Wales also made pottery during the domestic period. There are no basic geographical reasons why the industry should not have expanded there. What the region lacked, however, but which North Staffordshire possessed, was a cultural and industrial tradition and environment that bred people who found it rewarding to devote their energies and talents to perfecting the art of pottery making, rather than to developing techniques of iron, steel, and tin-plate production.

Recent developments in the industry

The Trent and Mersey Canal attracted industry to its banks, but transhipment remained necessary in the case of commodities destined for factories not located alongside it. The influence of the canal was weakened with the arrival of the railway, and to-day, with road transport well established, the waterway has virtually ceased to exist as a factor in the economic life of the region. This century has witnessed some dispersal of pottery manufacture to points outside the city, aided by more flexible forms of transport. A further development is also taking place which is likely to have far reaching consequences on the future of the industry, and which is also changing the face of the pottery towns themselves. This is the switch from coal to gas and electricity for kiln firing. The consumption of coal has declined from 1.5 million tons in 1939 to less than 100,000 tons per year at present. As a consequence, the old bottle ovens, over 1,000 in number twenty years ago, have now been reduced to a few dozen, and their places taken by smokeless, more efficient, but nondescript gas and electric kilns. Gas and electricity are more transportable forms of energy than coal, and the industry has thus been given the opportunity for the first time in its history of release from the coalfield that gave it birth. It is unlikely ever to move far from the Potteries—the labour skills, central research, and training facilities which exist there will ensure that—but only the future will show how many of the 200 or so firms will follow the example of the one or two that have taken advantage of the greater freedom of location that these new fuels permit to forsake the clutter of coal mines, spoil heaps, rubbish dumps, *shraff* tips, marl holes, brick and tile works, and steel mills, that now disfigure the city landscape, for the pleasanter conditions of the surrounding countryside.

Building materials

Clay, and the brick and tile industry.—Clay is an exceptionally common raw material, and its wide distribution has given rise to a well dispersed brick and tile manufacturing industry. This industry, however, has tended to become much more concentrated in recent years owing to improvements in the transport services, and the advantages that are to be realised from large scale operation.

The location of brick and tile works is influenced by the following factors:

1. By far the bulkicst raw material is clay, and works are almost invariably drawn to the site of the deposit.

2. Owing to the economies of scale that can be realised in the brick making industry, modern plants are tending to become very large. A clay deposit with many years' life ahead of it is therefore essential before such plants can be established.

3. Fuel consumption is high, and a location on a coalfield, or at a point where coal procurement costs are low, is very attractive.

4. Distribution costs are also high. Works are therefore situated close to the markets they serve.

Bricks are manufactured in enormous quantities in all the industrialised countries of the world. Several millions are made in Britain each day. In Britain, the centres of greatest importance lie on the outcrop of the Oxford clay at points where it is crossed by routeways (Fig 93). From rather fewer than twenty works between Bletchley and Peterborough comes more than half the output of the entire country. The remainder is produced by a few hundred small plants situated mainly on the northern and Midland coalfields.

Fire clay is obtained from open quarries in many coalfield regions. It is the raw material from which are made the refractory bricks used to line furnaces of all kinds where resistance to high temperatures and chemical corrosion is essential.

Building stones, sand, and gravel.—Limestone, sandstone, granite, and slate are among the most important of the natural building stones. In the pre-railway age, building materials, whether natural or manufactured, were produced locally, and buildings erected more than a century ago tend to mirror fairly accurately the nature of the underlying rock. Only when water transport was available, or when stone was needed for some particular purpose, was it carried for any distance. To-day, the high cost of quarrying and dressing natural stone, compared with the cost of manufacturing substitute products such as bricks and concrete blocks, has brought about a sharp reduction in the demand for building stone, even in areas where it is common.

On the other hand, there has been no decline in the volume of stone produced for other purposes. The consumption of limestone by the iron and steel, chemical, and agricultural industries has increased as those industries have expanded. Limestone and chalk are also essential ingredients in cement. Many hard rocks are crushed, and used as ballast on railways, and in road construction, and as aggregates in concrete. In addition, thousands of millions of tons of sand and gravel are quarried in the world each year, mainly for use by the building industries. Production in the U.S.A. alone exceeds 800 million tons annually.

The cement industry.—The cement industry is one of the giants of the modern age. Global production is now in the order of 400 million tons per annum (Table 91).

The manufacture of cement requires the assembly of a calcareous rock (chalk or limestone), an argillaceous rock (shale, clay, or silt), and small quantities of gypsum or anhydrite. The ingredients are finely ground, mixed in appropriate ratios, and then heated in a gas or coal fired rotary kiln. Most of the raw materials are extremely bulky and of low value. One works in the Derbyshire Peak District, which is typical of cement works generally, consumes annually in the order of 750,000 tons of limestone, 175,000 tons of

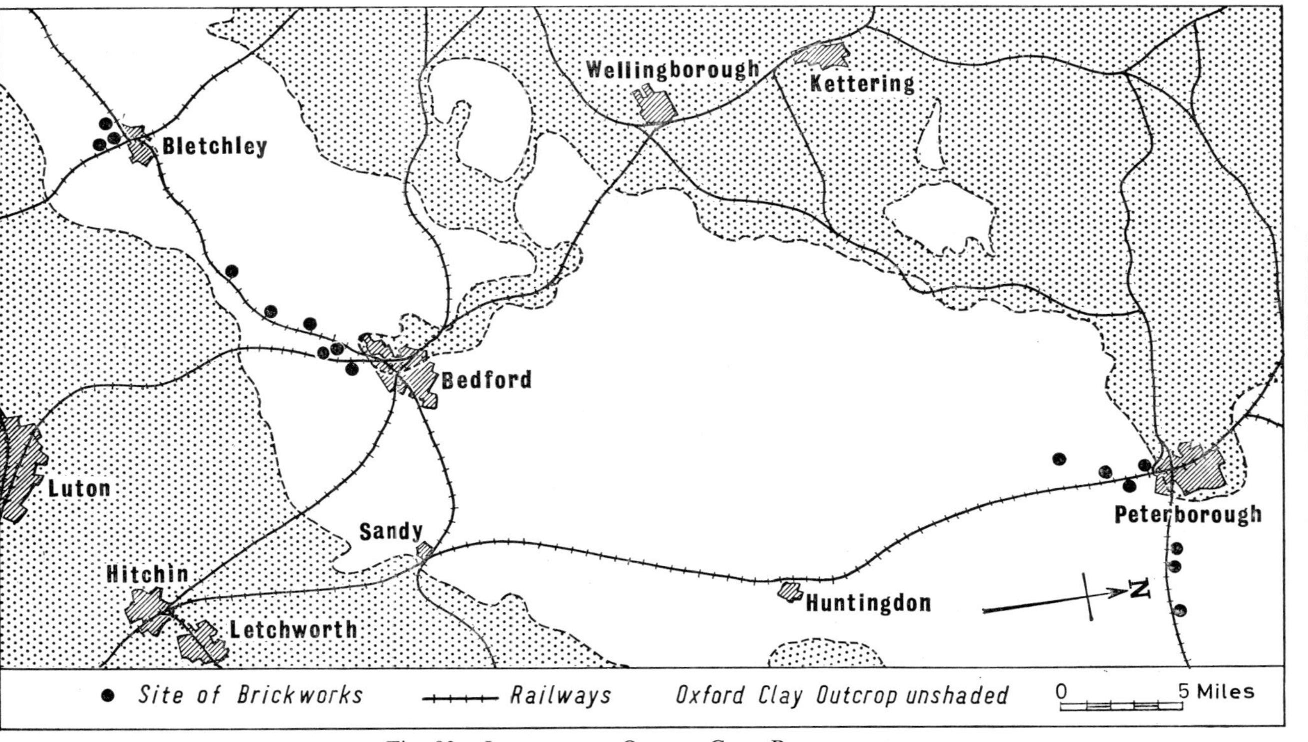

Fig. 93.—Location of Oxford Clay Brickworks.

shale, 45,000 tons of gypsum, and 160,000 tons of coal in order to produce some 600,000 tons of cement. Raw material procurement costs are at their lowest when works are situated adjacent to limestone (or chalk) and clay outcrops, and when they are linked to a coalfield by rail or water transport. The importance of low distribution costs is reflected in the siting of works near to large markets

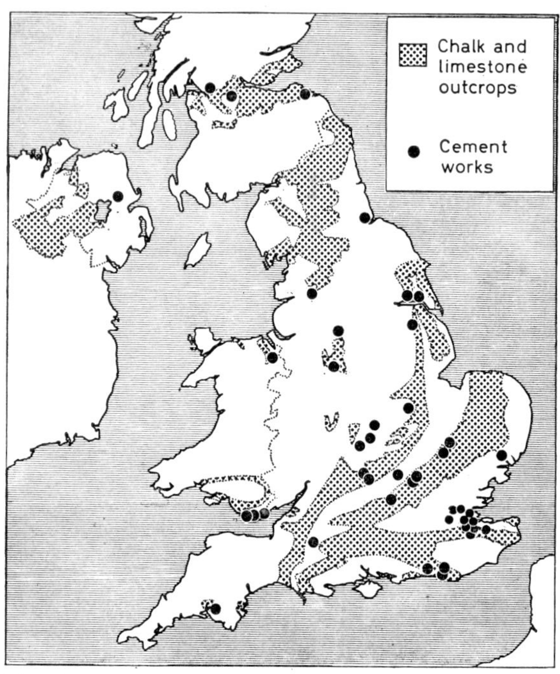

Fig. 94.—Location of Cement Works in the United Kingdom.

(Fig. 94). Approximately one-third of the output of British cement comes from works within about thirty miles of London.

Table 91

Production of Cement, 1966
(in thousands of metric tons)

U.S.S.R.	79,992	Italy	22,368
U.S.A.	67,176	United Kingdom	16,752
Japan	38,268	India	11,052
West Germany	34,740	China (mainland)	10,500*
France	23,436	Poland	10,044
World Total	450,000		

* Estimated.
Source: *U.N. Monthly Bulletin of Statistics.*

CHAPTER XVI

TEXTILES

Primitive textile manufacturing appears to have developed spontaneously in countries as far apart as Egypt, China, Peru, and Switzerland during the pre-historic period. The industry's early and widespread growth was due to the extensive distribution of natural fibres, to the ease with which those fibres could be spun and woven on simple equipment, and to the fact that textile production was concerned with the satisfaction of a basic human need, namely the need for clothing.

Textile industries to-day—factors affecting location

1. *Raw materials.*—All textile industries are engaged in the processing of non-perishable raw materials of a very high value-weight ratio. Such materials can be carried for long distances without transport charges amounting to more than a small fraction of the total costs of manufacture. The cost of bringing the quantity of raw cotton needed to make a shirt from the fields of Alabama to a British port, for instance, is only about threepence. Textile fibres suffer little loss of weight during the process of manufacture (except in the case of wool, where the weight is reduced by approximately half during the scouring operations). The volume used annually by each mill or by each operative is also small. It is perfectly feasible, therefore, for textile industries to be located in areas remote from the sources of the raw fibre.

It will be found that such locations are very common. The cotton mills of Britain, Western Europe, Japan, Hong Kong, and New England are situated in regions where not a single cotton fibre is grown commercially. Jute is carried 8,000 miles from the fields of India and Pakistan to factories in Dundee, Scotland. Little raw silk is now produced in Europe, and the silk industries of Lyons, the Swiss valleys, and the Alpine piedmont towns of northern Italy depend heavily on imports from the Far East and Asia Minor. The British silk industry relies almost wholly on imported fibre. The wool industries of the West Riding would shrink to a fraction of their present size if only the home clip were available to them. The Irish and Scottish linen centres obtain their supplies of flax from the Continent. These examples could be multiplied. Indeed, it is not uncommon for textiles to be shipped round the world between the raw material and the finished stages. Australian wool is spun and woven in Britain, and returned to Australia as cloth. Much Californian cotton is manufactured in Japan, sent to Britain for finishing, and then marketed in North America.

Furthermore, textile industries which are based on imported fibre are not essentially port industries, as are sugar refining, flour milling, and paper-making. Where they occupy sea board locations it is for reasons other than to save on freight charges.

The fibre-producing countries are not, of course, without textile industries of their own. Study will generally show, however, that in most cases these industries either developed before the days of easy transport, and have persisted down to the present, or more commonly, that they have been fostered by the developing countries who are themselves fibre producers, and who are anxious to retain within their borders the values added to the raw material at each successive stage of manufacture. The latter, rather than the aim of low-cost production based on proximity to the cotton fields, accounts for the modern mill industries in such centres as Bombay, Calcutta, Shanghai, Alexandria, and Kumasi.

2. *Power.*—Since the beginning of the Industrial Revolution, the location of centres of textile production has been greatly influenced by the distribution of energy supplies, and has responded to changes in geographical values resulting from the substitution of one type of energy for another. Inventions which harnessed the power of falling water brought about a concentration of spinning and weaving into small factory units on high gradient streams. Later, when steam driven plant was introduced to the mills, the coalfields became attractive, as large quantities of fuel had to be consumed by the rather inefficient steam engine of the day to produce an adequate output of power. Electricity has now superseded steam in most textile mills. Throughout Britain it is available from the national grid at prices which vary only slightly from one part of the country to another. Textile industries have thus to-day a very wide choice of location as far as the satisfaction of their power requirements are concerned, and the man-made fibre manufacturers have taken advantage of the fact to erect plants in areas where fifty years ago they could not have succeeded because of the expense involved in obtaining coal. There has been little tendency in this country, on the other hand, towards a dispersal of the cotton, wool, linen, and jute industries to points outside their traditional areas. Mills remain firmly rooted to sites appropriate to the steam age. The reason is that since 1914 the older textile industries of Britain have

gone into decline. Old mills have been demolished or turned over to other uses,[1] and few new ones have been built to replace them. The changes of location of the last two centuries occurred during periods of expansion and prosperity, not contraction and depression. Migration in a sense there has been since the First World War, but it has been to centres outside Britain altogether.

3. *Water supplies.*—All textile industries consume large quantities of water during the finishing processes. Water is also needed by the woollen and worsted industries for "scouring" or cleaning prior to spinning, and steam-driven mills are further dependent on water for their boilers. Hard or polluted supplies require treatment before use, which adds to operating expenses, and because of the quantities involved (a large print works consumes 20 million gallons per week), the public supply is normally inadequate, and too costly, except as a means of supplementing natural stream flow during a period of drought. Abundant supplies of pure soft water are available in the north and west of these islands, where rainfall is heavy and surface catchments extensive. On the newer rocks of the English Plain, and in the south, water is obtained from wells, or issues as springs from the lower slopes of the chalk and limestone uplands. This water is hard and generally unsuitable. Boulder clay cappings on the chalk of East Anglia, and sandstone formations within the predominantly calcareous rocks of the Cotswolds and the Wiltshire downlands, however, have given rise to numerous small soft-water streams upon which textile industries became based at a time when factory units were small and scattered, and the volume of water required was not great. The worsted industries of East Anglia and woollen industries of the West Country owed their origin in part to the existence of such streams.

As the textile industries expanded, they were drawn to regions where suitable water was more plentiful. The West Riding of Yorkshire, and east and south-east Lancashire had access to copious supplies from the peat covered Pennine moorlands and from Rossendale Forest. They also possessed water power and coal in abundance. The flanks of the limestone Pennines, with their hard-water rivers, and the New Red Sandstone plains of Yorkshire, Lancashire, and Cheshire which drew supplies from undergound (and which also lacked power) never became important. The vertically organised woollen industry is more stream based than the worsted industry which is organised horizontally, and is therefore

[1] Some Lancashire mills have been converted to the intensive production of poultry and eggs.

free to carry out many processes away from water. The finishing branches also became localised on soft-water streams, and although many of these streams are to-day so highly polluted that they furnish supplies which are neither soft nor pure, the location has tended to persist.

4. *Humidity.*—The importance of a moist climate as a localising factor in the textile industry has been over-stated. It is true that certain processes, *e.g.* cotton weaving, can only be performed satisfactorily in sheds where a high relative humidity is maintained. It is also true that this condition can be more easily attained if the outside air is moist than if it is dry. Flax spinning and weaving likewise demand a moist atmosphere. Cotton spinning, on the other hand, particularly the spinning of the lower counts, and wool spinning and weaving are not especially handicapped if relative humidities are much lower.

It must be stressed that it is the state of the atmosphere *inside* the building that is important. Textiles are not spun and woven in the open air. Internal and external relative humidities will approximate to each other only when there is no artificial heating in the building. If the mill is heated, as it must be in a cool temperate climate in winter, then the relative humidity of saturated air at 0° C. (32° F.) will be reduced to about 25 per cent. when its temperature is raised to 20°—25°C. (68°—77°F.), the level at which spinning mills and weaving sheds are maintained. Air as dry as this would cause too many breakages in the yarn, and would dislocate production: it must therefore be moistened artificially. Artificial humidification has in fact been practised since early times, originally by evaporating water from pans, or the floor, and later by blowing steam through the factory. To-day automatically controlled humidifiers are installed in every modern mill, and are effective no matter what the climate. That this is so is evident from the location of important cotton centres in regions such as the Nile Delta and the Punjab, where relative humidities of less than 10 per cent. are not uncommon.

5. *Labour.*—Textile industries are traditionally employers of low cost labour, and have tended to develop in regions where such labour is available. As the industries become more capital intensive, the importance of labour costs diminishes. This point is discussed on p. 355.

THE COTTON INDUSTRY

The cotton industry in Britain.—The Industrial Revolution began in Lancashire with the series of inventions that mechanised first the weaving and later the spinning branches of cotton manufacture. A factory industry soon became established in the south-east of the county, in the region where it is still entrenched. Nearly all the spindles, and 90 per cent. of the looms, running on cotton and mixed fabrics in 1964 were in Lancashire and the adjacent areas of Cheshire and the West Riding.

In Britain, cotton attached itself to existing wool and linen industries, but it never became as widely dispersed as the manufacture of these older fibres. It was once, however, more widely dispersed than it is to-day. The East Midlands had a brief period of prosperity during the water-power phase, but the region declined with the advent of the steam engine. Central Scotland and Northern Ireland also developed cotton industries. These remained important until about 1860.

The reasons for Lancashire's supremacy are well known. The region possessed during the period of the industry's most rapid growth, greater advantages for cotton yarn and cloth production than any other part of the British Isles, with the possible exception of Central Scotland. It had water power from the Pennines and the Rossendale Uplands, and abundant supplies of process water. It had coal. Twenty miles to the south lay the Cheshire salt fields, whose chemical industries supplied raw materials to the finishing trades. Thirty miles to the west, across a low flat plain that offered few obstacles to communications, stood Liverpool, which became the main port of entry for raw fibre once cotton cultivation had become established in the New World. In 1894 the Manchester Ship Canal was completed, and brought ocean transport into the heart of the region. Lancashire had a thrifty, hard-working population that had become skilled in the arts of spinning and weaving long before the idea of a factory industry was ever conceived. In common with the rest of western Britain, it boasted a damp climate. Finally, once the industry had become established, all the factors conspired towards further concentration. Factories which used each other's products, and took advantage of the same centralised buying and marketing facilities found it an advantage to be close to each other. The consequence was that it became increasingly difficult for mills erected outside the area to succeed, and once the Scottish industry had capitulated, Lancashire was left almost alone in the field.

Lancashire cotton is a classic example of a horizontally organised industry. The spinning, weaving, and finishing branches, with a few exceptions, are not only in the hands of different firms which confine themselves to a narrow range of activities, but are also localised in different parts of the cotton region.[1] The spinning towns lie in a crescent round Manchester. To the north, across an area of comparatively thinly populated moorland are the weaving centres. The bleach, dye, and print works occupy stream bank locations on the southern flanks of Rossendale Forest, and on the River Goyt between Stockport and Hayfield (Fig. 95). There exists a further sharp division between the so-called "Egyptian" section of the industry, which spins the long staple "Egyptian" cottons and which is centred on Bolton, and the "American" section spinning the

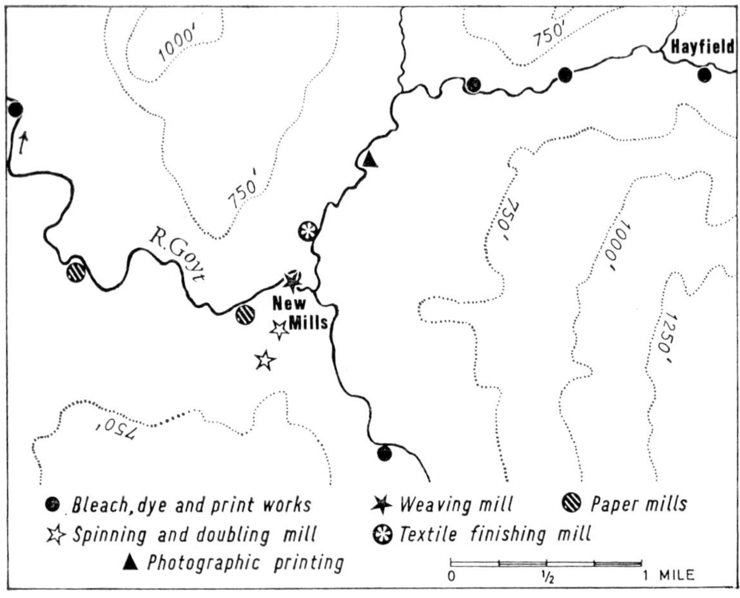

Fig. 95.—River Based Industry, Near New Mills, Derbyshire

coarser, short staple "American" cottons, centred on Oldham and Rochdale. Curiously, in an industry so fragmented, there is no corresponding division in the weaving section, and in almost all weaving sheds both "Egyptian" and "American" cottons are processed.

Horizontal organisation allows an almost endless degree of specialisation within the industry. It gives mills engaged in weaving

[1] According to the Cotton Industry Working Party's report, there were (1946) more than 130 firms that specialised in spinning, some 110 doubling firms, and more than 900 specialist weaving firms. Most of these were in Lancashire.

and finishing access to a far greater range of yarns and fabrics than would be possible if firms were organised vertically, unless those firms were very large, which the majority in Lancashire are not. On the other hand, a horizontal structure means that spinning mills have little or no control over the ultimate markets for their products, and the finishing branches over the production and supply of yarn and cloth. In the highly competitive situation of to-day this is a disadvantage, and the benefits that are to be gained by controlling the whole series of processes from bale-breaking to finishing are becoming appreciated. A number of large, vertically organised groups have, in fact, emerged since the reorganisation of the industry in 1959. Very little has been achieved in geographical integration, *i.e.* the bringing together of all processes on to the same site, and the physical separation of spinning, weaving, bleaching, dyeing, and printing are likely to remain a feature of the industry for many years.

THE GLASGOW REGION.—The manufacture of purely cotton fabrics developed in the Central Lowlands of Scotland during the eighteenth century. As in Lancashire, it grew out of existing wool and linen industries. The region is well favoured for textile production. Water flowing from the Southern Uplands is pure and soft, and the valleys provide many power sites. Glasgow offers port and trading facilities which are substantially equal to those of Liverpool and Manchester. Chemicals are produced in the region, and the climate is damp. The rise of the industry, therefore, is not surprising. It expanded rapidly during the early decades of the nineteenth century, and continued to prosper until supplies of raw cotton were cut off during the American Civil War. Thereafter it went into a rapid decline which cannot easily be explained. Glasgow was affected no more severely than Lancashire by the cotton famine of the 1860s, and yet Lancashire managed to recover once normal trading conditions were restored. Again, if Glasgow's decline were due (as has been suggested) to a tendency to specialise in the finer types of cloth for which demand was limited, why did it not switch to the production of the cheaper fabrics which had made Lancashire prosperous? It would not have been difficult during a period of expanding trade. A more plausible explanation of the decay of the Scottish textile industry is to be found in the rise of the iron and steel and engineering trades of the Central Lowlands. These were turning out to be more profitable enterprises than cotton, and were attracting increasing amounts of capital. What is difficult to understand is why they should have been so much *more* profitable when easy fortunes were being made by many Lancashire mill owners in a region no better endowed by nature for textile production. Engineering and textiles are also in one important respect complementary activities: while they may compete for capital, they do not compete to any serious degree for labour. Spinning and weaving are operations that can be, and are, performed equally well by women as by men. In the circumstances, therefore, the extent of Glasgow's decline is rather surprising.

The Central Lowlands still retain some of the finishing trades, now based on grey cloth imported from Lancashire. There is also a small weaving industry in Glasgow itself, but the spinning branch has virtually died out. The main activity is the production of cotton thread. Paisley is the chief centre.

The rise of foreign competitors, and the decline of Lancashire.—Between 1900 and 1914 the Lancashire cotton industry reached its zenith, although its rate of growth had been falling since the middle of the nineteenth century. In 1913 a labour force of nearly 600,000 men and women tended no fewer than 60 million spindles, and 700,000 looms, and produced nearly 60 per cent. (7,000 million yards) of all cotton piece goods entering international commerce. In a matter of 100 years Lancashire had built up the greatest export trade the world had ever known.

But in 1913 Lancashire was not alone in the textile business. The factory industries which had taken root in India and Japan during the previous decades were already well established. India was producing 1,000 million yards of cloth each year, and was supplying an ever increasing share of her own domestic requirements. Japan was exporting textiles to China and India, although as yet the volume of trade was small. Mills were being built in China, Mexico, Brazil, and in many other lands. Manufacturers on the continent of Europe and in the United States were also threatening Britain's export trade in markets for the finer type of cloth. During the First World War, and the depression years that followed, cotton manufacturing spread literally to dozens of countries, many of them in the tropics, and expanded at a rate little less than phenomenal in some of the established centres. Since 1945, Hong Kong, Pakistan, Formosa, and Korea have been added to the list of major producers, and more will certainly be added in the future. Mainland China also possesses one of the largest cotton textile industries in the world, and although she has been mainly engaged in satisfying her own very large internal market, a substantial overseas trade has developed in recent years (Table 92).

Table 92

UNITED KINGDOM FOREIGN TRADE IN COTTON PIECE GOODS
(in millions of square yards)

Exports to	1937-8	1960	1964
British West Africa	124·28 (British West Africa, Ghana, Nigeria, Sierra Leone)		
Ghana		24·76	6·28
Nigeria		36·8	15·04
Sierra Leone		10·0	7·88
Australia	149·16	44·36	17·72
South Africa	121·16	40·88	24·84
Irish Republic	31·84	17·76	21·84
Malawi, Zambia, Rhodesia	16·4	18·24	15·16
New Zealand	31·16	28·04	14·64
Canada	70·4	6·40	6·72
TOTAL U.K. EXPORTS	1,653·80	327·08	210·24

Imports* from	1937-8	1960	1964
India	1·68 (India and Pakistan)	231·16	247·6
Pakistan		39·6	48·16
Hong Kong	—	123·41	101·84
China (mainland)†	0·8	25·16	60·20
Korea	—	—	31·08
Portugal	n/a	18·12	27·72
Belgium	11·40	26·72	26·80
Canada	—	10·24	25·12
U.S.A.	—	16·76	5·68
Japan	20·44	52·04	5·36
TOTAL U.K. IMPORTS*	51·16	727·72	767·0

* Includes piece goods imported for finishing and re-export.
† 1937-8 figures include imports from Formosa.
Source: *Quarterly Statistical Review*. The Cotton Board, Manchester.

It is at the hands of the low-wage countries of the Far East that Britain has suffered most, partly because competition from producers having at their disposal almost unlimited reserves of cheap labour is very difficult to counter in an industry where wages comprise a large proportion of the total costs of manufacture, and partly because Far East production has concentrated on the coarser type of cloth, *i.e.* the type upon which Britain's export trade depended heavily. Nearly three-quarters of the spindles running in Lancashire in 1913 were spinning the comparatively cheap, short staple cottons destined almost exclusively for sale in India, China, and other lands where purchasing power was low. Initially Lancashire's markets were threatened in those countries which themselves had become producers. Later, traditional Lancashire markets in countries whose industries were not yet developed were invaded. New outlets were also found in many African, Asian, and Latin American territories, among people too poor to buy from Britain at all. After the Second World War, Commonwealth and Colonial producers took advantage of the terms of the Ottawa Agreement (1933) to export unlimited quantities of textiles duty free to Britain. At first, trade was mainly in grey cloth sent for finishing and re-export, but within a few years cotton piece goods for consumption in this country began to arrive. By 1959 Britain had become a net importer of cotton cloth, and to-day she stands as the largest importer of cotton goods in the world. The volume of imports is currently equivalent to 40 per cent. of the total home production. From Hong Kong alone Britain purchased made-up goods to the value of £50 million in 1964, including no fewer than 12 million woven shirts, 10 million knitted garments, and 22·5 million pairs of trousers. The implications of the situation for Lancashire, which fifty years ago dominated the textile markets of the world, hardly needs stating.

There are several reasons for the decline of the cotton industry in Britain. It has become fashionable to attribute its malaise to the great disparity in wage rates and working conditions which exist between this country and the lands of the Far East. The disparity cannot be denied and its significance belittled, but it is not the sole explanation. It must also be remembered that India, Hong Kong, and other developing countries, by taking advantage of their almost limitless supplies of low cost labour, are merely exploiting their most abundant factor of production, just as the economically advanced nations are making the fullest use of their main resource—abundant capital in the development of their own industries. To decline acceptance of imports from a country simply on the grounds that its labour is less generously rewarded than one's own is nothing less than economic stupidity, as well as being morally reprehensible, because if the practice became widespread it would bring international trade almost to a standstill, to the impoverishment of all. It would mean that Britain could only buy from the United States and a few other "Western" countries, while the United States, which has the highest wage rates in the world, could buy from no one. Britain, whose living standards depend to an exceptional degree on the buoyancy of foreign trade would be the greatest loser if this were to happen. In decrying the use of cheap labour in the undeveloped lands one should also remember that the opportunity for factory employment, however poorly rewarded by our own standards, represents a considerable economic and social advance for the majority of people who are fortunate enough to obtain such employment. Poorly paid mill work is better than casual work on a farm, and certainly better than no work at all.

Other factors which account for the severity of foreign competition are as follows:

1. Cotton textile industries are easy to establish. Before 1939, although the position has somewhat changed to-day, they could be started with a very small outlay of capital. Buildings did not have to be large and elaborate, machinery was comparatively inexpensive, and its operation called for no particular skill. There were few economies of scale to be realised, as small units of production were as efficient as the large. Output could be increased when opportunity

occurred by adding more machines rather than by re-equipping with larger ones, and consequently a mill owner could begin in a small way and expand out of profits. Since the war, equipment has increased in price, but even to-day a large, modern integrated spinning and weaving plant can be erected and brought into production at a cost of some £4-5 million, which is only a fraction of the cost of a steel works, motor vehicle plant, or oil refinery. Such a mill needs have access to only a a small market to achieve capacity working, while the steel works, etc., would have to command a very large market indeed before capacity operation, and therefore maximum efficiency, could be realised.

2. The two world wars hastened the movement towards economic self-sufficiency in the developing countries. In 1914, and again in 1939, the British textile industry was not considered essential to the war effort, and was forced to contract. Mills were closed, and labour dispersed into engineering and armament production. Shipping space was scarce, and manufacturers consequently experienced difficulty in securing supplies of raw cotton, and in exporting yarns and piece goods to overseas customers. The low quality cloth trade was the most severely affected as it was less able to bear the higher war-time freight and insurance charges. The outcome was that foreign buyers began to look elsewhere for cottons that they had previously bought from Lancashire, and all too readily found firms in their own country that were able to supply them.

3. Since 1945, there has been little less than a technological revolution in textile machinery. Before the war, equipment was likely to wear out before it was outmoded. Indeed there had been no fundamental change in textile machinery since 1895 when the automatic loom was invented. There was therefore little incentive for manufacturers to install new plant until the old could no longer be repaired. The position is very different to-day. Machines installed ten years ago, although still in good working order, are now obsolete. Until the re-organisation of the British cotton industry in 1959, many Lancashire firms were operating with plant that had not been renewed since the 1930s. By contrast, some of their most powerful competitors in the Far East had taken advantage of the reconstruction forced upon them as a result of wartime devastation to re-equip their factories along modern lines. Much Japanese equipment is of extremely advanced design, and in the mills of Hong Kong and Pakistan, which are essentially creations of the post-war period, two-thirds of the machines are less than five years old. The Indian industry, on the other hand, is still handicapped by much

antiquated equipment, and, in spite of low wage rates, labour costs per unit of production are high, probably as high as in Britain and double those of Japan.

4. Many overseas countries are now utilising their plant very intensively—an important factor in reducing production costs in an industry where equipment is now expensive and its economic life short. Factories operate on a two or three shift basis, while in Britain one-shift working is still the rule. Night work in the United Kingdom is forbidden for women by law, and opposition to it by men is difficult to overcome.

TABLE 93

AVERAGE NUMBER OF HOURS WORKED ANNUALLY BY ACTIVE SPINDLES AND LOOMS IN NINE COTTON TEXTILE PRODUCING COUNTRIES (1964)

	SPINDLES	LOOMS
Hong Kong	8,280	8,160
Egypt	7,492	6,611
Pakistan	6,838	6,062
U.S.A.	6,616	6,642
India	6,491	5,577
Japan	4,551	4,345
France	4,383	3,262
West Germany	3,528	3,226
United Kingdom	2,898	3,035

Source: *International Cotton Industry Statistics*, Zurich.

5. The industries of many developing countries are being assisted by government-sponsored, low interest loans. These loans are sometimes made conditional upon a certain quota of the production being exported.

The British cotton industry re-organisation scheme.—Faced with the melancholy prospect of a continuing fall in demand for British cottons both in foreign and domestic markets, the Cotton Board, in 1959, set about the task of streamlining the industry. The aim was to cut the industry down to a size more in keeping with present day needs, and at the same time to increase its competitive position. Surplus machinery was scrapped, and the less efficient firms were encouraged to go out of business. Compensation was offered by the government, and by firms remaining in the industry to all who responded. The government also contributed up to one-quarter of the cost of re-equipment. The extent of the changes which occurred within the space of a few months can be seen from Table 94.

The cotton industry is in a healthier position following the drastic surgery of recent years. Excess capacity has been largely eliminated

TABLE 94

THE EFFECT ON THE RE-ORGANISATION SCHEME ON THE NUMBER OF MACHINES IN BRITISH COTTON MILLS

	1959		Number scrapped April, 1959	Number remaining in 1960
	Number in place	Number running		
Spinning spindles	25,500,000	16,500,000	12,500,000	13,000,000
Doubling spindles	1,609,000	1,015,000	571,000	1,038,000
Looms	260,000	183,000	105,000	155,000*

* 40,600 of the looms remaining were fully automatic.

Number of mill closures between 1959 and 1965.

Spinning mills	151
Waste spinning mills ..	20
Doubling mills	79
Weaving sheds	320
Finishing mills	102

Source: The Cotton Board, Manchester.

and considerable progress made with modernisation schemes. However, long term prosperity depends on:

(*a*) More intensive utilisation of modern plant, which in effect means three-shift working, at least until the fully automated mill is developed and in operation.

(*b*) Concentration into larger, vertically organised firms with larger resources for research and marketing at their disposal.

(*c*) Some limitation on imports from the low-wage producers until (*a*) and (*b*) have been realised. India, Hong Kong, Pakistan, and others, have in fact agreed to a "voluntary" restriction on exports to the United Kingdom.

Cotton manufacturing industries in selected overseas countries

THE UNITED STATES.—The first New World cotton mill was erected at Pawtucket (Rhode Island) in 1790. The growth and prosperity of the New England centres in the decades that followed were based upon the exploitation of the region's considerable water-power resources, imports of cheap, water-borne coal, the labour skills of immigrants from Europe, abundant capital, and, as far as the coastal towns were concerned, easy access by sea to cotton-growing areas in many parts of the world.

The Southern States, on the other hand, were content until the 1870s merely to grow cotton, an activity that became very profitable after the invention of the gin in 1793. Four years of civil war, however, were sufficient to convince the South of its economic backwardness, and of the need to foster the industry that could utilise the one great raw material produced on its farms in such abundance. So great did the advantages of the South for the production of cotton textiles prove to be, that within half a century of the construction of the first mill, the region had outstripped New England in the output of yarn, and had acquired a substantial share of the weaving trade. By the middle of the twentieth century, some 95 per cent. of all cotton processed in the United States was being handled by Southern mills.

The industry became established in rural areas on the piedmont, on the Fall Line in the Carolinas and Georgia, and in the valleys of the southern Appalachians. Coal was drawn from the West Virginian and Kentucky fields, and from local sources. The hydro-electric potential of the region was greater than that of New England, and was later developed. The location of the mills within sight of the cotton fields permitted a slight saving on raw material transport costs, but these became insignificant with improvements in communications. The factories paid few or no state taxes, whereas taxation in the North was, by the standards of the time, high. The most important factor, however, was the low cost of Southern labour. Most of it was drawn from an under-employed and poverty-stricken farm-hand class which welcomed the opportunity of better paid work in the mill villages. It was conservative and docile, and unmoved by the blandishments of the Northern unions to restrict working hours, to refuse to operate certain machines (*e.g.* the automatic loom), and to indulge in strikes. The replacement of the complicated mule by the ring spindle offset the advantages that the North originally possessed in the matter of labour skills. Only the lower counts could be spun on the ring spindle, but this was of little consequence as the South was generally too poor to buy the more expensive fabrics. As the South gained in experience, and as its market expanded, the North's monopoly of the high quality cloth trade was broken. After the First World War the New England industry declined not only relatively but absolutely in face of Southern competition. At present, the North produces only about 15 per cent. of its 1914 output. Ninety-five per cent. of the spindles and looms running on cotton and mixed fabrics are to-day in the Southern States (Fig. 96).

The differences in labour costs between the two regions are less now than they used to be, and will eventually disappear. But Southern industry is progressive and efficient, and equipped with modern machinery which is being employed to capacity. This, as has been indicated earlier, is an important factor in reducing production costs in a capital-intensive economy.

New England still clings to a share of the high quality weaving and finishing trades. Its position close to New York, the main fashion centre of the continent, gives it a considerable advantage in this field. However, the mechanical and electrical engineering industries are now of far greater importance to the New England economy than cotton. The parallel with Lancashire is very close.

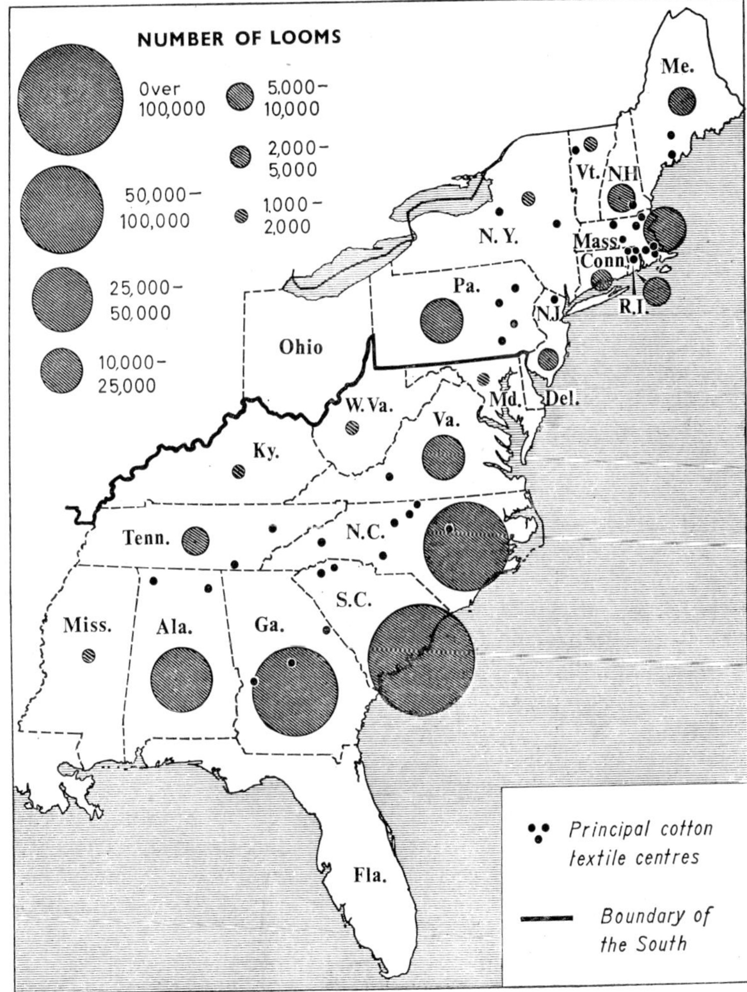

Fig. 96.—Looms Running on Cotton and Man-made Fibres in the United States, 1964

EUROPE.—The cotton textile industry is widely disseminated throughout a broad zone of continental Europe extending from France and the Low Countries, through Germany, Switzerland, Austria, and northern Italy into eastern Europe and the Soviet Union. As in the United Kingdom, it developed out of old established domestic woollen industries. Russia and some of the Balkan countries are producers of raw cotton, otherwise the European mills rely almost entirely on imported fibre. The combined yarn production of the continental European countries exceeds that of Asia. The Soviet Union, West Germany, France, and Italy are the leading textile nations (Table 95).

TABLE 95

CONSUMPTION OF RAW COTTON IN EUROPEAN MILLS
(in thousands of metric tons)

	1953	1960	1964
West Germany	248·8	323·7	283·5
France	264·1	300·9	282·4
United Kingdom	369·5	278·4	237·1
Italy	186·2	227·0	220·0
Belgium-Luxembourg	86·3	92·0	84·6
Netherlands	67·2	80·1	77·8
Austria	18·9	26·6	26·1
Sweden	28·2	27·8	21·0
Finland	13·4	17·6	16·8
Denmark	9·8	8·2	10·6
Norway	4·8	4·5	4·4

Source: *A Study of Cotton Textiles*, G.A.T.T., Geneva, 1966.

INDIA.—The factory industry in India dates from 1854 when the first spinning mill was built in Bombay. For centuries prior to this date an important hand spinning and weaving industry had flourished in the country. The hand weaving industry continued to prosper after the introduction of factory processes. It is still of sizeable dimensions, and some 2,000 million linear yards of cloth, or one-third of India's production, come off the hand looms annually.

The factory industry originated in and around Bombay, where access to the short stable cotton of the hinterland was easy, and where coal and machinery could be imported from Britain. Hydroelectricity, developed from streams descending the scarped slope of the Western Ghats, became a valuable source of power in later years. Much of the yarn from the Bombay mills was sent to China and Japan for weaving. Subsequently, with the rise of Japan as a competitor, the Indian industry spread to the interior, and became established in more than 600 factories across the peninsula and northern plains. With an eye on the export market, Bombay has begun to specialise in spinning and weaving better quality cottons, while the coarser cloths for home consumption are produced in the interior. With more than 14 million spindles, and 200,000 looms, India now has a spinning capacity surpassed only by the United States, and weaving capacity exceeded only by Japan. She is one of the largest producers of cotton cloth in the world.

TABLE 96

INDIAN FOREIGN TRADE IN COTTON PIECE GOODS
(in millions of linear yards)

Exports to—	1937-8	1955	1960	1964
United Kingdom ..	n/a	85·96	199·16	182·84
U.S.A.	n/a	1·88	35·04	35·64
British East Africa* ..	6·92	64·68	48·64	35·16
Ceylon	24·20	41·88	24·44	29·00
Afghanistan	n/a	13·08	22·72	25·52
Australia	n/a	41·68	48·60	25·32
Sudan	1·52	64·68	64·28	25·12
Aden	2·88	48·04	30·28	15·88
Canada	n/a	n/a	19·92	15·72
British West Africa ..	6·92	64·68	32·48	14·44
Singapore	20·96	29·28	23·48	4·76
Burma	76·76	10·80	22·44	2·76
TOTAL INDIAN EXPORTS	203·84	751·48	723·68	591·36

n/a—not available.

* Kenya, Uganda, Tanzania.

Source: *Quarterly Statistical Review*, The Cotton Board, Manchester.

PAKISTAN.—The partition of the Indian sub-continent in 1947 left Pakistan as an overwhelmingly agricultural nation, with only eighteen badly equipped, and poorly managed textile mills throughout her 365,000 square miles of territory. The development of manufacturing, therefore, become a keystone in the government's drive for economic expansion, and a measure of priority was given to industries that could process home-produced raw materials, particularly cotton and jute. The cotton industry grew rapidly. By 1961, 139 mills had been built, and 2 million spindles and 30,000 looms installed. Pakistan is now more or less self-sufficient in cotton cloth production, and has entered the export trade.

HONG KONG.—Hong Kong was founded as a free port in 1841, and grew to prosperity as a great entrepôt serving the western Pacific. The growth of significantly important manufacturing industry began before the Second World War, and expanded rapidly after it. The influx of refugees from communist China, which added to the colony's unemployment problems, and the decline in the value of the colony's entrepôt trade with the mainland, were major factors that stimulated the growth of industry. Among the many light consumer goods industries to be established were textiles. Certain aspects of the post-war developments in the field of cotton textile production are illustrated graphically in Fig. 97.

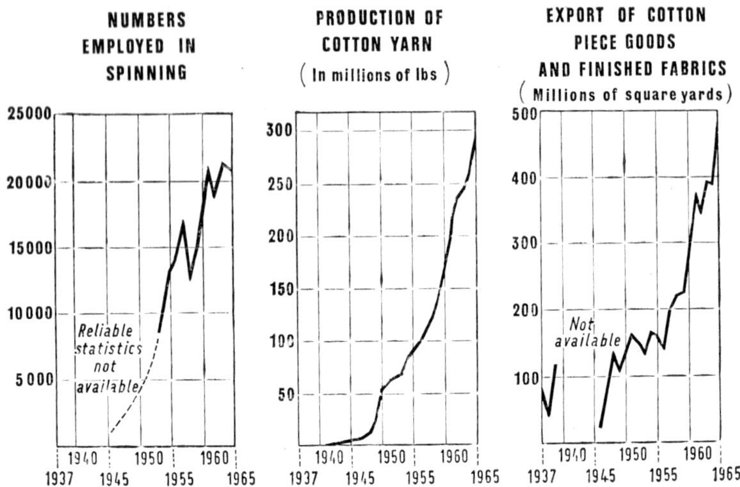

Fig. 97.—The Rise of the Hong Kong Cotton Industry.

Table 97

Production of Cotton Yarn
(in thousands of metric tons)

	1962	1965
U.S.A.	1,804·6	1,906·7
China (mainland)	1,632·6 (1960)*	n/a
U.S.S.R.	1,192·0	1,274·0
India	859·6	936·2
Japan	490·9	549·6
West Germany	318·8	294·6
France	260·5	231·7
United Kingdom	223·2	219·9
Poland	163·5	187·2
Italy	204·4	171·9
U.A.R.	121·1	131·2 (1964)
Hong Kong	106·8	131·1
Czechoslovakia	109·9	108·1
Spain	122·5	107·8

n/a—not available.

* Estimated.

Source: *World Cotton Statistics*.

TABLE 98.
PRODUCTION OF COTTON CLOTH
(in thousands of metric tons)

	1962	1965
U.S.A.	1,360·2	1,345·9
China (mainland)	1,150·0 (1960)*	n/a
India	829·1	925·3
U.S.S.R.	748·6	825·8 (1964)
Japan	409·7	400·2
West Germany	258·8	246·9
France	223·5	197·7
United Kingdom	153·2	148·5
Spain	101·9	102·0
Italy	136·8	96·9
U.A.R.	77·8	77·3 (1964)
Belgium	79·4	75·4

n/a—not available.

* Estimated.

Source: *World Cotton Statistics.*

THE WOOL TEXTILE INDUSTRIES

The manufacture of woollen cloth is an old occupation. During the pre-historic period it was carried on widely throughout the temperate and tropical highland regions of the world wherever sheep or other wool-bearing animals were to be found. Wool textile production, like cotton, became concentrated in factory workshops, and later in mills during the Industrial Revolution, although a primitive hand industry, employing techniques fundamentally no different from those known to and used by the ancients, still persists among many isolated communities.

Contrasts between wool and cotton textile industries

1. The processing of wool, to a greater extent than is the case with cotton, is concentrated in small factory units. It is an activity where diversity rather than uniformity is the rule, where operations are complex, and where careful supervision is needed at every stage of production. The woollen and worsted trades also differ fundamentally from cotton in that styling is done primarily in the early stages of manufacture. Cotton grey cloth can be mass produced, and then printed if need be in a thousand different patterns. The patterns of woollen and worsted cloth are determined by the type and colour of the yarn inserted into the weave, and sometimes by the mixtures of fibres in the yarn. Only to a limited extent are fabrics dyed and printed after weaving. In order to produce the great range of cloths in demand to-day, a very large number of short runs are therefore necessary. It is not uncommon for a loom to turn out

as few as three pieces, each of no more than sixty-five yards in length, before being re-set on a new weave. This is the antithesis of mass production. In such an industry there is an absence over a large section of it of any significant economies to be gained by large-scale operation, and the advantage tends to lie with the small, flexible firm that can respond quickly to changes in market conditions.

2. The uses of wool are more circumscribed than cotton. Wool has not been adopted as an industrial fibre and textile to the extent that cotton has. Furthermore, because of its high price (about three times the price of cotton), wool is beyond the means of large sections of the world's population, particularly those living in the

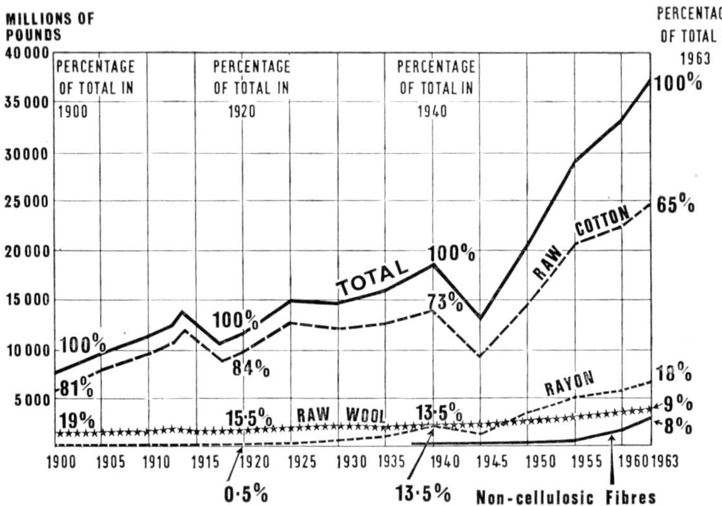

Fig. 98.—World Production of the Major Textile Fibres, 1900–63.

under-developed countries. In any case, woollen garments are generally inappropriate to the tropics where many of the under-developed countries are situated. The sheep too, is not a tropical animal, and the emerging nations cannot thus readily base a wool textile industry on a domestic raw material. For these reasons therefore, the mill consumption of raw wool lags far behind that of cotton, and currently accounts but for a small (and declining) share of total world usage of textile fibres (Fig. 98).

3. The important regions of cotton fibre production are with few exceptions also regions of cotton cloth production. The great sheep rearing lands, by contrast, are not themselves significant producers

of woollen goods, but ship raw wool for long distances to the mills of New England, Western Europe, Japan, and the Soviet Union. The sparsity of population in the areas of extensive grazing, which results both in a shortage of factory labour and a limited market, accounts for the general absence within them of important centres of wool manufacture.

Woollens and worsteds.—These terms are properly used to denote two quite distinct systems of spinning and weaving wool. Briefly the processes are as follows:

The woollen system.—Woollens are made from short staple virgin wool, wool that has been rejected during the combing process in worsted manufacture, and woollen wastes derived from spinning and weaving mills, torn up rags, tailors' clippings, etc., which are known in the trade as *shoddy* and *mungo*. A substantial quantity of cotton, mohair, alpaca and man-made fibres may also be added to the wool. After being sorted into grades, and scoured to remove grease, the wool is oiled to facilitate working. If a yarn mixture is required, wool is blended by mixing dyed and undyed material. The wool is then fed on to a carding machine, which mingles and mixes the fibres into a close criss-cross, web-like structure. The success of this process depends to some extent on the natural tendency of hairy wool fibres to adhere to each other. The wool comes off the carding machine in a smooth, soft rope known as a *sliver*. It is then loosely spun, normally on the mule spindle, and subsequently woven. Finally the cloth is milled or *fulled*, an operation which causes the further adherence of the fibres, and gives strength to the cloth.

The worsted system.—Worsteds are produced from long staple wool that has not previously been used. The processes involved are more numerous and complex than in woollen manufacture. After preparatory sorting, scouring, and oiling, the wool is combed in order to arrange the fibres parallel to each other and to remove the shorter fibres, or *noils*. The slivers which emerge from the comb are known as *tops*. The tops are stretched, and reduced to the diameter required for spinning by passing them through roving and drawing machines. In the spinning process, the wool is given a tight twist on either a cap or ring spindle. Tightly spun yarn is one of the characteristics of worsteds. The yarn is doubled if necessary, and then closely woven. There is no subsequent milling. Unlike woollen cloth, which has a felted appearance, the pattern of weave in a piece of worsted is clearly visible.

The geographical basis of the wool textile industry in Britain.—A domestic industry, turning out coarse wool yarn and cloth, had become well established in many parts of Britain even before the time of the Roman occupation. It owed its origin and early growth to the wide distribution of sheep in these islands, and to the damp, raw, northern climate against which a woollen garment afforded the best possible protection.

Very slowly during the early centuries of the Christian era, but at an accelerating pace after the Norman conquest, the industry began to expand. It continued to be broadly based, geographically, but the production of cloth for commercial, as distinct from purely subsistence purposes, began to show marked concentrations in those parts of the country where conditions were most favourable. By the year 1500, the West Country (notably the Cotswold area and Devon) and East Anglia had established themselves firmly as the leading regions. There were also small but important outlying areas in the Lake District and Leicestershire. Yorkshire at this time lagged far behind, and the quality of its cloth was poor. Both the West Country and East Anglia had ready access to wool, although in neither case was dependence on the local clip excessive. Even in those days it was quite feasible to carry wool over long distances by pack horse, or to import it from the Continent by sea. Soft water could be found in the quantities required by the industry of the day, even in the predominantly hard water chalk and limestone areas. Only the manufacture of woollens was dependent on water power (for the fulling process), and high gradient streams were common-place in the highly accidented West Country. On the drier, and more subdued East Anglian countryside, where water power was generally lacking, it was the worsted, rather than the woollen industry that took root. These regions too, derived great advantage from their position near the centres of the country's economic and social life, and from the commercial links that had been forged between southern England and the Continent, via London and the East Anglian ports. Throughout the Middle Ages raw wool had been a staple export to the Low Countries, whilst the finer types of woollen cloth had been imported. By the time of the Tudors the position had been reversed, and England was exporting cloth to the Continent at least equal in quality to that produced in Flanders. The changed fortunes had come about largely through the arrival in this country of a number of Flemish weavers during the fourteenth century. These immigrants dispersed themselves over the country: some settled in the Pennine regions of Yorkshire and Lancashire, but most made for the established wool towns of the south and south-east—London, Stroud, Winchester, and Norwich. Here they introduced the finer arts of weaving which were soon to make England one of the most important producers of high-quality cloth in Europe and the leading exporter of woollen goods in the world.

As the industry grew during the centuries before the Industrial Revolution, the natural advantages of the West Riding began to assert themselves. By 1800, before the use of machinery had made much impact on industry to the east of the Pennines, the West Riding had surpassed the West Country in woollen, and East Anglia in worsted, production. The introduction of power spinning and weaving, which came later to Yorkshire than to Lancashire, confirmed the West Riding's supremacy. By 1835, all but a small fraction of the power looms running on wool were in north of England. The advent of the steam engine sealed the fate of East Anglia, and forced the West Country, and other established regions of wool manufacture, into a high degree of specialisation, as the only means of survival in face of the overwhelming competitive advantages possessed by Yorkshire with a coalfield location.

THE WEST RIDING.—The factors which led to the rise of the West Riding to the position of leading wool manufacturing region need only be summarised. Long before the factory period, the eastern Pennine valleys had been the home of a domestic industry based on the wool clip from the neighbouring moorlands. Rough woollen cloths known as "kerseys" were the main product, but found little acceptance outside the area of manufacture. Imported fibre from Ireland, Scotland, and the English Midlands became a feature of the industry once it began to look beyond the West Riding boundaries for markets. During the nineteenth century, raw wool came to be imported in increasing quantities from the "new" countries—fine, long staple wool from Australia and South Africa, and shorter staple crossbred wool from the Argentine and New Zealand. To-day the region draws some 85 per cent. of its wool requirements from overseas.

The West Riding shared with Lancashire the rainy, peat-covered water gathering grounds of the Pennines. In deeply entrenched valleys carved from the sandstones and shales of the Millstone Grit Series flowed innumerable streams that brought process water to domestic workshops, and provided energy during the short water-power phase of the industry. The introduction of a steam drive resulted, as it had done in Lancashire, in the abandonment of many up-valley sites, and a concentration of manufacturing on the outcrop of the productive coal measures. The coalfield area between the Aire and the Calder-Colne became predominant. North of the Aire coal was absent, and the rivers which headed on Carboniferous limestone rocks brought down hard water. South of the Colne, beyond a region of thinly populated moorland, lay the Don Valley, where economic interests centred on the metallurgical industries. In this district, wool manufacturing never really gained a foothold.

Within the textile region, a broad distinction may be noted between the towns of the north-west—Keighley, Bradford, and Halifax, which are engaged primarily in the manufacture of worsteds, and those of the south-east—Huddersfield, Dewsbury, Batley, and Wakefield, where woollens rather than worsteds predominate (Fig. 99). Dewsbury and Batley are centres of the shoddy and mungo trades; the finishing branches are concentrated on Bradford—the main commercial and organising centre of the West Riding; blankets are made in the Calder Valley towns; and Leeds is the leading centre of the clothing industry. There is not the same degree of geographical or economic specialisation that is to be found in Lancashire, however. Woollen and worsted spinning and weaving are diffused throughout the region. The woollen industry has a vertical organisation, and it is common for each mill to undertake all the processes of manufacture, at least as far as the finishing operations. The worsted industry has a horizontal structure, but without the regional separation of spinning and weaving that is so characteristic of the cotton industry to the west of the Pennines.

OTHER BRITISH REGIONS.—Outside the West Riding, the worsted industry is of little importance, but the manufacture of woollens has persisted as a relic industry from the domestic period in a number of places. Except for a few centres in the English Midlands which produce yarn for hosiery and knitted goods, none of the remaining woollen regions is coalfield based. The absence of local coal deposits was the most important single factor which brought about their decline during the last century, although in the case of the West Country, the shortage of suitable process water, and the reluctance of the guilds to accept changes in production methods were contributary causes.

Scotland is famous for its tweeds and knitwear. Important centres are located in the Tweed Valley at Galashiels, Selkirk, Hawick, and Peebles. Handwoven tweeds are made on Harris and Lewis in the Outer Hebrides. There are also a number of woollen mills in the Aberdeen area, and the manufacture of carpet yarns is important at Kilmarnock. Most of the Shetland wool is machine spun at Aberdeen and returned to the Islands for knitting.

The West Country industry is small and scattered. Important centres are Stroud, Witney, Westbury, Frome, Totnes, and Ashburton. High quality woollens are specialities of the region—

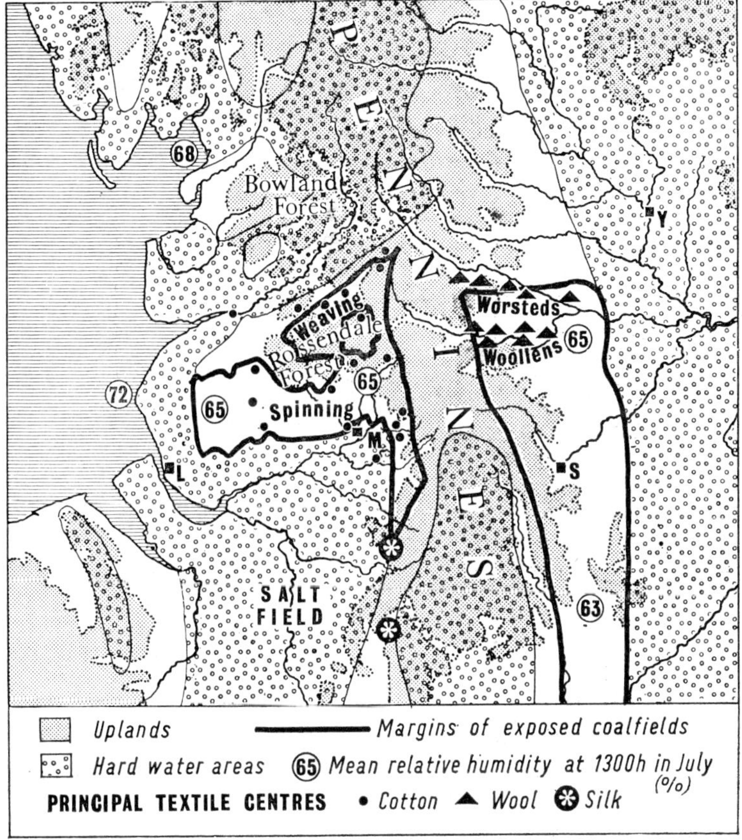

Fig. 99.—PHYSICAL BASIS OF THE LANCASHIRE AND YORKSHIRE TEXTILE INDUSTRIES

flannels, billiards cloths, blankets, tennis ball covers, meltons, and beavers. There is a little worsted weaving (employing yarns from the West Riding) and the finishing of worsted cloth. In Wales, mills in the Teifi Valley, Carmarthenshire, and in isolated centres elsewhere in the country produce blankets, travel rugs, and some tweeds. There is also a small woollen industry in Ireland.

Wool manufacturing regions overseas.—Wool cloth is essentially a product of the temperate lands. The countries of Europe, the Soviet Union, and the United States account for 70 per cent. of the world mill consumption of raw wool fibre. Outside these regions the only country possessing a major wool textile industry is Japan. Production from the tropics is very small.

TABLE 99

PRODUCTION OF WOVEN FABRICS BY THE WOOL TEXTILE INDUSTRY, WHOLLY OR PRINCIPALLY OF WOOL.

(in millions of square yards)

	1956	1960	1965
U.S.S.R.	292·8*	525·0	557·3
U.S.A.	547·0	476·7	434·2
United Kingdom ..	429·6	386·4	355·8
Japan	204·9	333·9	413·7
West Germany ..	189·8	202·1	185·3
France	204·8	199·2	193·0
Poland†	83·3	86·0	99·2
Netherlands	65·0	68·2	68·8
East Germany ..	31·7	56·9	45·0
Czechoslovakia† ..	40·2	50·5	47·9
Australia	37·5	39·5	35·5
Yugoslavia	32·7	39·2	46·2

* Linear yards in 1956. † Linear yards.

Source: Commonwealth Economic Committee.

TABLE 100

PRINCIPAL TRADING NATIONS IN WOVEN WOOL FABRICS, INCLUDING BLANKETS

(in millions of lbs.)

EXPORTING COUNTRIES	1957	1960	1965
Italy	104·98†	96·41*	133·04*
United Kingdom ..	68·96	60·76	50·91
Japan	17·71	18·40	27·02
Belgium	21·17	25·87	16·93
Netherlands	10·72	13·67	13·62
France	12·41	14·26	13·51
West Germany	6·20	6·20	7·60

* Fabrics whose predominant fibre is wool.

† Fabrics containing more than 12 per cent. wool.

IMPORTING COUNTRIES	1957	1960	1965
West Germany	43·43	47·81	60·70
U.S.A.	16·24	29·82	26·45
Netherlands	13·35	13·43	19·90
United Kingdom ..	19·34	15·04	16·30
France	10·58	7·30	13·47
Belgium	8·77	10·40	11·49
Sweden	6·44*	8·42	9·60

* Excludes blankets.

Source: Commonwealth Economic Committee.

Europe.—On the continent of Europe, as in Britain, the wool industry dates from antiquity. The wide dissemination of mills in almost every country is a consequence of the survival of many traditional centres from the domestic to the factory period. Important concentrations of yarn and cloth production do, of course, occur, notably on or near the coalfields of northern France, Belgium,

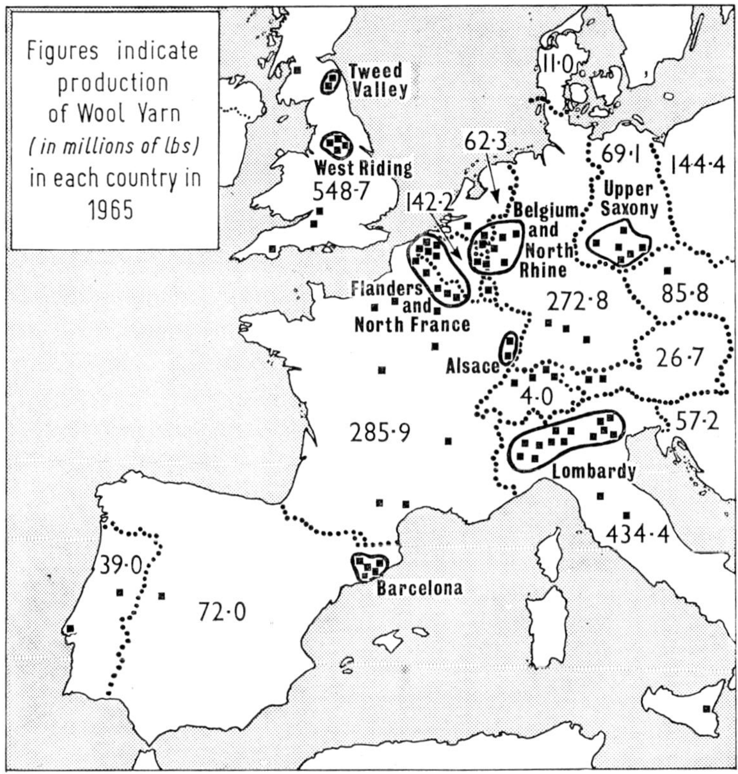

Fig. 100.—The Woollen Industry in Western Europe.

North Rhine-Westphalia, and Upper Saxony; and in regions where hydro-electric power is available, as, for example, on the Lombardy Plain and piedmont of northern Italy, and in and around Barcelona (Fig. 100). Originally based on the local wool clip, these and other European centres now lean heavily upon imported fibre.

The combined production from the countries of Western Europe accounts for more than a third of all manufactured wool products coming on to the world market. Most of the international trade in woollen goods originates in Western Europe. It is interesting to note too that European nations are also their own best customers (Table 100).

THE SOVIET UNION.—Upwards of one-third of the Soviet production of woven wool articles comes from mills in the Moscow area. Other important centres are situated in and around Leningrad; in the Kiev-Kharkov region of the Ukraine; in the Caucasus; and in Siberia at Alma-Ata (Kazakhstan).

THE UNITED STATES.—New England is the traditional centre of the wool textile industry of the United States. Wool from sheep raised in the east; the existence of numerous water power sites; access to Appalachian coal; the labour skills of immigrants; and the presence within, or in areas adjacent to, southern New England of relatively large and prosperous markets are some of the reasons for the industry's original development.

The shift to the South has been less dramatic than in the case of the cotton industry. The proportion of spindles running on wool in New England and the Middle Atlantic region has declined from more than 90 per cent. in 1940 to little more than two-thirds to-day, but this has been due rather to the closure of many small, uneconomic Northern mills than to any spectacular increase in activity in the South. Woollen and worsted cloth is less a mass-produced commodity than cotton. It is more subject to the dictates of changing fashion, and its production is therefore tied more effectively to locations near important centres of the clothing industry. The manufacture of clothing in the United States is concentrated in a remarkable way upon New York City, which has almost one-third of the nation's 1·3 million workers engaged in the "apparel and related products" trades.

THE SILK INDUSTRY

Silk is extruded by the silkworm as a ready-spun filament; hence the spinning operation which is essential to the production of other textiles employing natural fibres is absent from the silk industry.

The initial process in silk manufacture is known as *reeling*, and involves disentangling and unwinding the filaments from a number of cocoons (usually six, but sometimes as many as twenty) and joining them to give a stronger, but as yet scarcely visible thread. Cocoons unsuitable for reeling are utilised in the production of *spun silk*. Reeling is an extremely delicate task, requiring great patience and a high degree of manual dexterity, and is best suited to female labour. Once a domestic occupation, it is now commonly done in small factories, or filatures, in the regions where the silkworms are reared. The end product of reeling is raw silk, and as such it is exported to the silk manufacturing regions of the world.

Reeled silk is too fragile for most purposes, and is normally doubled or *thrown* in order to produce a yarn of more substantial thickness and strength. Throwing calls for little skill, and is an activity of manufacturing regions where cheap, easily-trained labour is available. Silk is now woven on the loom, as are other textile yarns, but because of the care with which silk filament must be treated, the hand loom persisted for much longer than in other textile industries. To-day, however, machine weaving is commonplace.

Spun silk.—Cocoons unsuitable for reeling, and broken and discarded filaments from the reeling machines and looms, are cleaned and separated into fibres of differing lengths by combing. They are then spun on the spindle, like cotton and wool fibres. Spun silk is used in the production of the cheaper fabrics.

The location of the silk industry.—Silk manufacturing is of importance in the Far East, where it originated at an early date. Southern Japan, central and southern China, and Korea are the principal regions. In Europe important centres exist in the Rhone Valley around Lyons, in northern Italy, and in the Rhinelands and at Krefeld (Germany). The British silk industry is located in a number of towns, but shows some degree of concentration in East Cheshire, particularly in and around Macclesfield. In the United States, New England, the New York area, and the anthracite coal mining region of eastern Pennsylvania are important.

Silk is a small-scale industry which is not amenable to mass production techniques. It has an affinity for regions where labour is cheap. It is an industry of the Far East, and certain rural and urban regions of Europe and North America where there is female labour with few alternative employment outlets. Silk too is a luxury product, and there is a tendency for silk manufacturing to be carried on near to the major fashion centres. Most of the American silk mills, for example, are within 200 miles of New York. The industries of southern Europe now depend upon the tourist trade for a substantial proportion of their sales.

Silk is a declining industry. Production of raw silk in recent years has averaged about 70 million pounds, an increase on the immediate post-war period, but still only a little more than half the output of the 1930s. The growing demand for man-made fibres by the clothing industries has steadily eroded the pure silk trade. Silk mills too have found it increasingly difficult to retain labour in competition with other industries, many of which can offer better paid employment. There are few silk manufacturers to-day who do not also use substantial quantities of rayon and other fibres.

THE LINEN INDUSTRY

Until the eighteenth century, the manufacture of linen cloth was an important activity throughout the flax growing regions of the North European Plain. North-central Russia, Saxony, the Low Countries, and Northern Ireland were then, as they are to-day, the principal regions.

As a major textile, linen failed to survive the Industrial Revolution. It was ousted by cotton, which is a more uniform and in some respects a stronger fibre. Cotton is also less easily damaged during the stages of manufacture that precede spinning. Furthermore, no complicated and disagreeable retting and scutching operations are involved in cotton fibre production as they are in the preparation of flax. However, it was the machine inventions of the early industrial period, particularly the gin, and the water frame and mule that were mainly responsible for the decline of the linen industry. The gin dramatically reduced the cost of cotton fibre production, while the water frame and mule spun a yarn so strong that it became possible for the first time to make all-cotton cloths easily and cheaply. Previously, cotton could only be used in mixed cotton-linen fabrics, as only a linen warp could impart sufficient strength to the cloth. The development of a technique for making all-cotton cloth thus dealt a blow to the linen industry from which it has never recovered.

The location of cotton and linen manufacturing is influenced by similar factors. The cotton industry developed in parts of Britain and Europe where linen was established, and within a short time overwhelmed it. Only in Northern Ireland did the linen trades successfully resist the encroachment of cotton. In Scotland they were forced out of the Glasgow region into the east coast towns of Dundee and Dunfermline, where with the allied jute and hemp industries they became concerned in the production of coarse fabrics—tarpaulins, sail cloth, canvas, etc., which do not compete directly with cotton. In northern England, only Manchester and Barnsley retained a linen industry of any significance.

The Northern Ireland industry, by far the most important in the world, is concentrated in the Belfast area, where female labour is available and where coal can be imported cheaply from Cumberland

and Ayrshire. It now relies entirely on imported flax, Irish flax production having ceased. Currently, Belgium supplies nearly four-fifths of the imports, and the remainder are obtained from France, the Low Countries, the U.S.S.R., and Egypt (Table 101). Rayon is employed extensively, and much of the output from the linen mills now consists of mixed fabrics. Approximately 40 per cent. of the linen and mixed cloth production is exported. The U.S.A., Canada, Australia, and Italy are the largest buyers (Table 102).

TABLE 101

FLAX FIBRE IMPORTS INTO THE UNITED KINGDOM
(in thousands of tons)

Imports from—	1961	1963	1964
Belgium	17·4	19·3	19·2
U.S.S.R.	4·6	3·0	2·6
France	2·1	2·1	2·0
Netherlands	1·7	2·0	1·7
Egypt	0·5	1·6	0·9
TOTAL IMPORTS	26·7	28·0	26·4

Source: *Review of the Linen Industry*, 1965 *Supplement*, Government of Northern Ireland.

TABLE 102

EXPORTS (BY VALUE) OF LINEN GOODS FROM THE UNITED KINGDOM
(in £ thousands)

Exports to—	1962	1963	1966
U.S.A.	5,382	5,668	5,836
Italy	664	887	550
Canada	1,014	834	712
Australia	867	785	661
West Germany ..	753	614	501
Hong Kong	202	297	412
South Africa	266	294	278
New Zealand	258	276	268
WORLD	12,646	12,739	12,595

Source: *Review of Linen Industry*, 1967, Government of Northern Ireland.

THE JUTE INDUSTRY

The modern jute industry was born in Dundee in the 1820s when raw jute fibre was introduced from the Far East. The establishment of the industry was assisted by the existence of a tradition of textile manufacturing in the city, and by the fact that Dundee at that time was associated with the whaling industry. Whale oil was used to soften the fibres before spinning.

The jute industry soon spread to the Continent, and later to the fibre growing countries themselves. The first Indian mill was built in Calcutta in 1855. Expansion thereafter was rapid, and Hooghlyside quickly developed into the largest jute manufacturing region in the world. The growth of the Pakistani jute industry after 1948 was hardly less spectacular: within a decade and a half it had attained a position of importance second only to that of India. India and Pakistan now produce a large proportion of the world's requirements of packaging materials—sacks, baling cloth, etc.—while Britain and the continental countries have come to specialise more in the production of high quality materials such as carpets, carpet and linoleum backings, upholstery lining, and stiffening material for book covers, in which competition from low wage producers is not so acute.

TABLE 103

PRODUCTION OF JUTE YARNS AND FABRICS IN THE O.E.C.D. COUNTRIES
(in thousands of metric tons)

	1958		1963	
	YARNS	FABRICS	YARNS	FABRICS
United Kingdom	130·1	78·7	136·4	86·0
France	93·7	72·9	82·1	64·7
West Germany	76·4	60·0	55·7	43·4
Italy	44·0	41·3	49·2	41·0
Spain	42·8	41·6	39·5	35·3
Belgium-Luxembourg	73·4	33·2	79·3	27·9
Netherlands	10·0	14·5	10·2	15·7
Portugal	11·9	9·6	21·1	14·7

Source: *Textile Industry in O.E.C.D. Countries*, O.E.C.D., Paris, 1965.

MAN-MADE FIBRES

Man-made fibres fall into two groups. First, in point of time and present day importance, are the cellulosic fibres derived from the cellulose of plants. Rayon is by far the most important member of this group. Secondly there are the true synthetic fibres—nylon, "Orlon" and "Terylene" which have been synthesised in the chemical laboratory from materials such as coal, petroleum, limestone, and even air.

The commercial production of rayon began towards the end of the last century (Fig. 98). Development was slow until the 1920s when a process for making rayon staple was perfected. Rayon and other man-made staples are fibres of rayon or the synthetics, produced by cutting filament yarns into short pieces. Staples can be made to resemble natural fibres in length and thickness, and can be spun on the cotton, woollen, or worsted system, or combined with natural fibres in the production of a mixed yarn. Their advent marked the beginning of a period of expansion in the man-made fibre industries which has continued down to the present day.

Nylon was introduced in 1938, and was followed after the Second World War by "Orlon" and "Terylene". New discoveries are constantly being made. About 3,000 million pounds of synthetic fibre is now produced in the world each year, of which nylon comprises more than half.

Some advantages of the man-made fibres

1. As both the cellulosic and synthetic fibres are products of the chemical industry, their composition and quality can be precisely controlled. Production can be tailored to fit market requirements, and the problems of gluts, shortages, and fluctuating prices largely eliminated. Output is neither dependent on the weather nor on the control of insect pests. Once in full production, the price of man-made fibres remains remarkably stable, in contrast to the price of natural fibres which is subject to sudden variations. Between 1951 and 1953, for instance, whilst the price of clean, cross-bred wool varied from 4s. 6d. to 12s. 8d. per lb., the price of rayon staple moved by less than 2s. per lb. Substantial changes in raw material costs create special problems for the textile manufacturer, who must sell on a market sensitive to price fluctuations. To some extent production costs and selling prices can be stabilised by mixing, for example, cotton with rayon or wool with "Terylene" in proportions that can be varied according to the relative cost of each fibre prevailing at the time.

2. For some purposes man-made fibres are superior to natural fibres, and have replaced or are in process of replacing them. The substitution of nylon for silk in women's hosiery and of rayon filament for cotton in motor tyre manufacture are examples of this trend. Man-made and natural fibres can also be blended to produce fabrics which resemble cotton, wool, linen, or silk, but which are in effect new products, possessing characteristics of strength, durability, and resistance to creasing, fire, and water to a greater degree than materials made from natural fibres alone. One consequence of the development of mixed fibres has been to increase, rather than to reduce, the demand for cotton and wool. The consumption of cotton has increased by 100 per cent. during the last forty years, and wool by nearly 50 per cent. Long term price trends, however, are likely to favour the man-made fibres, and it is possible ultimately that the natural fibres will be displaced entirely, or their uses confined to luxury goods as silk now is.

3. An increase in the output of man-made fibres at the expense of cotton, wool, flax, jute, hemp, sisal, etc., would increase the area

available for food production. If the present rate of population growth were to continue, there would be some 6,000 million inhabitants of the world by the year A.D. 2000 and 12,000 million by A.D. 2040; that is, within the lifetime of some people already born. After all allowance has been made for the higher yields that will result from the application of more intensive production techniques to agriculture, it is unlikely that numbers of this magnitude can be fed without a substantial increase in the area devoted to food crops. Natural fibre production makes a heavy demand on land resources. In the season 1964-5, approximately 81 million acres were under cotton alone in various parts of the world, a further 5·8 million acres devoted to flax cultivation, and 4·6 million to jute. Wool is in a different category, as sheep tend to occupy land of low agricultural value, and produce wool as a joint product with mutton. However, it is probable that 5,000 million acres in the several continents are given over wholly or in part to sheep rearing. By contrast, hardly any land at all is consumed in the production of the true synthetic fibres, and rayon (which uses as its main raw material the wood of the spruce, a tree of the cold temperate regions) can be produced without encroaching to any important extent on areas capable of supporting food crops.

The location of the man-made fibres industries.—More than thirty countries now manufacture man-made fibres. The United States is the leading producer, followed by Japan, West Germany, and Great Britain (Tables 104 and 105). Because of their association with the textile industries, the first rayon plants were erected near existing cotton and wool manufacturing centres. In Britain, before the Second World War, they were found at Greenfield and Wrexham, in North Wales, and at Preston, Liverpool, and Coventry. To-day

TABLE 104
PRODUCTION OF RAYON FILAMENT AND STAPLE
(in thousands of metric tons)

	1948	1960	1964*
U.S.A.	409·9	466·5	649·5
Japan	32·2	433·5	489·9
U.S.S.R.	n/a	196·2	304·2
West Germany	107·7†	228·4	296·8
United Kingdom	106·1	207·6	247·8
Italy	65·5	161·6	213·4
France	58·4	118·6	148·0
East Germany	—	137·6	141·1
India	nil	42·9	78·8
WORLD	1,113·4	2,600·0	3,317·0

* Estimated. † Includes East Germany. n/a—not available.
Source: *U.N. Statistical Yearbook.*

the synthetic fibres industries are relatively "footloose", using raw materials in comparatively small quantities, and obtaining electric power from the National Grid. The most important localising factor, as in so many industries, is a copious supply of pure soft water. Since the war there has been a dispersal of man-made fibre plants from the north-west and the Midlands, into South Wales (Pontypool), Northern Ireland (Carrickfergus), and the north-east (Wilton, Billingham, and Grimsby). These shifts in location have been facilitated by improvements in communications and by the policies of successive governments to encourage the movement of industry into areas of persistent unemployment.

TABLE 105
PRODUCTION OF NON-CELLULOSIC FIBRES
(in thousands of metric tons)

	1960	1964*
U.S.A.	307·2	638·1
Japan	138·3	342·3
West Germany	52·3	139·9
United Kingdom	60·9	126·4
Italy	33·7	100·2
France	45·3	92·6
U.S.S.R.	15·0	56·9
Canada	16·0	29·8
East Germany	7·7	17·1
WORLD	705·0	1,505·0

* Estimated.

Source: *U.N. Statistical Yearbook.*

CHAPTER XVII

INTERNATIONAL TRADE

Trade is concerned with the business of exchange, and is a natural consequence of economic specialisation. Regional and international specialisation occur because the various factors of production—"land" or natural resources, labour, and capital—are not distributed evenly over the face of the earth, and because they are not completely mobile. Goods which are produced as a result of the utilisation of these factors, on the other hand, are highly mobile, and consequently can be more easily transported and exchanged against one another.

The mobility of the factors of production.—*Natural resources*, including climate and soils, are obviously immobile. Tin can be mined only where there are deposits of tin ore. Natural rubber and rice can be produced only where climatic and soil conditions are appropriate to the cultivation of the rubber tree, and rice plant, and so on. A nation in need of tin, rubber, or rice, but lacking the resources which make their production possible, has no alternative but to resort to trade.

Over short distances *labour* is highly mobile. Men will readily travel twenty or thirty miles from home to their places of employment so long as fast and convenient transport is available. The same men would be less willing to accept work farther afield because it would involve them in the cost and inconvenience of moving house, and also possibly in the problem of readjustment to their new social environment. Regional mobility is higher among the young than the old, higher among the professional than the working classes, and generally higher among immigrant groups than among the native population. Labour is immobile across international frontiers, at least in the short term. Only a very small proportion of a nation's work force migrates to a foreign country in any given year. Differences in customs and languages, as well as restrictive immigration laws, are normally very effective barriers to a mass movement of labour to better-paid employment abroad.

Mobility of capital.—Economists distinguish between *liquid* or *free* capital which is mobile, and *fixed* capital which is not. Much of a country's capital is locked away in fixed assets such as buildings, industrial plant, agricultural land, etc.—assets which have relevance only to the production of a limited range of commodities, and which cannot be transferred from place to place or from industry to industry. Liquid capital (which is built up out of savings from current and past production) is available in a free society for investment in whatever enterprise its holder deems appropriate. Generally it will flow, after due consideration has been taken of the risks involved, into those industries where its marginal productivity will be highest, or, in other words, into industries where it can earn the highest interest rates. Normally these industries will be found in the expanding sectors of an economy.

Within a stable society the degree of capital mobility varies from industry to industry, rather than from region to region. Sound economic enterprises in politically mature countries have little difficulty in attracting investment. Investment in the developing countries, where risks are greater and where many projects in need of capital are unattractive on purely commercial grounds, is often channelled through government and international, rather than through private, agencies.

Conditions in which benefits can accrue from international trade.— To simplify the discussion which follows, we will assume that trade takes place only between two countries (we will call these countries A and B), and that only two commodities (wheat and potatoes) enter into trade between them. Such an assumption in no way invalidates the principles upon which international trade is based. Exchange will be to the advantage of each country in the following circumstances.

Case I. If A can produce only wheat, and B can produce only potatoes.

Case II. If A can produce wheat more cheaply than B, and B can produce potatoes more cheaply than A. If each country divides a given value of its productive resources (say £100 worth) equally between wheat and potatoes, then the result might be:

A produces	*B produces*
50 *units of wheat @ £1 per unit plus*	50 *units of potatoes @ £1 per unit plus*
25 *units of potatoes @ £2 per unit.*	20 *units of wheat @ £2·5 per unit.*

Total wheat production = 70 *units.*
Total potato production = 75 *units.*

Each country now specialises in the production of the commodity for which its comparative cost advantage is greater;

A produces	*B produces*
100 *units of wheat @ £1 per unit.*	100 *units of potatoes @ £1 per unit.*

Total wheat production = 100 *units.*
Total potato production = 100 *units.*

Case III. If A produces both wheat and potatoes more cheaply than B. If no specialisation takes place, and each country now devotes £100 of its resources to the production of each crop in the proportions that best meet its requirements, then:

A decides to produce	*B decides to produce*
75 *units of wheat* @ £1 *per unit plus*	20 *units of potatoes* @ £2 *per unit plus*
20 *units of potatoes* @ £1·25 *per unit.*	20 *units of wheat* @ £3 *per unit.*

Total wheat production = 95 *units.*
Total potato production = 40 *units.*

A now specialises in the production of wheat, for which its comparative cost advantage is greater, and B specialises in potatoes:

A produces	*B produces*
100 *units of wheat* @ £1 *per unit.*	50 *units of potatoes* @ £2 *per unit.*

In Cases II and III, the total production of each commodity has increased as a result of specialisation, and both A and B will gain, so long as they can exchange the commodity of which they have a surplus for the commodity they have elected not to produce at all. The rate at which wheat will be exchanged for potatoes will depend on production costs and the demand for wheat and potatoes in each country. In Case III, A will be prepared to exchange some of her wheat at a rate which gives her *more* than four units of potatoes for five units of wheat, because in order to produce four units of potatoes with her own resources (@ £1·25 per unit) she would have to forgo five units of wheat (@ £1 per unit). B, on the other hand, will be prepared to trade some of her potatoes for wheat at a rate which gives her *more* than two units of wheat for three units of potatoes since the cost of producing wheat in B is one and a half times the cost of producing potatoes. Expressed another way:

A will accept a rate which gives her *more than* 5 units of wheat to 4 units of potatoes, *i.e.* $1\frac{1}{4} : 1$.

B will accept a rate which gives her *not less than* 2 units of wheat for 3 units of potatoes, *i.e.* $\frac{2}{3} : 1$.

One unit of wheat will therefore exchange for between two-thirds of a unit, and one and a quarter units of potatoes. The precise rate will depend on the demand for each commodity in A and B.

The effect of transport costs.—The cost of transport will increase the price of a commodity in the importing country by an amount equivalent to the transport charge. In many instances this will be sufficient to offset any differences in production costs, and will therefore remove the advantages that would otherwise be gained from trade. On the other hand, transport costs on imported goods may be lower than on identical goods produced in a distant part of the importing country. Certain types of steel, for instance, can be carried more cheaply from Britain to Bombay than from Jamshedpur to Bombay. For the same reason a two-way trade in *identical* products sometimes develops between countries sharing a common frontier of great length. It is important, however, to note whether or not products appearing on both the export and import lists of a country are in fact identical, or whether they are merely grouped together under one heading for administrative convenience (see Table 100). The position can be illustrated by reference to the export trade in motor vehicles. Each day vessels leave British ports with shipments of vehicles bound for Continental markets, and the following day the same vessels return carrying cargoes of Continental vehicles for sale in Britain. The out-going and in-coming cargoes are, of course, actually made up of quite different products.

The terms of trade.—The rate at which exports exchange for imports is known as the *terms of trade.* A rise in the price of exports relative to the price of imports will result in an improvement in the terms of trade for the exporting country, as fewer exports will have to be given than formerly to obtain the same value of imports. During the last decade the terms of trade of the manufacturing countries, including the United Kingdom, have improved, while those of the primary producers have tended to worsen (Table 106).

TABLE 106

TERMS OF TRADE OF THE UNITED KINGDOM

1961 = 100

1954	87	1958	96	1962	102
1955	86	1959	96	1963	101
1956	87	1960	97	1964	99
1957	89	1961	100	1965	102

N.B.—A rise in the index represents a relative increase in the average price of exports. In 1954, for example, 100 units of exports were exchanged for 87 units of imports: in 1965, 100 units of exports purchased 102 units of imports.

Source: *Board of Trade Journal.*

Types of trade

BILATERAL TRADE.—Trade between two countries only, in which a given value of goods changes hands, is known as bilateral trade. No trade at all can develop on a bilateral basis unless each country has a surplus of the particular commodity the other is demanding, and the extent of the trade will be determined by the smaller of the two demands.

Bilateral trading increased considerably during the 1930s, when the pattern of world trade that had become established during the nineteenth and early twentieth centuries was disrupted by the great depression. As one country after another tried, usually without much success, to stimulate industrial activity and employment at home by cutting down the quantity of imported goods to a minimum, the volume of international trade shrank. The acceptance of imports was often made conditional upon a recriprocal agreement whereby exports were taken in direct exchange. Bilateral trading continued during the Second World War and into the difficult period that followed it, and was encouraged by the practice of state trading. In more recent times the proportion of goods traded bilaterally has declined, largely as a result of the activities of such organisations as G.A.T.T. (General Agreement on Tariffs and Trade), I.M.F. (International Monetary Fund), E.E.C., and E.F.T.A.

Barter is a form of bilateral trade in which goods are exchanged without the medium of money. It is of no importance to-day outside primitive societies.

MULTILATERAL TRADE.—The transfer of goods and services among several countries without any direct exchange being necessarily involved is known as multilateral trade. No basis for direct trade exists, for example, between any pair of countries in Fig. 101. Country A cannot purchase D's surplus cotton, which it needs, because it has nothing to offer D in return. Similarly, C has nothing acceptable to B in exchange for B's timber, and so on. If, however, the four countries agree to an exchange of surpluses as indicated in the diagram, trade can take place to the advantage of all.

Free trade and protection.—The doctrine of free trade stems from the belief that the maximum economic advantages are to be obtained only when all legitimate articles of commerce are permitted to move without restriction across international frontiers. The world, it is argued, can then function as a single economic unit in which each country has the greatest incentive to specialise in the production of those commodities for which it is best suited by nature. This state promotes a growth in efficiency, a reduction in costs, and a fall in prices.

Britain was a free trade country from the time of the Repeal of the Corn Laws until 1914. As the leading manufacturing nation in the world she found her interests best served by securing, as far as she was able, unrestricted access to foreign markets, and by allowing imports from overseas—which were mainly food and industrial raw materials—to enter without restraint. Abroad, however, the advantages of free trade were not so self-evident. Foreign industry found competition with established British producers very difficult, and clamoured for protection. Tariffs were erected in the United States to keep out manufactured goods from the Old World, and then in France, Germany, and other European countries to curtail agricultural imports from the New. Japan's growing manufacturing industries also sheltered behind a tariff barrier. Free trade also

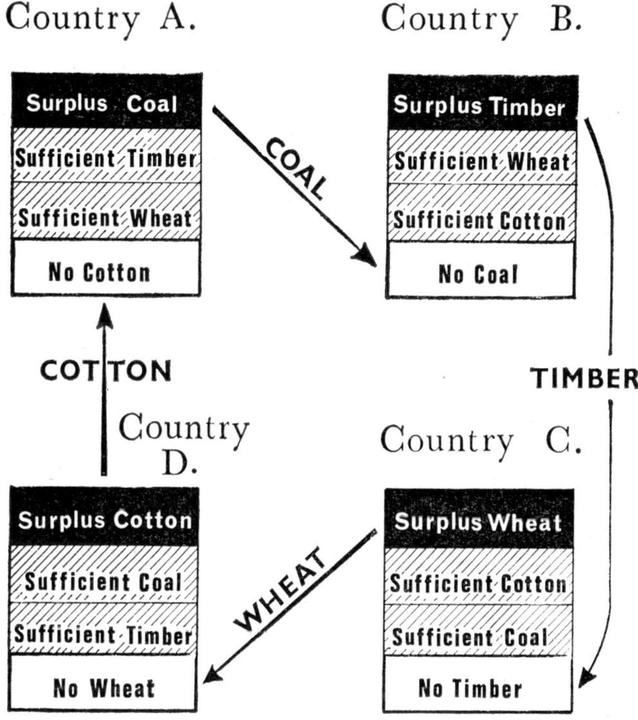

Fig. 101.—The Principle of Multilateral Trade.

began to lose much of its attraction as a practical policy during and after the First World War in Britain, and eventually had to be abandoned as world commerce became stifled during the 1930s. Protectionism became the order of the day, and so it remained until after 1945, when efforts were made to liberalise trade, both at a regional and international level.

Arguments for protection.—Advocates of economic protection would state their case as follows:

1. That in the present uncertain political situation it behoves a country to insulate itself as far as possible from the events of the outside world by attaining a fair measure of self-sufficiency. This argument carries considerable force. Twice during the present century world wars have severed international channels of trade with serious consequences for belligerents and neutral countries alike. Action can also be taken during peace time against a nation's economy for political reasons: the sanctions against Rhodesia and the American attempt to isolate Cuba are cases in point. It is usually conceded that protection in the interests of national security involves a cost to the community, but, it is argued, the cost is worth paying.

2. That protection helps to raise the level of employment at home. Thus, if domestic and foreign industry are in competition, the exclusion of the foreigner from the home market will stimulate activity in the domestic industry. The outcry for protection on these grounds in times of depression and unemployment is very difficult to resist, but the consequences of not resisting must be faced. They are, first, that the product which it is desired to exclude would not be imported at all unless it were cheaper than or of superior quality to the competing home product. A partial or total exclusion of imports, therefore, would serve only to raise the price of the product on the home market. Higher prices would result in a demand for higher wages, and higher wages in turn would increase production costs generally and so reduce the competitive advantage of the exporting industries. Secondly, protection of home industries would invite retaliation overseas. Thirdly, to the extent that protection were successful, it would transfer unemployment from the importing to the exporting country, and thereby reduce the ability of the latter to buy abroad.

3. That the exclusion of goods produced in countries employing "sweated" labour helps to maintain living standards in the developed countries. This is of course a fallacy, as the community as a whole cannot fail to be impoverished if denied access to cheap goods. It is also a mistake to suppose that import restrictions can do otherwise than depress wages in the poorer countries still further, by reducing the demand for labour in them. There is also a certain amount of special pleading in the "sweated labour" argument. It is always a curb on the import of goods in competition with home-produced goods that is demanded. No one in authority in Britain has yet advocated the exclusion of Far East rubber, palm oil, or tin on the

grounds that labour on the plantations and in the mines is not properly rewarded.

4. That many countries are destined to remain primary producers, dominated by the economically advanced nations and subject to the slumps and booms of the commodity markets, unless their developing industries are protected from open competition with the established manufacturers. This is the "infant industry" argument. Often, however, protection is given to industries that have little hope of ever becoming viable, and once given it is apt to be retained. Infant industries, in other words, do not always grow up.

Instruments of protection

TARIFFS.—A tariff is a levy on imported goods. Custom duties paid by travellers returning from overseas are tariffs. If imposed primarily to raise revenue, tariffs are normally restricted to goods having an inelastic demand, and are made to apply to the home produced as well as the imported product. The tax on petrol is an example. Most tariffs, however, are designed to reduce demand for imported goods by making them more expensive than similar home produced articles. Tariffs can be used to discriminate between groups of products and between producers. British tariffs are thus lower on food and raw materials than on manufactured articles. They amount to 30 per cent. on cars, watches, and clocks; 26 per cent. on clothing; 14 per cent. on steel, but no levy is imposed at all on imported newsprint and wheat. British tariffs are also lower on Commonwealth than on non-Commonwealth goods.[1] Unlike quotas, tariffs impose no absolute limit on the volume or value of goods that can enter. Provided the imports can surmount the tariff barrier, as they might do comfortably if costs of production in the exporting country were to fall, they can enter in any quantity.

QUOTAS.—A quota sets an upper limit on the volume of goods that are admitted into a country. Occasionally a global quota is fixed, in which case there is likely to be a free-for-all among exporters until the quota limits have been reached, but more commonly quotas are allocated among suppliers on a share basis. Quotas are more effective instruments of protection than tariffs, and distort the pattern of trade more completely. They were widely employed during the inter-war period, when tariffs by themselves failed to check imports of cheap foreign goods.

[1] Tariffs on imports of manufactured goods from the E.F.T.A. countries into Britain were finally abolished on 1st January, 1967.

SUBSIDIES.—Payments made by governments in order to reduce the price of a commodity on the home market, or alternatively to encourage its export, constitute another form of trade interference. The British farm subsidy outlined in Chapter V is in effect a form of discrimination against foreign suppliers of agricultural commodities, and its impact on trade is substantially the same as a tariff.

The balance of trade, and the balance of payments.—There is much misunderstanding about the precise meaning and significance of these terms. The *balance of trade* is the sum total of the differences between a country's *visible* exports and imports: it takes into account tangible items of trade only, *i.e.* merchandise. An excess of exports over imports is referred to as a *favourable* or *active balance*, and an excess of imports over exports as an *unfavourable* or *adverse balance.* A favourable balance is not necessarily good, and an unfavourable balance not necessarily bad, for the trading country. For a century prior to 1939 Britain had an adverse trade balance, and only after 1945, when her commercial problems really began, did the balance improve. The point of the matter is that a country's visible trade forms only a part, although normally a very substantial part, of its transactions with the outside world (Table 107).

The *balance of payments* represents the balance of *all* transactions with foreign countries. As well as merchandise it includes the invisible items for which payments are made and receipts taken in respect of services rendered. Earnings of shipping and airline companies engaged in carrying passengers and freight on behalf of other nations, the expenditure of visiting tourists, interest received on capital invested abroad, loans from foreign governments or private bodies, etc., bring money into a country, and are reckoned as *invisible exports.* On the other hand, payment made to foreign transport services, loans and gifts to other countries, the expenditure by a country's nationals travelling abroad, interest paid on foreign investments in the home country, etc., all involve outgoing payments, and thus rank as *invisible imports.* It was the income from invisible transactions, notably from interest received from investments made in the Commonwealth, the Argentine, and other overseas territories (in 1938 they brought in £205 million—equal to some £600 million at present day values) that made it possible for Britain to run a deficit on her balance of trade, without encountering the sort of economic crises that now seem to trouble us biennially.

A moment's thought will make it clear that a country must balance its accounts. Everything that it imports has to be paid for. The important issue for a nation's economic health is how these payments are made. Current debts may be settled in the following ways, some of which are manifestly more likely to lead to long term financial difficulties than others:

1. By selling goods and services to the value of those purchased.

2. By borrowing, on promise to pay later (long and short term loans).

3. By the transfer of gold or currencies of universal acceptance, or by the sale of overseas assets. (These are entered under the heading "Monetary Movements" in Table 107.)

TABLE 107

U.K. BALANCE OF PAYMENTS, 1963
(in £ millions)

	EXPORTS (Credits)	IMPORTS (Debits)
1. CURRENT ACCOUNT		
Visible trade:		
Merchandise (f.o.b.)[1]	4,286	4,335
Invisible Trade:		
Government[2]	42	429
Shipping	660	671
Civil Aviation	124	101
Travel	199	244
Other Services	494	275
Interest, Profits, and Dividends	782	405
Private Transfers	112	126
Total Invisible Trade	2,413	2,251
Total Trade, Visible + Invisible	6,699	6,586
2. LONG TERM CAPITAL ACCOUNT		
Inter-governmental Loans (net)		97
U.K. Subscription to I.F.C.[3]		
I.D.A.[4] and European Fund		9
Other U.K. Official Long Term Capital	1	
Private Investment abroad		309
Private Investment in the U.K.	259	
Total	260	415
Balancing Item[5]		111
Total Current and Long Term Trade and Transactions, Visible and Invisible	6,959	7,112
3. MONETARY MOVEMENTS		
Changes in Gold and Convertible Currencies, etc.	153	
BALANCE	7,112	7,112

NOTES.—[1] f.o.b.—"free on board", *i.e.* the value of the merchandise at the exporting port. Shipping and insurance charges are excluded.

[2] Government.—All transactions in goods and services between the U.K. Government and overseas countries not appropriate to other items in the accounts.

[3] I.F.C.—International Finance Corporation.

[4] I.D.A.—International Development Association.

[5] Balancing Item.—Many of the items in the Current and Long Term Capital Account are estimates. The Balancing Item represents the net total of all errors and omissions occurring elsewhere in the table.

Source: *United Kingdom Balance of Payments.* Central Statistical Office.

Common Markets and Free Trade areas.—The aim of a true common market is the economic fusion of a group of independent and more or less geographically contiguous states into a single customs union, in which all restrictions on the movement of goods, services, capital, and labour are eliminated. A common tariff, however, is maintained against the outside world. A Free Trade association, on the other hand, while it works for the removal of tariffs and other forms of trade restriction among member nations, does not seek to protect itself behind a common external tariff barrier.

The first real customs union took shape during the first half of the nineteenth century when all trade barriers between the several German states were abolished. This was the *Zollverein.* It paved the way for the rapid industrialisation of Germany, and was followed by political unification in 1871. The United States is another customs union, embracing a population of nearly 200 million. The Commonwealth, by contrast, has fallen far short of becoming a true economic union, for while its members have given preference to trade with one another, rather than to the rest of the world, they have not hesitated to impose tariffs against each other when it has suited them to do so.

The present trade blocs of Europe, Latin America, and Africa arose out of the changed economic relationships that developed after the Second World War. The new groupings tend to cut across the traditional trading patterns of the nineteenth and early twentieth centuries. Since 1945 manufacturing countries have sought integration with other manufacturing countries, and primary producing states with other primary producers.

The motives which inspired the setting up of the European Economic Community were complex, for as well as the desire to stimulate industry and raise living standards through the liberalisation of trade among its member nations, there was also the strongly held belief that economic integration, and ultimately a measure of political unification were necessary as the only means of healing the division of the continent that had twice plunged the world into war. In Latin America and Africa the reasons for integration were somewhat different. The Latin American and African countries are essentially primary producers whose traditional roles have been to supply the economically developed regions with food and raw materials. As appendages to one or other of the Western powers they were for ever likely to remain (or so they argued) hewers of wood and drawers of water. Acting individually they saw little hope for themselves, but collectively they felt capable of establishing closed but viable trading areas, in which they would be assured of a market from which outsiders would be excluded. In the case of the African states there was the added incentive to use their newly acquired independence to determine their own associations as they wished.

THE EUROPEAN ECONOMIC COMMUNITY (E.E.C., and also known simply as the "Common Market" or the "Six") is an organisation of six West European countries—Belgium, the Netherlands, Luxembourg, France, West Germany, and Italy—which was established by the Treaty of Rome in 1957. It is committed to a complete removal of all internal trade restrictions by 1969. In 1967 internal tariffs were reduced to 15 per cent. of their 1957 levels, and in the same year a common external tariff came into operation. The long term objective of E.E.C. is political unification. The productive capacity of the Community is second only to that of the United States. It is the most rapidly expanding economic region outside the communist world. One-quarter of all international trade originates in the region, and trade between member countries amounts to 10 per cent. of the world total.

Nineteen African states, including Nigeria and many of the former French colonies, are Associate Members of the Six. The agreement associating the African territories with Europe provides, among other advantages, for the progressive lowering of tariffs on African imports to the level where they will eventually enjoy unrestricted access to E.E.C. markets.

THE EUROPEAN FREE TRADE AREA (E.F.T.A. or the "Seven") consists of Britain, Norway, Sweden, Denmark, Austria, Switzerland, and Portugal (Fig. 102). Finland is associated with the group. E.F.T.A. was established in 1960 after negotiations for a wider free trade area embracing the E.E.C. states had failed. Its aim is the abolition of all tariffs between member countries, but unlike E.E.C. it has no intention of forming a closed trading area by setting up a common external tariff. With the exception of Norway, which was allowed to retain a few tariffs until 1969, and Portugal, which was permitted a slower rate of tariff removal because of its less developed state, the countries of E.F.T.A. became, on 1st January, 1967, a single market, free of internal trading restrictions on manufactured goods. The trade between the E.F.T.A. countries and the rest of the world is only slightly less in value than that of the E.E.C. members, while its per capita value exceeds that of any other economic grouping. About one-half of this trade originates in the United Kingdom.

C.O.M.E.C.O.N., or the Council for Mutual Economic Assistance, embraces the Soviet Union and the communist states of Eastern Europe. It was established in January, 1949, to liberalise trade among the member nations, and to act as an organisation through which credit could be made available for economic development. No real attempt has been made, however, to set up a true customs union or free trade area. Opposition to closer economic integration among some members is, in fact, strong.

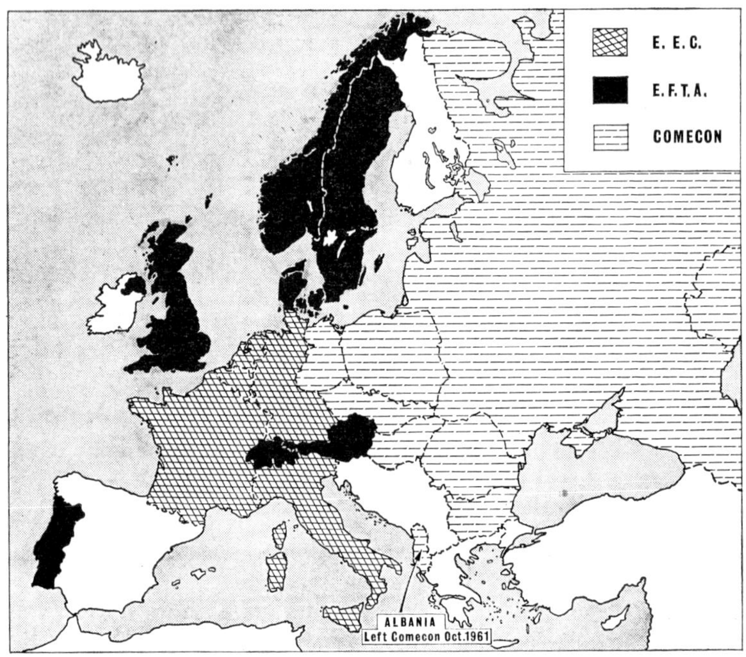

Fig. 102.—European Trade Groupings.

The Latin American Free Trade Association (L.A.F.T.A.) came into being in 1960 with the signing of the Treaty of Montevideo. Mexico and all the independent states of South America, with the exception of Venezuela (which has announced its intention of joining) and Bolivia, are members. The difficulties of integration are much more formidable than they are in Europe. The region is huge. Substantial parts of it lie outside the effective political control of the various national governments. No north to south transcontinental railway or motor road exists, and sea communications between Latin America and the countries of Europe are better developed than between the L.A.F.T.A. members themselves. Unlike the European countries which traded extensively with each other before they bound themselves together by economic treaties, those of Latin America have always traded primarily with the outside world (Tables 108 and 109), Only 7 per cent. of the total trade

Fig. 103.—TRADE GROUPINGS OF LATIN AMERICA.

of Latin America in 1960 was between states that signed the Treaty of Montevideo. The proportion has now risen to about 10 per cent. There are indications that the upward trend will continue, but it will still be many years before countries which are essentially primary producers can free themselves of economic dependence upon the manufacturing nations.

TABLE 108

LATIN AMERICAN FREE TRADE AREA

Member Countries	Area (square miles)	Population (in thousands)	Principal Exports	Main Export Destinations	Percentage of Export Trade with other Latin American Countries
Argentina	1,072,000	22,352	Livestock products, cereals, vegetable oils	Italy, U.K., Netherlands, West Germany, Brazil	15
Brazil	3,286,400	82,200	Coffee, iron ore, cotton ..	U.S.A., West Germany, Argentine, Netherlands, Italy	5
Chile	292,250	8,600	Copper, nitrates	U.S.A., West Germany, U.K., Japan, Netherlands	10
Colombia	439,500	17,482	Coffee, petroleum	U.S.A., West Germany, Netherlands, Trinidad	2
Ecuador	105,680	5,140	Bananas, coffee, cocoa ..	U.S.A., West Germany, Japan	1
Mexico	761,600	40,913	Cotton, coffee	U.S.A., Japan	4
Paraguay	157,050	1,949	Meat, timber, cotton, oilseeds, tobacco, quebracho extract	U.S.A., Argentine, U.K., Uruguay	28
Peru	469,200	11,351	Fish meal, copper, cotton, sugar, silver, lead	U.S.A., West Germany, Japan, Netherlands, U.K.	10
Uruguay	68,536	2,682	Meat, wool, hides, and skins	U.K., Netherlands, Italy, West Germany, U.S.A.	10

Source: *Britannica Book of the Year.*

TABLE 109

CENTRAL AMERICAN COMMON MARKET

Member Countries	Area (square miles)	Population (in thousands)	Principal Exports	Main Exports Destinations	Percentage of Export Trade with other Latin American Countries
Costa Rica	19,652	1,420	Coffee, bananas	U.S.A., West Germany, El Salvador	6
Guatemala	42,042	4,278	Coffee, cotton, bananas ..	U.S.A., West Germany, Japan	9
Honduras	43,277	2,163	Bananas, coffee, timber, silver	U.S.A., El Salvador, West Germany	16
Nicaragua	50,193	1,597	Cotton, coffee, gold	U.S.A., Japan, West Germany	16
El Salvador	8,260	2,918	Coffee, cotton	West Germany, U.S.A., Japan, Guatemala ..	20

Source: *Britannica Book of the Year.*

The Central America Common Market includes the republics of Costa Rica, El Salvador, Guatemala, Honduras, and Nicaragua. The total population of the group is only about 12 million. Lack of capital for development, exceedingly difficult internal lines of communication, political immaturity, and a low level of trade which is orientated almost entirely towards the outside world will make integration a very slow business. However, it is expected that as the economy of the region develops other countries may join, and that eventually the Central American Common Market will merge with L.A.F.T.A.

Africa.—Little more than a decade ago there was but a handful of independent countries on the whole of the African continent. Most African states were colonies of various European powers, particularly of Britain and France. When independence was granted to the colonial territories it was along the lines of existing political boundaries which took into little account factors of physical, human, or economic geography. Many of the newly independent states are too small to be viable entities. No fewer than nineteen have populations less than 4 million. All are primary producers, and maintain strong trading connections with the countries of industrial Europe—connections which have survived the changed political relationships. Self-government has resulted in a natural reluctance on the part of some states to submerge their identities in a larger grouping which would almost certainly be dominated by the more powerful members. A number of embryonic trade blocs are emerging, however, which have as their objects the economic co-operation of member states, and the strengthening of their hands against E.E.C. and E.F.T.A., viz.

1. The former British colonies.
2. The former French colonies, or the "Brazzaville Group".
3. The "Casablanca Group" which includes some of the former British and French colonies, *i.e.* Ghana, Guinea, Mali, Morocco, together with Egypt.
4. The "Monrovia Group" which includes members of the Brazzaville Group, as well as Ethiopia, Liberia, Libya, Nigeria, Sierra Leone, Somalia, Togo, and Tunisia.

The direction of world trade

In 1965 merchandise worth 184,000 million U.S. dollars (about £75,000 million) crossed international frontiers. Great as this figure undoubtedly is, it nevertheless represents only a very small fraction of the value of goods traded internally. Indeed, the total value of foreign trade is equal only to approximately one-half of the value of goods produced annually in the United States, and about two and a half times the value of all goods and services produced each year in the United Kingdom.

The several countries of the world do not share equally in the exchange of goods. Neither is the contribution of each nation related to its size, population, or productive capacity. The United Kingdom contributes a greater share of world exports than all the Latin American countries combined, although its population is only one-fifth as large. Approximately one-quarter of the United Kingdom's economic effort goes into the production of goods and services for consumption by people living abroad. The export industries, in fact, earn £85 worth of foreign currency each year for every man, woman, and child living in these islands. By contrast, foreign trade brings in about £15 per head to the people of Latin America as a whole. In Paraguay the figure is £10 and in Haiti, £3.

TABLE 110

VALUE OF WORLD EXPORTS
(in thousand million U.S. dollars, f.o.b.)

	1953	1957	1958	1959	1960
TOTAL	78·8	109·3	105·7	113·6	126·1
Primary products	41·8	53·2	49·8	52·2	56·2
Manufactured products ..	35·6	55·3	54·7	60·0	68·6
Manufactured products as percentage of total ..	45·5	50·4	51·7	52·8	54·5
	1961	**1962**	**1963**	**1964**	**1965**
TOTAL	131·9	139·0	151·7	169·8	186·2
Primary products	58·0	57·9	65·1	70·9	74·0
Manufactured products ..	72·4	77·9	84·6	97·6	108·0
Manufactured products as percentage of total ..	54·9	56·8	55·8	57·0	58·7

Source: *U.N. Yearbook of International Trade Statistics.*

N.B.—No allowance has been made in this table for changes in the value of money.

The pattern of world commerce that developed during the first half of the nineteenth century was based on an exchange of European manufactured goods for the raw materials of the undeveloped lands. The trade in primary products is still very important, and its value rises year by year, but its percentage share is steadily declining (Table 110). Very significant changes have also taken place in the primary producing lands themselves during the last 100 years. Many of them have become major industrial nations. One rarely thinks now-a-days of the United States as a primary producer, but the value of output from its farms and mines exceeds that of any other country in the world. The small volume of exports now generated by the under-developed primary producers—the countries of Africa, Latin America, and southern Asia—comes about because the bulk of the trade in raw materials originates today in parts of the world that are also highly industrialised (Table 111).

TABLE 111

DIRECTION OF WORLD TRADE. PERCENTAGE (BY VALUE) OF TOTAL TRADE BY ORIGIN AND DESTINATION, 1964

EXPORTS FROM: → / EXPORTS TO: ↓	Manufacturing Countries	Primary Producing Countries Group 1	Primary Producing Countries Group 2	Sino-Soviet Area	World
Manufacturing Countries	32·0	8·0	13·5	2·5	56·0
Primary Producing Countries Group 1 (Australia, New Zealand, South Africa, and Primary Producing Countries in Europe)	8·0	0·5	1·5	0·5	10·5
Primary Producing Countries Group 2 (all other Primary Producers) ..	14·0	1·5	4·0	1·5	21·0
Sino-Soviet Area	2·0	0·5	2·0	8·0	12·5
WORLD	56·0	10·5	21·0	12·5	100

Source: *Britannica Book of the Year.*

By far the most important trading region of the world is Western Europe. Some 40 per cent. of all exports originate in the countries of E.E.C. and E.F.T.A. The United Kingdom alone accounts for 7 per cent. of the world total. These values represent visible trade only. If the exports of services were added in, the European contribution would be even more impressive.

The great volume of trade generated in the countries of Europe stems from two causes. First, incomes and living standards are higher than in any other region of comparable size outside North America, and consequently economic demand is not only great in total volume but also in diversity. Even in countries well developed industrially there are many goods that cannot be produced as satisfactorily at home as abroad. Secondly, the European continent is very fragmented, politically. Countries are small and far from self-sufficient, especially in primary products. Britain, for example, must import (among many other items) 75 per cent. of her wheat and flour requirements, 70 per cent. of her sugar, half her iron ore, virtually all her metal ores, and every single fibre of raw cotton and jute. The home production of some commodities now brought from overseas could be increased—provided we were prepared to pay the price—and substitutes could be found for others, but there is a host of items on the import list of this country that could not be produced at home, for which there are no real substitutes, but which are, nevertheless, indispensable to a tolerable standard of life. Trade, of course, is vital to the Soviet Union and the U.S.A., but it is the volume of internal trade that matters most to them. International commerce may be more than a luxury in both cases, but in neither is it a matter of life and death. Transactions between the Ukraine and Siberia, or between New York State and Pennsylvania, however, do not appear in the international trade accounts. If Europe were ever united politically, the huge volume of goods that now passes among its separate states would also cease to be international in character, and would disappear from the statistics.

A noteworthy feature of the trading accounts of recent years has been in the imbalances in the trade of the United Kingdom and the United States. In spite of improvements in her *balance of trade* position since the Second World War, Britain has imported goods worth more than she exported, and has balanced her accounts by the export of "services", and in some years by borrowing heavily from abroad. The United States, on the other hand, has been a net importer of merchandise, and has corrected her trade balance by massive overseas investment programmes, and making gifts and loans to foreign countries.

The composition of world trade

TRADE IN MANUFACTURED GOODS.—It is not possible in a chapter of this length to discuss in detail the bewildering array of manufactured articles that pass into international trade. Students wishing to pursue the subject are referred to the Standard International Trade Classification Lists which appear in the *United Nations Yearbook of Trade Statistics* and in publications dealing with the commodity trade of individual countries. The *Annual Abstract of Statistics* gives a useful summary of the trade of the United Kingdom. The *Statistical Abstract of the United States* is an invaluable source of information on the U.S.A. These books are available in any good public library.

TABLE 112

EXPORTS OF PRODUCTS OF THE ENGINEERING INDUSTRIES, 1964
(in millions of U.S. dollars)

	Machinery		Transport	Total Engineering
	Non-electrical	Electrical	Equipment	Products
U.S.A.	4,719	1,654	2,978	9,350
West Germany	3,588	1,312	2,632	7,531
United Kingdom	2,403	882	1,828	5,113
France	911	499	943	2,302
Japan	481	638	839	1,958
Italy	863	342	641	1,846
U.S.S.R.	409	109	463	1,636
Netherlands	331	558	432	1,341
East Germany	712	258	325	1,296
Sweden	557	219	459	1,255
Czechoslovakia	n/a	n/a	n/a	1,241
Belgium-Luxembourg	374	233	430	1,037
Canada	435	118	393	946
Switzerland	603	181	11	795
Poland	201	72	212	716
Hungary	193	93	166	452
Denmark	240	85	106	430
Austria	161	86	48	295
Norway	57	23	107	187
Yugoslavia	49	39	64	152

Over 90 per cent. of the world exports in engineering products originate in countries shown in this table.

Source: *Bulletin of Statistics on World Trade in Engineering Products.*

TABLE 113

LEADING AGRICULTURAL PRODUCTS OF WORLD TRADE, 1964
(in millions of dollars)

Wheat and wheat flour	3,860
Raw sugar	2,475
Raw cotton	2,350
Coffee	2,330
Raw wool	2,200
Meat, fresh, chilled or frozen (all types)	1,960
Maize	1,260
Tobacco (unmanufactured)	1,170
Tea	670
Soya beans	610
Butter	580
Citrus fruit (all types)	530
Cocoa beans	525
Bananas	350

Source: *F.A.O. Trade Yearbook.*

Products of the engineering industries constitute the most valuable items of foreign trade. Electrical and non-electrical machinery, together with transport equipment, account for nearly 40 per cent. of all trade in manufactured articles. The twenty leading exporters of these products are listed in Table 112. The absence from the table of African, Latin American, and (with the single exception of Japan) Asian countries should be noted.

Other important groups of manufactured goods traded internationally on a large scale include textiles and clothing (valued at nearly 10,000 million dollars annually), chemicals and petroleum products, finished and semi-finished iron and steel products, and paper and paperboard.

TABLE 114

INTERNATIONAL COMMODITY TRADE OF THE UNITED KINGDOM AND THE UNITED STATES, 1964

S.I.T.C.*	UNITED KINGDOM (in £ millions)		UNITED STATES (in millions of dollars)	
	IMPORTS (c.i.f.)	EXPORTS (f.o.b.)	IMPORTS (f.o.b.)	EXPORTS (f.o.b.)
Food and live animals	1,624·6	159·2	3,486·3	3,982·6
Beverages and tobacco†	148·8	123·8	494·3	554·4
Crude materials, inedible (except fuel)	1,065·6	152·6	2,843·0	2,951·5
Mineral fuels and lubricants ..	584·9	138·8	1,996·1	911·5
Animal and vegetable oils and fats	53·6	5·8	114·2	433·7
Chemicals	252·5	412·2	706·7	2,374·8
Manufactured goods‡	920·6	983·0	4,523·6	3,201·1
Machinery and transport equipment	545·0	1,825·9	2,201·2	9,350·3
Miscellaneous manufactured articles	292·2	314·8	1,643·3	1,715·2
Commodities and transactions not elsewhere specified	25·7	138·1	591·3	610·9
TOTALS	5,513·5	4,254·2	18,600·0	26,086·0

Source: *Yearbook of International Trade Statistics*, United Nations.

* Standard International Trade Classification.

† Mainly alcoholic beverages; coffee, tea, and cocoa are included with "food and live animals".

‡ Iron and steel goods, textiles, etc.

NOTE.—[1] U.K. imports are given c.i.f. (cost, insurance, and freight), *i.e.* value of goods at the importing port. Exports are given f.o.b. (free on board), *i.e.* value at the port of exportation.

[2] Both U.S.A. imports and exports are given f.o.b.

[3] c.i.f. values are 10 per cent. to 15 per cent. above f.o.b. values.

TRADE IN PRIMARY COMMODITIES.—A primary commodity can be defined as a product that has undergone no fundamental change as a result of processing or manufacture. In this category are placed all unprocessed foodstuffs; all industrial raw materials produced from farm and forest land and from the sea; and all fuels and mineral ores.

The most valuable group of primary products are the foodstuffs. These were estimated to be worth more than 32,000 million dollars in 1964 (Table 113). Fuels made up the second most important commodity group, and were valued at 17,000 million dollars. Petroleum was by far the most important item in this group, both by value and weight. More than 500 million tons of petroleum now pass into international trade annually. By comparison, the export of solid fuels amounts to some 160 million tons. Of the mineral ores, iron ore is the leading commodity. More than 150 million tons were shipped abroad from the producing countries in 1964.

The commodity trade of two of the world's largest trading nations is set out in Table 114.

FURTHER READING

CHAPTER I

1. "The Earth's Capacity to Provide Food." COLIN CLARK, *New Scientist*, Vol. **8**, No. 195, August 1960.
2. "Must we all live in South East England?—The Location of New Employment." MICHAEL CHISHOLM, *Geography*, No. 222, Vol. **49**, Part 1, January 1964.
3. "Population Changes in England, 1951-61." M. F. TANNER, *Geography*, No. 213, Vol. **46**, Part 4, November 1961.
4. "The New Towns of Britain." K. C. EDWARDS, *Geography*, No. 224, Vol. **49**, Part 3, 1964.
5. "Metropolitan Influences in Oxford Region." D. I. SCARGILL, *Geography*, No. 235, Vol. **52**, Part 2, April 1967.
6. "Population Trends in the Soviet Union, 1959-64." C. THOMAS, *Geography*, No. 235, Vol. **52**, Part 2, April 1967.
7. "Population Growth and Urbanisation in Australia, 1961-6." R. J. JOHNSTON, *Geography*, No. 235, Vol. **52**, Part 2, April 1967.
8. "Pioneers in Canada's North." BARBARA WACE, *Geog. Mag.*, Vol. **38**, No. 12, April 1966.
9. "Iowa's Rural Revolution." Dr B. E. CRACKNELL, *Geog. Mag.*, Vol. **40**, No. 1, May 1967.
10. "Slaying the Malthusian Dragon: A Review." IAN BURTON and ROBERT W. KATES, *Economic Geography*, Vol. **40**, No. 1, 1964.

CHAPTER II

1. "Waterways of England and Wales." ROGER PILKINGTON, *Geog. Mag.*, Vol. **39**, No. 12, April 1967.
2. "Pipelines." R. E. WATKINS, *Geog. Mag.*, Vol. **39**, No. 7, November 1966.
3. "The Revolution in Air Communications." MICHAEL DONNE, *Geog. Mag.*, Vol. **37**, No. 6, October 1961.
4. "The Pipeline Revolution." GERALD MANNERS, *Geography*, No. 215, Vol. **47**, Part 2, April 1962.

5. "Air Freight becomes Big Business." E. COLSTON SHEPHERD, *New Scientist*, Vol. **28**, No. 469, November 1965.
6. "Britain's Road Problems." COLIN D. BUCHANAN, *Geog. Review*, Vol. **130**, Part 4, December, 1964.
7. "Road and Rail Transport in Great Britain." K. R. SEALY, *Geography*, No. 224, Vol. **49**, Part 3, July 1964.
8. "Channel Tunnel—The Way Ahead." DR I. B. THOMPSON, *Geog. Mag.*, Vol. **40**, No. 2, June 1967.
9. "Ships and Shipping: The Geographical Consequences of Technical Progress." S. H. BEAVER, *Geography*, No. 235, Vol. **52**, Part 2, April 1967.
10. "Moselle Waterway." ROGER PILKINGTON, *Geog. Mag.*, Vol. **40**, No. 3, July 1967.
11. "The Changing Role of Australian Coastal Shipping." G. R. WEBB, *Geography*, No. 221, Vol. **48**, Part 4, November 1963.
12. "Transport in Canada's Far North." G. W. ROWLEY, *Geog. Mag.*, Vol. **39**, No. 10, February 1967.
13. "Some Geographical Aspects of the Modernisation of British Railways." J. H. APPLETON, *Geography*, No. 237, Vol. **52**, Part 4, November 1967.

CHAPTER III

1. "Water in Britain." DR R. G. ALLEN, *Geog. Mag.*, Vol. **38**, No. 2, June 1965.
2. "The Morecambe Bay Barrage." PROF. GORDON MANLEY, *Geog. Mag.*, Vol. **37**, No. 7, November 1964.
3. "The Volta River Project." D. HILLING, *Geog. Mag.*, Vol. **37**, No. 11, March 1965.
4. "A New Method of Increasing Underground Water Storage." P. A. D. POWELL, *New Scientist*, Vol. **7**, No. 184, May 1960.
5. "Shadow on the Indus Plain." V. C. ROBERTSON, *Geog. Mag.*, Vol. **38**, No. 2, June 1964.
6. "Reducing Water Loss in South Australia." G. ROSS COCHRANE, *Geography*, No. 209, Vol. **45**, Part 4.
7. "The High Dam." BARRIE ST CLAIR MCBRIDE, *Geog. Mag.*, Vol. **38**, No. 3, July 1965.
8. "The Purification of Saline Water." PROF. W. G. V. BALCHIN, *New Scientist*, Vol. **4**, No. 103, November 1958.

9. "Irrigated Lands of the World." RICHARD M. HIGHSMITH, *Geog. Review*, Vol. **55**, No. 3, July 1965.
10. "The Columbia Basin Project—Expectations, Realisations, Implications." GEORGE MACINKO, *Geog. Review*, Vol. **53**, No. 3, April 1963.
11. "Measuring Potential Evapotranspiration." R. C. WARD, *Geography*, No. 218, Vol. **58**, Part 1, January 1963.
12. "Bringing Life to Arid Lands." TOM MARGERISON, *New Scientist*, Vol. **5**, No. 127, April 1959.

CHAPTER IV

1. "Planning the Use of the Land." PROF. L. DUDLEY STAMP, *New Scientist*, Vol. **8**, No. 197, August 1960.
2. "Agricultural Changes in Britain." J. T. COPPOCK, *Geography*, No. 224, Vol. **49**, Part 3, July 1964.
3. "The Changing Location of Intensive Crops in England and Wales." RUTH GASSON, *Geography*, No. 230, Vol. **51**, Part 1, January 1966.
4. "Mechanisation on the American Farm." PROF. B. A. STOUT, *New Scientist*, Vol. **29**, No. 481, February 1966.
5. "Farm Consolidation in Western Europe." AUDREY M. LAMBERT, *Geography*, No. 218, Vol. **48**, Part 1, January 1963.
6. "Co-operatives in Rumania." ALBERTO TESSORE, *Geog. Mag.*, Vol. **36**, No. 6, October 1963.
7. "Climate and the Australian Farmer." PROF. JOHN ANDREWS, *Geog. Mag.*, Vol. **34**, No. 12, April 1962.
8. "Cash Cropping in the Fijian Village." R. GERARD WARD, *Geog. Journal*, Vol. **130**, Part 4, December 1964.
9. "Plantation Agriculture in Victoria Division, West Cameroon—An Historical Introduction." S. H. BEDERMAN, *Geography*, No. 233, Vol. **51**, Part 4, November 1966.
10. "Among the Kashkai: A Tribal Migration." M. TH. ULLENS DE SCHOOTEN, *Geog. Mag.*, Vol. **27**, No. 2, June 1954.
11. "The Current Agricultural Revolution." A. N. DUCKHAM, *Geography*, No. 204, Vol. **44**, Part 2, April 1959.

CHAPTERS V, VI, and VII

1. "Cotton in Australia." E. M. BRIDGES, *Geography*, No. 234, Vol. **52**, Part 1, January 1967.
2. "Cotton goes West in the American South." J. FRASER HART, *Geography*, No. 203, Vol. **44**, Part 1, January 1959.
3. "Awakening in the Uboma Forests." L. E. VIRONE, *Geog. Mag.*, Vol. **40**, No. 3, July 1967.
4. "Rice Farming in Hongkong." ROBERT G. GROVES and KENNETH R. WALKER, *Geog. Mag.*, Vol. **39**, No. 9.
5. "Rice Revolution." W. J. RIDING, *Geography*, No. 214, Vol. **47**, Part 1, January 1962.
6. "Hybrid Corn Plantings in the United States." D. C. LARGE, *Geography*, Vol. **45**, Parts 1 and 2, January-April 1960.
7. "St Kilda." ROGER A. REDFERN, *Geog. Mag.*, Vol. **38**, No. 4, August 1965.
8. "Recent Developments in the Queensland Sugar Industry." E. M. DRISCOLL, *Geography*, No. 231, Vol. **51**, Part 2, April 1966.
9. "The Rhodesian Low Veld." D. E. HUSSEY, *Geog. Mag.*, Vol. **38**, No. 4, August 1965.
10. "New Tea Growing Areas in Kenya." D. R. F. TAYLOR, *Geography*, No. 229, Vol. **50**, Part 4, November 1965.

CHAPTER VIII

1. "New Ways in the Champagne World." PETER BRINSON, *Geog. Mag.*, Vol. **33**, No. 12, April 1961.
2. "The Useful Date Palm." F. G. HUCKLESBY, *Geog. Mag.*, Vol. **25**, No. 2, June 1952.
3. "Changes in the Lea Valley Glasshouse Industry." A. D. GRADY, *Geography*, No. 204, Vol. **44**, Part 2, April 1959.
4. "The Tasmanian Apple and Pear Industry." P. SCOTT, *Geography*, No. 203, Vol. **44**, Part 1, January 1959.
5. "The Huerta of the Levante." ALEXANDER RAINEY, *Geog. Mag.*, Vol. **36**, No. 6, October 1963.
6. "The Fat of the Land." TOM GIRTIN, *Geog. Mag.*, Vol. **39**, No. 7, November 1966.
7. "Sea-boots among the Daffodils." WILLIAM SANSON, *Geog. Mag.*, Vol. **35**, No. 1, May 1962.

8. "Pest and Disease Losses in Agriculture." A. H. STRICTLAND, *New Scientist*, Vol. **8**, No. 199, September 1960.

9. "Pesticides." DR NORMAN W. MOORE, *Geog. Mag.*, Vol. **38**, No. 12, April 1966.

10. "Pesticides and Health." JOHN HILLABY, *New Scientist*, Vol. **21**, No. 381, March 1964.

CHAPTER IX

1. "Death from a Fly: Tsetse Control in Northern Rhodesia." ELIZABETH BALNEAVES, *Geog. Mag.*, Vol. **34**, No. 10, February 1962.

2. "Climate and the Australian Farmer." PROF. JOHN WARHAM, *Geog. Mag.*, Vol. **34**, No. 12, April 1962.

3. "Longhorns of British Guiana." STANLEY E. BROCK, *Geog. Mag.*, Vol. **36**, No. 10, February 1964.

4. "Droving in New Zealand." G. MCDONALD, *Geog. Mag.*, Vol. **37**, No. 7, November 1964.

5. "The New Zealand Tussock Grasslands and the Mountain Lands Institute." L. W. MCCASKILL, *Geography*, No. 225, Vol. **49**, Part 4, November 1964.

6. "The Australian Merino." K. LOFTUS HILLS, *New Scientist*, Vol. **32**, No. 519, November 1966.

7. "Trends in the Australian Beef Industry." G. A. RICHARDSON, *Geography*, No. 238, Vol. **53**, Part 1, January 1968.

CHAPTER X

1. "Where the Green Gold is Minted: The Forests of Norway and Sweden." MICHAEL SALZER, *Geog. Mag.*, Vol. **33**, No. 11, March 1961.

2. "The Woodland Plantation as a Contemporary Occupance Type in the South." MERLE PRUNTY, *Geog. Review*, Vol. **53**, No. 1, January 1963.

3. "Irrigated Forests in West Pakistan." J. A. EDWARDS, *Geography*, No. 229, Vol. **50**, Part 4, November 1965.

4. "Britain's Woodlands and Afforestation." J. T. COPPOCK, *Geography*, No. 224, Vol. **49**, Part 3, July 1964.

5. "The Work of the Forestry Commission." PETER COLLINS, *Geog. Mag.*, Vol. **34**, No. 3, July 1961.

6. "Esparto: The Green Wealth of Algeria." D. TUDOR-POLE, *Geog. Mag.*, Vol. **24**, No. 3, July 1951.
7. "Manaus." DOUGLAS BOTTING, *Geog. Mag.*, Vol. **39**, No. 6, October 1966.

CHAPTER XI

1. "Farming the Sea." DR H. A. COLE, *Geog. Mag.*, Vol. **38**, No. 3, July 1965.
2. "The Search for New Fisheries." PETER WILLIAMS, *New Scientist*, Vol. **30**, No. 500, June 1966.
3. "The Growth of the Peruvian Fishing Industry." J. P. COLE, *Geography*, No. 215, Vol. **47**, Part 2, April 1962.
4. "The Sea Fisheries of the Southern United States." HERBERT R. PADGETH, *Geog. Review*, Vol. **53**, No. 1, January 1963.
5. "A Crop from the Sea." G. D. WAUGH, *Geog. Mag.*, Vol. **39**, No. 4, August 1966.
6. "Humpback Whaling in Australian Waters: A Declining Industry." W. E. GOODHAND, *Geography*, No. 220, Vol. **48**, Part 3, July 1963.
7. "Biological Problems in the Regulation of Whaling." DR N. A. MACKINTOSH, *New Scientist*, Vol. **5**, No. 133, June 1959.

CHAPTER XII

1. "Land Use and the Changing Power Industry in England and Wales." J. R. JAMES, SHEILA F. SCOTT, and E. C. WILLATS, *Geog. Journal*, Vol. **127**, Part 3, September 1961.
2. "Natural Gas and Britain." DR MICHAEL MORGAN, *Geog. Mag.*, Vol. **39**, No. 9, January 1967.
3. "The Source of North Sea Gas." DR TOM GASKELL, *Geog. Mag.*, Vol. **39**, No. 8, December 1966.
4. "The Production and Refining of Indigenous Oil in Britain." B. S. HOYLE, *Geography*, No. 213, Vol. **46**, Part 4, November 1961.
5. "The Location of Nuclear Power Stations in the United Kingdom." P. R. MOUNFIELD, *Geography*, No. 211, Vol. **46**, Part 2, April 1961.
6. "Electric Power in Britain." E. M. RAWSTRON, *Geography*, No. 224, Vol. **49**, Part 3, July 1964.

7. "The Kariba Project." MONICA M. COLE, *Geography*, No. 207, Vol. **45**, Parts 1 and 2, January-April, 1960.
8. "Exploration of the Athabasca Tar Sands, Alberta." T. M. THOMAS, *Geography*, No. 220, Vol. **48**, Part 3, July 1963.
9. "The Coal Industry in Mainland China since 1949." DR D. J. DWYER, *Geog. Journal*, Vol. **129**, Part 3, 1963.
10. "Kuwait Buys a Big Future." K. P. BARTON, *Geog. Mag.*, Vol. **39**, No. 9, January 1967.

CHAPTER XIII

1. "Sheffield: City of Steel." BRIAN DICKS, *Geog. Mag.*, Vol. **37**, No. 11, March 1965.
2. "Novosibirsk: The City." STEPHEN LE FLEMING, *Geog. Mag.*, Vol. **39**, No. 7, November 1966.
3. "A New Soviet Heartland?" DAVID J. M. HOOSON, *Geog. Journ.*, Vol. **128**, Part 1, March 1962.
4. "Britain's Post-War Iron Ore Industry." D. C. D. POCOCK, *Geography*, No. 230, Vol. **51**, Part 1, January 1966.
5. "The Size and Location of Steel Plants in the United Kingdom." *Steel Review*, No. 40, October 1965.
6. "The Scrap Trade." ELSBETH GANGUIN, *Steel Review*, No. 36, October, 1964.
7. "Home and Imported Ore." J. R. TOMLINSON and PETER WILSHER, *Steel Review*, No 38, April 1965.
8. "Locational Trends in the American Car Industry." B. P. BIRCH, *Geography*, No. 233, Vol. **51**, Part 4, November 1966.

CHAPTER XIV

1. "Map Interpretation and Industrial Location: The Example of Alkali Manufacture in Lancastria." K. L. WALLWORK, *Geography*, No. 235, Vol. **52**, Part 2, April 1967.
2. "Peru Profits from Sea Fowl." DR ROBERT CUSHMAN MURPHY, *Nat. Geog. Mag.*, Vol. **115**, No. 3, March 1959.
3. "Mining for Salt." *I.C.I. Mag.*, Vol. **45**, No. 334, February-March 1967.
4. "Tees-side's New Refinery." *I.C.I. Mag.*, Vol. **44**, No. 333, December 1966-January 1967.
5. "How to choose a Plant Site." GODFREY POWER, *I.C.I. Mag.*, Vol. **45**, No. 336, June-July 1967.

6. "Feedstocks for the Chemical Industry." SHIRLEY A. MANN, *Chemistry in Britain*, Vol. **2**, No. 1, January 1966.
7. "Chemistry in the Paper Industry." K. G. A. PANKHURST, *Chemistry in Britain*, Vol. **1**, No. 12, December 1965.
8. "The Superphosphate Industry in Uganda." W. H. DYSON, *Chemistry in Britain*, Vol. **1**, No. 11, November 1965.
9. "The Chemical Utilisation of the Natural Resources of Chile." C. G. TUBBS, *M. and B. Laboratory Bull*, Vol. **7**, No. 5, May 1967.

CHAPTER XV

1. "The Aluminium Industry in Australia." E. M. DRISCOLL, *Geography*, No. 237, Vol. **52**, Part 4, November 1967.
2. "The Wealth of Katanga." GEORGE MARTELLI, *Geog. Mag.*, Vol. **34**, No. 5, September 1961.
3. "Diamonds." JOHN BURLS, *Geog. Mag.*, Vol. **38**, No. 2, June 1965.
4. "Renewed Interest in Cornish Tin." J. C. GOODRIDGE, *Geography*, No. 214, Vol. **47**, Part 1, January 1962.
5. "The Earth's Mineral Resources." PROF. DUDLEY STAMP, *Steel Review, School Supplement*, 1961.
6. "Nickel Today." JOHN O. HITCHCOCK, *Steel Review*, No. **44**, October 1966.
7. "The Limestone Quarrying Industry of North Derbyshire." PHILIP K. BOWDEN, *Geog. Journ.*, Vol. **129**, Part 1, March 1963.
8. "The Nuclear Age in Canada." WILFRED EGGLESTON, *Canadian Geog. Journ.*, Vol. **71**, No. 6, December 1965.
9. "International Tin Restriction, and its Effects on the Malayan Tin Mining Industry." P. P. COURTENAY, *Geography*, No. 212, Vol. **46**, Part 3, July 1961.
10. "Portrait of Stoke on Trent." JOHN WAIN, *Geog. Mag.*, Vol. **33**, No. 1, May 1960.
11. "The U.K. Portland Cement Industry." P. N. GRIMSHAW, *Geography*, No. 238, Vol. **53**, Part 1, January 1968.

CHAPTER XVI

1. "The Future of Fibres." DR J. W. S. SEARLE, *New Scientist*, Vol **8**, No. 212, December 1960.

2. "British Nylon Spinners." G. F. WHITBY, *I.C.I. Mag.*, Vol. **42**, No. 319, August-September 1964.
3. "Changing Industrial Patterns of New England." R. C. ESTALL, *Geography*, No. 211, Vol. **46**, Part 2, April 1961.
4. "The Cotton Industry of N.W. England: 1941-1961." K. L. WALLWORK, *Geography*, No. 216, Vol. **47**, Part 3, July 1962.

CHAPTER XVII

1. "Smallest of the Six." JOHN LAMBERT, *Geog. Mag.*, Vol. **36**, No. 10, February 1964.
2. "Could Britain Feed Herself?" SIR WILLIAM SLATER, F.R.S., *New Scientist*, Vol. **28**, No. 470, November 1965.
3. "The Changing Significance of the Commonwealth in the Political Geography of Great Britain." C. A. FISHER, *Geography*, No. 219, Vol. **48**, Part 2, April 1963.
4. "The Common Market and the Changing Geography of Europe." M. J. WISE, *Geography*, No. 219, Vol. **48**, Part 2, April 1963.
5. "The Economics of Entry." *The Economist*, Vol. **223**, No. 6454, May 1967.

SUBJECT INDEX

PLACE NAME INDEX

PRINTED IN GREAT BRITAIN BY UNIVERSITY TUTORIAL PRESS LTD, FOXTON NEAR CAMBRIDGE